THE ISLAMIC TRADITIONS OF CIREBON

IBADAT AND ADAT AMONG JAVANESE MUSLIMS

A. G. Muhaimin

Department of Anthropology
Division of Society and Environment
Research School of Pacific and Asian Studies

July 1995

THE AUSTRALIAN NATIONAL UNIVERSITY

E PRESS

ANU
E PRESS

Published by ANU E Press
The Australian National University
Canberra ACT 0200, Australia
Email: anuepress@anu.edu.au
Web: http://epress.anu.edu.au

National Library of Australia
Cataloguing-in-Publication entry

Muhaimin, Abdul Ghoffir.
The Islamic traditions of Cirebon : ibadat and adat among
Javanese muslims.

Bibliography.
ISBN 1 920942 30 0 (pbk.)
ISBN 1 920942 31 9 (online)

1. Islam - Indonesia - Cirebon - Rituals. 2. Muslims -
Indonesia - Cirebon. 3. Rites and ceremonies - Indonesia -
Cirebon. I. Title.

297.5095982

Cover design by ANU E Press
Printed by University Printing Services, ANU

THE ISLAMIC TRADITIONS OF CIREBON

IBADAT AND ADAT AMONG JAVANESE MUSLIMS

Islam in Southeast Asia Series

Theses at The Australian National University are assessed by external examiners and students are expected to take into account the advice of their examiners before they submit to the University Library the final versions of their theses. For this series, this final version of the thesis has been used as the basis for publication, taking into account other changes that the author may have decided to undertake. In some cases, a few minor editorial revisions have made to the work. The acknowledgements in each of these publications provide information on the supervisors of the thesis and those who contributed to its development. For many of the authors in this series, English is a second language and their texts reflect an appropriate fluency.

Table Of Contents

Foreword xi

Acknowledgements xv

Abstract xvii

Preface xix

Chapter 1. Introduction

- Points Of Departure: Review Of Previous Studies 1
- The Study In Perspectives 5
- Theoretical Orientation 8
- The Field Work 12
- The Significance Of The Study 19

Chapter 2. Belief System

- The Idea Of God 29
- Belief In Spiritual Beings 38

Chapter 3. Mythology And Cosmology Of Cirebonese Traditions

- Introduction 53
- The Myth Of Creation 55
- Eschatological Ideas: The Calamity And The End Of The World 64
- Life After Death 66
- Takdir And Ikhtiar: The Problem Of Human Destiny 69
- Pitungan And Pena'asan: Javanese Numerology 72

Chapter 4. The Ritual Practice: Ibadat

- Prologue To The Analysis Of Cirebonese Ritual 79
- Ibadat: An Ambiguous Concept Of Ritual In Islam 81
- Ibadat Defined: Clarifying The Ambiguity 83
- The Practice Of Ibadat: Salat 91
- The Practice Of Ibadat: Fasting 104
- Charity And Other Practices Of Ibadat 108

Chapter 5. The Ritual Practice: Adat

- Introduction 115
- The Nature Of Adat 115
- The Commemoration Of Islamic Holy Days 119
- Celebration And Commemoration Of The Life Cycle: Slametan 135

Chapter 6. The Veneration Of Wali And Holy Men: Visits To The Shrines

- General Features Of Veneration: Introduction To Ziarah 159
- Babad Narrative Accounts Of Some Cirebonese Holy Men 162
- The Object Of Ziarah: Two Examples Of Kramat 176
- The Procedure Of Ziarah 191

Chapter 7. The Transmission Of Religious Traditions: The Role Of Pesantren

- Introduction 203
- The General Feature Of Religious Transmission 207
- The Role Of Pesantren: The Case Of Buntet 214
- The Rise And Development Of Pesantren Buntet 222

The Pesantren In Operation: An Example Of Daily Activities 241
Chapter 8. Pesantren And Tarekat: The Role Of Buntet
Introduction 247
Early Tarekat In Buntet: Syattariyah 248
Tarekat Tijaniyah 251
Chapter 9. Concluding Remarks 269
Bibliography 275

List of Tables

Table 3.1: Months of the Javanese and Islamic Calenders 73

Table 3.2: Naktu and Jejer of the Days of the Days of the Ordinary and the Pasaran Weeks 74

Table 3.3: Months of the Year and Years of the Windu and their Naktu 74

Table 3.4: Schedule of the Domination of Astronomical Objects 75

Table 3.5: First Day of the Months, the Lowong and the Raspatit (Year Alif) 77

Table 3.6: Sample of Lists of Good and Bad Days 78

Table 7.1: Number of Students/Santri at Buntet (1992) 217

Table 8.1: The Spiritual Genealogy (Silsilah) of Tarekat Syattariyah at Buntet 249

Table 8.2: Ancestral Genealogy of Abu Abbas Ahmad at-Tijani The founder of Tijaniyah order 252

Table 8.3: Spiritual genealogy of Syeikh Ali At-Thayyib al-Madani (West Java gate of Tijaniyah) 259

List of Maps

The Regency of Cirebon 6

Map of Desa Astana 178

Map of Desa Mertapada Kulon Kec. Astanajapura Kab. Cirebon 218

Pesantren Bunten Complex 233

List of Figures

Figure 4.1: Scope of Ibadat in Cirebonese popular conception. 88

Figure 6.1: Marriage alliance between Sunan Gunung Jati and Raden Fatah 169

Figure 6.2: Sketch of Astana Gunung Jati Grave Complex 184

Sketch of the site of Kramat Mbah Buyut Trusmi (1926). 187

Figure 6.3: Sketch of Kramat Mbah Buyut Trusmi (1995). 188

Figure 7.1: Genealogy of Sesepuh and Sohibul Wilayah (Buntent) 220

Figure 7.2: Intellectual Network of Kyai Abbas 230

Figure 7.3: Military Network of Pesantren Buntet under Kyai Abbas. 231

Figure 7.4: Political Network of Pesantren Buntet under Kyai Abbas. 234

Figure 7.5: Sample of Endogamous Marriage in Pesantren Buntet. 235
Figure 7.6: Genealogy of Some Kyai in Buntet. 237
Figure 8.1: Recruitment of Syattariyah Mursyid in Buntet 250
Figure 8.2: Main Entrance of Tijaniyah to Java. 260
Figure 8.3: Recruitment of Tijaniyah Muqaddam from Buntet 262
Figure 8.4: Spiritual Genealogy of Some Tijaniyah Muqaddam in Java 262

List of Plates

Plate 1: Kraton Kesuphuhan. 26
Plate 2: Pakuningrat S.H., Sultan Kesepuhan. 26
Plate 3: A business centre: a scene in the city of Cirebon. 27
Plate 4: A scene in the village. 27
Plate 5: Two children at play: a scene in the village. 28
Plate 6: Pak Shofie, his family and close kin. 28
Plate 7: Pak Shofie's hand writing copy of the manual of "Riyadhah Ayat Kursi" 49
Plate 8: Attending sermon at 'Id prayer. 113
Plate 9: Pak Shofie and his sons pray at Pak Shofie's mother's tomb after 'Id prayer. 113
Plate 10: Pagersari-kraton on "Muludan" ceremony prior to the "Panjang Jimat" procession. 153
Plate 11: Kraton religious officials on "Muludan" ceremony prior to the "Panjang Jimat" procession. 153
Plate 12: A group of circumcision grooms. 154
Plate 13: A circumcision groom on becak returns from "ngembang" at his elders' graves. 154
Plate 14: A circumcision ceremony. 155
Plate 15: A circumcision groom on display. 155
Plate 16: A carnival to fetch the groom for "munggah" ("marriage ceremony"). 156
Plate 17: The bride, the groom and the Penghulu at a marriage contract. 156
Plate 18: A seven month pregnant woman is bathed at "Ngrujaki" ceremony. 157

Plate 19: Water with flowers, and a young yellow hybrid coconut crafted with Qur'anic verses and coin inserted used at the "Ngrujaki" ceremony. 157

Plate 20: The bathed pregnant woman at "Ngrujaki" ceremony. 158

Plate 21: Chanting "Marhaba" to honour the pregnant woman. 158

Plate 22: A gate at Kramat Nyi Mas Gandasari. 175

Plate 23: The tomb of Nyi Mas Gandasari. 175

Plate 24: An entrance to Astana Gunung Jati grave complex. 199

Plate 25: Astana Gunung Jati custodians at the "Pekemitan" hall. 199

Plate 26: Pilgrims at Astana Gunung: the "Pesujudan" door is locked. 200

Plate 27: The "Pesujudan" door is open. (The ascending pathway leads to Sunan Gunung Jati's tomb.) 200

Plate 28: A "wong kraman" serves pilgrims. 201

Plate 29: Astana Gunung Jati custodians and Kecamatan Administrative officials pray together on a festival occasion. 201

Plate 30: Two Qur'anic learners at "khataman" ceremony to mark the completion of the whole Qur'an. 209

Plate 31: Demonstrating the melodious recital of the Qur'an. 209

Plate 32: Kyai Abbas. 238

Plate 33: Kyai Abdullah Abbas before "Haul" ceremony. 238

Plate 34: The main "pondok" of Pesantren Buntet. 243

Plate 35: Commemorating the Independence Day at Pesantren Buntet. 243

Plate 36: The Pesantren Mosque in Buntet. 244

Plate 37: Girlscouts of Pesantren Buntet on exercise. 244

Plate 38: A sample of "Ijazah" of Tarekat Syattiriyah at Buntet 245

Plate 39: Kyai Fahim Hawi, a Tijaniyah Muqaddam of Buntet. 265

Plate 40: Kyai Abdullah Syifa and his five year old son. 265

Plate 41: Kyai Fu'ad Hasyim. 266

Plate 42: Kyai Fahim Hawi among Tijaniyah followers. 266

Plate 43: Nyai Hammah, a Tijaniyah Muqaddam of Kuningan. 267

Plate 44: Nyai Hamnah, her followers and Kyai Imam Subki (Nyai Hamnah's husband). 267

Foreword

This volume, *The Islamic Traditions of Cirebon* by A. G. Muhaimin provides an excellent introduction to the practice of Islam in contemporary Java. Dr Muhaimin takes great care in presenting Islamic belief and practice as a living social reality. In Cirebon, religious and customary practices – *ibadat* and *adat* – blend together in a single rich historical Islamic tradition. It is the whole of this tradition that Dr Muhaimin is concerned to elucidate.

The setting for this study is particularly important. The coastal town of Cirebon with the region in which it is situated was a historical gateway for the coming of Islam to Java. Cirebon is thus redolent with Islamic traditions and notable for its numerous historic Islamic institutions. It is, for example, the site of a mausoleum complex in which one of the earliest founders of Islam, Syarif Hidayatullah, more commonly known as Sunan Gunung Jati, is buried. Sunan Gunung Jati is regarded as one of the nine *Wali* or 'Saints' of Java and the presence of his tomb in Cirebon has given the town great spiritual status and made it a place of pious visitation and special veneration. At the same time, the town has retained its courtly traditions – two courts, the Kesepuhan and Kanoman *kraton* – that have, for centuries, fostered Islamic learning and a distinctive tradition of art and performance. Not only is the Cirebon area replete with Islamic shrines – more than 300 according to the Department of Education and Culture – it is also one of oldest and most important centres for Islamic education in Java. According to the Department of Religion, there are 274 *pesantren* – Islamic boarding schools – in the region of Cirebon. Some of these claim to date to the 17th, others to the 18th century. Many of these *pesantren* were begun in connection with Sufi orders. Hence to this day, Cirebon is remarkable for the variety of different *tarekat*, some of the oldest as well as some of the newest in Java.

Given the importance of both *tarekat* and *pesantren*, this study focuses on both institutions. Dr Muhaimin provides a detailed examination of one of Cirebon's largest and most important *pesantren*, Buntet, that traces its foundations to *Kyai* Muqayim bin Abdul Hadi, the *Penghulu* of Kraton Kanoman, in the middle of the 18th century. The early history of *Pesantren* Buntet was intimately associated with the spread and development of *Tarekat* Syattariyah on Java and Buntet became a centre (*zawiyah*) for this order. Interestingly Pesantren Buntet is also a centre for *Tarekat* Tijaniyah which only became established on Java in the late 1920s. It is Tijaniyah that has become the most prominent *tarekat* in *Pesantren* Buntet.

The continuing promotion of Tijaniyah at Buntet, as described by Dr Muhaimin, reflects on the subtle and complex role of Nahdlatul Ulama (NU) in Indonesia as an organization based on a dense network of *pesantren* and on the *ulama* or *kyai* associated with them. Dr Muhaimin examines the many genealogies, both personal and spiritual, that link Buntet's *kyai* to other *pesantren* within the NU network. He also notes efforts by Buntet's *kyai* to gain official recognition from NU for Tijaniyah as a legitimate (*mu'tabarah*) *tarekat*. These efforts have been steadfastly rejected because this *tarekat*, founded by Ahmad at-Tijani in the 18th century lacks a spiritual genealogy (*silsilah*) of transmission like those of other Sufi orders. Despite this lack of official NU recognition, the *kyai* at Buntet continue to spread the teachings and practice of Tijaniyah. From Buntet, these practices of this *tarekat* have spread to other NU *pesantren* and have become particularly popular among the urban population of Java.

This book offers a rich mine of insights into the practice of Islam on Java. What is particularly valuable is the way that Dr Muhaimin consistently explicates a perspective on Islam associated with the mainstream of Nahdlatul Ulama – in effect, a Sufi notion of personal involvement in the world. From this perspective, there is no distinction between sacred and profane. By means of intention (*niyat*), religious pratice (*ibadat*) goes beyond the required ritual duties and encompasses all activities. Quoting Nasr [1] , he writes:

> Thus...`everything is essentially sacred and nothing is profane because everything bears within itself the fragrance of the Divine.' Therefore, *ibadat*, in this sense, may range from expressing daily courtesies to such things as the formal and solemn invocation both in and outside of formal prescribed prayers, and other forms of worship. It embraces a wide spectrum of actions and is akin to, and sometimes used inter-changeably with, *amal*, (*'aml*), meaning work, another word which points to the same thing referred to by *ibadat*. Thus, the distinction between *amal* [one's work] and *ibadat* becomes elusive. Both *ibadat* and *amal* require *niyat* (intention) which becomes the stamp that the work is for God. Another way to ensure intention is by uttering or murmuring *Basmalah* (a phrase, saying 'In the name of Allah, the Beneficient, the Merciful'). Thus doing any (good) thing, a religious or worldly matter, becomes *ibadat*, by merely preceding it with *Basmalah*.

In this view, all that is not forbidden (*haram*) can be made Islamic. For a traditionalist, 'islamizing' (*mengislamkan*) the world has more to do with consecrating the world than with transforming it. The exemplary methods cited for this process of 'islamizing' the world are those attributed to the earliest founders of Islam, the great *Wali* or Saints of Java, including Sunan Gunung Jati.

This is a study written with conviction and understanding. One of the ethnographic challenges that Cirebon poses to any observer is its depth of its local historical traditions and the multiple languages through which these

[1] S. H. Nasr, *Islamic Life and Thought*. Boston: George Allen and Unwin.1981:7.

traditions are expressed. Javanese, Sundanese, Cirebonese which is a distinctive dialect of Javanese, Indonesian and Arabic are the working languages of Cirebon and are used daily, in different contexts, by members of the area's diverse communities. Dr Muhaimin comes from Cirebon; he is fluent in its languages; he is also a graduate of *Pesantren* Buntet. As a consequence, he is able to present his study as an ethnographer and insider. This is a work that deserves a close reading to appreciate its many insights.

An Indonesian translation of this work was published in 2001 under the title, *Islam Dalam Bingkai Budaya Lokal: Potret Dari Cirebon*[2] and continues to be available in Indonesia. A limited English edition of this work was also published in Jakarta in 2004 by the Centre for Research and Development of Socio-Religious Affairs, Office of Religious Research, Development and In-Service Training, of the Ministry of Religious Affairs. The present publication of this volume within the ANU's *Islam in Southeast Asia* series provides the opportunity to make this work available to the wider international readership that it deserves.

James J. Fox

[2] Ciputat: Logos in cooperation with Yayasan Adikarya IKAPI and the Ford Foundation.

Acknowledgements

This work is based on my ANU PhD thesis which was submitted to the Department of Anthropology in the Research School of Pacific and Asian Studies in 1995. The completion of that thesis was made possible through a Columbo Plan scholarship award with financial support from the Australian International Development Assistance Bureau (AIDAB). I am grateful to the Australian Government for this funding and also for the kind assistance I received from AIDAB officers, especially Mr Hashem and Mrs Alicia Curtis of the ACT Regional Office in Canberra.

My supervisory committee that brought this work to fulfilment was made up of Professor Dr James J. Fox, Dr Soepomo and Dr Penelope Graham. To these persons I wish to convey my considerable thanks. In this respect, I owe an invaluable debt to my primary supervisor, Professor Fox, whose teaching and painstaking guidance contributed a great deal to the production of this thesis. His efforts in finding additional financial support meant very much in bringing this work to a conclusion. Moreover, to my family who stayed with me to share both happiness and sadness in Canberra, Professor Fox was more than my professional supervisor. My children prefer to call him as "Mbah Jim", meaning "grand-father Jim". When we were in Jakarta, I was rather jealous because for their own reasons, my children's personal attachment had been closer to their grand-parents than to my wife and myself, their own mother and father. Their reference of Mbah Jim to Professor Fox thus reflects their closeness to him. I am pleased and proud to have this "jealousy" repeated in Canberra. For all this, I can only express my greatest gratitude and *"nyuwun pangestunipun panjenengan dalem, nggih, Mbah Jim"*.

In many ways, especially through sharing ideas and perspectives, the staff and students in the Department of Anthropology in the Research School of Pacific and Asian Studies and the Department of Archeology and Anthropolgy in the Faculty of Arts have also contributed to this thesis. My first acquaintance with anthopology was through my teachers in the Faculty of Arts. Dr Nicolas Peterson, Dr Ian Keen, Dr Don Gardner Dr Douglas Miles and Dr C. Gregory, are among those to whom my respect will never cease. My thanks and gratitude is also extended to all individuals whose advice and suggestions have contributed to shaping this work. Among these are Dr Radin Fernando, Norma Chin, Dr Kathy Bellingham, Dr John Rudder, Don Porter and Dr Arlette Ottino, to mention only a few. Included in this list are my fellow Indonesians such as Yunita Winarto, Tom Therik, Jamhari Makruf and I Gde Pitana.

The help from the administrative staff in the Department of Anthropology, Research School of Pacific and Asian Studies have been equally instrumental. Considerable thanks go to Susan Toscan, Ria van de Zandt, Margaret Tyrie and

Anne Buller. Their share in providing facilities and technical support in an informal and familial atmosphere has been very impressive and without their assistance, this work would have been more difficult.

It is hard to imagine that I could have produced this thesis without enthusiastic support from many people in Cirebon where I carried out my research. Pak Shofie and his family, to whom I shared a home and to whom I express my thanks, occupy a place of special importance. It would be a long list if I mentioned here the names of all the distinguished *Kyai* from various *Pesantren, kramat* custodians, *kraton* personnel, government officials and generous villagers to whom I should also convey my thanks. I should, however, express my thanks for support and encouragement from Dr Zamakhsyari Dhofier, the reference from Professor Richard Pearse, my former supervisor at Macquarie University, and the permission from my superior in the Ministry of Religious Affairs in Jakarta to undertake this study.

Finally, I cannot conclude these acknowledgements without mentioning Nur Eko Prabawaningsih, my wife, Monita Cahyaningsih and Emmyliana Suryaningsih, my daughters, and Mohammad Heikal Ariestianto, my son. Their endless love, passion and patience as well as their sharing in both happiness and sadness have motivated my every effort and inspiration in producing this thesis. It is to them I also wish to convey my considerable thanks, and it is also to them I would like to dedicate this work.

A.G. Muhaimin

Abstract

This work deals with the socio-religious traditions of the Javanese Muslims living in Cirebon, a region on the north coast in the eastern part of West Java. It examines a wide range of popular traditional religious beliefs and practices. The diverse manifestations of these traditions are considered in an analysis of the belief system, mythology, cosmology and ritual practices in Cirebon. In addition, particular attention is directed to the formal and informal institutionalised transmission of all these traditions.

Detailed analyses of these popular traditions suggest that the Javanese socio-religious traditions can be best understood by tracing their roots in terms of traditional Islamic orthopraxy rather than resorting to other traditions such as a Hindu/Buddhist and an animistic past. Many of Cirebon's principal popular traditions even find their roots and justification in the Islamic doctrines embedded in the Islamic Scriptures: the Qur'an, the Hadiths and in the work of the *ulama*. Although there are indeed remnants of pre-Islamic influence, these lie outside the core of basic religious tenets and do not account for the formation of fundamental religious components.

The principal of Cirebonese belief system is to have faith (*iman*) in which the unity of God is its core. God is enunciated as the sole creator, the sovereign and the governor of the whole universe and the contents thereof. The mysteries of how the universe was created, governed and destined have become the subject of various cosmological myths and eschatological views. This includes the myth about the origin of the universe and mankind including the Javanese, the end of the world and the afterlife. Some themes of these myths follow the lines of theosophic speculation of specific *sufi-tarekat*, especially the Shattariyah, one version of which has been traditionally adopted by the *kraton* circle.

Verbal expressions of Cirebonese beliefs are manifest in various religious practices. The core is twofold: submission (*islam*) and deference (*ihsan*), both are inseparably intertwined. Anything springs up from the spirit of submission and deference is termed *ibadat*. Yet the term *ibadat*, is also used more specifically to refer to the enactment of the five pillars, the main rituals of Islam. Outside this main rituals, there are many others termed as *adat*. An *adat* ritual refers to additional rituals which have been part of the popular traditions by which people express a sense of piety and muslim identity. As there are some form of *adat* in the way of performing *ibadat* and there is a sense of *ibadat* within the *adat*, the difference between *ibadat* and *adat* sometimes becomes elusive and difficult to explain. Yet the way in which *ibadat* and *adat* are intertwined constitutes a general feature of the whole spectrum of the Javanese socio-religious tradition.

It is evident that the Javanese socio-religious tradition is Sunni Islam, acclaimed by its proponents as the "*Faham Ahlu Sunnah wa'l Jama'ah*" (School for the

Followers of the Prophetic Traditions and Concensus). This represents the full heritage of a classical tradition whose roots can be traced back to Ahmad ibn Hanbal (circa AD 855). Bringing with it an Ash'arite theology, the four *mazahib* of jurisprudence and Ghazalian sufism, its presence in Java is as old as Islam is in Java. Through various ways and means this tradition has been formally and informally transmitted from generation to generation. *Pesantren* and *tarekat* (sufi orders), however, are two main institutions which account for a major part for this overal preservation and transmission process. Unless carefully observed the intricacy of this tradition and its transmission tends to provoke misunderstanding.

Preface

This work contains many terms comprised of both precise and corrupted (Javanised) Arabic. In this context the transliteration issue is rather problematic. At the academic level there are, currently, no less than nine Latin-Arabic transliteration systems known in Indonesia. Among these systems two are worth mentioning: (a) the system announced by the Ministry of Religious Affairs in 1979 and (b) the system announced jointly by the Minister of Religious Affairs and the Minister of Education and Culture in 1987. The former legitimated the predominating contemporary transliteration system, the latter considered a much wider spectrum, including the systems used by the Encyclopaedia of Islam, the International Organization for Standardization (ISO), the American Library Association and the Library of Congress. The immediate aim of the 1987 joint decree system was twofold: precision and practicality in the sense that within one stroke of writing (typing) a transliteration symbol can be produced which represents a precise Arabic sound. Unfortunately this practical aim, in particular, was difficult to be achieved. Until now there is not a typewriter or computer which meets this practical need. The result is that the older systems, especially the 1979 system, are widely used with some inconsistent degree of application.

At the popular level inconsistency is even greater because at this level Latin-Arabic transliteration is dictated more by common sense and common understanding where most people rely more on context than on symbols. A simple example for this is the Arabic word: **صلاة** (meaning prayer), which is written as *shalat, sholat, salat* or *solat*. In the case of: **حي على الصلاة** (let us go to prayer), however, this word is written as *shalah, sholah* or *solah,* but rarely as, *salah,* because the latter could be confused with the Indonesian word meaning wrong'.

As the main concern of this work is to capture genuine local popular traditions, including oral, literary and verbal traditions, this work follows what was prevailing in the traditions (in which the context is more important than the transliteration symbols). With some variations and inconsistencies, the general features of this transliteration system employs no symbol that distinguishes long and short vowels; uses "h" to represent either ح or ه; uses a double consonant to indicate a **shaddah**; puts the definite article "**al-**" before words beginning with a lunar (**Qamariyah**) letter but when encountering words beginning with a solar (**Shamsiyah**) letter the **-lam- (l)** of the article is mostly changed into that solar letter to conform with its proper pronunciation (cf. Danner 1988:vi). In many cases an apostrophe of either (') or (ʻ) is used to indicate either ء (**hamzah**) or ع (**ʻain**).

In most cases, transliteration for some crucial Arabic letters are, as follows:

ث **: ts**	ظ **: z**	ظ **: zh**
ج : j	ش : sy	ع : 'a, 'i, 'u
ح : h	ص : sh	غ : gh
خ : kh	ض : dh	ق : q
ذ : dz	ط : th	ه : h

The Islamic law is frequently referred to as *syari'ah* or *syari'at*. The word referring to the Islamic Holy Book is "(al-)Qur'an"; my short reference to it is "QS" which stands for "Qur'an Surah", followed by the number of the referred verse. Thus QS 2:43, for example, means Qur'an Surah 2, verse 43. My own saying to mean the Tradition of the Prophet, which is locally written as "Hadits", when read as part of my narrative, "Hadith" is used. Most non-English words are put in *italics*, while some fairly "precise" Arabic (for explanatory purposes) are put in bold type. Unless indicated otherwise, the English translation of the Holy Qur'an that appears in this work is based on *The Holy Qur'an: English Translation of the Meanings and Commentary*, Medina: King Fahd Holy Qur'an Printing Complex (1411/1990).

The reference of "field-notes" is used to the records from the field that I put in my own words, whereas "interview" or "in-depth interview" is used to the translation into English of informants' words. In most cases the original Javanese words are put into the referred notes.

A.G. Muhaimin

Chapter 1: Introduction

POINTS OF DEPARTURE: REVIEW OF PREVIOUS STUDIES

> ...syncretism is very conspicuous in the religion of Java. This perhaps results from the flexibility of the Javanese people in accepting various incoming religions from the outside world. In historical times, upon their underlying animistic beliefs, Javanese had successively accepted Hinduism, Buddhism, Islam and Christianity, and "Javanized" them all. And as can be seen...worship of various spirits strongly exists in the deep stratum of folk psychology. It is said ... among the Javanese: "Sedaya agami sami kemawon" ... Although 90% of the inhabitants ...profess Islam, they all belong to ..."wong abangan", whose Islamic beliefs seem to cover the surface of their traditional concepts. This is well proved by the continuing existence of the various salamatans ...[1]

This quotation reflects a view adopted by some Indonesianists who hold as an axiom that Javanese Islam is syncretic. Its basis is a conviction that animism, Hinduism, Buddhism and Islam have formed layers of Javanese culture. From this conviction derives an approach of seeing Javanese Islam as founded on multi-layered syncretism. Everything is then analysed and explained in terms of this 'multi layered' schemata.

One version of this syncretic argument is championed by Clifford Geertz who developed an *abangan-santri-priyayi* trichotomy for seeing the socio-religious pattern and development of Java.[2] His approach has enjoyed currency among many Indonesianists for the last few decades. Subsequent work on Javanese socio-religious discourse cannot proceed without reference to him. For this reason, I wish to take his work as the focus of my initial discussion.

According to Geertz's historical representation, before the advent of Hinduism, the Javanese were animists. In about AD 400, Hinduism, and then Buddhism, began to gain a stronghold. Around AD 1500 Islam came through sea trade expansion.[3] The notion of essentially tolerant, accommodative and flexible Javanese is taken as another crucial point by which, instead of opposing any incoming religion, the Javanese were thought to have taken everything as necessary ingredients to form a new synthesis, i.e:

> ... the village religious system (which) commonly consists of a balanced integration of animistic, Hinduistic, and Islamic elements, a basic Javanese

[1] Bekki, A. (1975), "Socio Cultural Changes in a Traditional Javanese Village" in *Life in Indonesian Villages*, Institute of Asian Studies, Tokyo: Rikko (St. Pauls) University, p. 20.
[2] Geertz, C. (1960), *The Religion of Java*, Glencoe: The Free Press:. (My own reference is Phoenix Edition, 1976, Chicago: University of Chicago Press).
[3] Geertz, C. (1976), p. 5

> syncretism ... the island's true folk tradition, the basic stratum of its civilisation;[4]

The extent to which each religion has contributed to this syncretism was accounted for in a threefold manner: (a) the sequence and the time span of its presence in Java, (2) the basic nature of the religion; and (3) the group of people by whom the religion was initially brought and adopted. As animism was the first religion on Java that had long become an established tradition, it is argued accordingly that animism has made a major contribution. As animism is essentially a religion adopted by commoners, animism must have a stronghold among the village peasants and must have shaped their syncretism. Hinduism, which came and has been taken to constitute Javanese state craft and state polity for more than a thousand years, must also have been a contributory factor which had a major impact on overall Javanese cultural formation. As Hinduism, through its inherent caste doctrine, legitimates elite domination, its impact must have been the strongest among the court aristocrats because they benefited from this religion. Accordingly, Hinduism shaped these aristocrats' syncretism and world-view. Islam, on the other hand, which came late via trade expansion, and had its further spread hampered by the presence of European colonialism and the spread of Christianity, must have had less influence. It touched only the surface of the already existing Hindu/Buddhist animistic cultural rock. Consequently, Islam, according to Geertz,

> ... did not move into an essentially virgin area, ... but into one of Asia's greatest political, aesthetic, religious, and social creations, the Hindu-Buddhist Javanese state, which though it had by then begun to weaken, had cast its roots so deeply into Indonesian society (especially on Java, but not only there) ...[5]

Accordingly, in Java, "Islam did not construct a civilisation, it (only) appropriated one.'[6] To the Javanese, Islam was an alien tradition adopted and brought by unsettled traders in the coastal areas. Only after a long peaceful assimilation did Islam gradually form enclaves of trading communities in towns and among rich farmers. These Muslim communities adopted a syncretism which stressed Islamic cultural aspects. The net result of this overall process on Java is contemporary Javanese society with its intricate socio-religious groupings, consisting of:

> Abangan, representing a stress on the animistic aspects of the over-all Javanese syncretism and broadly related to the peasant element in the population; santri, representing a stress on the Islamic aspects of the

[4] *Ibid.* (The word between brackets is my own).
[5] Geertz, C. (1975), *Islam Observed*, Chicago: The University of Chicago Press, p. 11.
[6] *Ibid.*

> syncretism and generally related to the trading element (and to certain elements in the peasantry as well); and prijaji, stressing the Hinduist aspects and related to the bureaucratic element ...[7]

It was this schemata which, to my understanding, was taken by Geertz as his efficient, albeit simplistic, tool to analyse the abundant ethnographic data from Modjokuto, a small town in East Java. He partitioned the data according to this predetermined schemata, the *abangan-santri-priyayi* trichotomy. By adding a conflict scenario to his schemata he produced *The Religion of Java*, a controversial portrait of the socio-religious life of the Javanese.[8]

Response to Geertz

Response to Geertz's treatment varies from total and uncritical acceptance to strong rejection. In between these two extremes there have been some who accept it with caution and some others who merely repeat his jargon and use it for different purposes and different situations. Siddique (1977) perhaps, belongs to the later type. She uses the jargon of *abangan-santri-priyayi* especially to single out the participant group elements in the celebration of the birth of the Prophet Muhammad, the *Panjang-Jimat* ceremony, in the court of Cirebon.[9]

Strong criticism of this syncretic argument and the ensuing *abangan-santri-priyayi* trichotomy have come from a number of scholars. Bachtiar (1973), an Indonesian sociologist who knows much about Java, was one among those who spoke rigorously. To Bachtiar, *The Religion of Java* is an excellent work in the sense that it contains an abundance of detailed descriptive material concerning many aspects of Javanese religious beliefs and practices. As the work is put under scrutiny, major shortcomings readily appear at almost every point. Bachtiar points out among other things, the problems of Geertz's theoretical orientation, especially regarding what constitutes religion, and the way this precipitates confusion on how religion is distinguished from other governing values, codes of conduct and behaviour including, for example, *adat* or local traditions. Confusion also occurs in regard to the concept of religious syncretism and the sociological role of pluralism. Bachtiar explains that every Javanese is not just a Javanese. He is also a member of a household, *desa* community, the Indonesian

[7] Geertz, C. (1976), p. 6.

[8] This mode of analysis appears throughout *The Religion of Java*. The deterministic logic and the argument developed from it are evident in the 'Introduction.' The partitioning of ethnographic data appears in the division of the book into three parts, 'The "Abangan" Variant, The "Prijaji" Variant and The "Santri" Variant.' An example of the simple way of putting what belongs to which variant is: *slametan* for *abangan;* the prayers, the fast, the Pilgrimage, for *santri;* etiquette and mysticism, for *priyayi*. A person named Paidjan must be an *abangan*; Usman or H. Abdul must be a *santri*; Sosro must be a *priyayi*; etc. The terms 'abangan,' 'santri' and 'prijaji' are truly Javanese, but they are employed by Geertz, without full understanding of their meaning, to label his ingenuously predetermined animistic group, Hindu/Buddhistic group and Islamic syncretic group.

[9] See Chapter Five.

nation, the Muslim community, a political party, each with a certain position in it. Each position necessitates the performer to exhibit a certain mode of behaviour which does not necessarily reflect religious activity. Doing all these things at the same time, according to Bachtiar, does not reflect religious syncretism but rather the role of pluralism. Further, Geertz misunderstands the meaning of *abangan, santri* and *prijaji,* as the Javanese actually use these terms. In this respect, Geertz confuses the Javanese reference to certain religious behaviour (with reference to *abangan-santri*) and social strata (with reference to *priyayi-wong cilik*). With such confusions, it is therefore difficult to accept Geertz's major propositions.[10]

Other critics, such as Suparlan (1976), Koentjaraningrat (1963) and Nakamura (1984), also point out the inadequacy of the *abangan-santri-prijaji* theoretical framework and its use as a clear cut device to categorise Javanese society. With regard to doctrinal aspect, Dhofier (1985:6) points out that Geertz's claim that Javanese Islam is 'Hindu-Buddhist' is misleading and distorts the real situation. Hodgson (1974:551) states that Geertz made a major systematic error by taking only what the modernists and reformists happen to agree on and gratuitously labelling much of the Muslim religious life in Java, "Hindu." Geertz's comprehensive data intended to prove his contention, according to Hodgson, give no evidence that Islam in Java, even in its inner part, is "Hindu." Pranowo (1991) makes a definite claim that Geertz's theoretical framework does not work at all operationally when it is applied in a real situation. He found this when he studied traditional Muslims in a Central Javanese village. Woodward (1989) was also frustrated in trying to trace the Hindu/Buddhist elements of ideologies and ritual modalities even in the most allegedly Hinduistic ceremonies, such as *Grebeg Mulud* at the Yogyakarta court.

Javanese society is like other societies and the Javanese culture is as complex as others. My respect and appreciation of Geertz is for his ingenious contribution in bringing Java and Javanese issues to the academy. Enthusiastic responses from others, positive or negative, substantiate his success. All this has made the Javanese socio-religious discourse an outstanding subject of scholarship. Yet, as more and more scholars recognise that Geertz's treatment is ill-founded, the question is whether Javanese culture in general, and their socio-religious patterns and development in particular, can be fruitfully analysed based on such a 'deterministic' logic as Geertz has attempted.[11] In this regard I am also sceptical

[10] Bachtiar, H.W. (1973), "The Religion of Java: A Commentary," *Madjalah Ilmu-Ilmu Sastra Indonesia*, Djilid V, No. 1. (Written originally in 1964 in English, and published as it is without revision). The "*wong cilik*" is absent throughout Geertz's work.

[11] 'Determinism' is a philosophy which considers all events, including moral choices, are completely determined by previously existing causes that preclude free will and the possibility that man could have acted otherwise. In the 18th century, Pierre-Simon, Marquis de Laplace, for example, advocated that the present state of universe is the effect of its previous state and the cause of the state that follows. Omar Khayam, a Persian poet, also exhibits a similar tone in the concluding part of his quatrains by

as to whether the syncretic argument can be a useful tool to analyse the socio-religious traditions of the Javanese.

THE STUDY IN PERSPECTIVES

Being sceptical about syncretism, I wish to explore an alternative approach which renders a better understanding of Javanese socio-religious life. More specifically, I wish to seek an alternative understanding of the nature and dynamics of Islam on Java. In addition, I also wish to consider the genuine manifestations of Islam within the Javanese cultural context and thus, amidst the whole spectrum of Javanese cultural traditions, I shall attempt to make these manifestations identifiable and locate them in a single coherent frame work. This is an ambitious job and challenging endeavour. Before confronting the main issue, I wish to begin my discussion by recalling two considerations: the issue of demography and of the folk narratives regarding Islam that prevail among the Javanese.

The Demographic Issue: Statistical records

Statistical records, official or otherwise, indicate that the majority of Indonesians and the majority of Javanese (about 90 per cent), profess Islam. This means that even before considering whether the overall influence of Islam on Java is deep or rudimentary, this statistical data alone may provide grounds to assume that within the various Javanese socio-religious manifestations, there must be certain identifiable elements which can be considered as purely Islamic or which genuinely constitute parts of an Islamic tradition. Setting aside at the first stage, the extent to which Islam might have influenced Javanese socio-religious life, identifying and elucidating elements of an Islamic tradition within the Javanese society is a challenging task. With special reference to Cirebon, a region in north-coast Java, I would like to face this challenge and then explore the extent to which Islam has influenced Javanese social life.

saying that the First Morning of Creation is What the Last Dawn of Reckoning shall read (*Encyclopaedia Britannica: Micropaedia*, 1986, vol. 4, pp. 39–40).

The Regency of Cirebon

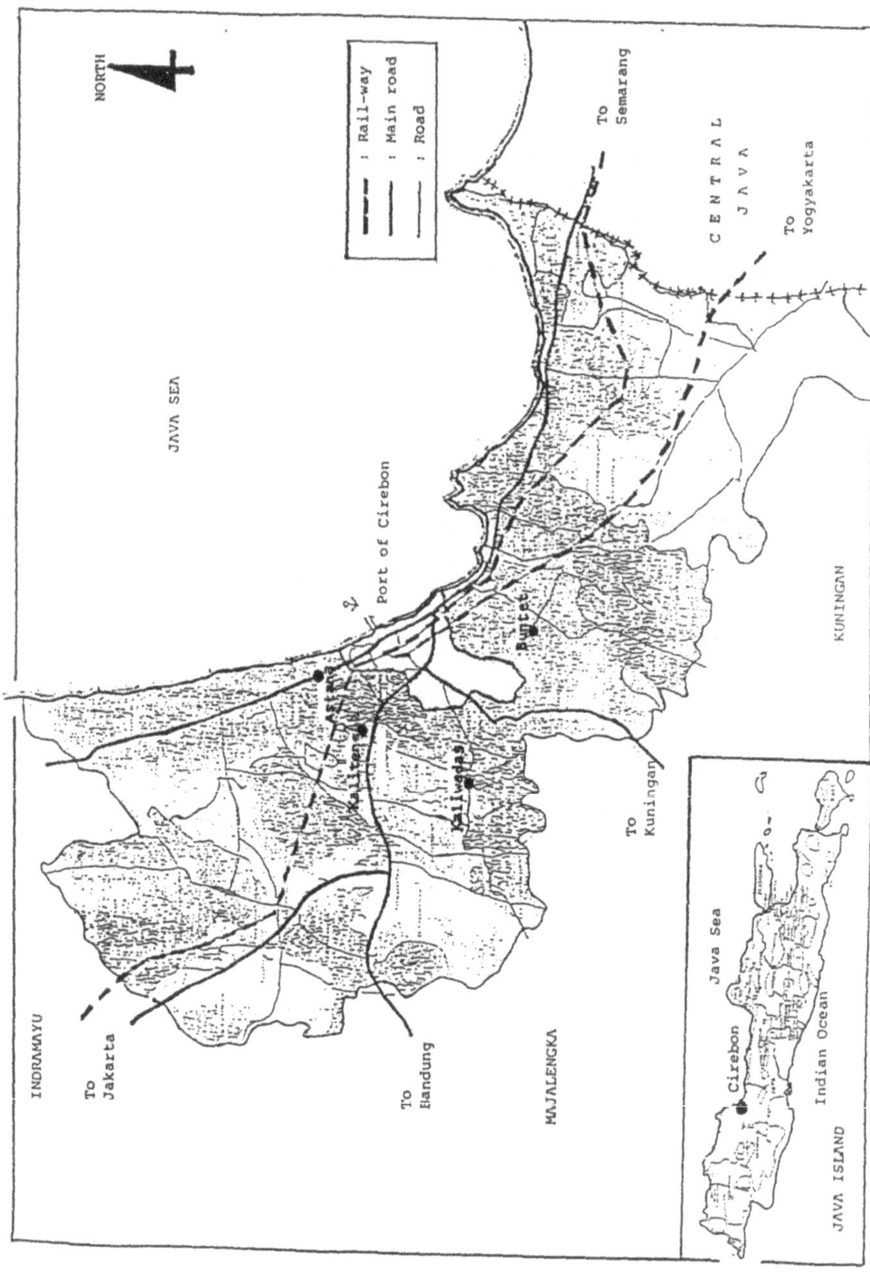

The Popular Narratives of Early Islam in Cirebon

Most historical accounts of Cirebon have always associated the region with the early development of Islam on Java and, in particular, in West Java. The rise of an Islamic kingdom, which has its roots in the 15th–16th century, would suggest that Cirebon has its own significant importance in the configuration of the Islamic era. The founder of the Islamic kingdom in Cirebon, Syarif Hidayatullah, later known as Sunan Gunung Jati, according to folk narratives is one of the *wali* or Islamic saints, the early propagators of Islam on Java. Although different traditions reveal different lists of *wali*, Sunan Gunung Jati is one whose name is always included on all *wali* lists. Older traditions such as the *Babad Tanah Jawi* and the *Babad Kraton* put forward eight *wali*, but each with different names. Those who are mentioned in the *Babad Tanah Jawi* are: Sunan Ampel, Sunan Giri, Sunan Bonang, Sunan **Gunung Jati**, Sunan Kalijaga, Sunan/Shekh Siti Jenar (Lemah Abang) and Sunan/Shekh Wali Lanang. The *Babad Kraton* on the other hand, mentions: Sunan (Ng)Ampel, Sunan Giri, Sunan Bonang, **Sunan Cirebon (Sunan Gunung Jati)**, Sunan Ngundung and Sunan Bantam.[12] At present the most widely accepted tradition mentions nine *wali* (*wali sanga*), namely: Maulana Malik Ibrahim, Sunan (Ng)Ampel, Sunan Bonang, Sunan Giri, **Sunan Gunung Jati**, Sunan Drajat, Sunan Kalijaga, Sunan Kudus, and Sunan Muria.[13] These *wali* are regarded as of 'foreign' origin, except for Sunan Kalijaga, who was a Javanese 'native.' At this stage, the narratives imply that Cirebon stood as an inseparable part of the whole and systematic network of Islam on Java. If the notion of 'foreign' and 'native' origin of the *wali* is drawn into a wider context, its implications crosscut the geographic boundaries of Java and the archipelago. It is concerned with a worldwide Islamic network centred in the Middle East. This network was maintained and has evolved over centuries even during the period when Indonesia was under foreign rules.[14] This network may have undergone up's and down's but it is certainly wrong to assume, as Geertz (1976) does, that Islam on Java was once totally cut off from the centre of Islamic learning in the Middle East and thus has lost its genuine genius and orthodoxy. It is this type of preserved Islam whose current manifestations I would like to identify.

According to local literary traditions, unlike other *wali*, who concern themselves mostly with religious matters while leaving other business to the king, Syarif Hidayatullah was himself a king beside being a *wali*.[15] He therefore, bore in his

[12] See also: Fox, J.J. (1991), "Ziarah Visits to the Tombs of Wali, the Founder of Islam on Java," in Ricklefs, M.C., ed., *Islam in Indonesian Social Context*, Melbourne: CSEAS, Monash University, p. 23).
[13] See also: Salam, S. (1960), *Sekitar Wali Sanga*, Kudus: Menara, p. 23.
[14] For the existence of continuous intellectual network between the Middle East and Java, see Azra, A. (1992), *The Transmission of Islamic Reformism to Indonesia: Network of Middle Eastern and Malay-Indonesian 'Ulama' in the Seventeenth and Eighteenth Century*, unpublished Ph D dissertation, Columbia: Columbia University.
[15] See also: Chapter Seven.

hands both religious as well as political power, and had the possibility, if he wished, of either institutionalising religion in the polity or of using religion to exercise political interest. Due to his sainthood, he chose the first rather than the second. He maintained contact with other leaders of Islam at that period, but was not intent on making Cirebon a political force. He even summoned his uncle Cakrabuana to return to Cirebon to attend a meeting of the religious leaders of Java, *wali sanga*, the nine *wali*. That is why, as far as those traditions indicate, Cirebon never developed into an important state, as De Graaf and Pigeaud (1989) noted. He was too religious to have strong ambitions of becoming a politically powerful king. Moreover, Syarif Hidayatullah had already had Sabakingking, a son from his marriage with a noble princess of Banten, a ruler in Banten. Sabakingking was later known as Sultan Hasanuddin. Thus, he was satisfied that his son in Banten was politically powerful enough that it was unnecessary for him to pursue politics in Cirebon, and he could, therefore, concentrate more on his religious mission. In addition, his sons in Cirebon, Jayakelana (who married Ratu Pembayun daughter of Raden Patah, King of Demak) and Bratakelana (who married Ratu Mas Nyawa, also a daughter of Raden Patah) preceded him, passing away soon after marriage. Later, Bratakelana's half brother, Pangeran Pasarean, who was supposed to be his direct successor, also died.[16] From these multiple grieves his sainthood grew stronger and he turned to focus more on religious matters, while at the same time, he expected his son in Banten to be even more powerful. His grandson, Pangeran Swarga, son of Pangeran Pasarean, who succeeded him in Cirebon was still a young child and thus could not exercise an effective leadership. When Panembahan Ratu succeeded Pangeran Swarga, Cirebon was left behind while Banten had already become an established empire vis-a-vis Mataram in Central Java.

Whether or not this narrative is warranted, my main concern at this stage is to suggest at least two things. One is that Islam in Cirebon may already have been long established at the early stage of Javanese conversion to Islam; the other is that Islam in Java has become part of folk tradition. These observations provide grounds to assume that Islam may have a strong influence on Javanese social life. Under such an assumption, looking at how Islam manifests itself and molds people's traditions is an interesting subject to deal with.

THEORETICAL ORIENTATION

Islam, like other religions, is a spiritual and moral force which influences, motivates and gives colour to individuals' behaviour. To elucidate the tradition of Islam within a particular society is to locate the Islamic traits which are manifest within the popular tradition. At this point, an immediate problem one encounters is what constitutes 'tradition,' and more importantly what constitutes

[16] See: 'the marriage alliance' between Sunan Gunung Jati and Raden Fatah in Chapter Six.

the 'Islamic Tradition.' I would like to suggest that the term 'tradition' is generally conceived as 'knowledge, doctrines, customs and practices, etc, transmitted from generation to generation as well as the transmission of such knowledge, doctrines and practices.[17] Islamic tradition is thus all the things which come from, are associated with, or bear the spirit of Islam. But how can we know that a certain tradition or elements of tradition come from, are associated with, or bear the spirit of Islam, and thus have become Islamic? In this context, it is interesting to refer to Barth who remarks on the relation between acts and intention in human interaction. He says among other things:

> "...the outcomes of (acts and) interaction are usually at variance with the intentions of the individual participants,..."[18]

Barth's point allows us to assume that a tradition or elements of tradition can be Islamic when the performer intends or claims that his act is performed within his Islamic spirit. This of course is simplistic and at best, it provides only a starting point. Barth however is a contemporary scholar who acknowledges the importance of intention in human action.

More than a millennium ago, long before Barth, the Prophet Muhammad, the founder of Islam, had put forward this point explicitly. He said among other things that the validity of actions is based on intention and thus the value of everything is dependent on the intention attached to it. If something is intended for a worldly end then its value is there, whereas if something is intended for the sake of God, then its value is a devotion to Him (which is very precious). This is both clear and authoritative indicating how important intention is for the Muslims.[19]

Now let us turn further to formal Islamic scholarly discourse. Here I would like to refer to remarks from Nasr (1981:1). He states that Islamic tradition is something which incorporates both the message received by the Prophet Muhammad in the form of the Scriptures as well as all that Islam, as a religion, absorbed according to its own genius and made its own through transformation and synthesis. It embraces all aspects of religion and its ramifications based upon sacred models. Further, Nasr argues that the Islamic tradition is like a tree. It has roots which are sunk in the Divine revelation, and from these roots grow over time trunk and branches. Islamic tradition is therefore a tree composed of

[17] Funk and Wagnalls (1984), *Standard Desk Dictionary*, Cambridge: Harper and Row.

[18] Barth, F. (1993), *Balinese Worlds*, The University of Chicago Press: Chicago.

[19] "**Innama'l-a'mal bi'l-niyat fainna likulli imrii ma nawa...** "This is a fairly long hadith but widely known, at least this part of the hadith. It is narrated by Muslim (Abu'l Husein Muslim bin al-Hajjaj bin Muslim al-Qushayriy al-Naisabury), one of the most reliable and authoritative hadith narrators. The hadith also appears on the first page of Nawawi's collection of 40 precious hadith and thus there is no need to explain its position and influence in shaping the view of (traditional) Javanese Muslims. For the complete text of the hadith see for example: Dahlan, A. (1988), *Hadits Arba'in Annawawiyyah*, Bandung: Al-Ma'arif.

roots, trunk and branches. Its core is religion, its sap incorporates God's grace (*barakah*), the sacred, the eternal and the immutable Truth, and the perennial wisdom and its continuous application according to various temporal and spatial conditions (Nasr, 1981:12).

Following Nasr's definition, Islamic tradition may be conceived as a vast embracing entity. It may include knowledge, world view, values and mode of behaviour where the Scriptures and the spirit of the Scriptures are the ultimate reference. Viewed in a technical context, it follows that to know to which religion a certain tradition belongs (Islamic, Christian, Hinduist, Buddhist, etc) is to find out in which religious Scriptures the tradition has its roots. By considering all these, it is also possible to draw the lexical meaning of 'tradition' into Islamic perspective and then to posit the tradition of Islam as something which involves 'tradition' wherein the owner or performer intends to do or claims that his action comes from, is associated with, or bears the spirit of, Islam; and that his intended or claimed behaviour is verifiable through, and finds its roots or justification in, Scriptures.

Taking Scriptures of various degrees of authority as a standard notion for justifying to which religion a certain tradition belongs should not be confused with using Scriptures to justify a legal and theological position as theologians, jurists and clergy do. Rather, we treat the society's reference to Scriptures directly or indirectly, consciously or unconsciously, as a sociological fact and empirically observable and testable phenomenon. Thus, when an observer sees that many things belonging to a society's beliefs and practices find their roots and justification in Scripture, he is neither collecting relics of revelation nor assembling a chronicle of error, as Geertz negatively implies.[20] As Graham points out, in a culture, the influence and importance of a scriptural text extends beyond the specifically religious sphere. One of the most obvious, according to Graham, is its effect upon language.[21] While this effect, as Graham says, is evident in Western Christendom, similar effects should not be ignored in Javanese Islam. The intrusion of an Islamic vocabulary and Arabic language upon the Javanese is enormous. As a tiny example, the prominent Javanese political jargon (Indonesian as well), the word *adil* (Arabic: **'Adl**) to mean just, such as in *Ratu adil* (the just king), is a word that appears many times in the Qur'an. So too is the word **salam** and **salamat** (pl. of **salamah**) meaning 'safe' which the Javanese slightly corrupt to *slamet*. No single Javanese word can replace **adl** (*adil*) and **salamah** (*slamet*). Even if for example, as Geertz (1976:14) tries in invoking a talk on etymology. He explains that in Javanese the word *slamet* means '*gak ana apa-apa*'--'there isn't anything' or, which according to Geertz 'more aptly'

[20] Geertz, C. (1975), *Islam Observed*, p. 19.
[21] Graham, W.A. (1987), "Scripture", in Eliade, Mircea, (ed), *The Encyclopedia of Religion*, New York: MacMillan.

(though not apt at all), 'nothing is going to happen (to anyone).' All these phrases and explanations, unfortunately, still do not reflect the real meaning of *slamet* as the original Arabic word implies. That is why the Javanese took it intact into their language. Even with such a simple thing, Geertz does not realise that the word he uses to refer to the core of *abangan* 'animistic ritual,' the '*slametan*,' is in fact, derived from the Qur'an and thus essentially Qur'anic. The *slametan*,' may be a religious symbol peculiar to Javanese Muslims. As we shall see however, it is not alien to the universal Islamic tradition; the name, the words recited in it, the procedures and the nature of its performance are after all Islamic.[22]

It is also from this point of view that a work like *The Religion of Java*, while stimulating, is also at the same time quite disappointing. Its author unhesitatingly judges various elements of Javanese tradition as belonging to a certain religion such as Hindu, Buddhist and animist, without a clear and definite standard for his judgement. This judgement appears to be based on the author's personal whims and simple rules of thumb. Throughout this work, not even a verse of formal Hindu or Buddhist Scriptures such as Veda or Theravada is cited. Geertz, the author, occasionally mentions the 'Ramayana' (p. 263) and 'Mahabarata' (pp. 263, 269ff, 278ff). Yet everyone knows that these epics, although they enjoy wide acceptance, are, like the *Kamasutra* and *Kakawin Arjunan Wiwaha*, not religious constituents of either Hinduism or Buddhism. Although these epics are enunciated through *wayang*, *wayang* takes more than these epics as its themes. *Wayang*, for a small fraction of Javanese, may be a ritual but for a majority of others, *wayang* belongs to the arts and the arts are entertainment and not a formal religious ritual as Geertz (1976:261ff) implies. Certainly, a deeply artistic entertainment like *wayang* may cause a certain degree of aura. To most Javanese (Muslims), all these things are part of their cultural heritage. The Javanese are proud to have them, good or bad, as signs of being a civilised society. Nevertheless, pride does not force an individual to take and mix them with his formal faith. What may be part of Islam —or other religions as well— is a respect for heritage, as respecting something, including a refined cultural heritage, is considered religiously meritorious and embedded deeply in Islamic Scriptures.

Kyai Fuad Hasyim, a religious orator of Pesantren Buntet, for example, is a genuine *santri* but he has been one of the fanatic lovers of *wayang* since his childhood.[23] On many occasions he unhesitatingly, even proudly, imitates a *dalang* to attract his audience, takes *wayang* figures to show both exemplary and derogatory behaviour, uses Sanskrit (Hindu/Buddhist) terms, vocabularies and wayang philosophies, to explain a theological or theosophical outlook and then finds the relevant Qur'anic verses, the Hadith or the work of *ulama* that enunciate

[22] See Chapter Five.

[23] Another *kyai's* appreciation and love of *wayang* as well as other arts is demonstrated quite clearly by Pranowo (1991).

the issues he is talking about. Is Kyai Fuad religiously syncretic? Few, if any, would consider him so.

While considering religion as a moral force which motivates human behaviour, I do not take the individual, household and community as units of analysis and then describe them based on predefined cultural traits. Rather, I stress action and behaviour. Thus, I identify and observe a certain behaviour, then trace it culturally within the sphere of a scriptural context. My approach therefore involves more 'contextual explanation' rather than that of social unit analysis.[24] Taking Scriptures into consideration in the study of Islam on Java has gained some currency. Studies that do this include the works by Dhofier (1985), Simuh (1988) and Woodward (1989). Through a detailed account based on my own data, I shall endeavour to demonstrate that the Javanese beliefs and practices, which are manifest in the life of the Javanese, including many things that Geertz claims as necessarily syncretic, are in fact genuinely part of an Islamic tradition, or an Islamic refinement of local tradition. Not only do the performers claim their tradition as Islamic but also find their roots and justification come from the basic sources of Islam: The Qur'an, the Hadith and the work of the *ulama*.

THE FIELD WORK

The field work on which this study is based was carried out in Cirebon, a region in the north-coast of eastern West Java, during the period between December 1991 to February 1993. Cirebon, which is located about 250 kilometres east of Jakarta, deserves a special attention for a number of reasons. Geographically the region is strategically located on the north-coast of Java and on the border between West and Central Java. Consequently, not only is it the gateway into and out of the two provinces but it is also the melting pot for Sundanese and Javanese sub-cultures. It forms a synthesis between the two cultures which is distinct from both, but bears in it the elements, influence and characteristics of both. This new synthesis is evident in the language the people speak, in some specific foods they eat and the specific arts they perform. *Bahasa Jawa Cerbon* or *Omong Cerbon* (the Cirebonese dialect of Javanese) for example, is unique. Although some claim that the language is *Omong Jawa* (Javanese language), ordinary Javanese-speaking people living in Central and East Java would not understand it, at least not initially. But as these Javanese would pay more attention to the language, they would soon recognise that the language is really similar to their own, or at least, they could understand it and be able to catch the main idea of what Cirebonese people are saying.

[24] Tjitrajaya, I. (1989), "Contextual explanations: A Methodological Examination," *Berita Antropologi*, Th XIII No. 45 Januari - Maret 1989, pp 1–10. Vayda, A.P. (1983), "Progressive Contextualization: Methods for Research on Human Ecology," in *Human Ecology*, 11, pp. 265–28.

Cirebon's location on the north-coast of Java entails some other implications. As one would expect, the sea has indeed provided a livelihood for the fishermen and sailors. Fish and other produces such as dried fish, *petis* (fish cream) and *terasi* (fish paste) are important trade goods. It is said that in ancient time *terasi* was also used as tribute. So many *rebon* or small shrimps were found in the area that according to literary tradition, this provided the name of the town and the region.[25] The nick name *Kota Udang* or Prawn Town is also used to refer to the city of Cirebon. In addition, the sea has certainly connected this region since long ago, not only with all corners of the archipelago but also with other nations and countries. Traders and other new comers from other parts of Java, Sumatra, Sulawesi as well as from China, India and other parts of Asia settled there.

Once, according to local literary traditions, the region was named *Caruban*, meaning the place where various people mixed and lived together and thus, the notion of melting pot takes on a wider spectrum.[26] The range of cultural elements it possibly accommodates becomes wider and goes beyond Javanese and Sundanese cultural boundaries, although these two cultural traditions are predominant.[27] In short, the geographic position has endowed the region with a richness of cultural traditions and access to continuous relations with other parts of the world. Currently, through the development efforts launched by the government and by the application of modern technology, especially in communications and transport, rural areas have been somewhat urbanised. Even the remote villages in the rural areas have now been linked with modern facilities. Paved streets, electricity, motor vehicles, radio, television and, to a much lesser extent, telephone, are within the reach of the common people; so are educational opportunities, at least at the primary level, and recently at junior secondary level. In some semi-urban dwelling areas, parabolic antenna to receive overseas T.V. broadcasts are used by well-to-do individuals. Urban-rural and coastal-inland differences in life-style and world-view therefore, have been narrowed but not been extinguished.

Geographic Descriptions

What is traditionally known as the Cirebon region was the former Dutch Residency (*Karesidenan*) of Cheribon which comprised the *Kotamadya* (Municipality) of Cirebon and the four *Kabupaten* (Regencies) of Indramayu,

[25] Cirebon means the water of tiny shrimps. It is a contraction of *Ci* and *rebon*; *ci* (or cai), in Sundanese, means water and *rebon* means tiny shrimps. The initial *ci* marks Sundanese names usually given to rivers: Cimanuk, Citarum, Ciliwung, etc; lakes or springs: Ciburuy, Cigugur, Cibulan, etc, and places associated with water: Cipanas, Cisaat, Ciawi, etc.

[26] The name *Caruban* and *Cirebon* represents an interesting linguistic phenomenon. Both are very close in pronunciation, used to refer to the same thing. But their lexical meaning, derivation and origin differ significantly. The first is Javanese the second is Sundanese.

[27] The influence of Chinese and Arab is quite marked in some forms of arts performance such as: the *Barong Sae* dance or the *Genjring* (flat drums) music.

Majalengka, Kuningan and Cirebon. The region covers an area of about 5,642,569 square kilometres and in 1990 had a population of about 4.5 million inhabitants. Lying on the border between West and Central Java, the region is bounded on the east by the Tegal regency in Central Java, by the sea on the north and the north-east, by Subang and Sumedang regencies on the west, and by the Ciamis regency on the south. Mount Ciremai, located to southwest of the city, is an active volcano. It is the highest mountain in West Java (3076 m) and the second highest on Java next to Semeru (3676 m). On its slopes there are a number of sulphur and hot water springs. The biggest are at Sangkanhurip (20 km south of Cirebon city) and at Gempol (10 km west of the city).

Administratively, the region of Cirebon is part of West Java province. Following the nationwide administrative system, each *kabupaten* and *kotamadya* has equal status. Each is under the West Java governor. Under the *kabupaten* and *kotamadya* are *kecamatan* (districts), each of which is headed by a *camat* (district chief). Some *kecamatan* have *kemantren,* headed by a *mantri,* a *camat's* assistant. A *kecamatan* usually consists of about 10 to 12 *desa* (villages) or *kelurahan,* the lowest level of administrative units. Each *desa* or *kelurahan* is headed by a *kades,* which stands for *kepala desa* or *lurah,* formerly known as a *kuwu* (chief). Although a *desa* is the lowest level of administration, it is not the smallest unit. A *desa* is usually divided into a number of *dusun* (hamlet), formerly *rukun warga (R.W.),* led by a *kadus,* which stands for *kepala dusun* (hamlet chief), who coordinates *rukun tetangga* (*R.T.* or neighbourhoods). An *R.T.* consists of a number of households; the maximum number is 70. It is the *R.T.*, headed by a *ketua R.T.* (*R.T.* chief), which constitutes the smallest unit within the *desa.*

Kabupaten and Kotamady Cirebon, in which the field work was conducted, lies between longitude 108° 40′ and 108° 50′ east meridian, and latitude 6° 30′ and 7° 00′ south of equator. It is an area of 984.15 square kilometres, or about 2.15 per cent of the West Java province. From west to east it extends for 54 kilometres and from north to south 39 kilometres. In 1991 the *kabupaten* had a population of 1.524.267 inhabitants whereas the city had 254.486. The proportion of male and female inhabitants in both areas was about 49 against 51 per cent. The population density in the *Kabupaten* was 1.549 per square kilometre, whereas in the *Kotamadya* it was 6.812. The Kabupsten had 21 *kecamatan,* 8 *kemantren,* and 424 *desa;* the city had only 5 *kecamatan* and 22 *kelurahan.*

The northern part of Kabupaten Cirebon is mostly a flat and marshy plain of less than 20 metres height above sea level. This plain areas constitutes about 80 per cent of the kabupaten, while the rest, at its southern part, is hilly. Most of the lands are agricultural land where 62.88 per cent of its total is wet rice terrace (*sawah*). Beside rice, peanuts, corn, cassava, vegetables and sugar-cane are also grown. Only 17 per cent of the land is used for settlement, 12 per cent for plantations to grow coffee, tobacco, rubber and tea. The rest is reserved forest

(4 per cent) and other (5 per cent). As can be expected, most people (about 52 per cent) are engaged in agriculture. This sector is the largest contributor (32 per cent) to the local GDP.[28] Trade, which involves only 12 per cent of the population, contributes almost as much and is the second largest contributor to GDP next to agriculture.[29] The city of Cirebon is an important producer of cigarettes. The biggest factory is owned by the British American Tobacco (BAT) Company. Among the other produce of the *Kabupaten* and *Kotamadya* of Cirebon are machine tools, chemicals, textiles (including batik), cement, pottery, furniture, cane crafts, sugar, fish and crude oil. All these things make the people of Cirebon an urbanised and mobile society.

The field work strategy

With anthropological training in mind, initially I was inclined to employ a holistic approach to a society in a particular locality. I chose a village in Plered, a small urban settlement about seven kilometres west of the city of Cirebon, to concentrate my research. I intended to work intensively and rigorously within the village milieu. I took residence at Pak Shofie's, a devout family living in a partly renovated old house with a small prayer house, in *Desa* Kalitengah, three kilometres north of Plered. I tried to get settled there and started working.[30]

As soon as I had started, I became dissatisfied. Neither in terms of socio-economic and political spheres nor in religion do the people of Plered belong to a self-contained society. They are dependent on, and affected by, many things that exist and occur in other places. For religious purposes, sometimes the people go many kilometres away from the village to *kramat* (shrines), at other times to the *kraton* (court). On one occasion they might go to a *pesantren* (a traditional boarding school), on another they might go across the village to attend a festival, a religious gathering or a *pengajian* (public speech). Still on another occasion they may invite a famous religious orator from in or outside Cirebon region to speak in the *desa* mosque. Considering the subject I would be dealing with, I

[28] Gunawan, W. (1992), *Industri Gula di Jawa Dalam Perspektif Model "Inti-Satelit," Kasus di Kabupaten Cirebon*, Bogor: Pusat Studi Pembangunan, IPB, p 4.

[29] Gunawan, W. et al. (1991), *Pembentukan Modal di Pedesaan, Kasus Kabupaten Cirebon*, Bogor: Pusat Studi Pembangunan, IPB. p. 9. (It is not stated, how much its contribution is to the local GDP).

[30] I thought Kalitengah was interesting in that, while most people are predominantly traditionalist, it has also become the centre of *Muhammadiyah*, the Modernists Muslim organisation, which began to appear in this *desa* in early 1960s. Here the Branch (*Cabang*), which coordinates the sub-branches (*Ranting*) of the surrounding *desa*, has its secretariat and has built a mosque. Traditionalist and Modernist tensions seemed to have been more apparent in Kalitengah than anywhere else in Cirebon and still appeared when I was there. Contrasting argumentations between the two sides around a number of practices often occurred where the traditionalists argued for keeping some practices, the Modernists argued against, even condemned, them. The Modernists are small in number but they tend to be militant and aggressive. The traditionalist, on the other hand, although sometimes militant, tend to be more defensive. Although claiming a larger number of members, through various gatherings, including formal meetings and rituals, I noticed that this organisation recruited no more than 300 supporters, including those from other surrounding *desa*. Compared with the population of Desa Kalitengah, which is more than 3000 inhabitants, Muhammadiyah is small but many of its members are rich.

felt it necessary to get a good understanding of what happened outside the village milieu in whatever the people of the village where I stayed were involved. Meanwhile it was impossible to find another village where all these things were available together at one place. In this situation, it was already clear that village traditions and religious life do not stand apart from other centres of tradition. What prevails in the village is confirmed in *kramat* or vice-versa; the roots of what occur both in the village and in *kramat* can be traced to *pesantren* and *kraton*; whereas, the sufistic nature and Islamic flavour of both the *kraton* and the *pesantren* is clearly evident in the village.

I was caught in a dilemma whether to concentrate on locality at the expense of losing sight of other relevant activities, or to study activities at the price of a probable insufficiency of a village-based ethnography. I decided to take the latter direction because I considered that relevance is more important than local detail. I initially wandered from one religious site to another throughout Cirebon, spending a couple of days or weeks at each place, leaving it for a couple of days or weeks and then coming again. All this was done to follow what was going on in the village, at *kramat* sites, in *pesantren, tarekat*, and at the *kraton* (Kanoman, Kesepuhan, Keceribonan and Kaprabonan). In the meantime I still kept my residence in Kalitengah as a base camp. At the same time I treated this village as a starting point to see an approximate model of the traditions of people's daily religious life. By so doing, and benefiting by being conversant in Javanese, Sundanese and the Cirebon vernacular (*Omong Cerbon*), I could establish good relationships and felt free to watch and get involved, as well as to observe and participate in many important activities as an outsider on some occasions, and as an insider on others.

According to the 1985 official statistics issued by the Department of Religious Affairs in Jakarta, there are at least 274 known *pesantren* throughout the region of Cirebon. They are scattered in various places, seven of which are in the *Kotamadya* (Municipality) and 91 in *Kabupaten* (Regency) of Cirebon. The rest are: 39 in Indramayu, 65 in Majalengka and 72 in Kuningan regencies. The latest figures for *pesantren* throughout the *kabupaten* and the city of Cirebon are also available at the local office of the Department of Religious Affairs. These show that there has been at least 30 per cent increase in *pesantren* in the last ten years; by 1992 the number of *pesantren* was 133.

I visited thirty *pesantren* before I decided to concentrate attention on only two. I stayed in both *pesantren*, first in Buntet, the biggest *pesantren* in Cirebon for quite a long time and only a couple of weeks in Tarbiyatul Banin. This is a newly established *pesantren* led by Ki Kuwu Nasir, who is a *kuwu*, a healer, a businessman and a *kyai* at the same time.[31] This *pesantren* specialises in educating pre-school and school age children.[32] When I stayed in Buntet I benefited in knowing about *Tarekat Syatariah* and *Tarekat Tijaniyah*, two important Sufi orders in Cirebon. In this work I only present a description of Pesantren Buntet and the Sufi orders operating within this *pesantren* precinct. It was readily apparent that *pesantren* and Sufi orders, *through ngaji pasaran* (public lectures) and *tarekat* gatherings, are major sources for the diffusion of Islamic orthodoxy among the mass populace of villagers.

Islamic learning in Cirebon may neither be as old nor have reached a comparable degree as in Acch. But there is enough grounds to assume that traditions of Islamic learning in Cirebon are not something new. Ignoring the *Babad*, which tells us about Shekh Datu Kahfi who started a formal *pesantren* at Gunung Jati, and without taking into account the *pesantren* within the court circle, traditions of Islamic learning could have been in existence since the sixteenth century. The oldest *pesantren* in Cirebon are Pesantren *Pusaka* in the Lemahabang District and *Nurul Huda* in Cilimus, each of which claims to have been established in the second half of the seventeenth century. Currently the largest *pesantren* in Cirebon, Pesantren Buntet, claims to have been first established in 1750. It is difficult to check these claims historically. But Hoadley (1975) may be right in maintaining that the one element contributing to the high esteem enjoyed by Cirebon was its reputation as the region's most revered centre of Islamic piety and learning, a reputation dating from the era of Java's conversion to Islam.[33] In addition, Cirebon as a coastal city may accord with John's assertion that coastal city states had the potential to become "centres for the diffusion of Islamic ideas to the peasant interior."[34]

Pijper describes Cirebon as a place where there are a large number of *kramat*.[35] According to the local authority at the local office of the Department of Education and Culture, the number of revered places known as *kramat* is more than 300. They are dispersed in many locations. I visited around forty of them but stayed a fairly long period at only some of them. Those places, mostly tombs of revered

[31] Certainly, this person poses a problem to the Geertzian framework as to which category Kuwu Nasir belongs. Is he an *abangan* because he is a healer, a *santri* because he is a *kyai*, or a *priyayi* because he is a *kuwu*? There are many others like Kuwu Nasir in Cirebon.

[32] During field work I visited this *pesantren* regularly at least once every two weeks to see my beloved son (who was 5 years old) staying in this *pesantren* to learn Qur'an for about 11 months. His stay, at least partly, contributed to my easy access of observing how a *pesantren* works. Although, after a fairly long adaptation, he enjoyed staying at this *pesantren*, I need to apologise for separating him at this early age from his beloved mother, sisters and peers in Jakarta.

[33] Hoadley, M.S. (1975), *History of the Cirebon-Priangan "Jaksa College", 1705–1735*, unpublished, Ph D dissertation, Cornell University, p.10.

[34] Johns, A.H. (1985), "Islam in Southeast Asia: Problems of Perspective", in Ibrahim, A., Siddique, S., and Husein, Y. (1985), *Readings On Islam in South East Asia*, ISEAS: Singapore, p.21

[35] Pijper, G.F. (1934), *Fragmenta Islamica* (Indonesian translation by Tujimah, 1987), Jakarta: U.I. Press. pp. 79–80.

figures of various standing, attract many visitors. One which is the most prominent is the *Astana Gunung Jati* grave complex, where Sunan Gunung Jati is buried. Visitors to this place come with various purposes and from various strata, ranging from ignorant laymen to famous scholars including *ulama* like Buya Hamka, from poor peasants to very rich Chinese businessman like Mas Agung, and from jobless individuals to famous politicians like former President Sukarno.[36] Until now, there are around one thousand people coming and going to visit this place every day. This number increases to five thousand or more on an ordinary Thursday evening (*Malam Jum'at*), twenty thousand or more on Thursday evening *Kliwon* (*Malam Jum'at Kliwon*), and hundreds of thousand at the time of festivals.

The second biggest *kramat* after Astana Gunung Jati, in terms of the number of visitors, is *Kramat Mbah Buyut Trusmi* at Trusmi. Next to Trusmi are *Lemah Tamba* at Lemah Tamba, *Nyi Mas Gandasari* at Panguragan, *Kramat Talun* at Cirebon Girang, and *Syekh Magelung* at Karangkendal, to mention only a few. After the Astana, it was to these places that I made my most frequent and longest visits. Unlike the Astana grave complex which stands under the direct control of the Cirebon *Kraton*, many other *kramat* stand more or less independently. Nevertheless, most of them in one way or another, still claim to be under the *wewengkon* (auspices) of either the *Kesepuhan* or *Kanoman* court, two of four *kraton* which still draw attraction to Cirebon.

Siddique has excelled herself in her study of the Cirebon *kraton*. By employing Berger and Luckman's sociological theories she has produced an interesting sociological analysis of the role of *kraton* in relation to the overall fabric of the Cirebonese social system.[37] My primary concern with the *kraton* was to explore whether there are traditions within the *kraton* circle which have some relation to village life. I found that some *kraton* traditions of ceremonies and feasts are in fact exemplary models for various feasts, including many forms of *slametan*, adopted by the people in the villages. In addition, through *Babad* and other literary traditions, the *kraton* are the major source of people's perception or knowledge about history and myths as well as ideal ethics and customs. In addition to this, *kraton-pesantren* differences can only be identified in terms of institutional and political orientation, not in basic Islamic orthodoxy.

While being sceptical about a syncretic argument on Javanese Islam, I am also rather sceptical about considering Islam in Arabia, Egypt or elsewhere as the sole standard by which to judge certain religious practices and traditions as Islamic or non-Islamic. I am convinced that it is necessary to consider a certain practice as Islamic if it is dominated by Islamic norms or spirit, regardless of its

[36] Buya Hamka refers to Prof Dr. H. Abdul Malik Karim Amrullah (Hamka), former chairman of Indonesian Council of Ulama (*Majelis Ulama Indonesia*).
[37] Siddique, S. (1977), *Relics of the Past?* Unpublished Ph D. dissertation, Bielfeld: Universitat Bielfeld.

origin. Take for example, the use of the *bedug* (large drum) and *kentong* (a hollowed log with slit hole in its centre) at the mosques and prayer houses in the villages, *kraton* and *pesantren*. They are Islamic in nature because they are used to inform people that the prayer time has come although their origin may be of the Hindu, Buddhist or some other tradition. Both of the objects and the sounds have become symbols of local Islamic identity.[38] This example can be expanded to many other objects and practices, including the *slametan*, Geertz's core *abangan* ritual which to him is indicative of animistic-Hindu-Buddhist syncretism.[39]

THE SIGNIFICANCE OF THE STUDY

Study on this subject and especially in this area is still very rare. Pijper (1934) however, has thrown interesting light on aspects of Islam in Cirebon. In the introductory to his account of the rise of *Tarekat Tijaniyah*, he mentions specifically: (1) that the areas of Banten and Cirebon are marked by many *kramat* and many *pesantren*; (2) that the influence of *kyai* or religious scholars among the villagers is very strong; (3) that traditional village religiosity is still evident; (4) that the modernist Islamic movements such as *Muhammadiyah* and *Sarekat Islam* were unable to make inroads in these areas; (5) that only the conservative *Nahdlatul Ulama* was able to do so; (6) that it was in Banten and Cirebon where the people's religious piety was the most clearly apparent; (7) that strict observation of religious duties, particularly in performing prescribed daily prayers when the time comes, even while being at work, were characteristic of people's religious life in the villages. To make things clearer, he illustrated that such practices as unhesitatingly doing prayer at the road side or in the midst of a paddy field or anywhere else that made it possible to do so were common among the villagers.[40] This study contributes to highlighting and substantiating Pijper's assertions.

Among the older generation in Cirebon, the term *Jawa* (Java or Malay) is inseparable from Islam. Being *wong Jawa* or Javanese is necessarily to be a Muslim; *wong-Jawa* is distinct from *wong Cina* or Chinese and *wong Welanda* or Dutch not only in terms of race as their appearances are different, but mainly in terms of religion as exemplified by the following informant's statement:

> "The Javanese are those whose religion is the religion of Java, that is Islam, worshipping Allah, praying at mosque; whilst the Chinese, their religion is the religion of Chinese worshipping Tao Peh Khong (idols),

[38] While a bell is used in the church, *bedug* and *kentong* are found in mosques or prayer houses.
[39] See Chapter Five.
[40] Pijper, G.F. (1987), *Fragmenta Islamica* (Indonesian translation), pp.80–81.

praying at temple; the Dutch, their religion is the Dutch religion, that is Christianity, worshipping Jesus, praying at Church.'[41]

Pijper's description about people's religious performances in Banten and particularly Cirebon which he calls "devout" but "still traditional", and under the "strong influence of *kyai*", is in marked contrast, for example, with what I found and experienced sometimes in Jakarta among fellow modern intellectuals, mostly modernist proponents. While discussing how Islam fits or can be fitted to modern times, that proposing the Muslims to do this and that in order that they become developed, arguing this and that will make Islam a moral force for modernisation, the call for prayer from the nearby mosque was treated as no better than the roar of motor vehicles in the nearby street. There was no sign that anyone in the group is being called upon to do a special (divine) duty. Some of us carelessly let prayer time pass and leave our duty undone although, according to our own standard of belief and knowledge, performing prayer is the core of being a good Muslim.

The situations are different, so are the contexts. My fellow intellectuals in the city have their own reasons, so do the villagers; both groups are more likely to claim themselves devout although they exhibit different expressions. Neither do I recall these contrasts to direct attention to traditional-modern issues. Rather, I want to recall to mind that now, in this era of globalisation, the largest segment of Indonesian society (around 90 per cent of the Muslims) keep professing and perceiving Islam differently from contemporary modernist intellectuals. Their form of Islam deserves our scrutiny.

It is already well known that many practices of traditional Islam in Java have been abandoned by the modernists-reformists, because according to them, these practices are not Islamic. On the other hand, the traditionalists see their modernists-reformists counterpart as attempting to deprive them of the meritorious practices which for them have real sacramental values. Currently, the major studies on Islam in Indonesia seem to favour the modernist-reformist discourse with tendencies to undermine the traditional one. To avoid showing contempt and to have sympathy for those who are caught in this undertow, some form of balancing attempt is worthwhile. Such an attempt has already appeared. Dhofier (1985) is a clear example. While pointing to the lack of serious study of traditional Islam, he criticises some writers who misjudged traditional Islam. He points out that such writers as Geertz, Samson and Noer who undermine traditional Islam by claiming it to be syncretic, Hindu-Buddhist, animistic,

[41] Field notes. During field-work I heard such expressions several times from different people. This version is from Mang Tumari (67 yrs), a blind massaseur. Its original Javanese is: "Wong Jawa iku agamae agama Jawa, yaiku agama Islam, nyembae ning Gusti Allah, sembayange ning mesigit; ari wong Cina, agamae ya agama Cina, nyembae ning tempekong, sembayange ning klenteng; wong Welanda, agamae agama Welanda, yaiku agama Kresten, nyembae ning Nabi Isa, sembayange ning greja".

conservative are, according to Dhofier, onesided, unfair and unwarranted because they tend to distort reality. Throughout his work he then shows how traditional Islam, particularly that which is maintained within the *pesantren* tradition, more specifically among the *Kyai*, has real vigour and vitality. It is because of its inherent vitality and dynamics that until now traditional Islam has never ceased from winning so many followers.[42]

The notion of 'followers' is one thing that I wish to underline in that traditional Islam is not only adopted by knowledgeable individuals like *kyai*, but also by the mass populace, the 'followers', whose knowledge of the Scriptures vary considerably, from not knowing to being very knowledgeable. The former group, is called *wong bodo* (ignorant), the second group is the small number of wong *alim* or *wong pinter* (knowledgeable people).[43] In between, the largest in number, are people with rudimentary or general knowledge. Part of this group are devout (*wong santri*), another part are non devout (*dudu wong santri* or *bli santri*). This religio-devotional categorisation is further complicated by moral or ethical categorisation in relation to daily conduct, ranging from *wong bener* (right or good people) to *wong mlaun* (sinners). *Wong bener* refers to those who keep from *malima* (the five sins): *madat* (taking opium), *maling* (stealing), *maen* (gambling), *madon* (womanising) and *mabok* (drinking alcohol); whereas the latter (*wong mlaun*) refers to those who commit one or more of the *malima*. This categorisation does not at all reflect a static and clearcut grouping but rather is dynamic in that a sinner at one time can later be very devout, or vice versa. These categories stand independently from each other. *Alim/pinter-bodo* is a grouping based on mastery of knowledge; *santri-bli/dudu santri* is based on devotion to God especially regarding the prescribed prayers; *bener-mlaun* is based on individual conduct and behaviour. Ideally, a *wong alim* is both a *wong santri* and *wong bener* at the same time, but this is not automatically so. In theory, it is quite possible to find an *alim* who is neither *santri* nor *bener*, or *wong bodo* who is *santri* and *bener*. In reality however, the former rarely occurs, the latter occurs frequently.

My concern in this work is to delineate the forms of Islam to which these people claim to belong. Such claims are manifest in their participation and commitment in various religious activities which to them are part of their tradition, the very tradition to which I personally claim to belong. I was born, raised and nurtured within this tradition. Thus I shared the feelings, knowledge and experience of these villagers. With rudimentary knowledge I also participated in village

[42] Dhofier, Z. (1985), *Tradisi Pesantren: Studi tentang Pandangan Hidup Kiyai*, LP3ES: Jakarta, pp.4–7.
[43] The term '*wong alim*' (Arabic: **'alim**, meaning knowledgeable individual, pl. **'ulama**) refers specifically to individuals with profound religious knowledge. *Wong pinter* (literally means clever people) refers to knowledgeable people in general in either religious or secular knowledge. The term *santri* is also applied to students of pesantren (traditional boarding school). Used in this way, its matching pair is *kyai* rather than *bli/dudu santri*. Thus, it is mostly used to refer to the student-teacher (*santri - kyai*), relationship. Going to a *pesantren* and becoming a *santri* (student at *pesantren*), in Cirebonese socio-linguistic context, implies a hope of growing into becoming a *wong santri* (devout individual). *Santri* are models of devout.

activities for the maintenance and preservation of the tradition. This work, therefore, represents a genuine observation from within. Being in this position, I was never trapped into what I would call an "elite cage" that I suspect many outside (especially foreign) observers usually find themselves in. Very often an outside observer becomes a "distinguished guest" who is given special treatment. In turn, this observer relies for much of his information on this elite host. In this situation, most elites, for their own interests, more often than not, temper the information they provide. In contrast, beside my being flexible as a participant observer, my informants are various individuals from various strata of the society, ranging from the wong *bodo* to very knowledgeable *kyai*; from the *wong mlaun* to *wong santri*; and from *priyayi* in the *kraton*, clerks and officials in the offices, to *wong beburu* (labourers), *wong tani* (farmers) and even people with uncertain occupations in the villages and streets; from the *wong sugih* (rich people) to the *wong mlarat* (poor people) and *wong bli duwe* (the have-nots). I was free to move in and out the mosques and prayer houses, sleep in *kramat* with pilgrims, participate in rituals and ceremonies, and mix amidst spectators. Despite the fact that my main concern was with the grassroots' tradition, inclusion of some elites (*kyai*, government and *kraton* officials) among my informants was inevitably necessary because in many cases, the *kyai* and the *priyayi* are in fact, masters of this tradition. Information from them was, however, confined to something relevant or related to their own roles and views, not about something else, unless it was needed for verification purposes.

This study, differs from other studies that have already appeared. Although it is closely related, it differs for example from Dhofier's. Dhofier's excellent work is concerned with knowledgeable *kyai*. In contrast, my concern is with the grassroots. In some way, it may be regarded as an expansion of Dhofier's with a much wider spectrum involving not only their world view, but also beliefs and practices. This study also differs from those such as Geertz's. Geertz is an outside observer who supposedly worked within a tradition similar to mine. Unfortunately, I think, he misconceived the real situation from the start, misunderstood as he went through and misinterpreted at the end. He, for example, took only the modernists' stance uncritically when he started working.[44] He speaks about *santri* but very little, if anything in his work, reflect *santri* traditions. Finally, he distorted part of what really occurs. In fact, except for a portion on Javanese *adat, The Religion of Java* reveals very little about Javanese religious tradition. Instead of seeing it as an account of the "religion" of Java, Geertz's stimulating work is much more concerned with 'adat ritual' and 'politics' in Java. It presents an interesting account about conflicting groups resulting

[44] Clifford Geertz, who studies Javanese Islam, takes the Modernists' stance and limits the scope of 'Islam' to only those things which the Modernists happen to approve of. This is why Hodgson (1974:551) refers to him as: "...caught to major systematic error."

from the intrusion of Western type political parties into Javanese village life.[45] It is Geertz's narrating talents which wrap everything up to look like religion.

Just as traditional Islam maintained in *pesantren* has been misunderstood and distorted by some observers, so too has been the traditional Islam of the populace, the 'popular Islam.'[46] Some modernists, including ignorant or 'popular' modernists, to which I also belonged during my High School period,[47] stigmatise the performers of this form of Islam by derogatory references such as ***jumud*** (static), ***taqlid*** (to follow others uncritically), ***bid'ah*** (innovations), and ***syirik-musyrik*** (equating God with something). These stigma are launched merely because these people rarely question the authority of the *ulama*, especially the *kyai* who preserve the *pesantren* tradition. Ironically, at the same time and in the same manner, these (ignorant) modernists rarely question the authority of the modernist orators. They only believe that these orators are true and the others are wrong. The beliefs and practices of the traditionalists are alleged as idolatrous, mingling with them the beliefs and practices of pre-Islamic past, merely because these beliefs and practices do not conform with the modernists'.[48] Yet for those performers who happen to be incapable of enunciating their ideas, almost all these condemned practices find their roots and justification in formal Scriptures. While standing between those who condemn these practices and the performers of these practices, it is interesting to delineate what the performers hold from their point of view. It is also here that I would like to make a contribution to an understanding of Islam on Java.

Malinowski (1935) rightly implies that doing genuine field work can be difficult, more so is organising its results into a readable coherent work. Faced with the difficulty in sorting out the wide range of popular tradition, I shall present this work in nine chapters which I think properly represent the popular tradition of Islam that prevails in the area under study. After this Introduction, which I designate as Chapter One, follows Chapter Two which discusses the Cirebonese

[45] Seen in this way the title of its Indonesion version "*Abangan, Santri, Priyayi Dalam Masyarakat Java*" (Abangan, Santri, Priyayi in Javanese Society), Jakarta: Pustaka Jaya, is much more appropriate than its original title, "The Religion of Java."

[46] I use the term 'popular Islam' to refer to the form of Islam which can generally be seen in the villages, *kramat* and other places especially outside the *pesantren* precincts.

[47] I was a fairly active member of "Pelajar Islam Indonesia (PII)" in Cirebon during my Junior High and in Bandung during my Senior High Schools. PII was an Indonesian Moslem Students Union, holding a Modernists' stance.

[48] Those attributes are commonly heard when modernists speakers refer in their speeches to the traditionalist's beliefs and ritual practices. Examples of such reference can be found in modernist's writings, one of which is Noer, D. (1973), *The Modernists Muslim Movement in Indonesia 1900–1942*, Oxford University Press, especially p. 300. As a modernist, Noer has made a significant contribution in delineating the nature, rise and development of Modernism in Indonesia. Unfortunately, he was tempted to get involved rather deeply in an unnecessary and unbalanced judgement of another group (the Traditionalists) to which Noer himself did not belong. Repeating Geertz, his subjective and sometimes emotional judgements of the Traditionalists in favour of the Modernists marred a great deal on the value of his scholarly work.

belief system. It discusses peoples' basic concept of and belief in God, spiritual as well as physical beings and their position in relation to God. Chapter Three is concerned with the mythology and cosmology of Cirebonese traditions. Included in this discussion are the myths of creation, both the creation of the universe and the creation of human beings, as well as the origin of the Javanese and their religion, the idea of calamity, the afterlife world and Cirebonese numerology. The latter is the science of the meaning that involves manipulating numbers to speculate about bad or good times to do certain work.

Chapters Four, Five and Six deal with ritual practices, the many religious practices in which most people in Cirebon are frequently involved. Chapter Four is concerned with *ibadat*, formal religious devotion to God, officially prescribed by Islam as everyone's duty so long as he or she is a Muslim. It is the commitment to this *ibadat*, especially daily prayers, by which a Muslim is locally considered as devout or non devout. Although failure to fulfil this duty is religiously considered sinful, in reality, due to various reasons, many people take the risk of being in this condition. Chapter Five discusses many forms of ceremonial undertakings, none of which is a formal religious duty and thus, failure to perform such activities are not considered sinful despite the fact that by local social standards, such non-performance may cause a sort of embarrassment. These ceremonial undertakings, regarded as *adat*, for those who like to do them and can afford them, are considered religiously meritorious. Many people use them either to express their Muslim identity or to ensure harmonious relationships among themselves in the light of God's mercy. Many forms of *slametan* fall into this category and for this reason these undertakings are discussed in detail in this chapter. Chapter Six contains a discussion of the veneration of *wali* and holy men. This form of ritual belongs to what is considered *adat*. While the *adat* discussed earlier is more concerned with relationships among the living, the *adat* discussed in this chapter concerns relationships between the living and the deceased, also in the light of God's mercy. The overall tenor of *wali* and holy men veneration is the belief in possible merits, in this world and in the hereafter, of establishing relationships with the venerated dead. As God loves the pious, establishing a good relationship with the pious, dead or alive, is itself considered a pious act. The dead, with whom a relationship is more likely to bring merit, are individuals who were known to have excelled themselves during their lifetime in pious acts and in extra devotion to God. The best known individuals of this kind are *wali* and holy men. It is these persons who, by their piety, are venerated. The widely practiced veneration of *wali* and holy men requires *ziarah* (visits) to their tombs, known as *kramat* (shrines). It is not clear when all these traditions began to appear but certainly they are as old as Islam on Java.

Seen from a wider context, *ibadat* and *adat*, including *wali* veneration cannot be separated from each other. Rather, as we shall see, there are mutual interrelationships because there are some forms of *adat* in the performance of *ibadat*, and ethically, there is a certain sense of *ibadat* in the *adat*. All these traditions, in one form or another, have been transmitted from generation to generation through various means and by various individuals. There are, however, certain institutions which are considered as most responsible for this transmission. These institutions are discussed in Chapter Seven which deals with *pesantren*, and Chapter Eight which deals with Sufi orders (*tarekat*). Both chapters lead to Chapter Nine, the conclusion of this thesis.

This work is neither perfect nor complete. There may be many things not included here. To the best of my effort, however, what I have put into this work constitutes the most essential parts of the manifestations of the Islamic tradition in Java and, in particular, in Cirebon. Hopefully, this work will provide a basis for further study and exploration as well as stimulate better understanding of the richness and intricacy of the long established tradition of Islam in Java.

Plate 1: Kraton Kesuphuhan.

Plate 2: Pakuningrat S.H., Sultan Kesepuhan.

Plate 3: A business centre: a scene in the city of Cirebon.

Plate 4: A scene in the village.

Plate 5: Two children at play: a scene in the village.

Plate 6: Pak Shofie (right), his family and close kin.

Chapter 2: Belief System

THE IDEA OF GOD

asyhadu al-la ilaha illallah,
wa asyhadu anna Muhammadar-Rasulullah.

isun anakseni kelawan atinisun,
setuhune oranana Pengeran anging Allah.
lan isun anakseni kelawan atinisun,
setuhune Nabi Muhammad iku utusane Allah.
tegese kang aran Pengeran, iku dzat kang agawe,

langit kelawanMbumi, sarta isine kabeh.
Isun anakseni setuhune Kanjeng Nabi Muhammad,
iku utusane Gusti Allah kanggo wong alam kabeh.

asyhadu an la ilaha illa Allah,
wa asyhadu anna Muhammadan Rasul Allah.

I bear witness in my heart,
that there is no Lord but Allah.
and I bear witness in my heart,
that Muhammad is the Messenger of Allah.

He who is called Lord is the Being who creates
heaven and earth and the contents thereof.
I bear witness that the most Excellent Prophet Muhammad
is the Apostle of Allah, for mankind throughout the whole world.

This poem is one sample of *puji-pujian* (praising God) I frequently heard from a *tajug* (prayer house) at Blok Kedawung, a village in Desa Kaliwadas of Weru District, about twelve kilometres south-west of the city of Cirebon.[1] The poem is in Cirebonese dialect, but somewhat surprisingly, on some occasions I heard the same poem chanted at a prayer house in the Sundanese village of Desa Brujul-Kulon, District of Jatiwangi in Majalengka Regency about 30 kilometres west of Cirebon. This would suggest that the poem is not only known by Javanese speaking people in Cirebon living in the plain close to the coastal area, but also by the inland Sundanese as well. The chanters were groups of people (*jama'ah*) consisting of children and adults, males and females, who were about to undertake the prescribed prayer. They usually do this chanting soon after one of them has sounded the *adzan* (call for prayer). During chanting, they recite

[1] *Puji-pujian* is a local term referring to chants in praise of God or the prophet Muhammad. It is a common practice among traditional Muslims in Java to chant *puji-pujian* after *adzan* or the call to prayer has sounded.

the verses repeatedly until the *imam* comes and prayer begins. The poem is not the only one recited in pre-prayer chanting; there are many others. I chose this particular poem because I think it is relevant to a discussion of the Cirebonese idea of God, the subject dealt with in this section.

Chanting *puji-pujian* at prayer time is a common practice among traditional Muslims, especially in Cirebon. Usually, the chanting goes on during the time between the call to prayer and the prayer itself, that is, during the time while people wait for their *imam* who will lead the prescribed daily prayer. The main idea of the chanting is that, in accordance with standards of piety, no time within the prayer session is without spiritual significance. All activities within this session are directed solely towards *ibadah* or *ibadat* (devotion to God); [2] and before the main *ibadah* (the prescribed prayer) begins, *puji-pujian* serves as a kind of warming up. In this context, the chanting, usually of verses that glorify God or that respect the Prophet Muhammad, or other similar verses, is considered a meritorious religious act. In addition, if the chanted verses are the **syahadah** (testimony of faith), they in fact, have at least a double function: for adults, the function is renewal and re-affirmation of the creed; for children, it is a kind of preparatory drill ensuring that they are conversant with pronouncing the words when the time comes to recite the creed formally.

The first couplet of the poem I have selected includes the Arabic words of the **syahadah** which the Cirebonese call *syahadat.* [3] Literally, *syahadat* means testimony. In religious use the term *syahadat* refers to the Muslim profession of faith stating that there is no God but God and that Muhammad is the Messenger of God. The second couplet is the translation of the *syahadat* in rather archaic Cirebonese Javanese dialect. In English it translates "I bear witness (in my heart) that there is no Lord but Allah, and I bear witness (in my heart that the most Excellent Prophet Muhammad is the Messenger of Allah." The third couplet contains a short description of the two main "characters" depicted in the *syahadat:* the first, explains the use of the term *Pengeran* (Lord) for God, a key point for me in determining the poem's relevance; the second, explains the function of Muhammad, whose prophethood is universal. The basic idea of Deity that prevails among most Cirebonese seems to conform to the message conveyed by this verse. It says that what is really meant by God is the Being who created heaven, and earth together with their contents. There is no doubt however, that the word *Pangeran* refers to Allah, the proper name of God among Muslims.

For Cirebonese, as well as for other Muslims, pronouncement of the Islamic creed, the *syahadat*, is a supreme religious act whose mere recitation suffices for entry into the community of believers.[4] The important position of *syahadat*

[2] In local usage, *ibadah* and *ibadat* make no difference, both are frequently used and interchangeable.
[3] Subsequently I shall use the Cirebonese word, the "*syahadat*."
[4] See also: "God in Islam", *Encyclopedia of Religion*.

among Cirebonese is manifest in the fact that almost without exception, all native Cirebonese are Muslim in the sense that everyone, recites the *syahadat* at least once during his/her lifetime. Interestingly, the formal recitation of the *syahadat* takes place at particularly crucial moments of the life cycle, that is, at the time of circumcision and marriage. Circumcision for a boy and marriage for a girl are of fundamental importance among Javanese.[5]

"Formally, in Islam, the obligation to recite syahadat is required only once during a lifetime", said Pak Shofie, my informant. He explained that when people finished reciting *syahadat*, they automatically become Muslim, whatever intention they might have in their hearts and whatever they will do after the recital. "We do not know what is in one's heart, we only know what one says." In Islam, Pak Shofie added, that to do good or bad, right or wrong is solely an individual's right; for that reason a person bears responsibility to God. But when a person falls into trouble or gets sick, other Muslims are obliged to help, and when a person dies it is the duty of other Muslims to care for the corpse, to pray at the burial and to bury the person at a Muslim burial complex. This statement does confirm that a mere recitation of *syahadat* suffices for entry into the *ummah*, the community of believers whose social bonds are based on the pronouncement of that very creed. Of course this is not to say that a mere oral pronouncement is enough to become a good Muslim. Deeper awareness in the heart of the reciter is also required; again, Pak Shofie explained:

> One who would truly recite *syahadat* is required to incorporate two things: the first is to pronounce it by the tongue and to fill the heart with earnestness while witnessing that there is no god that can be rightfully worshipped but Allah, and that Muhammad is the Messenger of Allah. He must be sure that Muhammad's prophethood is to teach jinn and humankind about the divine message written in the Holy Qur'an. Secondly, real recital of *syahadat* should be accompanied by *tasdiq, ta'dhim, khurmah* and *khilwah*. *Tasdiq* means affirming that Allah is the sole God; *ta'dhim* means glorifying God; *khurmah* means exalting God; and *khilwah* means being generous in accepting Allah as the sole God; that is the real *syahadat*. Ignoring those elements is to mar the recital of *syahadat* and one's becoming a Muslim is only superficial.[6]

[5] This is clearly illustrated by Geertz (1976), in *The Religion of Java*, Phoenix ed, Chicago: The University of Chicago Press pp. 51–67.

[6] Indepth interview, 28-2-1992: "Wong kang maca syahadate bener-bener iku kudu nyumponi rong perkara: siji, ngucapaken karo lesan lan nekadaken ning jero ati. Nakseni yen langka Pengeran maning kang wajib disembah sejene Gusti Allah, lan nakseni yen Nabi Muhammad iku dadi utusane Gusti Allah. Diutuse kanjeng Nabi Muhammad iku perlu kanggo nggawa prentah-prentahe Gusti Allah ta'ala kang ana ning Qur'an kanggo para jinn lan menusa. Keloro, wong kang syahadate bener-bener iku kudu dibarengi karo tasdik, ta'dzim, khurmat lan khilwat. Tasdik artine negesaken yen kang dadi pengeran iku mung Gusti Allah siji; ta'dzim yaiku ngagungaken Gusti Allah; khurmat artine mulyaaken Gusti Allah; khilwat yaiku ngrasa tenang lan nikmat atine merga duwe pengeran

Referring back to the poem that begins this section, God is firstly enunciated as *Kang gawe*, the creator of the universe: heaven, earth, and all the contents within them. This indicates that, in the first place, the Cirebonese idea of God is closely related to the concept of creation; professing that as creator, God creates what He likes and by His own will without interference from any other. Secondly, God is only one and the oneness of God is importantly emphasised: he has no companion, and has no equality. "*Gusti Allah iku Siji, oranana kang madani*" (the sovereign Lord Allah is One, none is equal to Him), Saefullah (37 years), a toy peddler, said. He affirmed the oneness of God by pointing out that it is in fact, depicted in the Holy Qur'an in *surat Qulhu* (QS: 112;1–4).[7] He recited the verses and then gave their meaning in *Bahasa Indonesia*, which translates as: "Say, He, Allah is One, the Eternal God. He begot none, nor was He begotten. None is equal to Him".

Some Cirebonese do recognise a variety of other deities: *dewa* (*deva*, male) and *dewi* (*devi*, female), *Betara* (*Bhatara*, male) and *Betari* (*Bhatari*, female), and also *Sang Hyang*. In general these terms are usually thought to have a relation to terms for Hindu deities.[8]

However, in Cirebon, the meaning of these words or the subjects referred to by such terms are vague. These terms are mainly heard in *wayang* (shadow-puppet) stories. Some *wayang* enthusiasts explain that *dewa-dewi, batara-betari* and *sang hyang* are the same things which refer to the earlier ancestors' deities predating Islam, but they do not believe that these divine beings now exist or ever existed. Some others say that these terms refer to superhuman beings, a mixture between jinn (genie) and man, each having a certain spiritual or magical power that enables them to become master of a certain element of the universe, such as wind, water, earth, or sky-and that some of our ancestors took them as deities. Some believe, and some do not believe, they existed at some time in history. Still others consider that they are only fictitious figures from *wayang* stories, created and inherited by an earlier generation to teach people about morality. The last view seems to be held most commonly.

The Cirebonese word for God is *Pa-ngeran* or *Pe-ngeran*.[9] This word is derived from Javanese and has two meanings: God, and lord referring to person of

siji yaiku Gusti Allah. Lamun maca syahadat bli karo mengkonon mangka dadi muslime bli pati temenan."

[7] This is so named because the surah starts with "Qul huwa' llah", yet to Cirebonese it is closer to "Qulhu-w' Allah". Moreover, they are used to noting the initial word of the Qur'an to refer to a particular surah, such as: Alamtara for Al-Fil (QS 105), Tabbat for Al-Lahab or Al-Masad (QS 111), and Inna a'thaina for Al-Kawthar (QS 108).

[8] The word *sembahyang* (to pray) which the Cirebonese use to translate the Arabic word *salat* is probably derived from *sembah-hyang* (to worship *hyang* or spirit). I explored this possibility with Pak Shofie and others but their answers were inconclusive. They insisted that the word *sembahyang* is another word from *solat*. The latter is derived from Arabic *salat* and that for them, *hyang* and *sembahyang* have no relation.

[9] Either Pa or Pe may be used without implying any different meaning.

nobility or of high rank. The Cirebonese use the word in distinct ways to mean either of these. *Pangeran* meaning lord, is used only as a title of the court families and is put before the person's name, for example, "Pangeran Diponegoro", "Pangeran Mangkurat Trusmi", "Pangeran Panjunan", and "Pangeran Jayakelana". For the common noun meaning lord they do not use *pangeran* but *pinangeran* (by inserting an infix 'in'); e.g: Pangeran Ardiningrat is a *pinangeran,* not a *pangeran;* there are many *pinangeran* (not *pangeran*) in a court ceremony. *Pangeran* to mean God, on the other hand, is used independently but not as a title preceding any name, not even God's name. Thus, the expression as "*Pangeran Allah*" is never found.

In Cirebonese vernacular, asking about a person's God can be phrased as: "*Sapa Pengeranira*?" ("Who is your God?"). The answer is "*Pengeranisun Gusti Allah*" ("My God is the Lord Allah"). The word *gusti* also comes from Javanese and can also be translated as "lord"; it is akin to, or sometimes used interchangeably with, the word "*kanjeng*" (excellency) to refer to nobility such as prophets, saints, kings or others. A reference using *gusti* however implies a patron-client or a master-slave relationship in which the referee is the patron or the master. *Kanjeng* and *gusti* are used for example in such references as: *Gusti Nabi* or *Kanjeng Nabi,* or *Kanjeng Gusti Nabi* Muhammad, *Gusti* or *Kanjeng* or *Kanjeng Gusti Sinuhun* Sultan Sepuh. *Kanjeng* is therefore, used only in reference to a person and never to God; hence there can be no expression such as: "*Kanjeng Pengeran*" or "*Kanjeng Allah*".

Along with regarding God as *Kang gawe* (the Creator), the Cirebonese also regard God as *Kang Kuasa* (the Sovereign) whose sovereignty is absolute and omnipotent, and *Kang ngatur* (the ruler). The notions of God as sovereign and ruler seem to be more frequently mentioned in daily life than the notion of God as creator. I did not further explore the reason for this, but it is probably for practical reasons; the matter of life after creation is of more concern than are matters before creation. As God is omnipotent everything is totally under His control and nothing in the universe is unseen to Him. The three-fold ideas of God as the Creator, the Sovereign and the Ruler are consistent with the ideas of God's absolute omnipotence over men on the one hand, and men's total dependence on Him on the other. The dependency relation of Creator-created is deeply imprinted; it manifests itself for example in oral traditions, and more apparently, in exclamations. When one begins to do something, especially something important, it is traditional to recite *Basmalah*, the pronouncement of *Bismillahir rahmanir rahim* (**Bism Allah ar-Rahman ar-Rahim**), in the name of Allah, the Beneficent, the Merciful. On the other hand, when facing something undesirable or unwanted or when frightened, one will spontaneously respond: "*ya Allah*!" ("oh God!"); or "*la ilaha illa'llah!*", even sometimes, "*Muhammad rasulu' llah*", with the full recital of the *syahadat* added; or "*masya Allah*" (**ma sya-a Allah**, meaning "Allah does not will that"); or "*Astaghfirullahal'adzim!*" (**astaghfir Allah al-'azhim** meaning I beg pardon of Allah the Greatest); or *"la hawla walaquwwata illa billahil 'aliyyil 'adzim"* (**la hawl wa la quwwah illa bi Allah al'aly al'azhim**, meaning "there is no power and strength except from Allah the Greatest"). Similarly, these expressions are used when shocked by something or by some accident. In a more precarious situation, when hearing that someone has died one will exclaim: *"Inna lillahi wa inna ilaihi roji'un"*, (**Inna li Allah wa inna ilaih raji'un** meaning, "lo, we belong to Allah and lo, unto Him we return"). But in contrast, that is, when facing desirable things or results, the response is: *"alhamdulillah"* (**al-hamd li Allah**, meaning "praise be to Allah"). These expressions are commonly enunciated not only by devout individuals and *santri*, but also by ignorant laymen. The only difference is in pronunciation. As one might expect, learned individuals will produce perfect or nearly perfect utterances of Arabic compared with laymen; for example, less learned laymen may pronounce *"la ilaha ill'Allah"* as "la ilaha ilelloh" instead of as "**la ilaha illa Allah**"; *"masya Allah"* as "masya olloh" rather than as "**ma sya-a Allah**"; *"Astaghfirullahal 'adzim"* as "astagpirulloh-al azhim" or even "astagailah", or just "astaga" instead of as "**astaghfir Allah al-'azhim**"; or *"la hawla walaquwwata illa billahil'aliyyil 'adzim"* as "la kaola wala kuwata ila billah" instead of as "**la hawl wa la quwwah illa bi Allah**".

Although these expressions do not necessarily reflect religiosity, in the sense that users need not necessarily be devout, these oral traditions are indications that Islam has indeed penetrated deeply into the traditions of Cirebonese social life.

Islam prohibits its followers from thinking about the substance of God or imagining His essence. Such questions as: "what does God look like" are strictly discouraged as they are beyond the reach of human understanding.[10] Not surprisingly, among the Cirebonese too, attempts to describe God end up with the identification of His names in terms of attributes called *sifat-sifate Gusti Allah* (Allah's attributes) which incorporate *sifat wajib* (the "must"- attributes), *sifat mustahil* (the "must not"-attributes) and *sifat jaiz* (the "may" attribute). The *sifat wajib* correspond to an affirmation of divine perfection, qualities that must be ascribed to God. There are twenty of these and hence they are known as *sifat rong puluh* (the twenty attributes). Thirteen of the attributes are said to be unanimously agreed on by theologians, while the other seven were added later by others.[11] The thirteen attributes are: *wujud* (existence); *qidam* (eternal);

[10] There is a hadith urging people to think only about creation and not about the Creator, because they will never be able to know God's Essence. It says: 'Ponder the creation of God, but do not take your meditation into the Divine essence, or you will perish' (See for example, Abduh, S.M. (1966), *Theology of Unity,* translated from Arabic into English by Ishak Musa'ad and K. Cragg, London George Allen & Unwin, p. 53. See also its Indonesian translation, *Risaiah Ilmu Tauhid,* by Firdaus, H. (1976), 6th edition, Jakarta: Bulan Bintang, especially p. 79–83.

[11] Ngah, Mohammad Nor Bin (1983), *Kitab Jawi: Islamic Thought of the Malay Muslim Scholars,* Singapore: Institute of Southeast Asian Studies, p. 10.

baqa' (permanence); *mukhalafatu lilhawaditsi* (dissimilarity with the created); *qiyamuhu binafsihi* (self-subsistence); *wahdaniyat* (oneness); *qudrat* (power); *iradat* (will); *'ilmu* ('knowledge), *hayat* (life); *sama'* (hearing); *bashar* (vision); *kalam* (speech). The other attributes do not intrinsically describe God's essence; they designate what God can do and usually does, they are *kaunuhu* (He is in a state of being: *qadiran* (powerful); *muridan* (willing); *'aliman* (knowing); *hayyan* (alive); *sami'an* (hearing); *bashiran* (seeing); *mutakalliman* (speaking). To assist memorisation, the Cirebonese put the list of twenty attributes into a poem chanted as follows:[12]

allah
Wujud, qidam, baqa,
mukhalafatu lilhawaditsi
qiyamuhu binafsihi,
wahdaniyat, qudrat, iradat, 'ilmu, hayat,
sama',bashar, kalam,
qadiran, muridan,
'aliman, hayyan, sami'an,
bashiran, mutakalliman.

The popularity of the poem is helped thanks to the modern recording technology and the current trend of people's religious commitment in Indonesia. Now the poem is beautifully chanted by some pop-singers and is available on records and cassettes, and can even be heard on some commercial radio stations.

The *sifat mustahil* (the "must not"-attributes), correspond to the negation of any defective qualities and, therefore, must not be ascribed to God. Standing in contrast with *sifat wajib*, there are also twenty *sifat mustahil: 'adam* (non-existence); *huduts* (recency); *fana'* (perishability); *mumatsalatu lilhawaditsi* (similarity with the created); *ikhtiyaju bighairihi* (non-self-sufficiency); *ta'addud* (plurality); *'ajzu* (weakness); *karahah* (unwillingness); *jahlu* (ignorance); *mawtu* (inanimated); *ashommu* (deafness); *a'ma* (blindness); *bukmun* (speechlessness); He, who or that which could be in a state of being: *'ajizan* (powerless); *karihan* (unwilling); *jahilan* (ignorant); *mayyitan* (dead); *ashomman* (deaf); *a'man* (blind), *abkaman* (non-speaking).

There is, however, only one *sifat jaiz* (the "may"-attribute): God's prerogative to do or not to do something.

As well as describing God in terms of these attributes, He can also be described in terms of Beautiful Names which are called *aran baguse Gusti Allah* or *asma'ul husna* (God's Beautiful Names). But this knowledge is prevalent only among

[12] All these attributes are taken directly from Arabic.

relatively learned individuals and is usually enunciated in Arabic terms. There are ninety-nine Names in total.[13]

In theological discourse, especially between the traditional Asy'arite schools on the one hand, and the rationalist Mu'tazilites on the other, there is disagreement about the appropriateness of describing God in terms of attributes. The Asy'arite proponents, including Al-Ghazali, argue in favour of attribution; while the Mu'tazilites stand against it. The Cirebonese clearly stand within the Asy'arite line. In accepting this doctrine, the Cirebonese however, in one way or another, also develop the necessary logical thinking they need to defend their faith. Mas'ud (26 years), a batik factory worker, used the existence of the universe as the basis for his argument on the existence of God:

> ...everything that exists must have come about because it has been created by its creator. The existence of clothes that we wear indicates that there is someone who makes them, that is, the tailor; the existence of chairs, tables and furniture indicates the existence of the maker, the carpenter; so too, the existence of plants, trees, animal, seas, earth, heaven, stars, moon, sun and all the things within the universe together with the well established structure and order would clearly indicate the existence of the Great Creator and Sustainer which we, Muslims, call Allah, the true God.[14]

When I further asked him, given that the universe exists because it was created by the Great Creator, and that this becomes the proof that God exists, who then, is the Creator of God?". Appearing slightly offended, he explained:

> You must realise that every rule in the world has an exception. You can see for example, in some offices there is a notice on the door saying: "NO ENTRANCE!" But why does the director go in and out of the room freely and carelessly despite the "no entrance" notice? It is because the "no entrance" notice does not apply to him; he is exempted from the rule because he is in fact, the master of the office and it is he who put up the notice. The same token also applies to God. Because God, the prime Creator, is not a thing and is not created, he is exempted from the rule stating that "everything is created." Above all, it will be evident when

[13] For list of the God's Beautiful Names, see for example, Brown, K. and Palmer, M. (1990), *The Essential Teachings of Islam*, Arrow Books: London, pp. 9–11.

[14] Indepth interview, 24-2-1992: "...apa bae kang ana iki bisa maujud krana digawe deng kang gawe. Anae anggoan kang isun kabeh ngenggo nuduhaken anane wong kang gawe, yaiku tukang jahit; anae korsi, meja karo sejene nuduhaken anae kang gawe, yaiku tukang kayu; semono uga dadie tanduran, anae wiwitan, satoan, segara, bumi, langit, lintang, wulan, srengenge lan segala rupa ning jagat kelawan wujude lan aturane kang tapis lan beres nuduhaken anae Kang Maha Agung Kang gawe lan Kang ngatur, kang munggu wong Islam diarani Gusti Allah, Pengeran kang estu."

> you also realise that the next two other attributes of Allah are *qidam* which means without beginning, and *baqa*, that is without ending.[15]

Mas'ud's explanation represents a layman's style. But considering that he is only a primary school graduate and has never been to a *pesantren*, that he has learned religion only from *ngaji* at the nearby *tajug*, where chanting *puji-pujian* is one of its media as well as its methods, his argument is remarkable. He accepts religious doctrine not in the form of dead dogma which must be accepted without question. He, instead, develops his creed with an enriched body of theological thinking. Not all people are of course like Mas'ud, but there are certainly many others like him, who may be taken as interesting examples showing that there are some cases in which assimilation of Islam amongst traditional people has produced a sort of 'popular rationalism.' The existence of God cannot be satisfactorily proven by any empirical enquiries, laboratory experiments or sophisticated logical manipulation, let alone by Mas'ud's explanation. Ghazali (in Au Zed 1974) warned that even the prophets were not sent to prove the existence of God and the origin of the world; they were only sent to teach His unity. Arguments for God's existence are permissible only if they are derived and sustained by the Qur'an.[16]

The description I have presented would suggest that the Cirebonese do not seem to have a unique concept of God. Their ides of God derives entirely from Islam wherein the concept of deity is recorded in the Holy Scripture, the Qur'an. The Scripture preaches that basic to the Islamic faith is the acceptance of the principle of absolute monotheism, the rejection of polytheism, and destruction of idols by bearing witness that Allah is the only one and unique God, and the Creator of all that exists. The Qur'an expresses and emphasises these basic tenets. This faith is the renewal of what the earlier prophets, Adam to Muhammad, recalled; it has also been validated and ratified by the pre-Islamic monotheistic believers where Abraham *khalil Allah*, or the friend of God, is notably described in the Qur'an as being: just and a prophet, a true believer (*hanif*), having surrendered himself (Muslim) to God without compromise with the *musyrikun* or polytheists, those who associate others with God.[17]

[15] Interview, 25-2-1992: "La sampean kudu ngerti ari aturan iku ana kalane bli kanggo. Contone ning kantor-kantor ana lawang kang ditempeli plang: "DILARANG MASUK!" Tapi dengapa ari kepala kantore manjing metu ora ya ora embuh bae bli perduli karo plang mau? Sebabe ya krana plang "dilarang masuk" iku munggu deweke bli kanggo; deweke bli dinisbataken karo aturan kang ning plang, krana deweke kang nguasani kantor lan ya deweke kang nempeli plang. Semono uga karo Pengeran. Pengeran iku suwijining zat kang gawe, dudu barang lan dudu gawean, dadi bli dinisbataken deng aturan kang munie "segala apa bae ana kang gawe." Tamba jelas maning, lamun sampean ngerti yen sifate Gusti Allah kang loro sawise wujud iku *qidam* kang tegese langka kawitane, lan *baqa*, kang tegese langka pungkasane."

[16] Abu Zayd, A.R. (1974), *Al Ghazali on Divine Predicates and Their Properties*, Lahore: SH. Muhammad Ashraf, pp. xxvii-xxviii.

[17] See: "God in Islam", in *Encyclopedia of Religion*.

BELIEF IN SPIRITUAL BEINGS

There is general agreement among Cirebonese on the existence of spiritual beings, although the details of these beings are perceived differently from individual to individual. The existence of spiritual beings is seen as a corollary of the existence of physical beings. If physical beings exist, why shouldn't non-physical or spiritual beings? Man Misna (52 yrs), an egg peddler, put the existence of physical vis a vis spiritual beings in a duality conceptual framework; he said:

> It is natural that everything be of two matching pairs; night-day, male-female, east-west, north-east, bad-good, physical-spiritual and so on. The physical beings like human beings, animals, trees and others do exist as they are clearly visible; the spiritual beings do also exist, but they are not visible due to their name, as spiritual ones. Men who deny the existence of spiritual beings are the silliest ones.[18]

The commonly known spiritual beings are: *malekat* (angels), Iblis (devils), *setan* (satans) and jinn (genies). However, detailed information about these beings is incomplete and speculative. Their nature, essence and actions are described differently by different people. A fairly coherent explanation was given by Fathoni, preferably called Toni (46 years), a hen-and-cock trader. His explanation seems to represent, more or less, the general Cirebonese conception of these beings. He claimed that what he said comes from what he could understand when he heard his *Kyai*, in *Pesantren* Benda, explain the subject on one occasion.[19] Firstly, he said that he did not know which spiritual beings were created first, but he felt certain that they already existed when Adam was created. *Malekat*, Iblis, *setan* and jinn were, in fact, of similar matter in that they are created from a kind of smokeless fire. Some people said that the *malekat* were created from *sorot* (light), while the rest (Iblis, *setan* and jinn) were created from fire.

Another kind of spiritual being, *mrekayangan* (ghost), was unclearly defined except that it was a type of *setan*. A *mrekayangan* scares people when it appears although it really does not intend to appear nor to scare. Some say that a *mrekayangan* is not really a *setan* because its origin is different from the real *setan*; rather, a *mrekayangan* is the bad spirit of a human being who has died improperly, for example, by suicide, by murder, or by accident while committing a sinful deed. Still others say that a *mrekayangan* is a type of jinn.

[18] Indepth interview, 21-3-1992: "Wis adate segala apa bae iku werna loro, pasang-pasangan; ana awan, ana bengi, ana lanang ana wadon, ana wetan ana kulon, ana lor ana kidul ana blesak ana bagus, sampe sateruse. Ari barang kasar kayadene menusa, satoan, wiwitan, karo sejen-sejene jelas ana merga katon, barang alus keding gan ana, mung bae bli katon, krana arane bae gan alus; boko wong kang bli percaya ning anae barang alus iku ya saking goblog-gobloge wong."

[19] Toni had not finished primary school but had been to *pesantren* for around two years.

Malekat

In Islam, the belief in angels constitutes the second Decrees of Creed (*Rukun Iman*).[20] It comes after the belief in the oneness of God, Allah. The other four are belief in His Messengers, the Holy Scriptures, the Day of Final Judgement or Resurrection, and God's Decree for Humanity. The Cirebonese certainly believe in these, but many people do not know that they constitute the Decrees of Creed. The last two decrees are mostly referred to as, respectively, *Kiyamat* (calamity) and *Kresane Pangeran* (the Will of God). In relation to the fourth and fifth decrees, Pak Shofie said that Muslims should believe that there are a large number of Messengers of God but every Muslim needs to know only twenty-five of them.[21] Most Cirebonese also know the names of the twenty-five prophets and frequently use them in naming their children. Nevertheless, few can list them perfectly, let alone in precise chronological order. Some put the list into a chant; hence, they can more easily list the names in the proper order. In contrast, there are only four Holy Scriptures: the *Zabur* (Psalms) revealed to *Nabi Dawud* (David), *Taurat* (Old Testament) revealed to *Nabi Musa* (Moses), *Injil* (Bible or New Testament) revealed to *Nabi Isa* (Jesus), and Qur'an revealed to the last apostle, Muhammad. Because there will not be any apostles after Muhammad, the Qur'an, which was revealed to him, is believed to perfect the three preceding Scriptures, covering therefore, the main things contained in them.

> ... the Scriptures revealed by God are four in number. First is the Psalm, revealed to his excellency Prophet David, second is the Old Testament revealed to his excellency Prophet Moses, third is the Bible revealed to his excellency Prophet Jesus, fourth is the Qur'an revealed to his excellency Prophet Muhammad, God exalts him and peace be upon him, the seal of the apostles, which concludes all the Scriptures revealed before. The prudence contained in those Scriptures are covered by the Qur'an.[22]

The word *malekat* known by Cirebonese comes from **malaika**, the Arabic plural form of **malak**, meaning angel. The term refers to the heavenly creatures, the servants of God who stand as intermediaries between the divine world and the

[20] The word *'rukun'* here is derived from Arabic **'rukn'** (pl. **arkan**) meaning 'pillar' It is used in such reference as *'rukun iman'* (the pillars of faith), *rukun Islam* (the five pillars of Islam), *rukun sembahyang* (the pillars of prayers) and *rukun wudlu* (the pillars of ablution). It is therefore, different from the Javanese word *'rukun'* meaning (to live) in harmony.

[21] See for example: Mahsun, K.T. (1958), *Qishashul Anbiya'*, Surabaya: Ahmad Nabhan.

[22] An address given by Pak Ubeid (49 years) at a routinely held *pengajian* (public speaking) at Kalitengah desa mosque. This quotation is from the 12-4-1992 occasion, saying: "... ari kitab-kitab kang diturunaken deng Gusti Allah iku ana papat. Siji kitab Zabur kang diturunakaen ning Kanjeng Nabi Dawud, loro kitab Taurat kang diturunaken ning Kanjeng Nabi Musa, telu kitab Injil kang diturunaken ning Kanjeng Nabi 'Isa, papat kitab Qur'an kang diturunaken ning Kanjeng Nabi Muhammad sall' Allahu 'alaihi wa sallam, nabi akhirul zaman, kanggo nyampurnaaken kitab-kitab kang diturunaken sedurunge. Syare'at-syare'at kang ana ning kitab kaen kabeh sekiyen wis dicakup ning Qur'an."

human world. Toni, seemed to represent a view widely held by many other people when he said that *malekat* were made of light, never sleep, are not born nor do they give birth, are neither male nor female, can neither eat nor drink, and have no passion nor lust. They are able to assume any form, can move virtually instantly, from one place to another over unlimited distance, and are always loyal to God and do what He wishes. They never forget nor feel tired. "The number of *malekat* is countless, only God knows, but every Muslim should know at least ten of them. Four are Archangels, each has a specific duty with countless subordinates", said Man Muklas, a 64 year old tobacco peddler and the *imam* at the Kedawung prayer house, (adding to Toni's explanation). He then named and described the ten *malekat*. The first and described at greatest length, including his appearance on earth in the form of unrecognised human being such as a beggar and a good looking man, was Jibril or Jibra'il or Jabara'il (Gabriel), whose duty it is to convey revelation to the apostles (*rusul*) of Allah.[23]

Man Muklas said that as far as he could remember from a *kitab* (book or written source of *santri* reference) he had read, Jibril had revealed God's words to Adam twelve times, to Idris four times, to Abraham forty times, to Jacob four times, to Moses four hundred times, to Ayyub three times and to Muhammad (peace be upon him), twenty-four thousand times. Jibril is a *malekat muqarrabun* [one of the angels who (is brought) close to God] and is the best known *malekat*.

Jibril is also known by names associated with *ruh* or spirit; *ar-ruh* (**al-ruh**, the spirit) who, with other angels, descends to the world to spread God's grace to the devotees who pray at *lailatul qadar* (**al-lail al-qadr**), the night of power (or blessing) during which a devotion is considered to be equal to or better than, continuous devotion for a thousand months, and is rewarded accordingly. The night of blessing occurs at the eve of *maleman* on odd-numbered nights after the twentieth day of Ramadhan (that is, the 21st, 23rd, 25th, 27th, and 29th nights).

Jibril is also called *ruhuna*, (Our spirit, that is, the spirit of God), the nickname assigned when he was sent to Mary and breathed upon her womb, making her pregnant without her having been impregnated by a man. Still another name is *ruhul amin* (**al-ruh al-amin**, the faithful spirit), for his main duty is as the angel of revelations. He brought down revelations in clear Arabic, to the prophet Muhammad (peace be upon him). The first revelation was brought down at the cave of Hira near Mecca, signifying the start of Muhammad's prophethood. Jibril came in his original form with wings. This caused a crisis for Muhammad (peace be upon him), who thought that he was possessed by the *jinn* of the cave. Jibril assured him that he really was sent by God and then read the revelation comprising the first to fifth verses of *surat Iqra'* (al-'Alaq), saying: "Recite in

[23] Field notes from after prayer informal discussions at Kedwung prayer house (5,6,8 March, 1992).

the name of the Lord who created; created man from clots of blood. Recite! Your Lord the Most Bountiful One, who taught man with pen; taught man what he knew not."[24]

Further it is said that prior to Jibril's full recitation of the five verses, there was a sort of short dialogue between him and Muhammad. Jibril instructed Muhammad to read, and Muhammad answered that he could not read. Jibril repeated the instruction once again but Muhammad repeated his answer; finally, Jibril read the verses for Muhammad. From that time on during Muhammad's prophethood, in response to the ongoing situation and demands, Jibril routinely came to Muhammad with revelations. Jibril also accompanied Muhammad on the night journey from Mecca to the mosque of *Al-Aqsa* in Palestine, and from Palestine to the seventh heaven up to *Sidratul Muntaha* (**Sidrah al-Muntaha**, the final destination). Here Muhammad received first hand-instruction from Allah to pray five times a day from whence comes the prescribed duty for all Muslims. Muhammad's night journey is known as *Isra'-Mi'raj*, which all Muslims commemorate annually on the 27th of Rajab, the third month of the Islamic calendar.[25]

The other angels after Jibril are: Mikail, Israfil, Izrail, Raqib, Atid, Munkar, Nakir, Malik and Ridwan. Mikail (Michael), has the duty of controlling rain, and distributing *rejeki* (fortune) such as food, nourishment and knowledge to all living creatures, particularly to mankind, whether believers or unbelievers.

[24] Al 'Alaq means the Clots of Blood (QS 96:1–5); it is referred to by the Cirebonese as *Surat Iqra'*. Beside talking about the original form of Jibril Man Muklas also spoke about Jibril assuming in human forms such as a beggar and a stranger. He said, it is not allowed to mistreat or coarse upon a beggar, especially who comes to our house, because *malekat* may assume in this personage to test someone's generosity. "If you cannot give something, just say your sorrow for it." Whilst his illustration of Jibril as a stranger which he claimed: "*ana ning kitab*" (available in a religious book) seemed to accord the *hadith* narrated by Muslim (Au 'l-Husayn Muslim bin al-Hajjaj, c. 202/817–261/875) from Umar which recounts that Jibril came to Muhammad as a dark, black-haired, unknown man in white clothing. He came mysteriously when Umar and other disciples were gathered together with Muhammad, the Messenger of God. Umar reported that he saw clearly, the man sit face to face with Muhammad, place his knees by Muhammad's knee, put his hands on Muhammad's thighs and ask Muhammad to tell him about *islam* (submission), *iman* (faith), *ihsan* (deference) and the (day of) *Kiyamat* (universal destruction). In reply, the Prophet related to the man the five pillars of Islam, the six decrees of faith. Regarding the principles of deference, the Prophet said that deference is 'to worship God as if you see Him as even if you do not see Him He sees you.' Umar was very surprised when the man commented, after each of the prophet's answers, 'You are right.' Umar thought, 'how could the man ask the prophet something and then respond in the style of an examiner, as if he knew better than the prophet does.' The hadith continues by recounting the *Kiyamat*, according to which Muhammad said that the questioned (he, Muhammad) knew no better than the questioner (the man). Then the man asked about the symptoms of universal destruction. The Prophet described some of its symptoms which were: when a man enslaves his own mother; when poor shepherds usually wore only old torn clothing are competing for luxurious houses and glamour. After this, the man went away mysteriously, leaving the gathering astonished. The prophet asked Umar if he knew who the man really was. Umar said that only Allah and His Messenger knew. The Prophet said that the man was Jibril, who came to teach them about religion. (For the text of this *hadith*, see for example: Dahlan, A. (1988), *Hadits Arba'in Annawawiah*, Bandung: Al-Ma'arif, pp. 12–15.

[25] *Isra'* refers to the journey from Mecca to Palestine whereas, *Mi'raj* refers to the journey from Palestine to the *Sidratul Muntaha* in the seventh heaven.

Thus, everything in the seas, and everything on earth that is useful for sustaining life (such as trees, fruits, grains and livestock) is under the control of Mikail. Another *malekat* is Israfil, the angel who will blow his trumpet on the day of resurrection. Actually, Israfil will blow his trumpet on three occasions: firstly to signal the calamity; secondly, when the earthly world has vanished altogether; and finally, on the day when the dead are resurrected to receive the Final Judgement. Izrail, the angel of death, is responsible for taking the soul away from living beings. When the time comes, no one can escape from death, or postpone it even a second; Izrail does his job strictly. These four *malekat*, Jibril, Mikail, Israfil and Izrail, are the Archangels (*malekat mukorobun*).[26]

Two further *malekat* often mentioned are Raqib and 'Atid, whose duty it is to record all human activities: words, actions and intentions, whether good or bad. Raqib records all the "good" ones while 'Atid records the "bad" ones. Everyone therefore has the two angels at guard at their sides. People with good intentions are credited with a minor "good" point; a full point is given when the intention materialises into action. By virtue of God's mercy, there are no minor points for bad intentions; a full "bad" point is given only when a bad deed is actually done. Still two more *malekat* are Munkar and Nakir, who come to examine the dead in their graves. The examination concerns God, the prophet and the path the dead followed while alive. The righteous and faithful will be able to answer all the questions, and Munkar and Nakir will release them in peace until the Day of Resurrection; the infidel however, will not be able to answer. Consequently they will experience severe suffering. Neither rationality nor intelligence works in answering Munkar and Nakir's question; indeed given the belief that the brain is where rationality and intelligence reside, these must also be dead when the body dies. In contrast, beliefs which are found in the soul, not in the body, will last forever.

The last two *malekat* are Malik and Ridwan. The former is the terrible angel responsible for controlling Hell which, generally, is kept by a large number of subordinate angels of hell called Zabaniyah. In contrast, Ridwan guards paradise and does his duty with thousands of subordinates called the angels of paradise.

Iblis, Setan and Mrekayangan

In Cirebon the term *setan* (satan) is used as a general term referring to any kind of bad spirit being who leads people to sin. When it appears to humans, it becomes a *weweden* or *memedi* (spook). But when the term is further elaborated upon, Cirebonese often classify *setan* into: Iblis, *setan*, and *mrekayangan*. The first two are species which can be vaguely distinguished from each other, but both were created, by God, from a kind of fire.

[26] Field notes (Arabic: *Al-Malak al-muqarrabun*).

Iblis and Setan

At a public speech (*pengajian*) routinely held every Sunday night at Kalitengah desa mosque, Pak Ubeid (49 years, engaged in construction) said that, early on during creation, Iblis lived in heaven with the *malekat*, but was then cursed and banished from heaven because of his arrogance, disobeying God's order to bow down before Adam when the latter had been completely created. The reasons for disobeying were firstly, Iblis thought that compared to Adam, he was the senior dweller of heaven, had been created and came earlier than Adam; secondly, Adam, who was created from the soil of earth must be lower in rank than Iblis, having been created from fire. Bowing down before Adam therefore, according to Iblis, was unfair, beneath his dignity and did not make any sense. Despite cursing and banishing Iblis, God still granted Iblis' request when he begged God to postpone his punishment until the Day of Resurrection, prior to which he would lead astray his rival Adam, and his descendants. God also deemed that those who stray and fall into Iblis' trap would become his followers, and after resurrection they would stay with him in Hell. Iblis did not waste any time and immediately started working. The first victims were Adam himself and his wife Eve, who were tempted when they were still in paradise.

In another *pengajian*, Kyai Fu'ad Hasyim from Buntet *Pesantren* interestingly dramatised the episode of how Adam and Eve fell into Iblis' trap. Coming in front of Adam and Eve, Iblis told Adam and Eve confidently that God's scenario of the universe put Adam and Eve in a bad position. Iblis told Adam and Eve that God did not really want them to stay in paradise forever; this was clearly evident when God prohibited their approaching a tree in paradise, the "eternity tree" (**syajarah al-khuld**), whose fruit, if eaten, entitled the eater to stay in paradise forever. God instead wished for them to leave paradise and to stay on earth where life would be hard. Adam, and particularly Eve, felt that Iblis' words were sensible and asked him if there was any way to stay in paradise forever and to avoid staying on earth.

Iblis was pleased that his deception had worked, but he did not show it. On the contrary, he pretended that he was very sad and deeply concerned about their problem. He then insisted that the only thing that might help would be to pick and to eat the prohibited fruit secretly, without God noticing. Tempted by his insistence, Eve and Adam approached the tree, picked its fruit, and then ate the fruit. But before they had fully swallowed the fruit, they found themselves already thrown onto the earth without clothing. One fruit eaten by Adam became stuck inside his throat; this turned into his "Adam's Apple", a sign of a mature male. The two fruits eaten and swallowed even earlier by Eve became stuck inside her at breast-level and they turned into breasts, a sign of a mature female. Adam was thrown to earth away from Eve. Only after a long search did they get together again. They repented to God who granted His forgiveness, but time could not be turned back; Adam and Eve had to continue living a hard life on earth.

After being banished from heaven Iblis generated descendants. Iblis' descendants are called *setan*, whereas Adam and Eve's descendants are called *menusa* (human beings). In turn, both *setan* and *menusa*, also gave rise to descendants, but, unlike human beings, none of Iblis, *setan*, or their descendants are mortal. Both Iblis and *setan* still exist and their number has multiplied tremendously. It is unclear whether Iblis and *setan* are differentiated by gender; but they are generally conceived to be hermaphrodites and to lay eggs. From the time Iblis succeeded in tempting Adam and Eve to follow his advice, Iblis and *setan* have been more and more zealous, working together hand in hand using all their power, intelligence and experience to lead Adam's descendants (human beings) astray. They rarely harm or scare humans as their only business is to tempt and trap human beings and jinn (see the next section) to follow their path and finally to lead them into being their companions in hell.

As part of their efforts, Iblis and *setan* often try to force information from *laukh-makhfudz* by spying on the scenarios of the universe,[27] especially those relating to individual human's lives, and using them effectively to establish co-operation with *tukang cempad* (fortune tellers) to lead their clients astray. Against such efforts, the guardian angel may take harsh measures and beat Iblis and *setan* severely. As a result, Iblis or the *setan* concerned has become weirdly shaped and is called by some people as *mrekayangan*.

Mrekayangan

Of the spiritual beings in which the Cirebonese believe, *mrekayangan* is one of the most vaguely defined. Unlike the terms such as *malekat*, Iblis, *setan* and jinn, which come from Arabic, *mrekayangan* is a local term, but no one knows its precise meaning. Its root is probably *yang*, which in Javanese means spirit. *Mrekayangan* is therefore a constructed word, referring to spiritual beings other than *malekat*, Iblis, *setan* and jinn.[28] According to Ki Hanan, what *mrekayangan* do is only to scare people when they appear to humans in the form of *memedi* or *weweden*. Different opinions persist on the origin of *mrekayangan*. Some say that they are really the beaten *setan*, who spy on human life. Others say that *mrekayangan* are the spirits of the dead who, for one or another reason, have difficulty or have lost their way in reaching their proper place (*roh kesasar*).[29]

[27] Field notes. This part and subsequent section on *mrekayangan* have been especially derived from a talk with Ki Hanan (67 years), an ex trader in Kaliwadas. *Laukh Makhfud* refers to the tablet where the record of the decisions of the divine are preserved (See: *Shorter Encyclopedia of Islam*, pp. 287-288).

[28] Possibly, the word *mrekayangan* is derived from the word *yang* (spirit). *Mrekayangan* is therefore a construction of *(m)reka-yang-an*, transforming into spiritual being, a word to refer to spiritual being other than *malekat*, Iblis, *setan* and *jin*.

[29] In Austronesian: "spirit of bad dead."

Still others combine these opinions saying that *mrekayangan* are of either origin. Reasons for the *mrekayangan*'s difficulties are by and large attributable to extremely bad conduct such as suicide, *nyupang* (profiting from contracts with *setan* or bad jinn), sudden death or being killed in an accident while committing the *ma-lima* (five sinful deeds: smoking opium, gambling, womanising, becoming intoxicated, stealing). In a state between consciousness and unconsciousness, a person may see *memedi* unintentionally, particularly when that person's mental condition is unstable. When consciousness returns the appearance of the *memedi* instantly disappears.

Memedi, be it *mrekayangan*, or jinn may take various forms. Some of the more widely acknowledged are: *setan gundul, wewe gombel, genderuwo, blegedeg treng, puntianak, jrangkong, kemangmang, wedon, kecik* and many others. *Setan gundul* is a spirit in human shape with all its hair shaved off. The *wewe gombel* or just *wewe* is a huge female spirit who hides children under her armpit, under her breasts or on huge trees). One way to release a child hidden by *wewe* is that a group of people must go around haunted places, bringing anything they can beat rhythmically in order to provoke the *wewe* to dance, thus freeing the hidden child from her control. The *Genderuwo* is a male *wewe*, whose name may be derived from *gandharva*, masculine embodiments of celestial light which, in Hindu belief, are musicians who accompany the dances of their female consorts.[30] *Blegedeg ireng* is a gigantic totally black figure; *puntianak* are female spirits, who eat babies' blood while they are being born by posing as a *dukun bayi* (a specialist who helps women giving birth). The *jrangkong* is a human skeleton; *kemangmang* is a fire haired figure, who walks on his hands (Central Java: *banaspati*); *wedon* is a ghost in white garments, wrapped like a corpse; *kecik* is a small spirit, who steals money for his master (Central Java: *tuyul*).

For some people, these spirits may cause some problem but for others, especially those who are acquainted with the Holy Qur'an, they may not. To avoid being scared (*'diwedeni'*) is easy enough. By *memacaan*, literally meaning reciting anything (verses or Surah of the Holy Qur'an), the appearance of these spirits can be avoided and their power can be nullified. Ki Hanan, for example, said: "... for anyone who is willing to perform *memacaan*, there is no way for being scared nor possessed."[31]

Among the verses and Surah for *memacaan* which are considered most effective are: *Ayat Kursi* (the verse of the Throne, QS 2:55), *Qulhu* (Al-Ikhlas, QS 112), *Qul a'udzu birabbil falaq* (Al-Falaq, QS 113), *Qul a'udzu birabbinnas* (Al-Nas, QS 114) and *Alhamdu* (Al-Fatihah, QS 1). For this practical purpose, it is advisable

[30] The name *genderuwo* is probably derived from *gandharva* (masculine embodiment of celestial light which, in Hindu divinity, are musicians who accompany the dances of their female consorts). See: "demons" in *Encyclopedia of Religion*.

[31] Field notes from informal talk at Kedawung prayer house, 17-3-1992. His Javanese statement is: "... ari wong kang gelem memacaan sih bli bakal diwedeni atawa kesurupan."

that everyone have some acquaintance with some of these verses or Surah. Ricital of the "*Bismillah*" (in the name of God) before doing something or going somewhere is one way to avoid the possible interference of these spirits.[32]

Jinn

The jinn are another species of spiritual being created from fire. They may be either male or female. They eat and drink, need a dwelling place, occupy space and can have children. Jinn also live in an established society and have a king. Azrak is referred to as the jinn's country although no one knows where Azrak is. On earth, jinn occupy haunted places, such as hills, caves, rivers, rocks, trees, certain lands, long unoccupied houses, certain bath houses, wells, bridges, lakes, mosques, ruins, cemeteries. When a person stays at a jinn-occupied place, especially if alone, the jinn may cause disturbances by producing unidentified sounds, making doors or windows close and open, moving articles or even a sleeping person from one place to another, making things disappear; causing strange incidents, etc. People who experience these kinds of incidents usually feel scared, and they call it *diwedeni* (being scared). In these cases the jinn probably does intend to frighten people so that they will leave and will not return to occupy that place again so that the jinn can claim the place for itself. Persuading jinn to leave an occupied place can be done by specialists, or indeed by non-specialists, through negotiation or by force. Intentionally or unintentionally disturbing or destroying the places occupied by jinn can be treated as serious offences to them. If so, they may lose their temper and take revenge; as a result the person concerned will suffer from some kind of illness (physical or mental). If appropriate measures are not taken to persuade the jinn to stop their action, the illness could end in death. Again, these measures can be taken by a specialist or by any one who can negotiate with, or force, the jinn to stop their action. Some informants told me about Man Makiyo who fought to exhaustion with jinns.[33]

Like human beings, jinn are subject to the temptations of Iblis and *setan*. There are some jinns, therefore, who are good, pious and faithful (*jin Islam*), and some others who are bad, sinful and infidel (*jin kapir*). Bad jinn may be malevolent to human, whereas good jinn may be benevolent by helping people do some hard work, or produce magical acts. Jinn can also assume many forms including that of human beings; but most usually they assume the form of an animal, for

[32] See for example the next section, especially on the merits of "*Ayat Kursi.*" Degrading efforts of the nature and power of spirits may be a reconciliation between older beliefs and Islam. Not to make the older beliefs variants of Islam, older spirits were taken as explanatory purposes for the existence of *setan* and jinn, which is part of the Islamic beliefs. Similar efforts also occur with regard to Hindu beliefs where Hindu deities were degraded into ancestors (see: Chapter Three).

[33] Man Makiyo was a *kemit* (mosque custodian) in Kalitengah. He was said as already died more than a year before I was in the field.

example, a snake, a lion, a donkey, a cat, or a dog. [34] A jinn who assumes the form of a cat may either have only one colour (totally white, brown or black) or have a combination of three colours (*belang telon*, meaning three stripes of different colours). Killing or beating such a pseudo-animal, (that is a transformed jinn) is risky because the jinn, its friends or its kin may take deadly revenge. The risk is more serious than when merely disturbing or destroying their places.[35]

The original shape of a jinn however, is thought of as a human-like figure of gigantic size. Its fingers, to illustrate size, are as big as *gedang ambon* (a type of large banana). Some people suggest the possibility of co-operation between humans and jinn for special purposes such as making friends, even marrying jinn and taking jinn as servants, in the case of benevolent jinn. This is possible for anyone who masters the mystery of jinn and learns *ilmu ghaib* (knowledge of the mysterious world). Some *kyai* are certainly known to have that mastery. There are a number of ways to acquire this mastery, one of which is by doing an exercise (*riyadlah*), aiming to gain the marvel and secret merits of the Verse of Throne (*ayat Kursiy*) of the Holy Qur'an (QS 2:255) as elaborated by al-Syeikh al-Buny.[36] The procedure of the exercise is as follows:

1. Cleanse the body by bathing and ablution, and the heart by generosity.
2. Wear clean clothing and surrender totally to God.
3. Find a quiet place such as a room, a cave or a place in the bush or mountain for seclusion where contemplation can be well performed.
4. Stay there for a couple of days from Tuesday morning before dawn on until dawn on Thursday (Friday morning).
5. Burn incense, then perform a dawn prayer (*salat fajar*). The incense should be kept burning all the time during the stay.
6. Recite a *du'a* of the *ayat kursiy* repeatedly 72 times after doing the five prescribed daily prayers and recite it also during contemplation.[37]

If everything is done well, according to al-Buny, on the first quiet night, around midnight, there will be a sound of a donkey. The performer must not worry, be scared, or nervous, as the sound will produce no harm. On the second quiet night, also around midnight, there will be a roar of a running horse. Again, the

[34] Lion and donkey are not found in Cirebon; probably the reference to these is the influence of Arabian beliefs. See also the next pages.

[35] It might be from this belief that drivers in Cirebon will avoid hitting a cat. Some drivers of city-passengers cars (suburban transportation) said that if a hitting does occur unavoidably, the driver will stop his vehicle, take the victim cat with sorrow and affection, and bury it properly; some may perform a simple *slametan* to prevent possible *na'as* (bad luck) or *blai* (accident).

[36] asy-Syeikh al-Buny, "... Riyadlah ayah al-Kursiy wa bayan da'swatiha" in an-Narly, Al-Ustadz as-Sayyid Muhammad (?), *Khazinat al-Asrar*, Syarikat an-Nur Asia, pp. 150-151. This book, with the date and place of publication were no longer readable, was shown to me by Pak Shofie. He read the chapter and I recorded his translation in local vernacular.

[37] The *du'a* is made up of the verse of the Throne (*ayat Kursiy*), modified by insertion of incantations, as prescribed in the text (see: plates at the end of this chapter).

performer must not worry, be scared or nervous, as it also will produce no harm. On the third night, around midnight there will be three cats, brown, white and black in colour, coming from the entrance of the niche where the contemplation is done. They will disappear mysteriously but again, the performer must not worry, be scared, or nervous, as the virtue of the *du'a* protects the performer from probable harm caused by them. Keep the incense burning and steadily recite the *du'a* facing the *Qibla* (*Ka'ba* in Mecca). On the fourth night, around midnight, there will be a smell of something. Soon there will come a servant made of light. Again the performer must not be scared, nervous or worried; but must make sure that the incense keeps burning, until a voice of greeting is heard. It says: "*Assalamu 'alaikum ya wali-Allah*" (Peace be upon you oh the friend of God) to which the performer has to answer with: "*Wa 'alaikumus Salam Warahmatullahi Wabarakatuh*" (Peace be upon you, and upon you the mercy of God and His blessing). Eventually, the servant will say: "What would you like to have from me oh the friend of God?" The performer should answer him by saying: "I do not expect anything from you, except that I hope you would like to be my servant during my life-time." Then the servant will give a gold ring carved with God's great names (*al-ism al-a'zham*). Probably he will also say: "Take this ring and wear it on your right hand finger as a sign of a pact between you and me. If you want my presence, recite the *du'a* three times, then say, oh king Kandiyas, I need your presence." The servant will come and can be asked to do what one wants.[38]

This procedure is said to be the way for a devout person to make a lawful pact with a good (Muslim) jinn. This pact must only be used for righteous and non-commercial purposes. Another pact, a condemned and unlawful one made

[38] Pak Shofie was reluctant to explain the probable efficacy of the *riyadhah*. He however, copied the text in hand writing and gave it to me while saying: "Just try and prove it by yourself."

with a bad jinn, is also said to exist. It is said that this pact is made by sinners through mediation by a *dukun* for unlawful and commercial purposes.

(فصل في رياضة اية الكرسي وبيان دعوتها)
ورياضتها صحيحة مجربة فانها مستجابة لمن يدعو بها ولكن لم يبلغ بالزيادة إلا بالرأي
قال الشيخ البوني قدس سره اذا اردت العمل بها فتوكل على الله وطهر قلبك ومكانك وثيابك
وخلص نيتك وتدخل الخلوة يوم الثلاثاء عند صلاة الفجر ويكون كثير من البخور عندك
وانت تتلو الدعوة دبر كل صلاة مكتوبة اثنين وسبعين مرة والبخور عمال.
اعلم يا بني وفقني الله واياك انك تسمع في الليلة الاولى في ركن الخلوة صوتا كنهيق الحمار
فلا تخف ولا تفزع فانهم لا يقدرون عليك. فاذا كانت الليلة الثانية فانك تسمع نصف الليل
فوق الخلوة صوتا كجري الخيل فلا تخف ولا تفزع. فاذا كانت الليلة الثالثة نصف الليل يدخلون
عليك ثلاث قطاط احمر وابيض واسود ويدخلون من الباب ويخرجون من صدر الخلوة فلا تخف
ولا تفزع فانهم لا يقدرون عليك. فان الدعوة مجاب. فاذا كانت الليلة الرابعة نصف الليل
اطلق البخور وانت مستقبل القبلة تدعو دعاء فان الحائط ينشق ويدخل عليك خادم
من النور فلا تخف ولا تقطع البخور حتى يقول السلام عليك يا ولي الله. فقل له وعليك
السلام ورحمة الله وبركاته. فيقول ما تريد منا يا ولي الله فقل له ما اريد منك إلا خادما
يخدمني ما بقي من عمري فيقول لك خذ هذا الخاتم الذهب منقوش فيه اسم الله الاعظم
هذا ميثاق بيني وبينك. فاذا اردت حضوري اجعل الخاتم في يدك اليمنى واقرأ
الدعوة ثلاثا ثم تقول يا ملك كنداياس اجبني بحضورك في كل ما تريد من طي المكان
والمشي على الماء وغيرهما من انواع الكرامات هذا مع التوكل ■ خزينة الاسرار ص ١٥٠
ارتيني: قال الشيخ البوني قدس سره. لمون سيرا ارف عرجاكن / عمالكن رياضة
اية الكرسي (دعاء اية كرسي سكع اسراري لن خواصي لن عزيمتي) ملك برتوكل نيغ كوستي الله
برسيهانا لن سوجي ناتي نيرا تمفت ايرا لن فكايني ايرا. لن اخلاص نيتة ايرا
سأ ويس ايكو كابيه بريس. نولي سيرا منجيفا نيغ تمفت كع سفي سأ دورونغي
فجر دينا ثلاثا. نولي سيرا غاكيماكن غوبوغ مينان / اوكوف لن تروس صلاة الفجر
لن سابان٢ تس صلاة فرض مجا دعاء (دعاء اية كرسي) فيغ ٧٢ لن تروس اوكوف٢.
كتهوي له هاي انك٢كو - موكا٢ كوستي الله متوكي نيغ ايسون لن نيغ سيرا
سأ تمني سيرا مغكو كروغو اعدالم بغي كع فرنام غدا وفنتو كادان سفي. كروغو نيغ
سوارا كيا برغيغيه حمار. نليكا ايكو سيرا اجا ودي لن اجا كليبسه. سبب بلي ارف
كغكو نيغ سيرا. فدا مالم كع كفندو يكتي سيرا كروغو نيغ سوارا كيا سوارا غلايوف
جران. غدا وغتو كادان سفي نيغ تغه مالم. سيرا انتف اجا ودي لن اجا كليبسه. لن فدا
مالم كع كفيغ تاو اناع تغه بغي. انا تلوغ ايكور كوجيغ (كوجيغ ابانغ - فوتيه لن ايرع)
منجيغ نيغ كامر ايرا. منجيغ سكع لاواغ لن متو سكع (دي تلان كسغين) ملك فدا
وقتو ايكو سيرا اجا ودي لن اجا كليبسه. سبب كوجيغ٢ ايكو بلي ككو نيغ سيرا. سبب

Pak Shofie's handwriting copy of the manual of Riyadhah Ayat Kursi

دعاء كڠ سيرا واجا ايكو كڠ غاليڠ ٢ فنى . لن نليكا بڠى كڠ كڠيڠ ففنت اناڠ تعه وڠى سيرا تتف
تروس اوكوف ٢ . لن سيرا تتف ماداف غبلة . لن تتف كلوان مجا دعاء اية كرسى ماؤ .
لن لمون سيرا كراسا انا امبون ٢ / ممبواف ناءف . تولى معكو انا خادم سكڠ نور
ممخيڠ . سيرا اجا ودى لن اجا فكوت اوكوف ٢ . سمڠى انا سوارا كڠ اولوڠ سلام نيڠ سيرا
كلوان اوجاف السلام عليك ياولى الله . تولى سيرا جاوابن وعليك السلام ورحمة الله
وبركاته . تولى خادم ماهو غوجف "ماتريد منا ياولى الله" . اف كڠ سيرا كهندا قى سڠ
اسون هو ولى الله . تولى سيرا جاوابن اسون بلى مفهندا قى اف ٢ كجوالى ابسون معهندا قى
سوفيا سيرا ادادى خادم كڠ عيكن ع اسون سلاما ايسون ماسه انا عمرى . تولى
خادم ماهو غوجف أمبلك (جلك) ايكى ألى ٢ مس (ألى ٢ مس كڠ انا اوكير ٢ اى اسم الله الاعظم)
ايكو فرجنجيا ن انترا ايسون لن سيرا . لمون سيرا معهندا قى كدا تڠانى ايسون . اغكوئ ألى ٢ ايكى
نيڠ تڠن ٢ ايرا لن واجانى دعاء . فيڠ تلو . تولى غوجف يا ملك كند ياس اجبنى بحضورك
مات خادم ماؤ تكا . اعدالم اف كڠ سيرا كهندا قى
(ايكى دوعاء اية الكرسى وخواصها .
(بسم الله الرحمن الرحيم) الحمد لله رب العالمين والصلاة والسلام على سيدنا محمد وعلى اله وصحبه
وسلم. اللهم إني اسئلك وأتوسل اليك يا الله يا الله يا الله يا الله يارحمن يارحمن يارحمن . يا رحيم
يارحيم يارحيم . ياه ياه ياه . ياربا ه ياربا ه يا رباه . ياسيداه ياسيداه ياسيداه ياهو ياهو ياهو
ياغياثي عند شدتي ياأنيسي عند وحدتي يا مجيبي عند دعوتي يا الله يا الله يا الله .(الله لا إله الا هو
الحي القيوم) ياحي يا قيوم يامن تقوم السموات والارض بأمره يا جامع المخلوقات تحت لطفه
وقهره . أسألك اللهم ان تسخر لي روحانية هذه الاية الشريفة تعينني على قضاء حوائجي
يامن (لا تأخذه سنة ولا نوم) اهدنا الى الحق والى طريق مستقيم حتى استريح من اللوم
لا إله الا انت سبحانك اني كنت من الظالمين يامن (له ما في السموات وما في الارض من الذي
يشفع عنده الا باذنه) اللهم اشفع لي وارشدني فيما اريد من قضاء حوائجي واثبات قولي
وفعلي وعملي وبارك لي في اهلي يامن (يعلم مابين ايديهم وما خلفهم ولا يحيطون بشيء من علمه)
يا من يعلم ضمير عباده سرا وجهرا أسألك اللهم ان تسخر لي خدام هذه الاية العظيمة والدعوة
المنيفة يكونون لي عونا على قضاء حوائجي هيلا هيلا جولا جولا ملكا ملكا يا من يتصرف في ملكه
(الا بما شاء وسع كرسيه السموات والارض) سخر لي عبدك كند ياس حتى يكلمني في حال
يقظتي ويعينني في جميع حوائجي يامن (ولا يؤده حفظهما وهو العلي العظيم) يا صمد ياحميد ياباعث
ياشهيد ياحق ياوكيل يا قوي يامتين كن لي عونا على قضاء حوائجي بالف الف لا حول ولا قوة الا بالله
العلي العظيم . اقسمت عليك ايها السيد الكندياس اجبني أنت وخدامك واعينوني في جميع أموري
بحق ما تعتقدونه من العظمة والكبرياء وبحق هذه الاية العظيمة بسيدنا محمد عليه الصلاة والسلام .

خزينة الاسرار ص ١٥١

كتاب خزينة الاسرار

خزينة الاسرار

جليلة الاذكار

للاستاذ السيد محمد حقي النازلي

نفع الله الناس بعلومه

امين

(وبهامشها كتاب الحصن الحصين من كلام سيد المرسلين)

(للعلامة شمس الدين محمد بن الجزري رحمه الله تعالى)

الناشر

شركة النور اسيا

Chapter 3: Mythology and Cosmology of Cirebonese Traditions

INTRODUCTION

> My son, Harlan, once decided to go to Jakarta via Puncak (Bogor). Because it was on an important business trip I told him to go on Wednesday Pahing. For certain reasons he firmly insisted on going the day before and I could do nothing but let him go and told him to be extra careful. Upon his leaving I tried not to think about him but I could not stop. Three days later I got a telegram from his office in Tangerang suggesting that I should see my son. Without knowing what had happened I set off immediately to Tangerang and found him lying in hospital after a not-so-serious injury in a bus crash ...[1]

One feature of Cirebon is its richness in myths and legends. Seldom is the name of a single place, locality or object such as a site, river, mountain and lake free from mythical or legendary tales. Each name bears its own folk-story of origin. It is a common knowledge that the name "Cirebon", meaning the water of tiny shrimps, is derived primarily from *Ci* or *Cai* meaning 'water' and *rebon* meaning 'tiny shrimps' and is associated with the development of the fishing industry pioneered by its first *Kuwu*, Ki Cakrabumi. Similar to this are the names of Kuningan, Indramayu and Majalengka, the other three regencies in the residency of Cirebon. They are also associated with mythical derivation and origin.

The name Kuningan, for example, refers to the legend of Pangeran Kuningan and Aria Kemuning. According to the local legend, Pangeran Kuningan was the son of 'Putri Cina' (Chinese Princess), daughter of a Chinese emperor.[2] When still in China she became pregnant not because of being impregnated by a man, but because of a brass bowl (*bokor kuningan*) attached to her belly to deceive Sunan Gunung Jati when he was invited to China. To judge Sunan Gunung Jati's sainthood the emperor summoned his daughter, and asked the Sunan to guess how advanced the *putri's* pregnancy was. Sunan Gunung Jati said that she was several months pregnant. Startled by this false statement the emperor became angry, accusing Sunan Gunung Jati as being a fraud rather than a saint, and instantly drove him out of his palace. When the *putri* went back to her room and took off her clothes to detach the brass bowl, she was frightened when she observed she was indeed pregnant. She cried from fear and called together her parents and other family members. Seeing his daughter's condition and deeply embarrassed by what had happened, the emperor was bewildered and, he decided

[1] Field notes: A statement given by Mang Atmo, a resident in Kalitengah, See the end this Chapter.
[2] Putri Cina probably refers to Nio Ong Tin, one of Sunan Gunung Jati's wives. See also Chapter Six.

to send his daughter to Java with a convoy of ships conveying a message acknowledging Sunan Gunung Jati's sainthood and with the request to take the *putri* as his wife. When the consort arrived at Cirebon, Sunan Gunung Jati was in Luragung, 20 kilometres east of the town of Kuningan, preaching the Islamic faith. Soon afterwards the *putri* bore a male child. Sunan Gunung Jati asked the local Ki Gedeng to care for the baby as a foster son. Meanwhile, about the same time the Ki Gedeng's wife also bore a male baby. Thus, Ki Gedeng had two newly born male children, one, his own and the other, a foster son, which gave the impression that they were twins. With Sunan Gunung Jati's permission Putri Cina's baby was named Pangeran Kuningan (the prince of brass) while his own son was named Aria Kemuning (from *kuning*, meaning 'yellow'). Later, when they had grown up, Pangeran Kuningan became Adipati Kuningan, ruler of Kuningan, whereas Aria Kemuning became his assistant.[3]

According to another tale, the name Indramayu is associated with the legend of Indang Darma Ayu and prince Wiralodra. Majalengka, whose name is derived from the expression *maja-e (wis) langka* ('the maja fruits have already disappeared'), is associated with the story of Aria Salingsingan, a local legendary figure. All myths and the figures in them are rooted in the process of Islamization and are directly or indirectly associated with Sunan Gunung Jati and his disciples. Even places like 'Pesalaran' and 'Weru', the district where I stayed, have their own distinct folk-tales. Pesalaran, which is now the centre of the small town of Plered, seven kilometres west of Cirebon, occupies only a small area in Kecamatan Weru. The name Pesalaran is associated with the word *nyalar* ('to ask'); while the name Weru comes from *weru(h)* meaning 'to know'. Both names are combined as in the expression, *weru sawise nyalar* (to know after having asked). The folk-tale tells of a small group of people, envoys of Talaga on behalf of the Galuh-Pajajaran Hindu Kingdom, who were sent to Cirebon to ask 'Kanjeng Sinuhun' to submit and render tribute to Galuh.[4] Half way to Cirebon they became confused and found themselves going around and around at one site for several days. After being frustrated in finding the right way, they saw a wood cutter with whom they started to ask a series of questions (*nyalar*). When the envoys asked the wood cutter, he did not give conclusive answers and referred them to another person who might be able to give further information. This person did the same thing; giving only an inconclusive answer and referring them to another one and so on. At last however, after a series of exhausting efforts they found someone, a wise man, who gave them advice and taught them wisdom as well as giving them the information about Cirebon and the right way to proceed. The man was Kanjeng Sinuhun himself from whom they finally embraced Islam and became his disciples. They did not go back to Talaga but

[3] Field notes which relied on a story told by Pak Sairoji (54 years), unclear occupation. He is a Kalitengah resident who travelled a lot.
[4] 'Kanjeng Sinuhun' is local reference to Sunan Gunung Jati.

stayed there. Since then, the site where they asked their questions is called Pesalaran meaning 'the place of *nyalar*' (asking), while the surrounding area where they finally gained knowledge is called Weru (knowing); the leader of the group then became Ki Gede Weru.[5]

THE MYTH OF CREATION

Among the legends and myths, however, none is more interesting than the myths of creation. These myths of creation, I think, have wide scope and bear philosophical significance. In this chapter I wish to consider three myths of creation: namely, the creation and origin of the universe, the creation of mankind, and the origin of Javanese inhabitants and their religion. Along with these myths I also include in this chapter the prevailing eschatological views especially those relating to the idea of calamity, life after death, the problem of human destiny, and attempts to resolve the mystery of life through the numerological system. I start with the first myth.[6]

Creation and Origin of The Universe

It is among the Cirebonese Court circle, particularly within the circle of *Pengguron Krapyak* led by Pangeran Sulaeman Sulendraningrat, that this myth of the creation of the universe prevails. It relates that once upon a time there was an *alam awang-uwung (ghoibul-ghuyub)*, a world of nothingness: no limit, no edge, no line, no boundary, no light, no sound. There was absolute quietness, nothing existed except God, the One, the Living, the Powerful and the Willing; at this stage His power and will were *la ta'yun*, not manifested. This is the earliest stage of the universe, the stage before creation, called *Martabat Ahadlah*, the stage when only One existed, only God. After an immeasurable duration came the second stage called *Martabat Wahdah*, the stage where the One God began to show His power and will in the form of bright light called *Nur-Allah*, the light of God which shone far brighter than a thousand suns. This stage is *ta'yun awal*, the first reality, in the sense that His intention to create was expressed in reality. The next stage occurred after another immeasurable duration, when a golden bright light called *Nur Muhammad*, the light of the praiseworthy, sprang up within the still shining brighter light, like an eggyolk within an eggwhite. The presence of *Nur Muhammad*, also called *Ruh al-A'zhom*, the greatest soul, constituted the *ta'yun-tsani* the second reality in which the intention of creation turned into a master design or master seed. It was the embryo of the complex

[5] Field notes. The story of Pesalaran was especially told by Man Sapi'i (62 years), an ex farmer at Trusmi.
[6] I owe Martin van Bruinessen, lecturer at IAIN Sunan Kalijaga (Yogyakarta), who had allowed me to copy from his disposal, five volumes type written manuscripts of Sulendraningrat's writing (Rama Guru at Pengguron Krapyak, Cirebon). This section relies a great deal on these manuscripts.

universe from which everything emerged. This latter stage is called *Martabat Wahidiyah*, the stage of the Greatest Union.[7]

The light of the praiseworthy (Nur Muhammad) was motionless for about 60,000 years until finally the light of the praiseworthy claimed to be God: "I am the God". Immediately Allah responded: "No, you are not God, you are the embryo of the whole universe I have created". Hearing God's decree *Nur Muhammad* trembled with fright and his whole body was covered with sweat; this event led to the next stage, the presence of the *Ruh Idhoft*, when the *Nur Muhammad's* sweat became *Durratul Baidla*, white pearl gems, the source of all souls of the universe. The sweat in his nose turned into the souls of angels; the sweat of his face turned into the souls of *'Arsy, Laukh Mahfud, Qalam*, and other heavenly creatures; the sweat of his chest turned into the souls of prophets, messengers, saints, scholars, and other selected individuals; the sweat of his back turned into the souls of Bait al-Ma'mur, Bait Allah, Bait al-Mukaddas and other prayer houses all over the world; the sweat of his eyebrows turned into the souls of faithful males and females; the sweat of his ears turned into the souls of infidels; the sweats of his legs turned into the souls of the whole universe. This is the stage when *Nur Muhammad*, the abstract design of creation, turned into a real one, *Ruh idhoft*, just as a developing photograph turns from a blur into a clear image. It is at this stage that the creation of every being became *mungkin*, or possible, depending on whether or not God Wills it.[8]

The next stage was the period of physical creation, that is the stage when God constructed the whole universe and its contents. The overall construction was completed within six divine days,[9] from Sunday through to the dawn on Friday. As each divine day is equal to 50,000 years, the six-day process was thus equal to 300,000 years. Within the first two days the globe of bare and bald earth was constructed; Over the next two days the earth was perfected giving it its finished structure and form furnished with continents, hills, mountains, rivers, lakes, seas, oceans, flora and fauna. The last two days was the completion of the galaxies; of the sun, moon, stars, other planets; of heaven and other heavenly things. In this stage God had created, among other things, 70,000 planets, each planet being 70 times the size of the earth. On each planet there were 70,000 inhabitants who were not angels, jinns, or humans. They worshipped God, but then they rebelled and God wiped them out. God created another 80,000 more planets, but these were smaller than the first 70,000 being only about ten times the size of earth. There were some kinds of birds living on the planets, but they finally vanished. After that, God created 20,000 human-like creatures out of

[7] Sulendraningrat, P.S. (1982), *Ghaib*, type written manuscript, Cirebon: Pengguron Caruban Krapyak, pp. 1–8; Sulendraningrat, P.S. (n.d.), *Babarnya Jimat Kalimasada Prabu Yudistira Amartapura*, type written manuscript, Cirebon: Pengguron Caruban Krapyak, Kaprabon, pp. 63–65, 80–86.
[8] Sulendraningrat, P.S. (n.d.), *Babarnya* ... pp.2–4.
[9] (QS 32:4); The Holy Qur'an: English Translation and its Commentary, p.1226.

light, but finally, they also vanished. After a pause of about 70,000 years, God created *Qalam, Laukh Mahfud, 'Arsy*, angels and finally, paradise and Hell. Thus, the creation of the whole universe was complete.[10]

Seventy thousand years after completing the universe, God created a human being called Adam, but not the Adam of our ancestors. He was the first Adam who lived on the earthly world long before the Adam of our ancestors was born. This earlier Adam gave rise to descendants but all were vanished; the last descendant died 10,000 years after the first Adam was born. God then created another Adam, but, again, he and his descendants vanished after 10,000 years. This was repeated again and again until 10,000 Adams had been created (the last one, the ten thousandth, was the Adam of our ancestors). It is unclear whether they lived here on our earth, or somewhere else. Supposing they really did live on this earth, it follows that since there had been 10,000 Adams (each Adam and his descendants lasting ten thousand years), our earth, according to this myth, has already been in existence for about 100,000 million years; whereas, the history of mankind since (our) Adam has been less than 10,000 years.[11]

Creation of mankind

The notion that the microcosm is a reflection of the macrocosm appears in Cirebonese myths of human creation. Within the court circle, the seven stages (*martabat pitu*) in the creation of the universe are used to describe the creation of human beings.[12] According to this tradition, long before people are born, they are in *Alam Ahadiyat*, the first stage. At this stage the existence of a person is still unthinkable because person is physically nonexistent. The second stage *Alam Wahdah* is reached when impregnation occurs, that is, at the moment when an ovum is fertilised by sperm. The third stage *Alam Wahidiyah* is then entered; at this stage the fertilised ovum multiplies and turns successively into a clot of thick liquid, then into a clot of blood, and then into a clot of flesh. The fourth stage, *Alam Arwah*, comes when the flesh-clot shows signs of movement, signifying that God has breathed life into the soul making it alive.[13] The fifth stage, *Alam Mitsal*, is when the flesh-clot becomes an embryo containing potential parts that will develop into specialised body parts. Then comes *Alam Ajsam*, the sixth stage when the embryo develops a complete physical structure with specialised body parts and organs: head, hair, body, hands, legs, finger and toe nails. On the whole it is still weak, until finally, at the seventh stage it reaches its final form and enters *Alam Insan Kamil*, the stage of a perfectly formed

[10] Sulendraningrat, P.S. (n.d.), *Babarnya* ... pp.4–6.
[11] *Ibid*, pp. 6–7.
[12] Kartapraja, K. (1978), "Ngelmu Sejati Cirebon", *Dialog*, Dep. Agama: Jakarta, Edisi Khusus, March 1973, pp.91–107.
[13] Cf: A hadith narrated by Bukhari and Muslim, from Ibn Mas'ud. See: Dahlan, A. (1988), *Hadits Arba'in Annawawiyah*, Bandung: Al Ma'arif, pp. 16–17.

human being. At this last stage the new human is ready to emerge from the womb and the mother is ready to give birth.[14]

Our species, humankind, is said as to be descended from Adam, who came to earth from heaven. Adam himself was created from clay and the process of his creation is another subject of mythology.[15] Mang Amin (54 years), a Batik factory worker said that the creation of Adam started when God ordered Gabriel to make a kind of seed by mixing the four elements (earth, fire, water and air) which he then planted in the soil of paradise. For a long time the seed grew steadily, just like an ordinary plant, but later it gradually turned into the human figure of Adam. When it reached about 30 metres high, God blew a spirit into it and Adam became animated. He moved and walked about, looking around the paradise as if surveying and recognising his environment. In the meantime God taught him the names of everything he found, and Adam mastered them well. Once, God introduced him to other heavenly creatures and ordered them to bow down to Adam. To show them Adam's worth, God ordered Adam to list the names and characteristics of a number of heavenly things which angels and other creatures knew nothing about. The angels were fascinated and respectfully bowed down to Adam. Iblis, another heavenly creature, was reluctant to do so; instead he looked down upon Adam, boastfully claiming himself to be superior to Adam. Due to this rebellion God pronounced His curse on Iblis and banished him to Hell forever. Nevertheless, God granted Iblis' plea for postponement of his punishment until the day of judgement; Iblis then swore to deceive Adam in order to lead him and his descendants astray.[16]

Adam had proved himself to be a clever being when God ordered him to name a number of heavenly things; the pity was, however, that he never talked because he had no one with whom he could talk. But when he was fast asleep in paradise, God ordered Gabriel to pull out one of Adam's left ribs, from which God created another being, Eve. After her creation was completed Adam woke up. He was surprised to see a lovely companion standing before him. He felt glad and thanked God for her presence. Adam and Eve then talked to each other, played together and started a new life until the time came when they had to leave paradise, and were thrown onto the earth because they had succumbed to Iblis' temptation. Adam was believed to be thrown down onto *Gunung* (Mount) Surandil (Adam's Peak in Ceylon, now Sri Lanka), while Eve was thrown down into Jeddah. After a long search for each other they finally met together at the Plain of Arafah in Saudi Arabia. With God's grace granted after their immediate repentance, Adam and Eve then started their earthly life, giving birth to descendants and becoming

[14] Field notes, derived from a talk with Pak Kusna, a personnel at *kraton* Kanoman (17-5-1992). *For Martabat Pitu*, see also: Kartapraja (1978), pp. 91–107; Sulendraningrat, S. (1980:78–84, 1982:80–86).
[15] See: (QS 4:1; 7:189).
[16] Field notes.

Khalifa, God's representatives on earth, to establish order, firstly among animals and later among both animals and their descendants.[17]

Origin of Javanese Inhabitants and Religion

The notion that mankind is descended from Adam is recounted in another myth that relates the link between the present generation and their ancestors.[18] According to this myth, the first time Adam begot descendants was when he was about 130 years old; Eve bore twins, a male and a female named Kabil and Aklima. In total Eve gave birth forty-two times, each time producing twins (a male and a female), except for the sixth time when she bore only one male child, Syis, and the forty-first time, when she bore only a female, Hunun. In all then, Adam and Eve's direct descendants numbered eighty-two. When Eve gave birth to the fifth set of children, Adam set a rule of marriage that said that a good-looking son had to marry an unattractive girl whereas an unattractive son had to marry a good-looking girl. Since both twins of each set borne by Eve were either good-looking or unattractive this rule ensured that no one could marry his or her twin.[19]

At this stage, Iblis who had caused them to be thrown from paradise, was ready with a new plan. He tried again to intrude on Adam and Eve, but could not do it in the same way as he had done in paradise, because their natures had become so different. Adam and Eve were physical beings, whereas he himself was a spiritual one. Iblis then entered Eve's heart and whispered to her to rebel against Adam by disagreeing with Adam's rule of marriage and imposing a contrary rule; that is, a good-looking person should marry another good-looking one, and an unattractive one should marry another unattractive one. To support their respective assertions, both Adam and Eve claimed rights over their children and, therefore, also the right to set the marriage rule. Each insisted that the children really originated from his or her own body; in the case of Adam, from his semen and in the case of Eve from her eggs. To solve the problem they agreed, however, to pour these substances into two different pitchers and to pray for God's guidance. After praying several days, a strong wind arose blowing away Eve's pitchers. When Adam was about 160 years old, there grew from his pitcher a nice boy baby. They understood then, that all this had happened from God's will and gave the baby the name Syis. Since then, the marriage rule set out by Adam became effective. The entire human population of the world, therefore is descended from Adam through his children (except for Hunun, who did not

[17] Sulendraningrat, P.S.(1982), *Ghaib*, pp. 16–25.
[18] Sulendraningrat, P.S. (1978), *Beralihnya Pulau Jawa Dari Agama Sanghyang Kepada Agama Islam*, type written manuscript, Cirebon: Pengguron Caruban Krapyak Kaprabon.
[19] *Ibid*, pp.2–5

marry because she was born without a twin, and Habil, who was killed before having children), including Syis, who got his wife in a different way.[20]

Failing with Eve, Iblis did not stop intruding; he moved on to her children. As a result of his efforts, out of the forty marriages between Adam's children, three couples were rebellious and married their good-looking twin partners. They were: the-first born, Kabil, to Aklima; the fifth-born, Harris, to Dayuna; and fifteenth-born, Lata, to Ujiah ('Uzza). Kabil married Aklima after killing her husband, Habil. To affirm their rebellion they left Adam's place; Kabil and Lata, with their partners, went separately south-westward to Africa, and Harris went eastward to China.[21]

Without specifying from which couple the Javanese population originated, the myth says that the first sea expedition to Java was made by the west Asian vizier of Alexander the Great. He intentionally sent as many as two thousand men and women to occupy Java. Unfortunately they encountered unfriendliness and most were killed by the native inhabitants, including several kinds of wild beasts, *lelembut* and *dedemit* (ghosts).[22] Fewer than one hundred people were left and these went back to west Asia. A second expedition was sent but with great caution, incorporating a number of wise elders and different ethnicities, particularly the people from south and south-east Asia (*Keling* and Campa). There were as many as 20,000 men and women, led by Syeikh Subakir who landed in Java. Soon Subakir went to Gunung Tidar where he met Semar and Togog,[23] the leaders of Javanese spiritual beings and negotiated with them. They finally reached an agreement allowing the newcomers to stay in Java on the condition that they should be aware that Java had, in fact, been inhabited by many spiritual beings so that both sides, especially the new settlers, had to make all possible efforts to sustain a peaceful coexistence (*rukun*) with each other. Since then Java has been inhabited by spirits as well as human beings.[24]

The position of Adam's descendant, Syis, is of specific significance. The myth says that Syis had been one of the most beloved children, and to him important legendary figures of later generations are attributed. He married Dewi Mulat, yet who she was, where she came from, and how Syis met her, are not described. Syis, on the other hand, is described as a nicely behaved child who later, after Adam had died at 960 years of age, inherited his prophecy. This provoked both admiration and jealousy of Idajil, king of jinns. Idajil wanted, and then attempted,

[20] Ibid, pp. 6–8

[21] Ibid, pp. 5–6.

[22] *Lelembut* and *dedemit* refer to spiritual beings which were supposedly jinn, occupying in certain places.

[23] *Semar* and *Togog* are *wayang* figures, referred to by this myth as coming from Eve's seed after her pitcher was blown by the wind. Idajil is said to have found the pitcher, and taken care of it (Sulendraningrat, Ibid p. 46).

[24] Ibid, pp. 43–47.

to have descendants who could take over or, at least, bear honour both Adam and Syis. He wanted Syis to marry his daughter, Delajah. Unfortunately, Syis had already married Dewi Mulat. Idajil however, did not despair; instead, he made all possible efforts to manifest his firm will. He insinuated his daughter, Delajah, into Dewi Mulat and secretly put her beside Syis. At the same time he took Dewi Mulat away. After knowing with certainty that Delajah had been impregnated he released her and immediately replaced Dewi Mulat for fear of eventually being caught.[25]

From her marriage to Syis, Dewi Mulat gave birth to twin children. One was a perfect human being named Anwas, the other was a light image of a human figure, a spiritual baby who was really the son of Delajah and Syis, named Anwar (the Arabic plural form of **Nur** meaning 'light'). The two babies (one human being and the other one, in fact, a jinn), were cared for with love and affection even when Adam realised that Idajil had interfered in the affair. During their childhood, they respected their parents and grandparents very much, and were proud of them, but later Anwas and Anwar showed markedly different habits and preferences. Anwas who clearly followed the wisdom of his father and grandfather, grew into a devout believer, being fond of learning the true faith. Anwar, however, was fond of wandering to seek wisdom through contemplation in quiet and strange places such as on mountains, in jungles and, in caves. Prior to his death Adam told Syis to be careful as his sons Anwas and Anwar would take different paths. This prediction came true after Adam died. Anwar was grieved upon seeing that human beings would finally die, become motionless and be buried. Syis told him that it was quite natural and that it would happen to everyone without exception. But Anwar's grief was unbearable and he made up his mind to leave his parents and to take any action that would enable him to avoid illness and death. He wandered in search of something that would ensure his wish. Idajil instantly took advantage of the opportunity; he met Anwar, really his grandson, and told him that his decision was good and he promised to help him. He led Anwar northward to Dulmat.[26] Here Idajil performed a magical act, first by producing thick clouds wrapping their bodies together. As the cloud disappeared, a spring of water appeared in front of them. He asked Anwar to drink as much as he could, and to bathe in the water called *tirta marta kamandalu* (or *banyu penguripan,* in Cirebonese), the water of everlasting life. He also gave Anwar Eve's pitcher, called *cupu manik astagina,* the gem pitcher of eight virtues, which he had found after it had been blown away by a strong wind. He asked Anwar to fill it with the water, as it might

[25] Ibid, pp. 6–7

[26] *Dulmat* probably comes from the Arabic word *dzulumat* (pl. *dzulm*) meaning darkness. In this myth the word is used to refer to an extremely cold sunless country, where the land consists of nothing but ice. Sulendraningrat (1978:9) explicitly mentions *Negeri Laut Es* (the country of icedsea) as *Kutub Utara* (Antarctica).

have some use in the future. One virtue of the pitcher was that the water in it could never be used up. Idajil then led him out of this place and told him to take a dying rewan plant he would find on his way; its roots, called *latamansadi*, were a useful remedy for any disease. He then disappeared, leaving Anwar alone and undecided about where to go. But at last Anwar found the *rewan* plant and he cheerfully took some of the roots, *latamansadi*, with him.[27]

By then Anwar had already found the important things he really wished for: the avoidance of illness, by possessing *latamansadi*, and the avoidance of death by drinking and bathing with the water of everlasting life. He had even more: the gem pitcher of eight virtues and some spare water of everlasting life. However, he wished for still more. The myth continues with the story of how Anwar, under Idajil's guidance, moved toward becoming a super spiritual being. For example, he was led to further adventures: to the sea of Iraq, where he met the banned angels Harut and Marut, who taught him to use astrology to learn what would happen in the future.[28] In Africa he met Lata and Ujiah ('Uzza), the rebellious son and daughter of Adam who taught him how to obtain a safe living with abundance. At the Cauldron Mountain at the upper end of the Nile River, he again met Idajil but without recognising him. Idajil gave him the mystical experience of seeing heaven; taught him to move faster than the wind; gave him the precious gift, *ratnadumilah*, a lamp-like shining diamond which could lead him to brighter paths; taught him, and authorised him, to teach the doctrine of everlasting life achieved through 'reincarnation', and the means to reach heaven for those who did not want to be reincarnated. Idajil also asked him to pursue further advanced knowledge as well as enlightenment in *Maladewa*, an island in the Indian Ocean, south-west of India.[29]

After following all of these instructions, Anwar moved on to his highest achievement; in a short clash with Nuradi, the king of jinns on the island of Maladewa, Nuradi surrendered to him and confessed that he, Anwar, was much more powerful. Nuradi surrendered his throne to Anwar. He asked his people to worship Anwar and to regard him as the true god. The people called the new king god Anwar, Sang (H)yang Nur Cahya meaning The Spirit of Super Light. Since Anwar gained power, the 'religion of Sang (H)yang' was formally established with reincarnation as its main doctrine. He married Nuradi's daughter, Dewi Rini, with whom he produced descendants. This Sang (H)yang religion was then brought to Java by Batara Guru, the fourth descendant of Sang (H)yang Nur Cahya. Batara Guru came to Java from India, married a Javanese woman and produced a son. When he went back to India, his position was taken by his native Javanese son. When Bhagawan Abiyasa and Pandu Dewanata, the 13th

[27] Ibid, pp. 7–10.
[28] For a short account on 'Harut-Marut,' see for example, *Shorter Encyclopaedia of Islam*.
[29] Ibid, pp. 10–16.

and 14th Javanese descendants of Nur Cahya from Bhatara Guru, took the leadership, this religion was spread more intensively. The religion was adopted by the Javanese until Islam came.[30]

Unlike Anwar, who was born as a spirit and who set up his own religion after long contemplation and a long search for wisdom under the guidance of Idajil, the jinn, Anwas was born as a real human being, who followed the prophetic religion of his father and grandfather. He produced descendants some of whom were also prophets, including Muhammad, the last prophet (peace be upon him). They passed on the religion of Allah to those willing to accept it.

According to the myth, Idajil's scenario did not end with Anwar, as his main concern was to have descendants who maintained Syis' honour among jinn or humans. From the intermarriage of Anwar's later generations with humans came the descendants who were either jinn, human, or half-jinn half-human. Some of them were honourable figures: among the jinn are the *Sang (H)yang*, among humans were the *Sang Prabu, Pandhita*, etc., and among the half-jinn half-human are the *Bhatara*, and *Bhagawan*. It was these descendants, with their religious tradition (religion of Sang Hyang), who occupied Java predating Islam.

In the Cirebonese court circle, the whole myth constitutes part of the literary tradition in which the link with their founding father, Sunan Gunung Jati, to Adam can be traced from both sides: Anwar's and Anwas'. Sunan Gunung Jati's mother, Rarasantang, was the daughter of Prabu Siliwangi, King of Pajajaran, the forty-first Javanese descendant of Batara Guru, and the forty-fifth descendant of Sang (H)yang Nurasa, son of Syis, son of Adam. Sunan Gunung Jati's father is Syarif Abdullah, vizier of the Turkish Empire in Egypt, the twenty-first descendant of the Prophet Muhammad, while the Prophet Muhammad himself is the thirty-seventh descendant of Anwas, son of Syis, son of Adam.

The message behind the myth is therefore clear: on the one hand, Sunan Gunung Jati and his descendants have a legitimate right to exercise leadership, both political and spiritual, over the Javanese population, be they Sang Hyang followers, Muslims, spirits, or human beings, as long as they are descendants of Adam or the jinns. Thus they all have to live in harmony (*rukun*) under his descendants' leadership. On the other hand, the myth implicitly asserts that Allah is the sole Supreme God. Other deities which are largely of Sang H(yang) type are nothing but our ancestors who deserve to be respected but not to be worshipped. They are powerless in the sense of having real and independent divine power. If they do have power, it is because God gives it to them. Their

[30] Along with Sang (H)yang Nur Cahya, Anwar is also accorded many other Javanese Sanskrit names, each of which is headed by the title Sang (H)Yang: Dewata, Dewa Pamungkas, Ngwatma Dewa, Sukma Kawekas, Sukma Wisesa, Amurbrengat, Manon, Warmana, Warmata, Mahawidi, Mahasidi, Mahasidem, Mahamulya, Mahatinggi, Mahaluhur, Kahanan Tunggal, Jagat Murtitaya, son of Sang Hyang Sita (Syis), son of Sang Hyang Athama (Adam).

power can be repealed any time God wills it. Moreover, just like us, they are only descendants of Syis, son of Adam. Adam himself was God's creation, who once had been punished. He survived after repenting and was granted a position as God's representative on earth, after being granted His grace. Still, he eventually died because he was only a creature.

Idajil, the powerful super jinn, who had contributed to the birth of Sang H(yang), was nothing but a creature, whose position was below Adam's, even below Syis'. Their common enemies are the devils, Iblis and *setan*, who always offer temptations to do evil and cause harm. Idajil however had fallen into this temptation.

ESCHATOLOGICAL IDEAS: THE CALAMITY AND THE END OF THE WORLD

The prevalence of popular beliefs in the inevitable ending of the world is easily understandable when we recall the notion of micro and macrocosm relations, and consider the commonly accepted fact that everyone is mortal. Death, seen as one thing that everyone must encounter, is the universal and inescapable end against which any power becomes powerless. Applying this perspective, Mang Marjuki (57 years), a farmer said:

> Just like everyone without exception will die, the whole world will also inevitably die; its death is its overall destruction and no one would know when, but certainly the time will come; that is what we call *kiyamat*.[31]

The local word *kiyamat* refers to the end of the world. This word comes from the Arabic **qiyamah**, which means "the arising". This term is used in religious discourse as a special reference to "the arising (of men at the Resurrection), a schematic statement of the order of events in Muslim eschatology", where all the dead are resurrected from their graves to receive the final judgment.[32] This event will take place after the universe is totally destroyed. Popular beliefs, however, put more emphasis on the total destruction of the world itself rather than on the resurrection. Commonly held ideas about *kiyamat* are: that it is the moment when tremendous floods appear everywhere, rising higher than the highest coconut trees and thereafter reaching all mountain peaks; all volcanoes will erupt; there will be terrible earthquakes; the earth will be rolled out like a carpet (*bumi digulung*) so that no one can live upon it; the stars, moon and sun will crash into each other; and the sky will break down and press upon the earth. In short, at *kiyamat* the world will be totally destroyed and no one will be saved.

[31] Indepth interview, 15-4-1992: "Apa binane kaya wong kang sapa bae pesti mati, kabeh jagat gan pesti mati; patine jagat iku ya rusake sing wong langka kang weruh kapan-kapane, tapi pesti ning rusake; kuwen iku kang diarani kiyamat."
[32] Shorter Encyclopedia of Islam, p.263.

It is also locally believed that the *kiyamat* will not come suddenly without notice. A number of signs will precede it, so that true believers detecting the signs and realising that *kiyamat* is about to come will have time to seek repentance. The non-believers however, because they have never recited *syahadat*, will not understand what is going on and will not know what to do. Instead, they will fall into vulnerable desperation. In local common belief, among the signs for the coming of *kiyamat* include: the appearance of smoke everywhere; the appearance of Dadjjal, followed by the descent of Imam Mahdi and Nabi Isa (Jesus); the coming of Ya'judj and Ma'judj (Gog and Magog). Sulendraningrat (n.d.) adds the signs with the appearance of three eclipses one in the west, one in the east, and one in Arabia; the rising of the sun in the west; the coming of *Dabbah* (the beast of the earth); the damage to the Ka'ba in Mecca; the prints of the Holy Qur'an disappear; and the spread of extreme cold air. Preceding these signs there will occur a long famine the world over, and civil war, which will break out in Turkey where two competing sides will fight to gain control over Istanbul.[33]

Local popular beliefs talk about catastrophic conditions preceded by various symptoms. Among the widely mentioned symptoms will be: when sons enslave their mothers; needy shepherds compete in unlawful luxuries (*bocah angon wis pada mabok ning barang kang bli karuan-karuan*);[34] time appears to be much shorter than ever; people no longer care whether they get things lawfully or unlawfully; there will be a general prevalence of arrogance and a craving for power; people will become careless with regard to their faith; adultery will seem natural, sinless, and be in common practice; the world will be caught in a long lasting darkness; the sun will rise in the west and Dadjjal will appear. Imam Mahdi and then Jesus will descend to refresh the Islamic faith; monstrous beasts will appear; the whole universe will shake violently.

Among these signs, the legend of Dadjjal is worth mentioning briefly. Dadjjal, which means the super liar, is a name that refers to a satanic human figure who leads people astray. He is identified as a descendant of Medina Jews, born when the Prophet Muhammad was still alive. During his childhood his name was Ibnu Shayyad or Ibnu Shaid. He is believed to be still alive and chained somewhere. Now he is more than 1400 years old. His first appearance will be in Khurasan, a town in Persia. His body will be huge and corpulent with reddish, frizzy hair, and with a wide throat. One of his eyes will look like a floating grape, as if made of green glass. On his forehead and between his eyes (some others describe him as one-eyed), will be written three unconnected Arabic letters *kaf* [**K**], *fa* [**F**], and *ra* [**R**]. If they are combined it will read "*kufur*" (unbelieving) or "*kafir*" (unbeliever). He will appear bringing supplies of food, water and fire, conquering

[33] Fairly lengthy accounts on the signs of *kiyamat* also appear in Sulendraningrat (n.d.), *Babarnya Jimat Kalimasada ...*, pp. 87-123 and Sulendraningrat (1982), *Ghaib*, pp. 30-66.
[34] This accords with the hadith narrated by Abu'l Husayn Muslim bin al-Hajjaj (known as Muslim) cited earlier (see: Chapter One, which recounts the appearance of Jibril).

the whole world by both coercive and fascinating magical acts. Although he will succeed in seizing most parts of the world and gaining many followers, he will not be able to seize Mecca and Medina. He will exercise power causing unbearable chaos for some time (some say forty days, others say forty years).[35]

The legend also mentions that Imam Mahdi and Jesus will appear preceding *Kiyamat*. They are two figures who will refresh the Islamic faith. Imam Mahdi is said to be the descendant of Sayid Husein, grandson of the Prophet Muhammad, born in Mecca on 15th of Sya'ban (the fourth month of Islamic calendar), AH 255/AD 834, that is, more than one thousand years ago. He disappeared miraculously and will reappear in Mecca sometime on the tenth of Dzulhijjah in an uneven year of the Muslim calendar, for approximately ten years, to fight against Dajjal and to establish order. At that time the Muslim army will not be strong enough, Imam Mahdi will probably be defeated and killed by Dajjal, but will have paved the way for Jesus to achieve a great victory. Jesus, however, will descend and work with Imam Mahdi, and upon Mahdi's death he will succeed to his leadership. Jesus will defeat Dajjal and the latter will perish in Syria or Palestine at Jesus' hand. After Jesus' time the situation will deteriorate. Most believers will pass away and finally only unbelievers will be left. At that time there will be no longer heard people pronouncing the words: "Allah, Allah". The day of ending will come even closer, the world will be caught in uncertainty, then Israfil will blow his trumpet; all living creatures will vanish.[36]

LIFE AFTER DEATH

Akin to the ideas of the end of individual life and of the world is the idea of life after death. This belief is also embedded in the fifth decree of faith. It incorporates the process of questioning by Munkar and Nakir; preliminary reward and punishment at the grave until the Day of Resurrection, the Day of Resurrection for final judgment; the *syafa'at* or intercession for the believers; passing the *sirat* and, finally, the everlasting life of the hereafter (the reward of paradise or the punishment of hell). Mang Sutaro (57 years), a Batik factory worker who held a common perception concerning life after death, told me about it coherently. A part of his account is recorded here:

> When the last men have left about three steps after burial, two angels, Munkar and Nakir, will visit the dead person in the grave and ask: Who is your God? Your Prophet? Your leader, and so on? If the dead is a good

[35] Sulendraningrat, P.S. (1982), *Ghoib*, pp. 33-46.

[36] *Ibid*, pp 41-66. These are not written explicitly in the Scriptures although in principle, the belief in the end of the world is implied in the scriptural doctrine embedded in the fifth decree of the Islamic faith, belief in the Day of Resurrection or Judgement. The uncertainty and catasthropic situation at the moment of universal destruction, however, is clearly indicated in the Qur'an (see for example: QS 99, al-Zalzalah).

> person he will certainly be able to answer quite easily, as the angels come in a fine appearance using polite words. But when the dead is a bad person, the angels come in scary appearance using harsh words causing the dead who is questioned to tremble, be bewildered and be unable to utter a word; in this situation the angels unhesitatingly beat him: bum, bum, bum, then leave him unaccompanied but later there come big snakes, centipedes, and scorpions to bite and bite him endlessly ...[37]

In the remainder of his narration Mang Sutaro described the first eschatological world of life after death that one will find while staying in *alam barzakh*.[38] It starts from the time of death until the Day of Resurrection. When Israfil has blown his trumpet and all the earthly world ends, all the dead will be resurrected, given a new body, and will be led to an assemblage at the *mahsyar* (vast plain) by their respective prophets, to receive absolutely fair judgment. Along with the two angels, Raqib's and 'Atid's detailed record of everything one has done in the world, one's body organs will become fair witnesses to everything. The hand for example, will say: "Yes, really, I have done or have been used to doing this and that at that place and time". The mouth will say: "Yes, I have said or have been used to say this and that or ate this and that at that place and time". Similarly, the other organs of the body such as eyes, ears, legs and brain will also give their confessions. In short, at that time nothing will be able to be hidden from God. In such a situation, therefore, everyone will anticipate either reward or punishment. At that time, absolute individualism will prevail; no one will have the time to care for others, not even children for parents nor vice-versa. Everyone's motto will be *Nafsi-nafsi* (literally meaning myself-myself) implying no one will be available for others because each person will be completely occupied in thinking about his/her own affairs. For sinners the only hope will be to beg for intercession by their own prophets, but none except the Prophet Muhammad, who has a special position at God's side, will be entitled to be an intercessor. It follows that only his followers will have the possibility of gaining beneficial weight in the *mizan* (or balance).[39]

[37] Interview (3-7-1992): "Wong mati baka wis dikubur terus ditinggal kira-kira telung tindak deng wong kang terakhir ngateraken, bakal ditekani deng malekat loro, Munkar wa Nakir, terus ditakoni: manarobbuka, mannabiyyuka, waimammuka, sampe seteruse. Boko mayid iku wong bagus, deweke ya gampang bae njawabe; nekanane uga srese, ngomonge alus. Tapi lamun mayid iku wong blesak apa maning wong kafir malekat mau nekanane nyentak petekusan, toli mayid mau bli kejagan wedie, keder, boro-boro arep bisa njawab; ari wis konon ya terus bae diganden deng malekat mau: bleg, bleg bleg, terus ditinggal bature mung ula, klabang, kala jengking gede-gede, mbari nyokoti terus-terusan ...".

[38] Some informants explain *alam barzakh* simply as *alam kubur* or the world of grave. In eschatology *alam barzakh* refers to the boundary of the world of human beings which consists of heavens, the earth and the nether regions and its separation from the world of pure spirits and God (Cf: 'Barzakh,' in *Shorter Encyclopedia of Islam*)

[39] *Mizan* refers to the process of weighing the good and the bad deeds in the Day of Judgement.

When the judgment is over, everyone will be required to pass *wot sirotol mustakim,* the **Sirath** or the path, which leads to either *Suarga* (paradise) or to *Neraka* (Hell). The width of the path is believed to be one-seventh of a hair's thickness, but each individual will find it to be different. Eventually, no unbeliever will be able to pass down the path because they will find it to be its real size. For the believers, the size, and the apparent construction of the path, and, therefore, the convenience of passing down the path will be commensurate with the balance between the "good and bad" accounted for in the judgement. The more the balance favours "good" acts, the better, and the more convenient the path will be and, therefore, the greater the likelihood of reaching *Suarga.* In contrast, the more the balance is towards "bad" acts, the narrower the path will be and the less convenient it will be to pass down it and therefore the smaller the likelihood of reaching paradise. There are seven suarga and seven neraka to reward and punish in the *alam akherat,* the real hereafter. The *suarga* are: *Jannatul Ma'wa, Jannatun Na'im, Jannatul Firdaus, Jannatu 'Adnin, Jannatul Khuldi, Darul Qarar, Darul Bawar.* The seven *neraka* are: *Jahannam, Sa'ir, Huthamah, Hawiyah, Saqar, Jahim* and *Wail.*[40]

The Cirebonese describe *Suarga* and *Neraka* mostly in materialistic terms. The former is a place of absolute happiness and joy wherein faithful believers are rewarded, whereas the latter, on the contrary, is a place of absolute suffering and misery wherein unbelievers and sinners are punished. *Suarga* is illustrated as a beautifully ornamented building with nice gardens and untainted rivers; everything there constitutes an incomparably joyful place to live in. Delightful foods and drinks of various flavours, as well as all recreational means and objects with an everincreasing delight, are unceasingly served by exceedingly charming men and women. All negative conditions such as exhaustion, boredom, depression and the like are totally absent. The elect shall remain always at their best age, never getting old and men will become as handsome as Joseph while women will become even more beautiful than *widadari* (heavenly nymphs). The greatest joy in paradise, however, will be felt upon seeing God.

In contrast to *Suarga,* the conceptions of *Neraka* are extraordinarily unpleasant. In addition to excessive beatings by Zabaniya, the angel of hell, the fire wherein the punished dwell will be terribly hot; the ash from it would boil seven oceans. The foods one will be forced to eat will be the bitterest *kestuba* and *jakum* woods, while drink will be boiling bismuth. Each time the body is shattered from drinking or being beaten, its smithereens will instantly reform into a new one to be beaten or forced to drink again with ever increasing severity. Unbelievers will stay there forever, while sinful believers will stay there for a duration commensurate with their sins. The hereafter, therefore, consists of striking contrasts; that is, between reward and punishment, happiness and misery, joy

[40] These names are all derived from Arabic.

and suffering. These are nothing but results of what everyone does in this world. Wrong doers (to God, to humans, or to nature) may be able to escape from responsibility and to remain safe in this world but can never escape from punishment after death. Similarly, a generous and good person may obtain nothing in this world but will certainly be rewarded in the next. In short, death is regarded not as an end; rather, it is a rung on the eschatological ladder by which human beings move from their present abode, worldly life (*alam dunya*) to their last abode, the hereafter (*alam akhirat*). Above all, life after death is contingent on absolute justice.

TAKDIR AND IKHTIAR: THE PROBLEM OF HUMAN DESTINY

Like most other Muslims, the Cirebonese conceive human destiny, good or bad, desirable or undesirable, as essentially determined by God. In other words, something happens because God wills it. This belief is, in fact, embedded in the sixth decree of the Islamic faith: belief in *Qadla*, or predetermination, and *Qadar*, or fixed human destiny. In more popular terms both *Qadla* and *Qadar* are referred to by a single term *Takdir*, meaning Divine decree or predestination. Classic examples used to argue for the existence of predestination, as Pak Shofie put it, are that we cannot decide where and when we are born; we cannot choose who shall become our mother and our father; we can neither choose nor decide to become male or female, tall or short, good-looking or bad-looking; we cannot choose or decide how, where, and when we shall die. Given these things, Pak Shofie said, we must just accept what we are. Someone may want to die because of a miserable life or because they cannot bear a long painful illness, but still they keep living. On the other hand, most people want to live longer and do many things to try to achieve that, but nevertheless might die suddenly. Because death is predestined, suicide is regarded as an act against predestination, which, therefore, is heavily condemned, promising severe punishment in Hell.[41]

[41] Due to the fact that Qur'anic verses put stress on predestination on the one hand and on the importance, even the obligation, of 'making effort' or free will on the other, the issue of the relative position of each has given rise to theological debates with contenders from different schools: Murji'ah, Jabariyah, Qadariyah, Mu'tazilah, Ahl al-Sunna wa'l-Jama'ah. The first two maintain the extreme dominance of predestination while negating the role of free will; the second two, on the contrary, invert this position and view free will as the sole determinant of human destiny while negating the importance of predestination; the last school occupies position between these two extremes, arguing that human destiny basically is predetermined, but there are some areas in which God bestows a role for free will. Indeed, the problem of free will and predestination has been one of the most controversial issues in Islamic theology from the earliest time. Ormsby implies that Al-Ghazali himself, at the possible risk of being rebuked, tended to see the problem of predestination as a divine mystery which for ordinary people is better not to be discussed as it would dazzle the weak, the ignorant and the unprepared. This subject, according Al-Ghazali, belongs to the **'ilm al-mukashafat** (subject of illuminationists) which may not be treated in detail in a work for ordinary people. As cited by Ormsby, Al-Ghazali said that one should not lift the curtains which hide the sun from the gaze of the bats lest they perish. (See: Ormsby, E.L, 1984, *Theodicy of Islamic Tought: The Dispute Over Al-Ghazali's "Best of All Possible Worlds"*, New Jersey: Princeton University Press, especially pp. 69–74.

Following from this principle of predestination is the view, held also by the Cirebonese, that insists that mankind's fortune or misfortune is the result of 'the will of God' (*Kresane Gusti Allah*). Sudika (38 years), a newspaper-agent, explains:

> Principally, what happens in the world, whether it be good or bad, liked or disliked, is dependent on the Lord God's will. Man can only propose, but God disposes ...[42]

This view clearly reflects the uncompromising Cirebonese belief in the power and omnipotence of God, especially regarding human fate. Theoretically, this sense of dependency on God's will, according to Goldziher, tipped the scales in favour of denying the freedom of the will, so that virtue and vice, and reward and punishment are exclusively predestined by God; humans have no role to play.[43] In practice, however, further explanations enunciated by Sudika do not fully fit this standard because, beside predestination, there is also an obligation of *ikhtiar* (effort). Not only is *ikhtiar* necessary because God obliges mankind to do so, but it is also necessary for their own sake because *ikhtiar* is a precondition for the realisation of God's Mercy, Beneficence and Bounty. In this regard Sudika further explained:

> Men should believe that the Lord God is Beneficent, Merciful and Bountiful, He will never let men be miserable. But His mercy and bounty will never fall automatically from heaven; His mercy and its bestowal must be acquired and their coming must be obtained by effort. Men are bestowed with a perfect body and mind to enable them to make an effort; those who do not use their bodies and minds to make an effort are thankless individuals, negating God's gift and kill themselves. Reluctance of making such efforts is, as the *santri* would call, a great sin ..[44]

Setting aside the theological arguments, Cirebonese ideas seem to conform to the common Javanese belief indicated by Suparlan that one's fate has really been determined from the time when the person was in the mother's womb.[45] According to this Cirebonese idea of human creation, the designation of one's fate (including one's livelihood, death, actions, fortune and misfortune), occurs

[42] Interview (11-6-1992): "Pokoke apa bae kang kedadian ning dunya, mbuh blesak mbuh bagus, disenengi atawa beli, iku kabeh kresane Gusti Allah siji. Memusa mung bisa ikhtiar, kasil belie apa jare Pengeran ...

[43] Goldziher, I. (1981), *Introduction to Islamic Theology and Law*, New Jersey: Princeton University Press. p.81.

[44] Interview (11-6-1992): "Wong iku kudu percaya, Gusti Allah iku luwih murah, luwih welas, luwih asih, bli bakal nyengsaraaken menusa. Mung bae welas asihe Gusti Allah iku bli bakal tigel dewek seng langit, tapi kudu digulati lan disababi kelawan usaha. Menusa diupai awak sampurna karo pikiran deng Pengeran, maksude supaya dienggo usaha; boko wong kang bli gelem ngenggo awak karo pikirane kanggo usaha lan luru sabab, wong iku kena diarani nyingkur, lan bli gelem mulang trima ning peparingane Pengeran mbari mateni awake dewek; kang mengkonon iku jare wong santrie dosa gede ..."

[45] Suparlan, P. (1991), *The Javanese Dukun*, Jakarta: Peka Publication, p.7.

when the process of creation is at the stage of *alam arwah*; that is, when the foetus is about four months old and when God sends Gabriel to blow a soul into it, after which time the young foetus starts to become animated. This fate, according to Suparlan (1991:7) is influenced by the combination of the mother's and father's power which form the foetus, by the soul which animates the foetus, by the extent to which the soul fits the foetus, by the mother's power and activities; by the conditions of the womb, by the efforts and attainment of the foetus during its stay in the womb; and by the time and place of birth. In addition, Suparlan also claims that fate can still be changed, within certain limitations, through one's acts and relations with one's surroundings. A simple example is of someone who is fortunate, born to well-to-do parents and, thus, likely to grow well and healthy but who is then unfortunate because his parents do not realise it when he falls into his friend's temptations. Instead of becoming a good and successful man, he becomes a delinquent, and is sent to jail. Converse examples may be cited. The main point is that fate, to some extent, may change through an individual's "efforts" and through using certain powers and capacities bestowed by God. In this context Sudika added that since no one knows with certainty one's own fate, or what God will actually decide, the making of *ikhtiar* (efforts) is absolutely necessary". In other words, we only know something is predestined, *takdir*, either after our own "efforts" have been carried out or after being assured that the thing under consideration is beyond the capacity of humans to control. Sudika illustrates this with the following example:

> ... we have to call it a neglect, our fault, instead of *takdir* if we fail an exam which we are not prepared for; it may be a *takdir* if adequate preparation has been made, but at the time of examination a certain illness comes and obstructs our concentration; or, due to one or other reasons the marker intentionally or unintentionally gives an unfair mark and thus, makes us fail. In some cases you can protest and prove your ability, this is another form of *ikhtiar*, if it works it may improve your position but in other cases your protest does not work because any decision made is final. If the latter be the case, the best thing you can do is to realise it and thus accept it as *takdir*.[46]

Ordinary people of Cirebon seem to be wiser in treating the contradiction between "predestination" and "free will". Some intellectuals put the questions of free will and predestination at two poles that bear inherent tensions. By contrast, the ordinary people consider them simultaneously as tied up together in the sphere of *rukun*. Pak Shofie had this to say on the subject:

> Predestination and personal effort [free will] need not be disputed, both exist, both come from the Holy Qur'an, both can be used simultaneously;

[46] Field notes from casual talk with Sudika 13-6-1992.

thus, predestination and [free will] can co-exist in harmony. What problem will arise, if you just take the true belief that God is omnipotent, He has the right to decide anything for His creatures? At the same time make maximum "efforts", since doing so is ordered by God. In doing so, may God bestow on you safety and loftiness.[47]

PITUNGAN AND PENA'ASAN: JAVANESE NUMEROLOGY

Pitungan is a local term constructed from the word *itung* meaning to count. The prefix *pe-* and suffix *-an* are added to mean the way of calculating, or, simply the numerological system. Associated with the term *pitungan* is *pena'asan,* derived from the word *na'as* meaning bad luck; thus, *pitungan* and *pena'asan* mean calculating the value of the number in a numerological system to avoid bad luck. In practice the Cirebonese numerological system has two main objectives. The first is to determine the beginning of the new Javanese calendar year, and the second is to determine preferred dates and times to do important jobs. Both are done mainly by manipulating certain values attached to each calendar unit, for example: day, month, year.

The Cirebonese, as do other Javanese, use a traditional lunar calendar along with the official solar one. Unlike the months and the new years of the solar calendar whose beginning are easily ascertained, determining the new months and, therefore, the new year in the lunar calendar is rather problematic. The moon's orbit (and, therefore, the interval between new moons) is about 29.5 days. Hence, a month is calculated as either 29 or 30 days. Unfortunately, which month should take 29 and which should take 30 cannot be fixed precisely. Each individual month could have either. A certain month may take 29 days one year but the next year it may take 30. This gives rise to difficulty in determining the new months and in turn the new year. To reconcile the differences a certain calculation is employed. This reconciliation is important as most communal feasts are held on the basis of this calendar, and this calendar is the basis for *pena'asan* too.

[47] Personal interview 12-6-1992: "Takdir karo ikhtiar, bli perlu dadi perkara kanggo genceng-cewengan, karo-karone bener anane, karo-karone njukut seng Qur'an, loro-lorone bisa dienggo; dadi takdir karo ikhtiar bisa rukun. Apa angele, lamun percaya-a bae kang temenan setuhune Gusti Allah iku kuwasa, wenang nemtokaken segals apa bae karo makhluke; ikhtiar-a kang temenan krana ikhtiar iku wis dadi prentabe Gusti Allah. Inaya Allah Gusti Allah maringi keslametan lan kamulyan." Muslim Ibn Yasar (d. 100 or 101/718 or 720) never visited Cirebon nor preached there, and I doubt that Cirebonese like Sudika have read his work. But Ibu Yasar's attempt to find a compromise between strict predestinarians and advocates of free will meets with the spirit of *rukun* in Cirebon. Ormsby, cites Ibn Yasar from van Ess, as follows: "[Free will and pre destination] are two deep valleys where people stray without ever reaching bottom. Act therefore like someone who knows that only his own acts can still save him; and trust in God like someone who knows that only that will strike him which was meant for him." See: Ormsby, E.L. (1984), *Theodicy in Islamic Thought*, p. 71.

Table 3.1: Months of the Javanese and Islamic Calendars

Javanese	Islamic
Sura	Muharram
Sapar	Safar
Mulud	Rabi'al-Awwal
Sawal Mulud	Rabi'al-Akhir
Jumadilawal	Jumadi'l-Awwal
Jumadilakir	Jumadi'l-Akhir
Rejep	Rajab
Ruwah	Sya'ban
Puasa	Ramadan
Syawal	Syawwal
Kapit	Dzu'l-Qa'idah
Raya Agung	Dzu'l-Hijjah

In Cirebon, as well as in most parts of Java, there are two ways of calculating weeks: one is the seven-day week, the other is the five-day *pasaran* (market-day) week. For each method, each day has its own *jejer*, or ordinal standing, and *naktu* (Central Java: *neptu*). *Naktu*, a specific value attached to the names of people and calendar units: days of the week, the *pasaran*, months, years, is a crucial element on which calculations are based. The *naktu* for the days of the ordinary week and the *pasaran* week are puit in Table 3.2.

The Cirebonese consider Friday as the most important day of the week and, in relation to *pitungan*, it is put at the first *jejer* and, thus, the seven-day week goes from Friday to Thursday. In the *pasaran* week, on the other hand, Kliwon is considered to be the most important day and is put at the first *jejer* and, thus, the five-day *pasaran* week proceeds from Kliwon to Manis, Pahing, Pon and Wage. A most significant moment occurs once every thirty-five days; that is, on *Jemuah Kliwon* where the first *jejer* of the seven-day week (Friday) meets the first *jejer* of the five-day *pasaran* week (Kliwon). Friday's significance seems to come from the Islamic tradition that regards Friday as the master of the days (*Sayidul Ayyam*) for doing religious service. It is unclear, why *Kliwon* is considered significant although it must be of Javanese tradition. Local literary traditions mention that Friday-Kliwon was traditionally taken by Sunan Gunung Jati as a court assembly day because the day is good for detecting one's intention whether it is good or bad (*bisa niteni ala becike niyate wong*). It also happens that Sunan Gunung Jati died on "Friday-Kliwon."

Table 3.2: *Naktu* and *Jejer* of the Days of the Days of the Ordinary and the *Pasaran* Weeks

Week day	Naktu	Jejer	Pasaran	Naktu	Jejer
Jum'ah (Friday)	6	1	Kliwon	8	1
Septu (Saturday)	9	2	Manis	5	2
Akad (Sunday)	5	3	Pahing	9	3
Senen (Monday)	4	4	Pon	7	4
Selasa (Tuesday)	3	5	Wage	4	5
Rebo (Wednesday)	7	6			
Kemis (Thursday)	8	7			

Javanese numerological books (*primbon*), however, do not place any special importance on *Jemuah or Jum'ah Kliwon*, nor do they put it on any list of bad days. Friday appears often on lists of good days. It is the day of *kemresik* (cleansing), an auspicious time for weddings or other feasts during the months of Mulud, Bakdomulud (Cirebon: Sawal Mulud) and Jumadilawal. Friday appears as fair days during Sura and Sapar, whereas in Jumadilakir Friday is inauspicious. A woman born on Jemuah Kliwon is expected to have the characteristics of being ambitious, has the potential for acquiring abundance, and should be careful and frugal, faithful and considerate to her husband (*gedhe butarepane, sinung ing rejeki, setiti lan ngatiati, bekti mring wong lanang, waskita kareping wong lanang*).[48]

Table 3.3: Months of the Year and Years of the *Windu* and their *Naktu*

Month	Naktu	Year	Naktu
Sura	2	Alif	3
Sapar	2	He	2
Mulud	1	Jimawal	2
Sawalmulud	1	Ze	1
Jumadilawal	5	Dal	5
Jumadilakir	5	Be	5
Rejep	4	Wawu	4
Ruwah	4	Jimakir	3
Puasa	3		
Syawal	3		
Kapit	2		
Raya Agung	2		

Although of less importance, *naktu* is also calculated for the months of the year and for the years of the *windu*.[49] By manipulating these *naktu*, calculations have been made. In order to establish that the first day of the month Sura of year Alif shall always fall on Rebo (Wednesday) Wage. This is known as the *ABOGE* system which stands for A-(lif), (Re)-bo, (Wa)-ge. The *Aboge* is then taken as a fixed point and is used as the basis for subsequent calculations for specific purposes.

48 Ki Sura (n.d.), ed., *Buku Primbon Jawa Jangkep*, Solo: U.D. Mayasari

49 See Table 3.3. A *windu* is eight years cycle, each name of the year within the *windu* has been selected from the Arabic alphabet.

Aside from *jejer* and *naktu* it is also believed that the position of astronomical objects brings about an ethereal influence on the characteristics of particular times (years, months, days, and even hours). The ethereal condition of certain times will, in turn, affect the result of work done on particular occasions. Certain times which are under the domination of certain astronomical objects will, therefore, be fitting and beneficial for particular jobs, but not necessarily for others. Finding the best time for doing particular jobs is the second main concern of Cirebonese *pitungan* and *pena'asan*.

Table 3.4: Schedule of the Domination of Astronomical Objects

	Hour	Sun	Mon	Tue	Wed	Thu	Fri	Sat
am	06-07	Sun	Moo	Mar	Mer	Jup	Ven	Sat
	07-08	Ven	Sat	Sun	Moo	Mar	Mer	Jup
	08-09	Mer	Jup	Ven	Sat	Sun	Moo	Mar
	09-10	Moo	Mars	Mer	Jup	Ven	Sat	Sun
	10-11	Sat	Sun	Moo	Mar	Mer	Jup	Ven
	11-12	Jup	Ven	Sat	Sun	Moo	Mar	Mer
pm	12-01	Mar	Mer	Jup	Ven	Sat	Sun	Moo
	01-02	Sun	Moo	Mar	Mer	Jup	Ven	Sat
	02-03	Ven	Sat	Sun	Moo	Mar	Mer	Jup
	03-04	Mer	Jup	Ven	Sat	Sun	Moo	Mar
	04-05	Moo	Mar	Mer	Jup	Ven	Sat	Sun
	05-06	Sat	Sun	Mo	Mar	Mer	Jup	Ven

Remarks on the names of astronomical objects:

Sun = Sun
Moo = Moon
Mar = Mars
Mer = Mercury
Jup = Jupiter
Ven = Venus
Sat = Saturn

There are seven astronomical objects that many Cirebonese think have an influence on the work of humans: *Syams* (Sun), *Qamar* (Moon), *Mirik* (Mars), *Athorid* (Mercury), *Musytari* (Jupiter), *Zuhro* (Venus), and *Zuhal* (Saturn).[50] The influence of these object are: the Sun, good for almost any work except going to war; Moon, good for any work; Mars, good mainly for making weapons or amulets; Jupiter, not good for any work, although it may be good for going to war; Mercury, like the Sun, good for any work except for going to war, for risky business, or for venturing the chance of large profits; Venus, especially good for religious services and Saturn, good only for making wells. Everyday of the week from six o'clock in the morning until six o'clock in the afternoon is under their astronomical influence. Each of these 'planets' come successively hour after

[50] These astronomical objects are referred to in Arabic; probably it is of Arabic influence.

hour to exert temporal dominance. So regularly are their comings that these can be put into an ordered schedule. By merely consulting the schedule one can decide the time at which an important job should be started on a particular day.

For important undertakings, particularly marriages and house building, the month is also of special importance. Of the twelve months, only three are good for marriage, and only four for house building. The months good for marriage are: Raya Agung, Ruwah and Jumadil Akhir. Raya Agung leads the couple to real happiness whereas Ruwah and Jumadil Akhir can bring God's bestowal of abundance. The other months may engender unwanted consequences such as: Sura, a broken marriage; Sapar, overt domination of lust, which may cause betrayal; Mulud, many obstacles; Sawal Mulud, easily being tempted by gossips; Jumadil Awal, frequent loss of belongings; Rejeb, repression; Puasa, betrayal; Syawal, serious debts and Kapit, frequent illness. The months good for building houses and the expected benefit are: Puasa, acquiring precious valuables; Raya Agung, bringing abundance; Kapit, good for farms and raising livestock and Jumadil Awwal, attracting many friends; Jumadil Akhir, facing no serious trouble. Fair months for building a house are: Rejep, which causes a tendency of staying indoors and provokes laziness and a feeling of isolation; Ruwah, makes people hesitant to approach the occupants. Bad months are: Sura, and Sawal Mulud, which will cause the builder to encounter some trouble; Sapar and Mulud are even worse.

In some cases, one cannot wait until a good time comes, but one must avoid the dangerous day called *Raspati*.[51] In this case it may be preferable to choose a neutral time called a *dina lowong* (literally, meaning vacant day) when neither advantageous nor disadvantageous consequences may result. To this end, a person has to find out either the neutral day on which he could do a job or the *Raspati* on which he is to avoid doing a job. *Dina lowong* is basically any day of the month which does not coincide with *pasaran Kliwon*. Determining this day can be done by calculation, by memory, or by consulting written records of the first *pasaran* day of the month under consideration, then by counting from this *pasaran* day to Pahing. An example for the use of this method is: the first day of Sura year Alif must fall on Rebo (Wednesday) Wage; count the *pasaran* starting from the day after Wage. This makes three days, that is: Wage (uncounted), Kliwon, Manis and Pahing. Three days after Wednesday is Saturday (Pahing). However, if the first day of the month falls on Pahing, the next Pahing (the sixth day of the month) will be a neutral day, a day when one can do a job without a fear of bad consequences or a hope of good ones: *paduasal slamet bae* (just safe only).

[51] Probably the word *raspati* is a construction from an archaic local Javanese *rasa-pati* (containing death). It refers to bad days for doing important undertakings, contrary to the good days. It may cause bad luck (accidents, serious loss, illness, even death). See the next page for its occurrence.

Sometimes a person is very uneasy with *Raspati*, and he is eager to determine its occurrence in order to avoid it. The formula is simple: *Raspati* occurs when the value of *naktu* of the particular month combined with the *naktu* of the day is either twelve or five. Take twelve, for the first example. Subtract twelve by *naktu* of the month, the rest is equal to *naktu* of the day, that is the *raspati*. Thus, *naktu* of Syawal is seven. Twelve minus seven makes five; find out a day whose *naktu* is five (Sunday), which is the *raspati* for that month. One must therefore, avoid doing important jobs on the Sunday of Syawal. The *naktu* of Sapar is two; five minus two makes three which is the *naktu* of Tuesday; one must avoid doing important jobs on Tuesday of Sapar. After doing long and laborious calculations for a few years, Mang Atmo, who is not a *dukun*, produced a number of comprehensive *pena'asan* tables applicable for entire years. As one of the custodians of *Kramat Uma Gede* (The Great House) at Trusmi, he has many guests, some of whom consult him about *pena'asan*. Instead of doing laborious calculations he simply consults his ready made hand written tables to serve his clients. For the year Alif, for example, the expected first day of the months, the *lowong* (neutral) and the *raspati* (dangerous) days is put in following table.

Table 3.5: First Day of the Months, the Lowong and the Raspatit (Year Alif)

Month	First day	Lowong	Raspati
Sura	Wednesday-Wage	Saturday	Sunday
Sapar	Friday-Wage	Monday	Tuesday
Mulud	Saturday-Pon	Wednesday	Saturday
Syawal Mulud	Monday-Pon	Friday	Wednesday
Jumadilawal	Tuesday-Pahing	Sunday	Friday
Jumadilakir	Thursday-Pahing	Tuesday	Monday
Rejep	Friday-Manis	Thursday	Tuesday
Ruwah	Sunday-Manis	Saturday	Thursday
Puasa	Sunday-Kliwon	Wednesday	Wednesday
Syawal	Wednesday-Kliwon	Friday	Sunday
Kapit	Thursday-Wage	Sunday	Monday
Raya Agung	Saturday-Wage	Tuesday	Saturday

In addition, by taking the influence of the astronomical objects into account (the items appear in table 3.5), Mang Atmo has also a long list which says about the recommended (good) days, the forbidden (bad) days, dates and *pasaran*, even hours, for doing important work throughout the entire *windu*. An example of this list appears in table 3.6.[52]

In relation to the current use of *pitungan*, Mang Atmo however claimed that the *pitungan* system is nothing more than man's *ikhtiar*, or efforts to follow where nature seems to go, and that we should therefore not try to go against it. It was invented by our ancestors when our life was so much more dependent on nature.

[52] In Mang Atmo's version, table 3.5 and 3.6 are mixed together. I necessitate to present it separately because I think, his version is rather difficult to catch, at least by a quick reading. A specimen for portions of his table see appendix.

Now our lives are different; people are knowledgeable and do not seem so dependent on nature. He says that when he was a child the harvest occurred only once a year because most *sawah* relied totally on rain. One had to be careful to catch the best time to start working a *sawah,* otherwise the work would be ruined; that is why the *pitungan* system was needed. Now, by virtue of irrigation, harvests occur twice a year and the starting times are far more flexible. In working *sawah* people no longer care about *mangsa* (seasons) for agricultural *pitungan*. However, there are still many aspects of our lives where people think that *pitungan* is still needed. He then warned that those who believe in *pitungan* should keep it in proper perspective because it is not the only factor determining good results. Along with individual characteristics including ability, resources and other influencing factors, there is still the final and unavoidable factor, that is, *kresane Gusti Allah* (God's will). Nevertheless, *"bli arep ndingini kresane pengeran"* ("without intending to preempt God's will"), he said that he himself still adheres to the *pitungan* system because sometimes it shows its worth.

To illustrate the worth of *pitungan* and *pena'asan* Mang Atmo told about his own son, Harlan, who got into trouble.[53] In this example Mang Atmo probably wished to imply that if his son had followed his advice based on the *pitungan* system his son probably would not have fallen into trouble. In other words he wanted to illustrate how *pitungan* could be a useful means of avoiding unexpected results. This, of course, does not necessarily imply that the *pitungan* is the only prerequisite for doing something safely. There are many other factors that contribute to failure or success, such as ability, tools, conditions and the atmosphere by which and in which the work is carried out. But if other variables are held constant, the *pitungan* system is an additional help. In other words, if two persons have to do something, each having about equal ability, using similar tools, working in the same conditions, facing similar difficulties, the one who takes account of the *pitungan* system is thought of as having a better chance of coming to a better end.

Table 3.6: Sample of Lists of Good and Bad Days

Sura, year Alif.	
Good:	Monday, 6 Wage and 27 Kliwon; 06.00, 08.00 a.m, 01.00, 03.00 p.m.
	Tuesday, 21 Wage; 10.00 a.m, 12.00 noon, 05.00 p.m.
	Wednesday, 29 Pahing; 07.00, 09.00 a.m, 02.00, 04.00 p.m.
	Thursday, 23 Manis and 9 Pahing; 06.00, 11.00 a.m, 01.00 p.m.
	Friday, 17 Kliwon and 24 Pahing; 08.00, 10.00 a.m, 03.00, 05.00 p.m.
Bad:	during the 11th, 14th, 15th; any date of Saturday and Sunday Manis[54]

[54] Hours for bad days are not specified.

[53] See the quotation at the beginning of this Chapter

Chapter 4: The Ritual Practice: Ibadat

PROLOGUE TO THE ANALYSIS OF CIREBONESE RITUAL

Any attempt to identify precisely the activity belonging to ritual in the Cirebonese context encounters semantic problems. There is no such word in the local language which precisely translates the English word "ritual". In Cirebon, ritual activities, religious or otherwise, are singled out by their names; each name corresponds to the nature and purpose of the ritual concerned.

The lexical meaning of ritual is defined as "a prescribed form or method for the performance of a religious or solemn ceremony, or, any body of rites and ceremonies."[1] This basic meaning implies that, on the one hand, ritual activity differs from ordinary activity, by the presence or absence of a religious or a solemn character. Ritual activity, on the other hand, differs from technical activity by the presence or absence of a ceremonial character. Anthropologists, however, have different opinions about what constitutes ritual and thus what ritual really is. Some argue for narrow definitions, some others argue for broad ones. After showing the diversity of opinions and definitions set forth by anthropologists, Seymour-Smith proposes that perhaps it is ultimately unnecessary to define ritual, or to delimit it from ceremony on the one hand and from instrumental or practical action on the other.[2] Seymour-Smith thus, takes a position much closer to Leach than to Gluckman. Gluckman (1962) defines ceremony as any complex organisation of human activity which is not specifically technical or recreational but that involves the use of modes of behaviour which are expressive of social relationships. Ritual, on the other hand, according to Gluckman, is a more limited category of ceremony but symbolically more complex because, in ritual, deeper social and psychological concerns are involved. Moreover, ritual is characterised by its reference to a mystical or religious nature and purpose.[3]

Leach, in contrast, asserts ritual to be any behaviour that "serves to express the individual's status as a social person in the structural system in which he [*the person concerned*] finds himself for the time being."[4] Following this same line of thinking Lessa and Vogt suggest that ritual may comprise all symbolic actions, profane or sacred, technical or aesthetic, simple or elaborate. It may range from the etiquette of daily greetings such as saying 'How are you?' to the solemn

[1] Funk & Wagnalls (1984), *Standard Desk Dictionary*, Cambridge: Harper and Row.
[2] Seymour-Smith, C. (1990), *Macmillan Dictionary of Anthropology*, London: MacMillan.
[3] Seymour-Smith, C. (1990), p.248
[4] Leach, E.R. (1964), *Political Systems of Highland Burma: A Study of Kachin Social Structure*, London: The Athlon Press, p. 10

utterance of a magical spell or any form of dignified ceremony.[5] Leach considers that the great majority of human actions fall into place on a continuous scale. He suggests that at one extreme actions are entirely profane, entirely functional, or purely technical and simple; at another extreme, actions are entirely sacred, strictly aesthetic, technically non functional and elaborate. He argues that most social actions fit between the two extremes, being partly of the one sphere, and partly of the other, and that the distinction among phenomena are therefore arbitrary and not always neatly classifiable.[6] In contrast with some other scholars, Leach regards ritual not as a category of behaviour but as an aspect of behaviour. He writes:

> "... technique and ritual, profane and sacred do not denote types of action but aspects of almost any kind of action. Technique has economic material consequences which are measurable and predictable; ritual on the other hand is a symbolic statement which 'says' something about the individual involved in the action."[7]

In other words, Leach maintains that any behaviour may have both ritual and non-ritual aspects. The degree to which a particular behaviour bears within it ritual and non-ritual aspects depends on the extent to which the individual concerned expresses in his action, both his status or symbolic value and his practical objectives and utilities. Leach therefore departs from conventional Durkheimian perspectives which categorise human actions in terms of the sacred-profane dichotomy, avoids putting rigidly religious rites in the sacred domain and technical acts in the profane, and disregards those who use the word ritual only to describe the social actions occurring in sacred situations.[8]

For a different purpose and in a different manner I want to make use of Leach's perspectives to explain the ritual behaviour in the traditions of Islam in Cirebon.

[5] Lessa, W.A. and Vogt, E.Z., ed (1979), *Reader in Comparative Religion: An Anthropological Approach*, 4th ed, New York: Harper and Row, p.220.

[6] Leach, E. (1964), pp. 11–13

[7] Leach, E. (1964), p.13.

[8] Leach goes further when he treats ritual in relation to the symbolisation of time. With special reference to Greek mythology, "Cronus and Chronos" he sets out the standard notion of time both in terms of repetition and irreversible natural phenomena. He suggests that we tend to think of time in terms of repetition in that, certain phenomena of nature repeat themselves; at the same time we also think that life changes —to be born, grow and die— is an irreversible process. Based on this recognition of repetition and aging. Leach then resolves the puzzle of why men all over the world mark out their calendars by means of festivals. He suggests that as people satisfy themselves in festivals through formality, masquerade or role reversal, festivals have a variety of functions. Among these he includes the ordering of time, where between the two successive festivals of the same type there will be a period, usually a named period such as "week" or "year". Without the festivals, according to Leach, such periods would not exist and all order would go out of social life. See: Leach, E.R., 1961), "Two Essays Concerning The Symbolic Representation of Time", in Lessa, W.A. and Vogt, E.Z., ed (1979), pp. 221–229.

IBADAT: AN AMBIGUOUS CONCEPT OF RITUAL IN ISLAM

To some writers, Islam provides a clear enunciation of ritual. They simply equate ritual (in Islam) with *'ibadat*, and *'ibadat* with the five pillars. The Arabic word **'ibadat** (sing. **'ibada**) which literally means to enslave oneself (to God), when it is used as a religious term, refers to the ordinances of divine worship.[9] For example, Bousquet prefers to define *'ibadat* as:

> submissive obedience to a master, and therefore, religious practice, corresponds, together with its synonyms *ta'a*, in the works of *fikh*, approximately to the ritual of Muslim law ..., as opposed to the *mu'amala* ...[10]

Bousquet's definition of *'ibadat* to denote ritual in Islam is strongly *'fiqh'* (Islamic jurisprudence) orientated. He even warns us not to translate *'ibadat* as 'cult' if we are to follow credible theoretical understanding. He urges:

> If we translate *'ibadat* with 'cult' we are committing something of theoretical error ... for it has quite correctly been said that, strictly speaking, Islam knows no more of a cult, properly speaking, than ... it does of law; nor, we should add, of ethics. *Fikh* is, in fact, a deontology (the statement of the whole corpus of duties, of acts whether obligatory, forbidden or recommended, etc.) which is imposed upon man.[11]

At the point at which the *fiqh* is concerned, it is clear indeed, as all Muslims unanimously agree that the enactment of the five pillars is undeniably and undoubtedly *'ibadat*. Nevertheless, Islam cannot be reduced to *fiqh* and thus, *ibadat* is more than the enactment of the five pillars. There are many other activities which are not set down in *fiqh*. The equation of ritual in Islam with *'ibadat* and then *'ibadat* with the five pillars to some extent is warranted but should not be overemphasised because seen in a different context it could be misleading. As far as Islam is concerned the concept of *'ibadat* entails some different connotations. I would argue that, with special reference to Cirebon, *'ibadat* is an ambiguous concept. Therefore, especially in dealing with the ritual practice of traditional Islam, a strict equation of *'ibadat* with the five pillars deserves further scrutiny.

Owing to Bousquet's definition it is not surprising that Rippin (1990) asserts that ritual in Islam centres on the five pillars. Rippin considers the notion of the five pillars represents the epitome of the revealed law as enacted through ritual activity. The five actions embedded in the five pillars —the witness to faith (*syahadat*), prayer (*salat*), charity (*zakat*), fasting (*sawm*), and pilgrimage (*hajj*)—

[9] See: 'Ibadat' in *Shorter Encyclopedia of Islam*. Further use of the word *'ibadat'* represents its use in Cirebon which refers to either singular or plural forms.
[10] See: 'Ibadat' in *Encyclopedia of Islam*, new edition.
[11] *Ibid.*

being an integral part of the belief system and a part of the explication of theological statements of belief, are duties for which each individual is responsible, separate from general ethics and rules of interpersonal relationship.[12] At this stage Rippin implies that what he meant with his statement that ritual in Islam 'centres' on the five pillars refers to what is found in the treatises of *fiqh*. In *fiqh* books *'ibadat* is discussed separately from other subjects such as *mu'amalat* (rules of economic contract), *munakahat* (rules of marriage), *jinayat* (rules of expiation), *hudud* (rules of punishment), *faraidl* (rules of inheritance) and *jihad* (rules of warfare).

Another writer also adopts a similar perspective. Denny (1985:69) points out that the most 'basic' term for ritual in Islam is *'ibadat*, meaning worship or service of inferiors toward their superior, their Lord. Denny clearly uses the term *'ibadat* to refer to the same activities noted by Rippin. Denny says that all of the official duties of Islam are subsumed under *'ibadat*, the five Pillars. *Ibadat*, Denny claims, constitutes the 'main' categories of Islamic ritual and 'lesser' activities are arranged under the five pillars in orderly fashion. Examples given by Denny for Islamic ritual under the 'lesser' category of the five pillars are such activities as *'Id* of Sacrifice (*'Id al-adha*) which is inextricably rooted in Hajj, the festival of fast-breaking (*'Id al-fitr*) which serves to punctuate the ending of *Ramadan* fast, and the special *Salat* for earth-quake or eclipse which are 'variations' of the standard form, as is the *Salat* at the graveside.[13]

Actually, Rippin and Denny are not unaware of Bosquet's over-statement on the issue. Rippin's words that *ibadat* is the 'centre' and Denny's use of the word 'basic' or 'main' in referring to *ibadat*, in the context of ritual in Islam, indicate their awareness of the existence of other *ibadat* which do not belong to this 'central', 'basic' or 'main' category. Rippin's position becomes clearer when he also states that to the extent to which Muslim identity is expressed, ritual is not limited to the five pillars although the prominence of the grouping is obviously high. He notes that the *mawlid* festival celebrating the birth of the prophet Muhammad, various informal *du'a* prayer (invocations), and visits to tombs are 'additional' ritual-type activities which are considered by many Muslims to be significant for the expression of their faith.[14] It is true that many Muslims deny that these 'additional' practices which go beyond the enactment of the five pillars belong to *'ibadat* or Islamic ritual.[15] They even denounce these activities as sinful innovations and condemn their observants for committing sin.

[12] Rippin, A. (1990), *Muslims: Their Religious Beliefs and Practices*, Vol.1, London: Rutledge.
[13] Denny, F.M. (1985), 'Islamic Ritual: Perspectives and Theories' in Martin, R.C., ed (1985), *Approaches to Islam in Religious Studies*, Tucson: The University of Arizona Press.
[14] Rippin, A. (1990), p.98.
[15] Throughout his work, Rippin uses only the term 'ritual', but it is quite clear that what he means with ritual refers to *'ibadat*, which specifically refers to the enactment of the five pillars.

There are many others, including most people in Cirebon, who think otherwise and justify these 'additional' activities as essentially *'ibadat*. Pak Soleh (44 years), a thoughtful trader said:

> It is true that such work as *reciting the Qur'an, tahlil, tahmid,* visits to tombs and the like are not *ibadat* in the narrower sense, but from the broader perspectives of Islam it is essentially *ibadat*, depending on our intention, whether we do it for Allah, for others or only for fun.[16]

It is clear that the Cirebonese see *'ibadat* from two different perspectives, specific (*khusus*) or narrow and general (*umum*) or broad, and thus bring the concept of *ibadat* into ambiguity. The Cirebonese, however, have a complex enunciation of how this ambiguity is clarified and understood, at least for themselves.

IBADAT DEFINED: CLARIFYING THE AMBIGUITY

Islam, in its ideal form does not distinguish the sacred from the profane. Nasr claims that within the unitary perspectives of Islam, all aspects of life, as well as degrees of cosmic manifestation, are governed by a single principle and are unified by a common centre. Everything is essentially sacred and nothing profane because everything bears within itself the fragrance of the Divine.[17] Nasr seems to justify a contention that Islam looks at the individual as a whole and requires the individual to submit himself completely to God, as is witnessed in the fact that every Muslim utters in his *salat*: my prayer, my sacrifice, my life and my death belong to Allah; He has no partner and I am ordered to be among those who submit (Muslim).[18] A true Muslim thus should always be thinking, saying and acting solely for the pleasure of God, as his life and death have been submitted to Him. This contention presupposes the conception of worship or *ibadat* in Islam to be comprehensive, to include almost everything of any individual's activity. Worship is an all inclusive term for all that God loves of external and internal sayings and actions of a person. It includes rituals as well as beliefs, social activities, and personal contributions to the welfare of fellow human beings.

Nasr and the other commentators are, of course, speaking about norms or ideals. In reality perhaps, not many Muslims, can achieve this condition or maintain continuously for twenty-four hours this spirit of worship. Actually, as Denny says, Islam defines itself not only based on norms, but also by its acts, that is,

[16] Indepth interview, 3-5-1992. Its original Javanese expression is: "Pancen bener yen pegawean kaya done maca Qur'an, tahlil, tahmid, ziarah kubur karo sejen-sejene iku dudu ibadah munggu pengertian kang khusus. Tapi munggu pengertian Agama Islam kang umum, kabeh iku ya ibadah, tergantung niyate apa krana Allah apa mung kanggo plangguran bae, atawa krana sejene."
[17] Nasr, S.H. (1981), *Islamic Life and Thought*, Boston: George Allen & Unwin, p.7.
[18] This utterance can be found in most *fiqh* books.

Muslims define Islam in its various forms without even being conscious of doing so.[19]

The Kaula-Gusti Relationship

The popular argument over the broader and narrower meaning of *ibadat* incorporates both semantic and verbal considerations. The local term *ibadat* or *ibadah,* is a direct borrowing from Arabic **'ibada**. It means, according to Pak Sholeh, "to enslave oneself to God (*ngaula ning Gusti Allah*)." Semantically (*munggu logat*), the notion of *ngaula* (to enslave) entails at least two implications. The first is affirmation of the existing bond between man and God in a slave-Master (*kaula-Gusti*) relationship where man is the slave or servant (*kaula*) and God is the Master (*Gusti*); the second is an affirmation that man, the servant (*kaula*), has the task of obeying the Master (*Gusti*), both by doing continuously what the Master orders and by avoiding what the Master forbids. However, acknowledging that the God is the Master who, despite His absolute power and omnipotence, is exceedingly beneficent and merciful, giving the servants life and invaluable nourishment, has a third implication; that is, that the servant has a moral obligation to express thankfulness, to do his utmost in his service, and to be generous in his obedience. The semantic implications of *ngaula* match properly the three principles on which the religion of Islam is founded. The first is 'to have faith' (*iman*), from which the Decree of Faith comes and later becomes the subject of elaborate discussion in theology (*ilmu tauhid* or **kalam**). The second principle is 'total obedience' (*islam*), the outward manifestation of faith which is subsumed under the Five Pillars and from which emerged the Divine Law (*hukum syara'* or **syari'ah**) set down by the scholars (*ulama*) into Islamic Jurisprudence (*pekih or* **fiqh**). To ensure and verify this outward manifestation of obedience comes the third principle, 'deference' (*ihsan*), from which *tasawuf* (cleansing the heart), which incorporates both Islamic ethic (*akhlaq*) and Sufism, derive. *Tasawuf* and *hukum syara'*, stand in a mode of complementary validation to each other. Pak Sholeh concluded that *ibadat,* in the broader sense, brings into practice the three founding principles of Islamic religion by way of *ngaula;* whereas, in the narrower sense, *ibadat* refers to the observance of required duties, subsumed under the five pillars; that is, the formal outward manifestation of faith.[20]

The second argument about the broader and narrower meaning of *ibadat* reflects a somewhat operational argument. It starts from the belief that one's faith is in constant oscillation between maximum and minimum, from high to low and vice-versa. For this, again Pak Sholeh said:

[19] Denny, F.M. (1985), *'Islamic Ritual'*, p 77.
[20] Field notes.

> ... man's faith is of course unstable, on one occasion it is thick, on another it is thin. When it is thick, one's awareness of God is intact, and thus a person keeps remembering God while thinking, saying and working. But when a person's faith is thin he forgets God, not only while working but also while doing nothing.[21]

The corollary is that one's devotion to God may alternate between being full and being partial. When the faith is at its height, one will be fully aware of one's status as a slave of God (*kaulane Gusti Allah*) and submit oneself, one's life, and one's death, solely to God. The person eventually devotes what he thinks, says and does solely for the sake of God, thence everything becomes *'ibadat* in the broader sense. Indication of this kind of devotion, and at the same time its minimum requirement, is the presence of awareness which manifests itself as intention (*niyat*). According to Pak Sholeh, it is enough to have intention in one's heart but it is much better to pronounce it vocally. In Islam, the role of intention is crucial without which one's work will not be an *ibadat*.[22] It is in the presence of intention that everything, irrespective whether it is a worldly or afterlife activity (*bli perduli apa urusan dunya atawa urusan akherat*), is religious and thus, in Nasr words, 'everything is essentially sacred and nothing is profane because everything bears within itself the fragrance of the Divine.' Therefore, *ibadat*, in this sense, may range from expressing daily courtesies to such things as the formal and solemn invocation both in and outside of formal prescribed prayers, and other forms of worship. It embraces a wide spectrum of actions and is akin to, and sometimes used interchangeably with, *amal* (**'aml**), meaning work, another word which points to the same thing referred to by *ibadat*. Thus, the distinction between *amal* and *ibadat* becomes elusive. Both *ibadat* and *amal* require *niyat* (intention) which becomes the stamp that the work is for God. Another way to ensure intention is by uttering or murmuring *Basmalah* (a phrase, saying 'In the name of Allah, the Beneficent, the Merciful'). Thus, doing any (good) thing, a religious or worldly matter, becomes *ibadat*, by merely preceding it with *Basmalah*.

Usually an activity referred to by *amal* is technical and focussed on social action such as helping others and giving charity. In *ibadat*, on the other hand, the activity is usually of individual concern yet not necessarily related to the five pillars of Islam, such as reciting the Qur'an, *du'a* (invocation) and exalting God. As the difference is elusive, it cannot be precisely explained. People, for example, often say that *du'a* is undeniably *ibadat*, feeding an orphan is *amal* but, other ordinary technical and mundane acts such as going to work, going to school and

[21] Indepth interview, 5-5-1992. Its Javanese expression is: "... imane wong iku ya bli tetep, ana kalane kandel ana kalane tipis. Lamun imane lagi kandel ya elinge ning Gusti Allah bli ucul, awit krentege ati, metune pengucap, sampe pragat menggawe tetep kelingen ning Gusti Allah. Tapi ari imane lagi tipis, aja maning lagi menggawe, lagi meneng bae gan ya klalen."
[22] See Chapter One.

participation in social gatherings, are also said to be *ibadat* because doing these things, from the broader perspective, is essentially a religious duty; hence, not doing these things is a neglect and thus, can be sinful. Moreover, *amal* and *ibadat* are frequently combined to become a compound word, *amal-ibadat*, used either with an emphasis on or in reference to a more general notion covering both.

The notion of *amal* and *ibadat* attached to one's action diminishes, even disappears, when, at other times, a person's faith lessens, and the person concerned is no longer aware of his faith. This is the situation about which God warned through His testimony of time: "By the time, Verily man is in loss, Except such as have Faith"[23] This warning, according to Pak Sholeh, implies God's mercifulness. Acknowledging man's faith is in constant alternation (from high to low), He is always willing to save man from loss. The enforcement of (formal) *'ibadat*, especially the prescribed prayer five times a day, and other worships of the five pillars, helps man to remember Him periodically so that what he thinks, says and does has spiritual value and becomes *amal* and *ibadat*.[24]

When one officially becomes a member of the community of believers (*ummat Islam*),[25] his membership card is the pronouncement of *syahadat*, the first pillar of Islam; the standing rule is the *syari'ah* (canon law in Islam); and the prescribed duty is observance of the other four pillars, the *ibadat* in the narrower sense. It is narrow in the strictest sense because it is the prerequisite, the minimum requirement for being a true Muslim. In addition, if one would like to be generous and obtain more merit than he can obtain from the prescribed duties, one is welcome to do so by performing the 'religiously recommended (*sunna*) activities.'

A recommended activity may not necessarily derive from the *fiqh* books; it may find its roots in *tasawuf*. The *ulama tasawuf* (tasawuf scholars, mostly enunciators of Sufism) who attempted to get close to God, according to the Cirebonese belief, have set forth various meritorious activities that are supposed to enable a person to establish a better relationship with God (*hablum minallah* or **habl min Allah**) as well as with his fellow human beings (*hablumminan nas* or **habl min al-nas**), dead or alive. Reciting the Qur'an outside the prescribed prayer, for example, is not set down in *fiqh* but it is encouraged by *tasawuf*; so too is helping other people. Pak Sholeh said that according to the principle of *tasawuf*, reciting the Qur'an, even without knowing the meaning, reflects sympathy and relish for God's words; uttering *kalimah tayibah* (good phrases), such as exalting and praising God, shows a sort of courtesy to Him; so also is reciting *salawat* in reverence for His messengers. All these things are considered as attempts to

[23] QS 103:1–3.

[24] Field notes.

[25] One informant in Kalitengah compared the community of believers to a club (*perkumpulan*). The most familiar perkumpulan for him was a cooperative (*koopearsi*), especially Batik Cooperative, in which membership is the key to access to rights to communal property.

establish a better relationship with God. Visiting the tombs of pious figures, praying at grave sides for the welfare of the deceased involve establishing good relations with the dead; whereas, teaching, helping others by such means as giving material support, showing sympathy, giving advice and showing courtesy, all belong to attempts to establish good relations with the living. God will never be jealous if a person has good relations with his fellows, dead or alive; on the contrary, He will be pleased because establishing good relations with others is part of His order, and reward is provided for those who do so. Moreover, doing those things can even be used as a means to seek His pleasure and thence it is part of *ibadat* in the broader sense. In Cirebon, these types of activities are said to belong to the recommended activities and thereby are *ibadat* in the broader sense.

Following Pak Sholeh, the Cirebonese seem to conceive human actions as having a complex configuration. Diagram 4.1 shows how the configuration may seem to be. In the first place, actions may either be *ibadat* or non-*ibadat*, depending on whether or not they are based on faith. Further, faith-based actions (*ibadat*) fall into two categories: the formal submission (*islam*) and showing deference (*ihsan*). The formal submission (*islam*) transforms into *syari'ah* and is set down in *fiqh*. The *fiqh* enunciates both the laws and rules of 'formal duties or worship' (*ibadat* in the narrower sense), subsumed in the five pillars, and rules of interpersonal contracts (*mu'amalat*) such as those regarding marriage and inheritance. Showing deference, on the other hand, transforms into *tasawuf* which encourages good relations either with God in the form of additional *ibadat*, or with other creatures, human or non human, dead or alive, in the form of, among other things, ethics and *amal saleh*. As *islam* and *ihsan* are inseparable, both explicate the faith (*iman*), so too do formal obedience and showing deference, the *fiqh* and the *tasawuf*.[26]

[26] Ki Dulah gave a long illustration to explain the relationship between *ibadat* usually set forth in *fiqh* (*'ibadat syare'at* or formal *ibadat*') and *ibadat* developed in *tasawuf* (*'ibadat suftyah.*'). He said among other things that the 'formal' nature of the former and the 'informal' or 'courteous' nature in the latter. Two parties, for example, may have a deal straightforwardly to the points they are dealing with. But such a relationship is arid because it touches only the rational or physical aspect of human nature, without taking into account the emotional or spiritual aspects. To make a relationship lively and sensuous, courtesies are needed. Thus, a pre-prayer *puji-pujian*, for example, is a kind of courtesy, before formal 'meeting' with the Lord (*madep ning Pengeran*) proceeds. In fact, according to Ki Dulah, Islam involves both ratio and emotion of man. (See further sections).

Figure 4.1: Scope of Ibadat in Cirebonese popular conception.

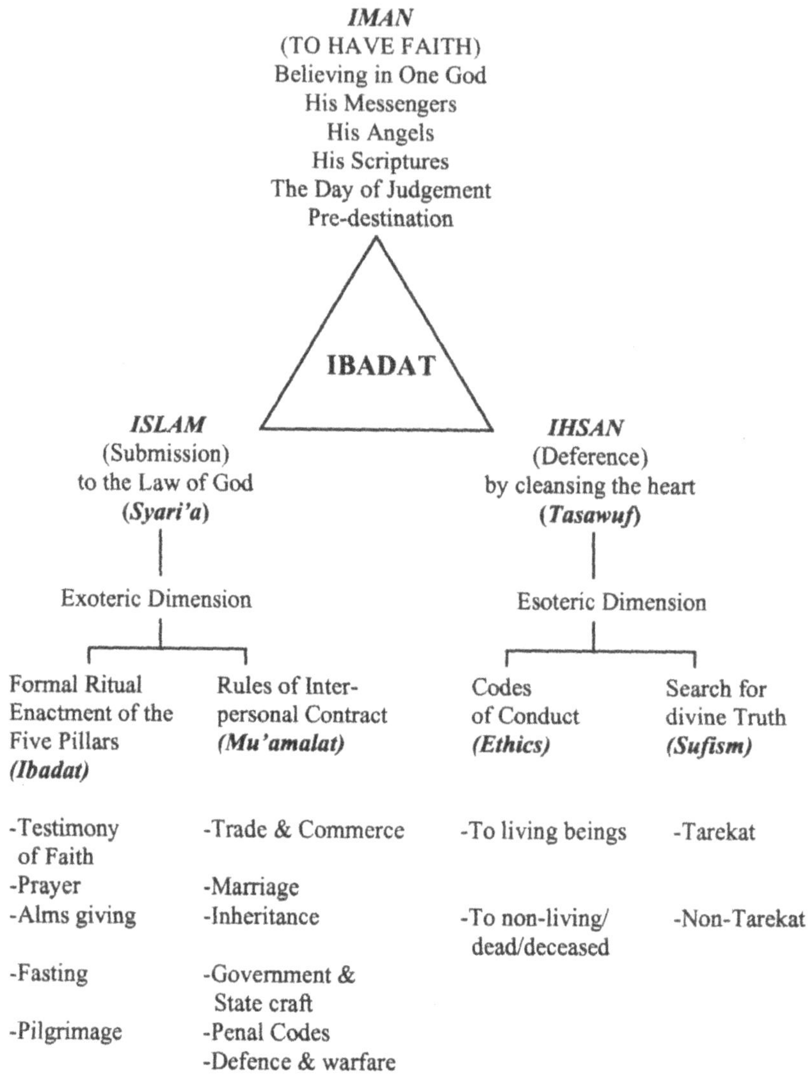

Fiqh and Tasawuf: Dual aspects of ibadat

Following the above explanation, activities belonging to *ibadat* (in the narrower sense) can be divided into two kinds, one derived from jurisprudence (*fiqh*), the other from *tasawuf*. Each is dialectically related to the other in a mode of complementary validation. In fact, *fiqh* is a prerequisite and thus it comes first before *tasawuf*, but enactment of *fiqh* without *tasawuf* is incomplete. Similarly, enactment of *tasawuf* without *fiqh* is invalid. *Fiqh* and *tasawuf* are thus like two sides of the same coin. K.H. Abdullah Abbas (affectionately known as Ki Dulah) of Pesantren Buntet, quoted Al-Ghazali's words in Aabic and then the translation in Cirebonese:

> One who observes only those things set down in *fiqh* without observing *tasawuf*, (still) commits sins. And one who observes only *tasawuf* without observing those things set down in *fiqh*, commits heresies.[27]

In addition, *ibadat* or worship, according to Ki Dulah, is working with God (Allah). The *fiqh* (Islamic Jurisprudence) which explicates the Divine Law (*syari'ah*) identifies what is obligatory (*wajib*), recommended (*sunna*), licit (*mubah*), illicit (*makruh*), and forbidden (*haram*). Bound up in these legal constrains, man usually tends to fulfil only the obligatory, unwilling to do the recommended, and desires the illicit or the forbidden. Man, however, is probably safe enough if he can fulfil the obligatory and do only the licit, but the temptation for doing the illicit and forbidden is so great that, without special effort, man is quite unlikely to be able to avoid the illicit and the forbidden completely because those things are present everywhere, in and outside the body. *Tasawuf* provides ways to counterbalance this tendency with encouragement and training to do the obligatory work properly and earnestly, and separate man from what is illicit and forbidden.

The obligatory duty required in *fiqh*, Ki Dulah said, accounts for only a small portion of man's life. Strict fulfilment of what is required is like working part time, while *tasawuf* makes it full time. The prescribed prayer (*salat*) is the most pressing duty one may think of because it must be observed five times a day. But, the time to do it takes only less than five minutes. The total time required for it is thus, less than 25 minutes a day, or about 1.7 per cent of the 24 hour period. The second hardest is fasting, once a year for 29 or 30 days, each day takes about 13 or 14 hours. The approximate time taken for fasting is therefore 360 hours or less, or about 4.0 per cent of the total hours of a year. *Zakat*, amount to just 2.5 per cent a year, taken from the surplus one keeps; whereas the hajj is required only once during a life time, and only for those who can afford it. Thus, even if we do the prescribed duties perfectly, according to Ki Dulah, we

[27] Indepth interview, 11-8-1992. Its Javanese expression is: "Sapa wonge kang nglakoni amalan feqih bae bli karo nglakoni amalan tasawuf, wongiku faseq. Lan sapa wonge kang nglakoni tasawuf bae bli karo nglakoni amalan feqih wongiku zindiq."

can count that the proportion of our life-time intentionally directed to God is very minimal, while outside that proportion, Iblis and *setan* are working restlessly to lead man astray. Indeed the greatest proportion of man's worldly life is unsecured. The danger of falling astray is clearly evident. Greed, snobbery, arrogance, unguided lusts and passions, according to Ki Dulah, penetrate quite easily into the heart of everyone at anytime and at any place. God's testimony *in 'Surat Wal'asri,'* saying that man is in constant loss unless he has faith, does righteous deeds, joins together in the mutual enjoining of truth, patience and constancy, shows its relevance in this context; and, it is here the *tasawuf* beneficially comes.[28]

Speaking about *tasawuf*, Ki Dulah said, does not necessarily mean speaking about being an ascetic or following the advanced mystical path, the **tharlqa** (*tarekat*) developed by certain Sufi orders, although certainly following this path is one of the significant outward indications of a commitment to *tasawuf*. In its broader sense, *tasawuf* is to cleanse the heart from contaminations occurring in daily life. From the perspective of *tasawuf*, the expression of *ibadat* may take various forms ranging from the earnest belief in the Oneness of God to the removing of even the smallest obstacles from people's way. Doing good to people and to nature with generosity for the sake of God (*lillahi ta'ala*) is already doing *tasawuf*. Earnest and generous submission of a wife to her husband and a husband to his wife in a harmonious relationship is also *tasawuf*. So is eating with an awareness that by means of eating one can maintain energetic work and thereby a person can support his family.

In addition, within *ibadat* of either the broader or narrower sense, there is not only a burden, but a joy. Most *ibadat* bears an atmosphere of cheer and festivity. An earnest person, after doing certain *ibadat*, would feel some sort of release from tension. The joy of fasting and the excitement of the *hajj* are claimed by many people. Thus, Ki Dulah remarked, there is no ground to think that *ibadat* is burdensome. On the contrary, for some, especially those who have been accustomed, *ibadat*, both from the perspective of *syari'ah* and from *tasawuf* is a pleasant undertaking, simple and easy to do. It might be a burden for some, who prefer thinking rather than doing, but *ibadat* is to be done, not (only) to be thought.

In short, when one is willing to observe the required duties earnestly, the person is performing *syari'ah* and *tasawuf* at the same time. In addition, anyone can make everything religiously meritorious by simply adding an intention, even if it is only in the heart, that what one does is for the sake of God. It is in this way that any action can become *ibadat*. In other words, if doing something is preceded by an intention to please God, that is *ibadat*. Indeed intention brings

[28] Surat *Wal'asri* refers to QS 103: 1–3 (Al-'Asr).

the worldly life into the religious; it needs nothing but a remembrance of God and earnestness. *Tasawuf* is, primarily, maintaining this awareness to achieve earnestness of obedience.[29]

THE PRACTICE OF IBADAT: SALAT

Sukardi (46 years), a shop owner in Plered said: "ISLAM stands for *(I)-sa, (S)-ubuh, (L)-uhur, (A)-sar, (M)-agrib*"; that is, the prescribed daily prayers five times a day for every Muslim who supposes himself to be devout. *Isya* (**'Isha**) is the duty of undertaking night prayer, *Subuh* (**Subh**) morning prayer, *Luhur* (**Dhuhr**) noon prayer, *Asar* (**'Asr**) afternoon prayer and *Magrib* (**Maghrib**) sunset prayer. I asked Sukardi whether he was serious in saying so, and he was not. He urged me not to take his words seriously because what he had just said was only a frivolous tautology *(kirata, dikira-[kira] nya-[ta])*, which he had heard from his friends. He insisted that what he had said did not have any sort of textual basis: "it is not available in books" (*langka ning kitabe*).

Sukardi's remark is a manipulation of five Roman letters: 'I', 'S, 'L', 'A' and 'M', forming the word "ISLAM"; each individual letter is said to represent the initial —in local language— the time and the name of the five daily prayers. This would make the five prayers a summation of the meaning of Islam. I realised later that in fact, such a joke is not strange and is already known by local people. Knowing that Islam was born in Arabia they are quite aware that Islam has no relation with the Roman letters. This fabrication is, however, interesting in that it reflects a genuine intelligible folk explanation of the position of the prescribed daily prayers in Islam.

The prescribed daily prayers (**salat**<phrase role="bold-ital">), which Watt (1979:185) prefers to call "public worship" rather than "prayer" is really the heart of Islamic worship.[30] Watt's preference to use "public" is understandable given that the Muslims speak of two distinct sets of acts for worship, referred to in English by the word "prayer". One is the so called *du'a* (in Cirebon: *donga*),

[29] In this context, "ritual" is a very interesting subject for scholarship. Anthropology has contributed much to unpacking its intricacy. Studies on this issue have been considerable but the more it is studied the more intricate it seems to be. The very notion of ritual as a particular kind of social action poses crucial questions revolving around the value of dichotomisation, whether sacred or profane, collective or individual, static or dynamic, action or thought, structure or antistructure (Bell, C. 1992). Seymour-Smith's suggestion cited earlier that perhaps ultimately it is unnecessary to define ritual, or to delimit it from ceremony on the one hand or from instrumental or practical action on the other because of the extreme difficulty of doing so, does not seem to resolve the problems of ritual automatically. This is more apparent, I think, when the subject is related to Islam, more specifically, traditional Islam in Cirebon where people consider any action intended to please God to be *ibadat* (worship including ritual). The boundary between activities which are religiously valid and those which invalid, is only one of an intention. Without intention, an activity, even the most ritualised and formalised one, becomes profane in Durkheimian sense. Similarly, even the most profane or technical action becomes sacred merely because of the intention. It is the intention which brings the profane into the sacred, and the sacred becomes profane when intention is absent.

[30] Watt, W.M. (1979), *What is Islam?*, 2nd ed, London: Longman.

an expression of thought, hopes or needs directed to God either in Arabic or in any other language, by heart or by tongue. This is usually done when the performer is either sitting, reclining, standing, walking or any other position, and can occur at any time; whereas *Salat* (in Cirebon: *sembayang* or *solat*), consists of various coordinated actions, such as standing, bowing and prostration, accompanied by appropriate exclamations of praise and recitations from the Qur'an, and performed only at the prescribed time. Owing to its important position to the Muslims, I shall focus the discussion concerning the practice of worship (*ibadat*), mainly on prayer. Other forms of *ibadat* are discussed in conjunction with this prayer. In addition, without disregarding Watt's suggestion, the use of the word "prayer" to mean *salat*, is widely used.[31] For practical reasons, I will use both *salat* and prayer interchangeably.

Based on people's commitment to the prescribed prayer, there is a wide prevalence in Cirebon to categorise people roughly and yet arbitrarily into *wong sembayang* (those who observe the prayer) and *wong bli sembayang* (those who do not observe the prayer). This categorisation has nothing to do with structuring people into particular positions, neither has it any effect on any form of personal rights, although one who observes is considered better from the religious point of view than a non-observer. This categorisation is quite arbitrary in the sense that a non-observer, even without other people's notice, can become observer at will and at any time. Sooner or later, other people will notice. In the same way, an observer can become a non-observer.

There is no written record about the number of people who move from being non-observers to being observers or vice-versa. However, the tendency of people moving from being non-observers to observers is much greater than the reverse, especially when they find themselves getting older. In addition, most of those who may be considered as non-observers go at least once or twice a year to the *'Id* prayer (*sembayang raya*), the congregation prayer at the end of Ramadan and the tenth of Dzu'l-Hijjah. This suggests that the categorisation between observer and non-observer can better be regarded as involving a continuous process rather than a discrete dichotomy. Its practical implication is behavioural rather than social in that, it indicates the crucial position of prayer relative to other forms of *ibadat* in determining one's religiosity. It makes prayer into a kind of public acceptance which is distinct from, for example, alms-giving. This is true because, unlike with other worship activities, people consider prayer as everyone's duty without exception, be that person healthy or sick, rich or poor. This formal acceptance does not necessarily mean actual commitment. Yet, it is quite common, in Cirebon, to hear gossip about someone's commitment to prayer. In contrast, there is no question of whether or not someone has pronounced

[31] It is also used for example, by Juynboll (See: "Prayer", in *Encyclopedia of Religion and Ethics*, pp. 196–199.

syahadat, (testimony) although *syahadat* is the foundation of all other worship activities and the key to being a Muslim. Probably, it is taken for granted that everyone born to a Muslim family is automatically a Muslim. Considering that *salat* is a matter of public concern, Watt's preference of referring to *salat* as a "public worship" rather than as "prayer" is actually quite sensible.

The daily life in Cirebon, as in other societies, consists mainly of sleeping, working and leisure. There is, of course, a great diversity between individuals as well as between groups regarding the time and duration of each activity. The normal situation dictates that sleeping is at night, working occurs during day time, and leisure in between. Some exceptions occur among those who work as village security, fishermen and sometimes among those who are traders.

A snapshot which illustrates a segment of the daily life of the Cirebonese village in the morning, wherein *ibadat* becomes a part, may be useful. Here, I want to refer to the case of Pak Shofie's and the surrounding households with whom I had become a part:

> Pak Shofie and his wife Nafsiyah usually wake up around four o'clock in the morning. They wake up their five sons and two daughters who sleep in their separate rooms or in other parts of the house wherever they like. Sometimes Pak Shofie uses a stick for a light beating to awake his sons. He and his wife take a bath immediately, make ritual ablution (*banyu wulu*), and get dressed. Pak Shofie wears a *sarung*, usually the same sarung he has already worn for sleeping, a shirt and a *topong* (black velvet cap). His sons follow what Pak Shofie does. His wife and daughters, on the other hand, wear a *tapi* (garment) or *sarung*, usually of batik, and a blouse with a *mukena* to wrap the head, showing only the face while the lower part of the *mukena* rests around the shoulders; the mukena hangs in front of the body and covers the chest and abdomen. While their sons and daughters are taking a bath and getting dressed Pak Shofie and his wife undertake *sembayang sunnah* (recommended prayer) in the private praying niche in the house.[32]

This is the way they prepare for morning-prayer (*sembayang subuh*), the earliest daily activity done by Pak Shofie's family and many others. The most important of these activities is making the ceremonial ablution (*banyu wulu*), which is a prerequisite before offering any prayer. The formal function of ablution is self-purification (*nyuceni awak dewek*) which is particularly required for everyone who does holy work, such as undertaking the prescribed prayer. As the nature of prayer is to have communion and communication with God, the Holiest and Purest Being, praying requires the performer to be in a state of purity.

[32] Field notes.

Ablution is a kind of ceremonial bathing that involves washing parts of the body generally exposed to dirt, dust or smog. Officially, it consists of the declaration of intention, the washing of face and hands, the wetting of a part of the head and the washing of legs; all are done in successive order. Usually, however, it is performed as follows: (1) utter the *Basmalah*: "In the name of Allah the Beneficent, the Merciful" (2) wash the hands up to the wrists (3) rinse out the mouth with water three times (4) cleanse the nostrils of the nose by sniffing water into them three times (5) declare an intention that the act is for the purpose of worship and purity (6) wash the whole face three times with both hands from the top of the forehead to the bottom of the chin and from ear to ear (7) wash the right and the left arms up to the far end of the elbow, three times each (8) wipe the whole head or any part of it with a wet hand (9) wipe the inner sides of the ears with the wet forefingers and the outer sides with the wet thumbs (10) wash the two feet, three times each, first the right and then the left, up to the ankles. When all these thing are completed, one is ready to offer prayer unless the purification is nullified by things such as vomiting, falling asleep and natural discharges: urine, stools, gas.

This ablution actually exceeds formal ablution requirements (*fardlu*). There are only six of these, comprising: intention, washing the face, washing the hands up to the elbows, rubbing the head with a wet hand, washing the feet up to the ankles and keeping these activities in the proper order. The additional practices belong to the *sunnah*. Pak Shofie teaches his students about ablution through a chant which he claimed as his father's creation. The chant is as follows:

Ferdune wudlu iku nenem kabehe
Wong wis baleg kudu weruh sekabehe
Siji niyat iku ana ning atine
Loro mbasuh rahining barengane

Telu mbasuh tangan teka ning sikute
Papat mbasuh sirah ning enggon rambute
Lima mbasuh sikil teka ning kiyonge
Nenem kudu karo tartib nglakonane.

The obligations in ablution are six in number
All the grown up people should know these obligations
The first is intention which resides in the heart
The second is washing the face accompanying the intention

The third is washing the hands up to the elbows
The fourth is wetting the head where the hair grows
The fifth is washing the feet up to the ankles
The sixth is putting those things in the proper order

Along with its formal functions, some informants insist on the symbolic meaning of ablution as a sort of self-reminder (*ngelingaken*), introspection (*ngrumangsani*) and, at the same time, expression of repentance (*tobat*), expecting God to nullify any bad effects coming from improper activity by the misuse of those organs. Washing the mouth signifies an expectation for nullifying any disgrace from improper or unlawful saying and eating; washing the face is to nullify improper seeing, facing and directing of any activity; washing the hands is to nullify improper holding and doing; washing the head is to nullify improper thinking; washing the ears is to nullify improper hearing; washing the legs is to nullify improper places that the legs have taken the body. Some other informants emphasise an even wider meaning. Any action involving the ablution of those organs is a symbol of the basic tenet of Islamic ethics. It is not only to nullify what is already done but more importantly, ablution is a refreshing instrument which reminds everyone to be careful in using those organs and thence avoid any probable misuse for having or doing illicit and forbidden actions. Ablution is therefore, interpreted by some as an encompassing framework which, ideally, guides an individual as well as a social activity for the preservation of a safe and peaceful life.

Early in the morning, people's activities throughout the hamlet centre mainly around the wells located outside the house. Since not every household has their own bathroom and source of water supply, the well becomes a place of rendezvous for a number of households. The well is usually owned by one household but it becomes public, used by the others, for bathing and washing either clothes or dishes. Ablution is taken from the *padasan* (a jar propped on a pillar, usually stone or brick, at knee height with a small water outlet near the bottom). Upon their return they take with them a bucket or two of water for cooking and other necessities. In the meantime the religious atmosphere accompanying the early morning in a village is approximately as follows:

> Since early in the morning, the sounds faintly heard from the prayer house in far hamlets begin to reverberate with the recital of the Qur'an, *salawat* (reverence to the Prophet) or *puji-pujian*. In no time, sounds from another prayer house follows, also reverberating with the same sounds, vocally or from records. Later, more and more sounds come, including the one from some nearby hamlet. The climax happens at about 4.30 a.m when the time for morning-prayer (*subuh*) is marked by the rhythmical beating of the *kentong*, followed by the call to prayer (*adzan*).[33] The sounds of *kentong* and *adzan* are heard one after another, and some

[33] The *kentong* is a cut of log, about 1.5 metres long with a long resonance hole in the centre. It is hung vertically in most prayer houses and mosques to be beaten rhythmically with a certain tempo, softly and strongly to signal to the surrounding people the prayer time.

> are even heard about the same time as if orchestrating a religious symphony, which has already started in the previous hour.[34]

Some argue that all sounds heard in the morning are an offence to private individuals concern, causing only a nuisance rather than convenience, obstructing the nicest sleeping time. Such an issue, Pak Nasuha (52 years) said, was raised sometimes in the 1960s by PKI (Indonesian Communist Party) members. The argument finally stopped without causing any more problems, after the PKI was banned in 1966. According to Pak Nasuha, the "nuisance", for those who think so, is now intensified by the wide-spread use of sound systems in many *tajug*, even the small ones like Pak Shofie's. Some, particularly among the modernists in Kalitengah, besides claiming that it is an innovation (*bid'ah*), call the contents and usefulness of the sounds into question, asking whether it has any educative value for the people given that the sound is almost totally Arabic and thus, not understandable. While denouncing this practice they claim that only the *adzan* is acceptable. Most people however, think about it differently. For example, I asked Bi Rukila (52 years), a woman snack peddler from the neighbouring house to Pak Shofie, if she knows the meaning of the sound coming from the prayer houses and, how she feels about it. Her comment was as follows:

> ... I do not know anything about the meaning and, I think, very few people know it. For me, in particular, it is not the meaning which is important though. The tone, the rhythm and the lyrics which, by local taste, penetrate into the heart and exuberantly invoke an atmosphere of religiosity is much more meaningful than any words can say. Also, its aim is not to tell people something, but to help them awaken, to get up early, and it will be better for those who are willing, to come to God by doing prayer early in the morning. Our elders said that getting up early in the morning is good; it may brings fortune closer (*gampang oli rejeki*), and enlighten the mind (*njembaraken pikiran*)...[35]

Pak Shofie's prayer house also contributes to the creation of the morning's religious atmosphere. This starts when someone strikes the *kentong* hanging in the verandah of the *tajug* adjacent to Pak Shofie's house. It instantly wakes any young boys sleeping in it. There are four or more boys from nearby households who often use the *tajug* to sleep in. Usually, there are two or three of Pak Shofie's neighbours who come to the *tajug* quite early and strike the *kentong*. Then if there is a man among them he turns on the *tajug*'s sound systems and sounds the *adzan*. If there are no men present, a woman beats the *kentong, and* the *adzan* is not immediately sounded. Pak Shofie's sons will understand the situation and

[34] Field notes.
[35] Field notes from a set of informal talks.

one of them will suspend bathing, take only ablution, and go off to the *tajug* to sound the *adzan*. After *adzan*, the congregation (*jama'ah*) in the *tajug* chants *puji-pujian* in chorus, while more and more people come to join the chorus and the group grows bigger and bigger. Some do pre-morning prayer in the midst of the chorus. The most frequent chant sounded in this *tajug* is the "Cry of Adam and Eve for Repentance". It was said that Adam uttered it soon after being thrown from paradise. According to Pak Shofie, it teaches us to be a *kesatriya* (an open-minded individual) in that, when something goes wrong, the first thing to do is to reflect and to look for one's own fault rather than blaming others, and then generously confess that it is really one's own fault not the fault of others. The chant is in Arabic and translates as follows:

Rabbana ya rabbana
Rabbana dzalamna anfusana
Wa in lam taghfirlana
Lanakunanna min al-khasirin

Our Lord, oh our Lord.
We have oppressed ourselves.
If thou forgive us not,
We certainly belong to the disadvantaged.

After doing pre-morning prayer at home, Pak Shofie goes to the *tajug*; a person of the group, usually the one who sounded the *adzan*, stands up again to sound the *iqamat*, a shorter form of *adzan*, commanding the group into prayer. All people stand, the women loosen the lower part of the *mukena*, so that it covers all parts of the body; only the face and palms of the hands are visible. Pak Shofie enters, walks across to the 1.5 square metre niche (*pengimaman* or **mihrab**), located at the centre of west-wall inside the *tajug* cube, and stands there facing Mecca.

Just before the morning prayer begins Pak Shofie, who is about to start to lead the prayer, first turns to the group and reminds them to stand properly and form straight lines. They stand behind him, shoulder to shoulder and foot to foot to form straight lines. Usually, there are four to seven lines in the congregation, each line consists of five or six people. Men and women are separated by the line. The front lines consist only of men and boys, behind them are lines consisting only of women and girls.

The prayer starts when Pak Shofie, who leads the prayer (*imam*), pronounces *takbir*, saying "Allah the Greatest" ("*Allahu Akbar*"), with his hands open on each side of the face and with his palms facing the front, very near, almost or even touching the lobes of the ears. This act is followed by the others. But before the *takbir*, everyone, including the leader, concentrates his/her mind individually and utters an intention (*niat*) in Arabic softly in a whispered tone: "I intend to undertake morning prayer two *raka'at* (unit of prayer) facing the *Qiblat* (in Mecca) for the sake of Allah alone." After *takbir*, the hands are folded, the right palm is put over the left, against the front of the body; this position is kept while standing. A set of opening words (**Iftitah**) is recited softly which translates:

> I turn my face, to the Creator of the heavens and earth. And I am not of the polytheists. Surely, my prayer, my devotion, my life and my death, belong (solely) to Allah, master of the whole universe. None is companion to Him, and for that I am ordered, and I (certainly) belong to the Muslims.

Following the *iftitah*, the *Imam* recites the first Surah of the Holy Qur'an (Fatihah) audibly, while the others listen or follow it by heart. When the Fatihah ends, everyone responds in chorus: "Amen." After the Fatihah comes recital of a short *surah*, or few verses of the Qur'an. After that the further practice is as follows: (1) Bowing down from the hips (*ruku*), with the head and back parallel to the ground; the hands hold the knees and a phrase is softly uttered three times: "Glory to my God the Great". (2) Straightening up after bowing, returning to the upright position, saying: "Allah hears those who praise Him" followed by "Our God, to thee be the praise." (3) Sliding to the knees and doing the first prostration with the knees, forehead and nose touch the ground, saying: "Glory to my God, the Highest", also three times. (4) First sitting on the heels with one foot up and the other flat; the head is raised from the first prostration, the back is erect and the hands rest on the knees, saying: "God, please forgive me and give me thy mercy" (5) Repeating the prostration, again with saying: "Glory to my God, the Highest," three times and then coming back to a standing position. After that the Fatihah and short verses are again recited. The observances from Fatihah to the second prostration constitutes a unit (*raka'at* or **raka'at**). The morning prayer proceeds in two units concluded by the utterance of reverence (*Tahiyat*) or witness-bearing (*Tasyahud*). At the upright position, after straightening up from *ruku* of the second unit, a *qunut* is read.[36] The *Tahiyat* or *Tasyahud* consists of two parts; each translates as follows:

> (1) All reverence, all blessing, all sanctity are due to God. Peace be upon you, O Prophet, and the mercy of God and His Blessings. Peace be upon us all and on the righteous servants of God. I bear witness that there is no God but Allah, and I bear witness that Muhammad is His Messenger.
>
> (2) Oh, God! Exalt our Master Muhammad and the people of our Master Muhammad, as Thou didst exalt our master Abraham and the people of our Master Abraham. And bless our Master Muhammad and the people of our Master Muhammad, as Thou didst bless our Master Abraham and

[36] *Qunut* invocation is normally read only at morning prescribed prayer and *witr*, the recommended night prayer of the 16th day onward of the Fasting month (*Ramadan*). Along with the soft verbal utterance of the intention (*niyat*), qunut is strongly recommended by the traditionalists but has been abandoned by the modernists.

the people of our Master Abraham. Verily, in the worlds, Thou art the praiseworthy, and glorious.

It appears that within the *tahiyat* there is a pronouncement of *syahadat* (from which the name *tasyahud* is derived). When it is pronounced, the person praying raises his index finger as if he is pointing to the west, although, according to one informant, it is not pointing to the West but gesturing and affirming the oneness of God as pronounced in the *syahadat*. At the end of *tahiyat* everyone turns their faces right and then left, each turn being accompanied by a greeting (*salam*), saying: "Peace be upon you, so be (upon you) God's grace and His blessing" This greeting marks the completion of the prayer. At this moment young boys and girls instantly stand up and go out of the prayer house, whereas most adults and some youngsters sit there still to attend *wiridan* or simply, *wirid* (litany or a set of after-prayer invocations). Pak Shofie, the *Imam*, turns around to face the group and starts loading the *wirid*. Unlike the prayer which is solemn and formal, *wirid* is more relaxed. Basically *wirid* is a prayer formulae comprising a set of invocations; its essence is to glorify God *(tasbih)* 33 times, praise God *(tahmid)* 33 times and exalt God *(takbir)* 33 times, concluding with an invocation. Sometimes, *tahlil* (negation of any deity but Allah) 21, 41 or 100 times is also included before the conclusion. The invocation or **du'a** (*donga*) to conclude the *wirid* is recited by the *Imam*, begging God for everyone's beneficial and safe life in this world and in the hereafter. Everyone raises up the palms in front of their faces, responding to the leader repeatedly, with "Amen", in chorus. At the end of the **du'a** everyone rubs their palms against their faces, then everyone gets up to shake each other's hands; the congregation breaks up at about five o'clock a.m., which indicates that the whole process lasts about a half hour. While shaking hands, a fare-well chant is uttered. The most frequent chant for this occasion is "The Cry of Prophet Ayyub" in local Arabic pronunciation and translates as follows:

Ilahi lastu li 'l-firdawsi ahla
Wa lal aqwa 'alan-naril-jahimi
Fahabli tawbata waghfir dzunubi
Fa innaka ghafirudzdzanbi 'l-'adzimi.

My God, I am not (eligible to be) an occupant of paradise,
But I (certainly) can not bear against the fire of Jahim.
So, give me repentance, and forgive all my sins,
Surely, Thou art the forgiver of sin (even) a great one.

Pak Shofie's prayer house is small (4.5×6 square metres) compared with the other 11 prayer houses in the *desa*, but what usually goes on at other prayer houses follows the same pattern. The same practices are also carried out at other prayer houses in the villages outside the *desa*, in the *desa* mosques, around the shrines (*kramat*), and in *pesantren*. It is a common pattern followed by traditionalists in Cirebon and elsewhere in Java. This pattern may extend to what happens at other prayer times as well. The difference between this and other prayer times is (as *Fiqh* dictates), the number of units (*raka'at*). The morning prayer, proceeds in two units; noon, afternoon and night prayers respectively, four units and two *tahiyat*, one *tahiyat* comes after the first two units and another one after the fourth. Sunset prayer proceeds in three units and two *tahiyat*. The first *tahiyat* follows the first two units and the second after the third, the last unit. Another difference is in the recital of *Fatihah* and other *surah* of the Qur'an which is audible in the morning, and at the first two units of sunset as well as night prayers, but it is spoken softly at noon and afternoon prayers.

Not all people do their prayer at a prayer house and in congregation (*jama'ah*). Most of them do it at their homes, individually or in a group with their family members; there are even some who do not do it at all. Whether or not people observe the duty, the religious atmosphere undoubtedly dominates the early morning of village life. This atmosphere is further enriched by religious programmes (public lectures or *pengajian*) from several radio stations and, more recently, from the regional TV broadcast transmitted from Bandung.

Among Pak Shofie's family only his wife and Yazid, (26 years), his oldest son, a recent graduate of a state university in Solo (Central Java), stay at the *tajug* to attend the *wirid* until the end. The others return home earlier, read the Qur'an for a while and do some house work. Yayuk, the older daughter, younger sister of Yazid, works in the kitchen to prepare morning tea or coffee, clean the dishes or do her washing. Her sister, Titiek (8 years), is too young to be able to join in her work. After reciting the Qur'an she goes to her bedroom to listen to the radio. Didin and Fadlan the two sons clean the floor. After having some tea and snacks, they kiss their father's and mother's right hands for permission to go to school for morning class at 7.00 a.m., Imran goes to the market to open Pak Shofie's kiosk, preceding another boy of the neighbouring household who will join him a bit later to work as an assistant in the kiosk.

It is after the break up of the morning prayer that people begin to engage in the daily business. In the village daily routine, the first thing to do is household work, and then they do work for a living. School children go to schools, adults go to the markets, to the offices, to the factories and workshops, to the agricultural lands. Aside from the few who are involved in formal official jobs, working hours are quite flexible. Normally, for most people however, work stretches from sunrise to around 5.00 p.m, with two intervals, one for meal around 9.00–10.00 a.m and for a snack (*njabur*), usually a big one, and one for prayer, between 12.00 noon and 1.30 p.m.[37] For those who do not rely on a

[37] Normally, meal in Cirebon is of two kinds, *mangan* (to have meal) and *njabur* (to have snack). *Mangan* is to have or to eat rice with dishes, twice a day, in the morning and in the afternoon (between 9.00–10.00

clock, noon is signified by the sound of *bedug*, and *adzan* from the mosques, informing people that the prayer time has come.[38] Only noon and Thursday afternoon prayer-time is signified by *bedug*; other times are indicated by the sound of *kentong* from the mosques as well as from other prayer houses.

Among the prescribed daily prayers held in congregation, sunset prayer attracts the largest numbers. The second largest attendance is at night prayer and then after these comes the morning prayer time. These congregations are not compulsory, although they are recommended. From the break up of night prayer until late, a class for learning to read the Qur'an (*ngaji*) for boys, girls and children, is held, either at the prayer house or at the teacher's house. At his prayer house Pak Shofie also teaches some grown up boys to read *Kitab*, the *Safinah* and *Sulam Taufiq*.[39] Bed-time begins soon after the children have come back from *ngaji*, but because of the presence of television, bed-time has become more flexible, often it is suspended until eleven or even twelve midnight. The class for learning to read the Qur'an usually ceases during, and for a few days after, the Fasting month.

Formal congregation, which is compulsory for Muslims, is held once a week at noon on Friday in the mosque. It is compulsory only for men; women are allowed to go but are not compelled. This congregation is a substitute for noon prayer but consists only of two units instead of four, and the recitation of the *Fatihah* and other verses of the Qur'an by the leader (*imam*) is made out loud. A sermon (*khutbah*) given by a *khatib* (who may be the same person as the *imam*) should precede the prayer, and the congregation should not be less than forty people, including the *imam*. This is the basic pattern of Friday prayer in Islam. There are some who say that four people is enough to make up a Friday congregation, but this never happens in Cirebon.

In Cirebon, the religious atmosphere in the village is most apparent on Friday. According to local belief, Friday is the master of the days (*sayidul ayyam* or **sayid al-ayyam**). It is the most gracious day for religious service. On Thursday, the day before, the time for afternoon prayer is signalled by the *bedug*, implying that after sunset of that day, it will be Friday. By sunset on Thursday, some people buy flowers to be scattered on their beds and some burn incense (*ukup-ukup*). The real purpose of burning incense is not known except there are

a.m and 4.00–5.00 p.m). *Njabur* which means to have or to eat *jaburan* (any foods other than rice and dishes), also twice a day, in the morning and at noon (between 6.30–7.30 a.m and 12.00 at noon - 1.30 p.m). *Njabur* is usually with tea, coffee or other drinks. Bread, toast, biscuits, various cakes and snacks belong to *jaburan*. Casual buying of *jaburan* to be eaten instantly is called *jajan*. Eating dishes (meat, fish, soup, etc) without rice is called *njambal* or *njambal iwak*.

[38] The *bedug* is a huge drum, made of a cut of huge log about 1.5 - 2 metres long and about 1.25 metres diameter covered with cow or buffalo leather on both sides. It is hung in the mosques to be beaten at certain times, particularly at noon and on certain occasions.

[39] *Safinah* refers to *Safinatun Najah* (**Safina al-Najah**), an elementary *Figh* book, whereas *Sulam Taufiq* (**Al Sullam al-Taufiq**) is an elementary *Tasawuf*, both written in Arabic by Nawawi of Banten.

some who say that it is to drive *setan* away; some others say that they only follow their elders; still other say that it is to signal (*tengeran*, literally, the sign) that it is Friday. While the burning of incense is mostly done inside the house its fragrance carries some distance.

On Friday some visit their elders' graves to pray for God's mercy and forgiveness on them. After sunset prayers, they read the Holy Qur'an, especially *Yasin* (QS 36), *Waqi'ah* (QS 56) and *Tabarok* (**Al-Mulk**, QS 67). By reading these Surah they expect God's forgiveness, a safe life and merit in the world and the hereafter. After night (*Isya*) prayer there are gatherings for a *Marhaba chant* (poetry reading taken from *Barzanji* to revere the Prophet Muhammad); some others hold *Hadiwan* or *Manaqib* (special invocations by reference to *wali*).[40] At the end of either *Marhaba* or *Hadiwan*, usually around 10.00 p.m., foods are served and the people eat together.

Every Friday around ten o'clock in the morning the *bedug* in the mosque is beaten in a way which is different from the ordinary beating at noon. This beating, called *penatag* (reminder), is aimed to remind people that it is Friday, and that there might be some who need to make necessary arrangements for Friday congregation. Older people are probably those who are mostly concerned as it is they who usually go to the mosque early around 11.00 o'clock a.m. The popular belief prevails that the earlier one goes to Friday congregation the better, and hence more, the reward that can be expected. Metaphorically it is explained that the relative merit of coming to congregation early, coming just on time, or coming late is like getting a cow compared to a chicken, or compared to an egg.

The activity of those who come early centres on uttering invocations, reading the Qur'an, *salawat* or just sitting calmly. As soon as anyone arrives at the mosque, they do a voluntary two unit prayer individually in reverence of the mosque (*tahiyatul masjid*). About fifteen minutes before noon, *salawat* is chanted repeatedly saying: "Oh Allah, assuage our mentor Muhammad and give thy grace to our mentor Muhammad."[41] The chanting is brought to a high pitch when the *bedug* is beaten signalling the prayer time. The beating of *bedug* takes two or three minutes ending simultaneously with the termination of the chanting. One who is in charge as *muadzin* (one who sound the *adzan*) or *bilal*, stands up to sound *adzan*.[42] After the *adzan* he urges, in Arabic, those attending the congregation to do a two unit voluntary prayer, the pre-congregational prayer (*qabliyah Jum'ah*). After having finished doing the prayer, the second *muadzin* (who may also be the same person as the first) stands up, takes a walking stick or a spear from the pulpit beside the *mihrab* and, keeping it in his hand, turns

[40] For further elaboration of burning incense, *Marhaba, Hadiwan* and *Manaqib*, see Chapter Six.

[41] In local Arabic it says: "Allahumma salli wa sallim 'ala sayyidina Muhammad."

[42] In the Great Mosque of *Kraton* Kesepuhan, where a sound system is not used, this *adzan* is done by seven people in chorus.

around facing the congregation telling them (in Arabic) that within a few seconds the sermon will be spoken. He is the second *muadzin*, one who sounds the (second) *adzan*. He urges the audience to follow the sermon solemnly by reciting a *Hadith* narrated by Bukhari and Muslim which states that speaking or talking while the sermon is spoken is disdain. In the meantime someone sitting among the congregation stands up and walks towards the *muadzin*, takes the walking stick or spear and goes to the podium. He is the *khatib*, who is in charge of giving the sermon. When the *khotib* reaches the podium he does not immediately turn to face the congregation but stand still for few seconds as the *muadzin* utters a *du'a* (invocation) for the safety of all Muslims and believers, men and women, alive and dead. Everyone raises their hands, puts the palms of their hands in front of their faces responding "Amen" in chorus repeatedly and rubs their palms against their faces when the *du'a* is finished. The *khatib* turns around to stand on the podium, facing the congregation with the greeting: "Peace be upon you, so be the mercy of Allah and His Blessing" (*Assalamu'alaikum warahmatullahi wabarokatuh* or **al-salam 'alaykum wa rahmah Allah wa barakatuh**<phrase role="bold-ital">) then he sits down on the podium seat. When he is sitting the *muadzin* sounds the (second) *adzan*. After sounding the *adzan* the *muadzin* sits down and the sermon starts.

A sermon consists of two parts. Each part starts with praising God and praying to God to bless the Prophet Muhammad. In the first part, a Qur'anic passage is recited and explained for the purpose of exhortation and admonition. A call to devotion and piety is the main theme of every sermon, calling upon all Muslims to follow the true path, do good things, and avoid sins. News of the current situation in the Muslim world and its relevance for the local community is also offered. At the end of the first part of the sermon the *khatib* takes a short rest by sitting on the podium seat, then stands up again to give the second sermon. Although general affairs may be discussed in either one or both parts of most sermons, in several mosques I attended, the *khatib* used only the first part for such a purpose. At the end of the second part, which is usually entirely in Arabic, the *khatib* prays for the general welfare of all Muslims. Since mid-1992 many *khatib* in Cirebon explicitly expressed, in their invocations, the hope for the safety and welfare of the Bosnian people who were in chaos. This substantiates the sense of Muslim brotherhood within the community of believers transcending the geographic, national, ethnic and racial boundaries. Throughout the praying the audience responds repeatedly with "Amen."

After the sermon is concluded, the *iqamat* is made and the two units of obligatory prayer are led by the *imam*. The *Fatihah* and the Qur'anic passage are, on this occasion, read in an audible voice. All procedures used for this prayer follow the ordinary prayer pattern.

At some *desa* mosques, including that in Kalitengah, the sermon is delivered in a local language, whereas in the city and some urban areas outside the city of Cirebon, it is mostly given in Bahasa Indonesia. There are some *desa* mosques where the *khutbah* is fully spoken in Arabic but preceding the formal *khutbah*, before prayer-time comes, the public speech (*pengajian*) is usually made in the local language by local *kyai* or *ustadz*. There are also mosques, including the Great Mosque of *Kraton* Kesepuhan, the mosque within Pesantren Buntet, Kramat Astana Gunung Jati, Cirebon Girang, Kalijaga and many others, where the sermon is fully spoken in Arabic without any public speech preceding it. These certainly represent the most conservative line. The reasons behind this conservativeness varies from one place to another. Some informants gave one or more of the following reasons: (a) an anxiety to conserve an original or antique form of the prayer began by the early propagators of Islam and thus maintain the solemn nature of the prayer (b) to keep the congregation's activities to a short time so that everyone can get back to work without losing too much time or feeling constrained by attending Friday congregation (c) to enhance the spiritual atmosphere of the Friday congregation (d) to avoid any probable conflict arising from misunderstanding or misuse of the *khutbah* by certain individuals, who might take advantage of the prayers to enunciate their own views in the guise of religious truth.[43]

THE PRACTICE OF IBADAT: FASTING

The intensity of the religious atmosphere of the weekly cycle, which culminates on Friday, finds its match in the yearly cycle which culminates on the Fasting Month (*Ulan Puasa* or **Ramadan**). The Fasting Month, being the zenith for the annual pulse of religious life, falls on the ninth month of the Islamic calendar. During the month all Muslims abstain from food, drink, cigarettes and sexual intercourse from dawn until sunset, for the period of 29 or 30 days each year depending on the moon's position. Exempted from fasting are women in menstruation or with (child-birth) bleeding, any person on a sick bed or on a journey, men and women who are too old and children under the age of puberty.

In Cirebon, the popular tradition for the beginning of Fasting month is signalled by the sound of *peteter*, a distinct melodic style in the beating of the *bedug* in the mosque. *Peteter* is sounded at 4.00 or 8.00 p.m. at the end of *Ruwah* (or **Sya'ban**) the month that precedes the Fasting. *Peteter* sounds at 4.00 p.m on the 30th day of *Ruwah*, but when the Ruwah is 29 days (*brandangan*) the sound of *peteter* is suspended until 8.00 p.m. after the National Team for visual observation

[43] Some may use the sermon as a media to enunciate certain primordial or political views or interest in the guise of religion, resulting in tensions between opposing and supporting groups. This happened for example, in Kalitengah, when traditionalists and modernists *(Muhammadiyah)* were competing to gain control over the mosque. In Kaliwadas, tensions occurred concerning the correct direction of *Kiblat* of the mosque.

(*ru'yat*) from the Ministry of Religious Affairs announces its judgement. When *peteter* is sounded children throughout the village go running eagerly to the mosque to see how the *peteter* is sounded. In Indonesia, however, the beginning and the ending of the Fasting Month is officially announced by the Minister of Religious Affairs via evening radio and TV broadcasts, followed by a speech about the merit of the Fasting month that urges everyone to do his utmost, to do good and avoid evil.

The daily period of observance starts before the break of the dawn (*imsak*) and ends immediately after sunset. Currently, there are many calendars which give the exact time of each day and this is also included with daily information from newspapers, radio and TV broadcasts. Prior to fasting, early in the morning before dawn, people anticipate their fast by having an early morning meal (*sahur*). After *sahur* they go to the mosque or prayer house for morning prayer. On their return from morning prayer, most youngsters do not immediately go back home; they spend the morning walking to and fro, making the mornings throughout the month exceedingly exciting.

During the day time the situation is not much different from other days, except that most coffee shops, canteens and restaurants are closed. Some, however, are secretly open to cater to those who cannot fast for a variety of reasons, such as those who are doing hard physical work. *Becak* drivers and porters are examples among those who usually do not fast. The appearance of weakness and exhaustion is felt by workers at the *batik* factory, shoe making and cane craft workshops. Around 10.00–11.00 a.m., Marnisah (19 years), a young woman working at a cane workshop, said that she is nervous on the first day of fasting; she suffers from exhaustion around 10.00 a.m. but it soon passes without causing any problem. Other informants talk about the same thing and tell of the great excitement at having a bite to eat at break time. Among the clerical workers exhaustion appears at lunch time, around 12.00 at noon when, after doing noon prayer, they lie weakly on the mat at *mushalla* (prayer room) of their offices, some are even falling asleep and go back to work at 1.30 p.m.

The time to break the fast at sunset, is signified by the sound of *bedug, kentong,* and *adzan* from the prayer houses, radio and TV broadcasts. People take *ta'jil* (a quick small bite of something to break the fast), usually dates or sweets, but most commonly *kolak* (foods, usually fruits, cooked with sweetened thick liquid or coconut milk). A full meal is served after sunset prayer.

From the first evening of the fasting month, people swarm to prayer houses (*tajug* and mosques) for evening prayer and *traweh* (**tarawlh**), a set of prayers which are not compulsory but strongly recommended (*sunnah muakkad*) to be done throughout the fasting month. Included in the notion of *traweh* is *witir* (**witr**), another recommended prayer done at night with an uneven number, mostly three, of units (*raka'at*). At *Ramadan, witr* is performed following *traweh.*

People who go to *traweh* therefore, are usually involved in the observance of three consecutive prayers: the prescribed evening prayer (*'Isya*) performed in four *raka'at*; the *traweh* itself which is mostly performed in 20 *raka'at* (10×2) or, especially among the modernists, eight *raka'at* (4×2 or 2×4) and *witr* three *raka'at. Traweh* (with *witir*), therefore, may be either 23 or 11 raka'at. The 23 *traweh,* which is predominant in Cirebon, represent the hallmark of proper practice among the traditionalists, whereas the *11 traweh* represents the practice of the modernists. For those who practice 23 *traweh,* beginning from the sixteenth day onward, the *qunut,* an invocation uttered at morning prayer, is also uttered at the last *raka'at* of *witr.*

In the practice of *traweh* the traditionalists and the modernists exhibit their differences quite publicly, although at present, unlike in the last two decades, the differences do not cause any conflict. The traditionalists regard *traweh* as *sunna* (recommended, not compulsory) which, according to (their) *syari'ah,* may be observed in either 8, 20 or 36 *raka'at,* plus *witr.* Not doing *traweh* at all is not counted as a sin, but if someone would like to do it, the more the better. Doing *traweh* 8 units, plus *witr,* is essentially good and lawful but it is only a minimum and therefore, implies laziness; doing 20 is better than 8, while doing 36 is the best but too exhausting. Thus, according to their view, 20 is the most reasonable practice (*paling maslahat*).

The local modernists, in contrast, while agreeing that *traweh* is *sunnah,* regard only the 8 *raka'at* as prescribed by law. Practicing *traweh* 20 or 36 units is, according to their view, an innovation and therefore, sinful. Even if it is lawful, the work is useless because, unlike their practice which is done slowly and well, the 20 *traweh* are usually done badly by hurrying every portion recited in the prayer.[44]

Along with practicing 20 *raka'at,* the traditionalists have more elaborate procedures. Following each of their two units, the *bilal* shouts glorification of God and/or praises the prophet Muhammad, to which the others respond in chorus. Moreover, after completing the *traweh,* the *imam* leads his congregation to utter the intention (*niyat*) for their fasting. He utters the *niyat,* portion by portion in respondable lengths, first in Arabic, followed by the congregation in chorus, and then in Javanese also followed by the others in chorus. The *niyat* translates as follow:

> I intend to do fasting tomorrow, for the fulfilment of the duty during the fasting month this year, to obey the order from God, the One.[45]

[44] I found however, actions and movements of prayer in some *tajug* and *pesantren* even slower and in much better Arabic utterance than at *Muhammadiyah* mosque in Kalitengah.

[45] Its Javanese is: *"Niyat isun puasa ing dina besuk iki, saking anekani fardune ulan Ramdhan ing taun iki, krana miturut prentahe Gusti Allah ta'ala."*

They do this to prevent someone in the congregation from missing his *niyat*, because *niyat* in any worship, according to them, is very important for the validity of the worship, in this case, fasting. After speaking the *niyat* in chorus, the *traweh* congregation breaks up, accompanied by chanting *puji-pujian*. All these practices are considered to be additional work which, if God will accept them (and they hope He will), can gain merit for them. To the local modernists, however, all these things are nothing but sinful innovations.

The elaborate *traweh* done in prayer houses, which takes approximately 45 minutes, is still followed by another activity. The next activity is *darusan* or *tadarus* where a group of around six people sit around facing each other on mats for *nderes* (a reading exercise), with their legs folded (*sila*). Each person has a small bench in the front of him on which the Qur'an is placed. One of the group reads the Qur'an while the others follow him by memory and correct any misread verse or wrong utterance. When reading pauses between consecutive verses the others yell: "Allah", or "Allah ya rasul Allah." When a reader feels tired he stops reading and someone else in the group takes a turn; the former reader becomes a corrector. When someone becomes tired after reading and correcting, he may quit the group and another may enter.

Darusan may proceed until late in the evening or until early morning. This depends very much on the number and desire of those attending. When the whole Qur'an is read, a special invocation (*do'a*) called *khataman* (completion), is recited and rice mounts (*tumpeng*) with other dishes are served. The service comes from a volunteering household(s) that wants to serve it. Some snacks (*jaburan*) are even served everyday at the mosques for *ta'jil*, and for supper after *darusan*. More abundant food is served at *maleman*, the uneven night of the twentieth (21st, 23rd, 25th, 27th and 29th). On these nights villages are lit up by *damar malem* (a sort of candlelight especially lit on this occasion).

The frequency of completion of the reading of the Qur'an varies from one group to another; in some, it is targeted, in another it is not. Sometimes, completions are achieved through alternate and concurrent reading. This is what is normally done; yet during the later stages, some groups are eager to make more frequent completions and then, instead of reading the Qur'an alternately in the regular way, they take the 30 divisions (*juz*) of the Qur'an, then divide them by the number of the group. This results in each member having a certain number of *juz* to read. This procedure is usually adopted when the fasting month has almost reached its end.

Along with *darusan* more devout individuals attempt to complete reading the Qur'an individually at home, at least once during the Fasting month. Reading the Qur'an in the Fasting month is considered very meritorious. A visit to the mosque (*i'tikaf*), even just for a short stop, also has merit, much more so when combined with praying or reading the Qur'an.

CHARITY AND OTHER PRACTICES OF IBADAT

The glory of Fasting reaches its climax on *Riaya*, the first day of *Syawal* (**Shawwal**), the tenth month of the Islamic calendar. It marks the end of *Puasa*, where requirement of abstinence from eating, drinking, smoking and sexual intercourse during the day time is removed. At *riaya* every single household has a feast. Preparation for this, of such things as new clothing, nice food and special dishes are made a few days earlier. Funding for this is anticipated for several months. Since everyone does the same thing, from the middle of Fasting month onward, market activities increase considerably (*mremaan*) and culminate a few days before *riaya*. Their peak is two days before *riaya* on what is called *mrema cilik* and one day before on what is called *mrema gede*. The village environment is cleansed; houses and fences are painted. Of particular importance is *tipar* (cleansing the cemeteries from weeds and grass). Every household has a share in cleaning the graves of relatives and elders to make the visit on *riaya* comfortable. Like the beginning of *Puasa*, *riaya* is signified by the sound of *peteter* from the mosque but unlike *Puasa* where the sound of *peteter* takes only about ten to fifteen minutes, at Riaya *peteter* is sounded continuously on three periods, from 4.00 p.m. of the last day of *Ramadan* until sunset, from the break after evening prayer (*'Isya*) to twelve midnight, and from the break after *'Id* prayer in the morning until noon of *riaya*. In the evening, accompanying the incessant sound of *peteter*, a group of people gather at mosques and prayer houses for *takbiran* (to chant a long version of *takbir*, exalting God in Arabic). The verse of the *takbir* follows the tradition of other parts of the Muslim world although the chanting melody must be peculiarly local. The verse of the *takbir* translates as follows:

God is the Greatest (three times),
There is no god but (the true) God.
God is the Greatest, God is the Greatest,
and His is the praise.

Surely God is the Greatest.
His is the abundant praise,
Glory to Him, day and night,
There is no god but God, the One true God,
He fulfilled His promise, supported His servant,
granted His soldiers a manifest victory,
and inflicted decisive defeat on the allied enemies,
There is no god but God,
and we worship none but Him, with sincere devotion,
even though the disbelievers may resent it.

O God! Exalt and have blessings on our Master Muhammad,
And on the people of our Master Muhammad,

And on the supporters of our Master Muhammad,
And on the wives of our Master Muhammad,
And on the descendants of our Master Muhammad,
All salute all of them with much peace.[46]

Takbiran is also performed by groups of people who march around throughout the village with candlelight and fire-sparkles; some others use trucks, large and small, equipped with sound systems, by which they go around forming mobile groups of *takbiran* (*takbir keliling*). The sound of takbiran ceases at dawn when the call to morning prayer is sounded. It starts again after morning prayer through the commencement of **'Id** prayer, and from the break up of **'Id** prayer until noon.

Meanwhile, since the first beat of *peteter*, exchanges of foods occur between households. Women and girls do almost all the work in the preparation for exchanging food; an example of the short courtesies which occur in the exchange of food is as follows:

> ... a girl from a neighbouring house comes to Man Pingi's house with a large tray on her left shoulder. Her left hand supports the tray from below and her right hand crosses her chest holding the tray at the edge. She is bringing food for Man Pingi (a Qur'anic teacher). She stops at the door saying: "kula nuwun" ("may I enter"); then Bu Pingi (Man Pingi's wife), the hostess, answers in a smiling welcome: "mangga" ("please"), and she asks the girl to come in. The girl puts the tray down on the table and waits until the food is taken from the tray. While emptying the food onto her plates and bowls Bu Pingi smiles and says: "Girl, is it riaya? Where are you going for a picnic in riaya?" The girl answers: "I really don't know, Mum, that is what people say and I have not decided yet where to go." Then she asks for permission to leave the house and brings the empty dishes back with her. Bu Pingi answers with thanks and accompanies her up to the door. Man Pingi's family gets various kinds of food from others; in return his wife (Bu Pingi) also sends her own to neighbouring households.[47]

Along with the exchange of foods, *riaya* in the village is marked by the crisscrossing of people who go and return from paying *zakat*. Zakat, which is either staple food (*zakat fitrah*) or wealth (*zakat pekaya* or **mal**) constitutes the third pillar of Islam. *Zakat fitrah* is a must and a duty imposed on all Muslim household heads who possess the amount of *zakat* after providing food for himself and those whom he feeds for a day and a night, together with the expenditure which he incurs for his dependants such as wife and children. It is

[46] Abdalati, H. (1991), *Islam in Focus*, Singapore: The Muslim Converts' Association, p 77.
[47] Field notes.

paid in staple food (3.5 litres of rice per person) as purification for the one who fasts from vain things, and as a help and sustenance to the poor. *Zakat pekaya* is imposed by Islam for those who have a surplus. It comes from the assumption that within the abundance we get, there is a certain amount which is not really ours. Roughly, *zakat pekaya* amounts to 2.5 per cent of the surplus one keeps throughout the year, excluding non commercial things such as private abode, personal clothing, furniture, means of transport and equipment. Unlike *zakat pekaya* which by and large is paid in money and usually handled by adults or parents a few days before riaya, *zakat fitrah* is handed from parents and taken by boys and girls directly to the individual recipient whom the parents have already ascertained. Sometimes it is sent indirectly via an *amil* at the evening of *riaya* until dawn in the morning before going to **'Id** prayer (*sembayang riaya*).[48]

As soon as they have finished morning prayer, men, women, boys and girls, in their finest clothes and perfume (including those who usually known as non-observers) go to the *desa* mosques, prayer houses and public squares where the congregation for **'Id** prayer is held. In Kalitengah, some prayer houses also hold a congregation but the largest, attended by more than 1,500 people, is at the *desa* mosque. In Kalitengah, *Muhammadiyah* holds its own congregation at the public square and this is attended by around 200 followers, including the members from the neighbouring *desa*. The prayer starts at 7.30 a.m., two *raka'at*, led by an *Imam*. The prayer is no different from ordinary prayers except that at the beginning of the first and second *raka'at*, *takbir* is uttered nine and seven times respectively in an audible voice, instead of only once as at the ordinary prayer. The prayer is followed by a sermon which stresses the meaning and merits of *zakat*, more specifically the *fitrah*.[49] Concluded by *du'a* the sermon ends and everyone gets up to return home. While standing they shake each other's hands and thus, almost instantly, the congregation turns into a mass of people shaking hands. The act of shaking hands, called *pangapuraan* (pardoning each other) does not stop here but continues thereafter, everywhere and anywhere they meet each other. Returning from congregation, older people stay at home, whereas teenagers form groups, large and small. The members of each group are usually peers who are acquainted with each other. They go around the hamlets cheerfully, from door to door to see everyone they know, particularly elders, shake their hands and ask their pardon, saying: "*Nyuwun pangapunten*

[48] *Amil* is a person or a group of persons who, on ad hoc basis, collect and distribute the *zakat*. In Kalitengah, there were two *amil*, each was formed by both *Muhammadiyah* and NU. Each distributed money and rice to about 140 recipients who were local poor residents. Some received only from Muhammadiyah, some only from NU but mostly received from both. Muhammadiyah distributed Rp 12,500.00 and around a kilo and a half of rice per recipient. NU which had slightly more recipients than Muhammadiyah distributed Rp.12,000.00 and one kilo of rice per recipient. In fact, most recipients were NU members or sympathisers.

[49] The same process is repeated about two months later on the occasion of 'Id al-Adha but instead of *zakat* and *fitrah*, the sermon focuses its discussion on the nature, history and merits of sacrifice and its relevance to the current situation faced by the Muslims.

kula Man/Bi/Ki/Nyi..." ("I beg your pardon Mr/Mrs..."). If the person being visited is someone with whom they are well acquainted or another group of about the same age the phrase is less formal: "*Njaluk pangapura isun ya Man/Bi or* ...(I ask for your pardon Mr/Mrs or ... name); the person being visited or met answers in courtesies: "*Sewangsule ya cung, nok, ... ayo njagong dingin, njabur.*" ("So do I, boy, girl, ... please sit down and have a bite). In return the visitors reply: "*Kesuhun, mengkin malih mawon, kulae ajeng mrika krihin.*" ("Thank you but we have to visit others first, we shall come again later"). In some households where they are well known, however, they drop in for some time, to be served with food and drinks while talking, chatting, joking and teasing, sharing happiness and cheer with each other.

While teenagers are going around the hamlets rushing from house to house to ask for pardon and forgiveness from the occupants, adult married men and some older people, sometimes with their grown up male children, visit the graves of their deceased relatives and elders to *ngembang* or *nyekar* (to put flowers on the graves). They pray for the deceased's well being and for the mercy of God, concluding by putting *kembang selasih* on the graves, between the grave stones.[50] After *ngembang*, they go around with their family members, especially wife and children, visiting their living elders and relatives on both the husband's and the wife's sides. For those who have many relatives the visits by family members may take a few days. To miss visiting a particular family especially an elder on *riaya* (or the subsequent days) without reason is considered contemptuous and something that everyone should avoid. Sending cards by mail is not enough and this is common only between friends and relatives living at different localities. It is even considered an insult to send a card to a father or mother in-law. An ordinary handwritten letter, not a card, however, is acceptable for those who live in the *tanah sebrang* (outside Java) or in Java but have difficulties that make a visit impossible. Along with its religious sacredness, *Riaya* or *Lebaran* or *Iedul Fitri* (**'Id al Fitr**) is thus used by Cirebonese as an occasion by which solidarity and kinship ties, which may have loosened over the previous months, are reaffirmed.

Muslims everywhere, including the Cirebonese have in fact, two main Holidays known throughout Java as *Riaya* or *Lebaran*; one is **'Id al-Fitr**, the festival at the end of the Fast and the other is **'Id al-Adha**, the Festival for Sacrifice. In Cirebon they are called *R(i)aya Kecil* and *R(i)aya Agung*.[51] *Riaya Kecil* refers to the celebration at the end of the Fast, whereas *Riaya Agung*, which falls on the 10th day of *Raya Agung*. (**Dzu'l-Hijjah**), the twelfth month of either Javanese

[50] *Kembang selasih* is a special species of flower, used only for this purpose and at this special occasion (*riaya*); it is not used on visits on other occasions. This flower is used, probably because of its name *sel(asih)*, as a symbolic expression of *asih* (love).
[51] In Bahasa Indonesia the *riaya* are respectively, known as *Idul or Iedul Fitri* and *Lebaran* and *Idul or Iedul Adha* or *Lebaran Haji*

or Islamic calendar, follows on the completion of the course of pilgrimage to Mecca (*Hajj*). People do the same things and observe the same traditions on both *Riaya Kecil* and *Riaya Agung* but unlike *Riaya Kecil* which is marked by *zakat, Riaya Agung* is marked by sacrificing cattle (goats, sheeps, buffaloes and oxen). The animals for sacrifice must be male, healthy and in perfect condition with reasonable weight. They can be obtained quite easily everywhere because for the **'Id** occasion, many people take the opportunity to become casual retailers. The price of cattle generally increases by more than double; a good sheep for sacrifice, which usually costs Rp 160,000.00 becomes Rp 350.000.00 two days before *Riaya Agung*.

The slaughtering which occurs on three consecutive days from the break up of **'Id** prayer is done individually or in mass, organised mainly by the mosques and prayer houses.

In Kalitengah, at the time when the **'Id** prayer was performed, I saw seven sheep and one water buffalo slaughtered in the yard of *desa* mosque. Whereas Pak Shofie had only one sheep of his own to be slaughtered individually at his prayer house. He invited his neighbours to witness the slaughtering, help him skin the animal, have *satay* (barbecue) and distribute the meat. Except for a few seconds at the moment of slaughtering, when the knife is applied to the animal's neck, at which time *Basmalah* and *Salawat* are uttered in a murmur by the slaughterer preceding the flow of the animal's blood, everything seems to be very technical; neither a solemn nor a sacred expression is exhibited by those who attend. Unless one knows that it has a transcendental basis (God's order, rooted in the story of Abraham and Ismael, and coinciding with other Muslims who are doing pilgrimage in Mecca) the sacrifice, at the first glance, is no more than a process of butchery and distribution of meat. So is *zakat*, both *zakat pekaya* and *zakat fitrah*, no more than the collection and distribution of money and rice. To the people nevertheless, these rituals are both *ibadat* and *adat* at the same time.

Plate 8: Attending sermon at 'Id prayer.

Plate 9: Pak Shofie (third from left) and his sons pray at Pak Shofie's mother's tomb after 'Id prayer (at left is the researcher).

Chapter 5: The Ritual Practice: Adat

INTRODUCTION

"Ma ra-a hul mu 'minuna hasanan
Fa huwa 'indallahi hasanun"

"What the faithful believers find good,
is [presumably] good on the side of God."

(Hadith transmitted by Ahmad).

This Chapter deals with the ritual practice of *adat* which is nearly the same thing as what Rippin called the "additional ritual", the ritual outside the enactment of the Five-pillars, used by the Muslims to express their identity. It thus, lies outside the domain of *ibadat* in the narrower sense. Some of the *adat* activities are undeniably Muslim creations, some others have unclear origins but all of these practices have an Islamic flavour. Other activities refer to indigenous ceremonies which are likely to have a non-Islamic origin but are tolerated or retained because they have been Islamised in that they have undergone modification from their original form. Their existence in their present form is harmless to the Islamic faith or has even been incorporated into it and is used as an expression of particular local Muslim identity. Among *adat* rituals belonging to the first type are commemorations of the Islamic holy days; those belonging to the second are thanksgivings (*syukuran* or *tasyakuran*) and *slametan* related to the individual life cycle and the commemoration of the death of a person. Examples of those belonging to the third are the communal feasts related to the agricultural season.

THE NATURE OF ADAT

Before going further into a description of *adat* rituals in Cirebon, it is worthwhile to take a brief look at the nature of *adat* and how they relate to the Cirebonese context. This is important because the relation between *adat* and Islam is an interesting subject of analytical discourse.

The word *adat* is derived from Arabic **'adat** (plural form of **'adah**) meaning custom, or habit and is considered as synonymous with **'urf**, something which is commonly known or accepted. It generally refers to the result of long-standing convention, either deliberately adopted or the result of unconscious adaptation to circumstances, that has been followed where practical considerations have been uppermost.[1] By this definition, even an animal is said to have its own *adat*.[2] The early Sunni scholars considered some **'urf** as the roots of the *fiqh*, but in

[1] Levy, R. (1957), *The Social Structure of Islam*, London: Cambridge University Press, p. 248.
[2] See: "Adat Law" in *Encyclopedia of Islam*.

Wahhabi Arabia, **'urf**, if contrary to the rigid code held by the rulers, is stigmatised as a *taghut*, the mistaken conduct of the ungodly *Jahiliya* way.[3] Since the nineteenth century, especially due to the influence of Van Vollenhoven, ter Haar and Snouck Hurgronje *adat* has been used by colonial government in Indonesia as a legal term designating a prescriptive right, which was given currency as an independent legal entity apart from the canon law of Islam (*syari'ah*).[4] Local *adat* was encoded into units of jural management, whereby legal pluralism in colonial Indonesia was introduced.[5] Under this scheme, based on a classification of *adat* systems as cultural geographic units, the Dutch divided Indonesia into at least nineteen *adat* law areas.[6] So called *adat law* rather than *syari'ah*, was then imposed wherever possible in an attempt to divorce the indigenous people from Islam. *Adat* law, however, was applied inconsistently as at the same time, under the 1854 Constitution (article 75, para 3), the application of *adat* rules which were in conflict with generally recognised principles of justice in European terms was strictly forbidden.[7]

Meanwhile, the ensuing discourse on South-East Asian Muslim societies concerning the relation between Islam and *adat* has become unclear. *Adat* is sometimes described as either mingling, suggesting an unstructured mixing, or as conflicting, suggesting the reification and existence of two separate bodies of knowledge and practice. Either view, according to Ellen, is a profoundly misleading over-simplification.[8]

In Cirebon, the word *adat* is generally used precisely to refer to custom, habit or any form of ordinary behaviour commonly adhered to by many people (*barang apa bae kang wis biasa dilakoni deng wong akeh*). To illustrate this meaning, the following expressions may be helpful:

> Different places have different *adat* (customs); the *adat* of people here is like this, whereas the *adat* of people over there is like that.[9]
>
> It is the people's *adat* (customs) here to wear *sarung* and *topong* at prayer.[10]

Commenting to someone who complains about the demanding and frequent crying child, one says:

[3] Levy, R. (1957), pp. 248–249.
[4] See: "Ada", in *The Shorter Encyclopedia of Islam*.
[5] Ellen, R.F. (1983), "Social Theory, Ethnography and the Understanding of Practical Islam in South-East Asia", in Hooker, M.B. (1983) ed, *Islam in South-East Asia*, Leiden: E.J. Brill. p. 52. ter Haar, B. (1948), *Adat Law in Indonesia*, New York: Institute of Pacific Relations.
[6] Hooker, M.B. (1978), *Adat Law in Modern Indonesia*, Kuala Lumpur: Oxford University Press, pp. 16, 30.
[7] Ibid, p. 46.
[8] Ellen, R.F. (1983), "Social Theory, Ethnography and the Understanding of Practical Islam in South-East Asia", p. 64.
[9] "Sejen tempat ya sejen adat; wong kene adate mengkenen, wong kana adate mengkonon."
[10] " *Adate wong kene iku ari sembayang ya sarungan karo topongan.*"

> It is its *adat* (nature) if a child likes crying (so do not complain nor be startled).[11]

Many other examples can be put forward but the point is that *adat*, from the Cirebonese perspective, is no more than custom. While like in other parts of Java there is no such a thing as *desa adat*, neither is there an *adat* official, nor is there, at least in contemporary Cirebon, any jural implication of such so-called *adat*. Rather, *adat* is conceived as a natural phenomenon whose occurrence commonly and inherently contributes to human conduct, to the way of doing things such as religious duties or social behaviour. Some *adat* may be genuinely of local creation while other *adat* may be of foreign origin. Some is ritualised and other *adat* is loosely technical. Most people are hardly aware of when *adat* came into being or where it came from. From their religious view point, some *adat* is good and other *adat* is bad; some matches precisely with the *syari'ah* set forth in *fiqh*, other *adat* matches the ethical spirit emanating from Islam. Still other *adat* just parallels Islam, while some other *adat* may stand in opposition to Islam. The *sepikulan-segendongan* principle in the Javanese rules of inheritance whereby a male sibling gets twice that of a female is an example of *adat* belonging to the first.[12] Many forms of feasts may be the example of the second, the use of local clothing to cover *'awrat* at prayer is an example for the third, whereas such activities as cock-fighting, betting and gambling at the *lebaran* festival are examples of the fourth. Given that *adat* may either be good or bad, its treatment, whether one wishes to keep it or avoid it, is subject to an individual's own ethical consideration be they of Islamic, Christian, or any other origin.

The quotation from the *hadith* at the begining of this Chapter comes from Pak Soleh (44 years), the thoughtful trader already acknowledged in the preceding chapter, the one who enunciated the broader and narrower meaning of *ibadat*.[13] He claimed that the *hadith* is one of the scriptural bases that guides him whether to accept or reject certain *adat*. In relation to a number of ritual and ceremonial activities belonging to *adat*, it is the true believers, represented by *ulama* and pious figures, who attest to a practice's Islamic validity. He asserted, that such activities as the commemoration of Islamic holy days and many forms of *slametan* have gained support from, and have become part of the favourable work of many *ulama*, pious figures and *kyai*. It is enough to say that these activities, according to Pak Soleh, have become good Muslims' *adat* (*wis dadi adate wong Islam kang bagus*) and have a certain Islamic significance. It is thus, unnecessary and, sometimes even difficult, to set a clear boundary between *adat* and *syari'ah*.

[11] Its Javanese reads: "*Ya* adate *ari bocah iku ya doyan nangis*."

[12] Some informants said that the *sepikulan-segendongan* is *hukum* (Islamic law) which has become *adat*, and is commonly practiced even by ignorant people, although there are some who apply an equal division of inheritance.

[13] The hadith can be found, for example in, Ad-Dairabi, Al-'Alim al-' Alama asy-Syeikh (n.d.), *Al-Mujarrabah ad-Dairabi al-Kabir*, Semarang: Al-Munawar, p. 74.

To clarify the relationship between the two, Pak Soleh gave the following illustration:

> The case of *adat* and *syari'ah* is just like doing prayer and wearing *sarung* and *topong*. Prayer belongs to *syari'ah*, wearing *sarung* and *topong* belong to Javanese *adat*. How then, should they be separated? It is true that doing prayer is valid without wearing *sarung* and *topong* provided the *awrat* is covered. But clearly, doing prayer and wearing *sarung* and *topong* are united, they are not opposed to *syari'ah*; rather, in our taste, it even looks better as it indicates more humbleness to God.[14]

Pak Soleh's approach to *adat* vis-a-vis *syari'ah* undeniably represents the position of many traditionalist Muslim villagers. Unfortunately, this position stands against the main stream of *Indologie* scholarship put forward by Snouck Hurgronje and others who, under the guise of scholarship, exploited *adat* and Islam as a means to enable the colonial government to exercise easier political control. In dealing with Islam in South-East Asia, Hurgronje and others have successfully enjoyed esteem for arguing for the necessary separation and opposition between *adat* and *syari'ah* (Islam).[15] Virtually, the reliability of this colonial scholarship is now under siege from the current trend of more objective research.

Based on a strong denial of the significance of Islam in Dutch colonial policy and in the interest of preventing the emergence of a national integrity in the colonial state, ethnic divisions were fostered. In the meantime, the European colonial cultures, especially British and Dutch, misunderstood and distorted Islam from the very start when they made systematic descriptions of it. Ironically, it is this confusion and distortion which provided the framework for the scholarship of Islam in South-East Asia that followed.[16]

Leaving aside this issue for a while, it might be useful to echo Hooker's assertion that Islam, being the youngest of the world's monotheistic religions, in its own view, is intended to complete the great Judeo-Christian traditions. Also in its own view, Islam prescribes a complete scheme for the temporal and spiritual worlds and thereby it does not separate religion from daily life, something that the secular West can hardly comprehend.[17] Yet, to understand the local manifestations of great traditions such as Islam, it is not enough to simply focus

[14] Interview 3-4-1992: "Ari antarane adat karo syare'at iku ya kayadene sembayang ngenggo sarung karo topong. Sembayang iku syare'at, sarungan karo topongan iku adate wong Jawa. La priben kudu misahe? Ya bener, wong sembayang sih, bli sarungan karo topongan maning gan, asal nutup 'aurat ya sah. Tapi, sembayang ngenggo sarung iku wis dadi siji, bli bertentangan karo syare'at; malah, munggu pengrasane wong kene, luwih bagus sabab nuduhaken luwih ta'dzim Ningi Gusti Allah."

[15] Hooker, M.B. (1983) ed, *Islam in South East Asia*, Leiden: E.J. Brill, pp. 59–60.

[16] Ellen, R.F. (1983), "Social Theory, Ethnography and the Understanding of Practical Islam in South-East Asia", pp. 52–53.

[17] Hooker, M.B. (1983) ed, p. vii.

on ethnographic particularities alone, especially the ethnography of colonial vintage which, according to Ellen, has failed to make valuable contribution in analysing Muslim belief and practice other than as a part of a cultural assemblage.[18] It is true, as Ellen holds, that an initial recognition of distinctive Muslim culture within the totality of Islamic tradition is a prerequisite before one starts to grapple with an understanding of the local expression of the Islamic faith. Muslims all over the world live within diverse cultural niches whose expressions of identity bear the colour of their diversity, one of which is in the form of various *adat*. With these convictions, I shall start my discussions of *adat* to include the following items.

THE COMMEMORATION OF ISLAMIC HOLY DAYS

The genuine Islamic nature of ritualised *adat* is probably best seen in the commemoration of either Islamic holy days or holy months. It is difficult to trace historically, when this type of ritual began. Rippin indicates that activities such as *mawlid* festivals for celebrating the birth of Prophet Muhammad were not fully established until about the thirteenth century A.D.[19] But commemoration of other days have explicit scriptural roots in the Qur'an and the Hadith, suggesting that it was already being practiced when the Prophet was still alive.

In dealing with this subject, I am more concerned with how the commemorations are performed than with their historical origins, although the latter can not be ignored. There are at least four months in Islam which bear commemorative significance because they are claimed as sacred; they are: Dzu'l-Qa'idah (*Kapit*), Dzu'l-Hijjah (*Raya Agung*), Muharram (*Sura*) and Rajab (*Rejep*). These are respectively the eleventh, the twelfth, the first and the seventh month of the Islamic and Javanese lunar calendar.[20] During these months Muslims are forbidden to engage in warfare unless forced into it for reasons of self-defence. This reckoning is rooted in the Holy Qur'an, saying:

> "The number of months (in a year) in the sight of Allah is twelve; so ordained by Him the day He created the heavens and the earth. Of them four are sacred; That is the right religion, so wrong not yourself therein ..."[21]

The Qur'an, in fact, does not mention these specific months, it is the commentators who instigated so.

Along with these sacred months there are other months in which certain day(s) are held by many Muslims as being holy and on which they make celebration.

[18] Ibid, p. 53.
[19] Rippin, A. (1990), p. 98.
[20] *The Holy Qur'an, English Translation of the Meanings and Commentary*, p 510; Adnan, K.H.M. (1969), *Peringatan Hari-Hari Besar Islam*, Sala: A.B. Siti Syamsijah, p. 6.
[21] (QS 9:36).

They are: Safar (*Sapar*), Rabi' al-Awwal (*Mulud*), Sya'ban (*Ruwah*) and Ramadhan (*Puasa*), being respectively the second, the third, the eighth and the ninth months of the Javanese calendar. This makes eight out of the twelve months that have commemorative significance of one form or another. By means of commemoration or celebration, attachment to a Muslim identity is expressed. The significance, of these months can be traced in Islamic history rather than in any formal scriptural ordinance. The general pattern of commemoration and celebration of Islamic holy days consists of one, or a combination, of the following: invocation, fasting, non-obligatory prayer, recital of the Qur'an, recital of the biography of certain religious figures or of the related stories which sanctify that particular day or month, and offerings of food or other material. Although not necessarily, more often than not, celebration is accompanied by some form of feast. Currently, as a result of recent development, the commemoration of Islamic holy days focuses on *pengajian* (a public speech) given by an orator intentionally called for this purpose. *Pengajian* reduces the many different forms of commemoration to a uniformity in which variations and differences are apparent only in the references, content and messages of the speaker.

Suroan

Suroan means celebrating or commemorating *Suro* or *Sura*. Etymologically, the word *sura*, in old Javanese (*Kawi*), means giant; in Sanskrit it means god or goddess, powerful, brave, warrior, monkey.[22] It is difficult to relate directly these meanings to this context. The most likely explanation is that it is local reference to the Arabic term *'Asyura* referring to the tenth (day) of Muharram. The first day of the month is, therefore, the new year and its celebration commemorates the new year of the Islamic lunar calendar. Its reckoning started on the day when the Prophet Muhammad and his companions fled from Mecca to seek refuge in Medina in AD 622. This refuge is referred to as ***hijrah***, hence the calendar's name is derived and usually linked with the starting point for the rise of Islam and its historical upheaval.[23] A wise adaptation of the older Javanese calendrical system (*tahun Saka*) into the Islamic one was made in 1663 by Sultan Agung of Mataram with the Javanese starting point set at AD 78.[24] Under the new system the first month of the Javanese calendar coincided with the first month of the Islamic ones.

[22] Dirdjosiswojo (1957), *Kawi-Djinarya*, Djilid 1, Klaten: Pertjetakan Republik Indonesia, p. 215.

[23] Citing *Wedyaprada*, Adnan claims that the Islamic calendar was firstly adopted in Java in AD 1443 when Raden Fatah, under the supervision of Sunan Giri, one of the nine Javanese *wali* who settled in Gresik, set up a settlement called Bintara. See: Adnan, K.H.M. (1969), *Peringatan Hari-Hari Besar Islam*, pp. 12–13.

[24] Simuh (1988), *Mistik Islam Kejawen Raden Ngabehi Ranggawarsita*, Jakarta: University of Indonesia Press, pp 11–12. The reckoning of *Tahun Saka* refers to a legendary figure of Ajisaka, probably an Indian, who came to Java in AD 78 and created (or introduced) the Javanese alphabet. In Cirebonese literary tradition Ajisaka is referred to as Syeikh Subakir (see Chapter Three).

In Cirebon, *Suroan* refers to either the first or the tenth day of *Sura* or Muharram. Along with the New Year celebration of the Javanese Islamic calendar the first of *Sura* is also acclaimed as the *Hari Jadi* (the Founding Day) of the city of Cirebon. The story goes back to the legend of 15th century Cirebon when Walangsungsang, son of Prabu Siliwangi, King of Pajajaran, and his younger sister Rarasantang, left the Pajajaran palace. In his nine-month adventure Walangsungsang obtained a wife, Indang Geulis, daughter of Sang Hyang Danuwarsih, a Hermit at the mount of Maarapi. He, his wife and his sister reached Pasambangan where they studied the Islamic faith with Syeikh Datu Kahfi and Syeikh Nurjati, religious teachers of Arab origin. After two years of study, Walangsungsang established a settlement at Kebon Pesisir on the southern side of Amparan Jati hill near the shore, some 5 km east of Pasambangan. A calculation made by the Committee for the history of Cirebon determined that this establishment occurred on 1 Sura around AD 1445. Walangsungsang also built a place of worship named Tajug Jalagrahan, the oldest prayer house in Cirebon. Later, the settlement grew into a busy village and was visited and settled by people of various races, religions, languages, customs and means of livelihood. The village was then called Caruban which means the melting pot of various people.

The celebration of the New Year and the *Hari Jadi* of Cirebon is, however, significant only among the *kraton* (court) circle and, currently, the local Government. Among the *kraton* circle, as Siddique noted, the celebration is performed by the reading of *Babad* Cirebon (Cirebon Chronicle) at the *kraton* and a procession to the grave complex at Astana Gunung Sembung. For the local government, on the other hand, *Hari Jadi* is more like a civil festival than a religious one. Its celebration, which is officially organised by a committee specially set up for that purpose, takes a few weeks. Sports competitions and arts festivals, especially local arts such as *Tarling* opera, *wayang golek, topeng* dance and *serimpi,* are the most important parts of the program. It culminates at night when a ceremony and display is held for the competition and festival winners. On the same night there are also open stages in front of Kecamatan and other government offices where these entertainments are performed.

The sanctity of Muharram appears from the very name of the month in that, the Arabic word Muharram, exactly means "that which is made sacred" (derived from *haram,* meaning sacred). In addition, there is also a possibility that the name *'Asyura* is related to *'asyu-nura* (also Arabic) meaning those who have obtained divine light.[25] According to local belief, the day of *'Asyura,* which falls on the tenth of Muharram, recalls a number of important events. It traces the history of the great monotheistic traditions. On 10 Muharram the first apostle of God, Adam, was sent to earth; God gave His grace to Adam and Eve when

[25] Adnan, K.H.M. (1969), p. 12.

they sought repentance after being thrown out of paradise; Henoch (Idris) was endowed by God with a noble position; Noah and his disciples touched land safely with their ark; Abraham was saved without harm after being burned by the King Namrud of Babylon; Moses got revelation directly from God in the Sinai desert; Joseph was set free from jail and his name was cleared of the accusation of having raped Zulaikha, the then Egyptian King's wife. Yacob recovered from serious eye disease; Jonas came out safely from the belly of a sea monster (the giant *khut/nun* fish). The day of *'Asyura* also coincides with the recovery of Job (Ayyub) from serious cholera; it is the reunion of Jacob and Joseph after separation for forty years; it is the birth day of Jesus and his Ascension to heaven; it is also the day when the Prophet Muhammad married Khadijah; it is the day of the creation of the heavens, the earth, the Pen (*Qalam*), and of Adam and Eve.[26]

To commemorate so many important events the Cirebonese perform *slametan* or *sedekah*, which according to their belief is one form of *ibadat* (in the broader sense). They offer *bubur sura* or *bubur slabrak* to be distributed to neighbours and close kin. *Bubur sura* or *bubur slabrak* is a rice flour porridge with coconut milk containing various food-stuffs. The message behind this act is clear. The porridge (*bubur*) itself, which is white in colour, symbolises the day of *'Asyura*, which is holy, whereas the various foodstuffs contained in the *bubur* symbolise the various events that occurred on the day they are celebrating. But who, when and where the *adat* of offering *bubur sura* in celebrating *'Asyura* was began is unclear. Man Kasman (57 years), a batik maker, speculates that it was initiated by a *wali*.

While claiming that there is nothing wrong in having a *slametan* by offering *bubur sura*, even it is considered good because it is basically *sedekah*, and has become good *adat*, some fairly knowledgeable and devout individuals like Man **Hawari** (42 years) a thoughtful trader at Sumber Market, and others, suggested that the celebration of *'Asyura* would be better if it were conducted by performing some devotional undertaking such as fasting, voluntary prayer, reciting special invocations (*du'a*) called *du'a 'Asyura* after sunset prayer, feeding orphans and giving other forms of *sedekah*. He said that according to his *Kyai* when he was in *Pesantren* Leler in Banyumas (Central Java), doing these things

[26] Cf: Asy-Syafi'i, Abdur-Rahman as-Safuri, (n.d.), *Nazhat al Majalis*, vol. 1, Beirut: Al-Maktaba as-Sa'baniya, p. 174. Among the Syi'ite-which seems to be less significant for people in Cirebon- the *'Asyura* is the day for the commemoration of the death of Husein, son of 'Ali. The latter was the fourth Caliph, thus Husein was a grandson of the Prophet Muhammad). Husein was counted as the third *imam*. The first two *imams* are the Prophet Muhammad and Ali themselves. Husein was cruelly killed by Umayyad Caliph of Damascus at Karbela in A.H 61 (October 10, AD 680). The difference between the Sunni and Syi'ite tradition regarding 'Asyura is therefore, among the Sunni *'Asyura* is joyous, whereas among the Syi'ite it is apprehensive.

on the day of *'Asyura* is religiously meritorious.[27] *Slametan*, practiced by offering *bubur sura*, are still common in Trusmi. Pak Satira (38 years), a kerosene peddler, rarely does the prescribed prayers but he feels obliged to offer *bubur sura* to his neighbours and close kin because he thinks it is the easiest and most convenient way with which to express his obligation to remember God (*kanga isling Ningi Pyengana*).

Saparan

Saparan commemorates *Sapar* (**Safar**), the second month of the Javanese Islamic calendar. *Sapar* is locally known as the mating season for dogs, the locally considered unclean animal, and thus marriage is not recommended. Beside this, Sapar is believed to be the month in the year where frequent accidents, disasters and bad luck may occur (*wulan kang akeh blai*) especially on the last Wednesday of the month (*Rebo Wekasan*). It is not clear why or how this belief arose, but referring to the warning of some gnostics (**ahl al-Kashf**), Al-Dairaby declares that each year God reveals 350,000 accidents or disasters; most of which occur on the last Wednesday of Sapar. This makes the day the most precarious day of the year. A suggested attempt to avoid disaster is to perform a four-unit prayer, at each unit, after the *Fatiha*, the practice is to recite respectively Surah **al-Kautsar** (QS:108) 17 times at the first unit, **al-Ikhlas** (QS:112) five times at the second unit, **al-Falaq** (QS:113) once and **an-Nas** (QS:114) once respectively at the third and fourth unit and conclude with a special *du'a* of *'Asyura*.[28]

People take extra caution on this month by minimising long distant travel, dangerous work and sinful acts. Doing religiously good work such as helping others and giving *sedekah*, especially to orphans and widows, is highly recommended. In accordance with this, during the month of *Sapar* the Cirebonese have three peculiar popular traditions of commemoration: *Ngapem, Ngirab*, and *Rebo Wekasan*.

Ngapem refers to *apem*, baked or steamed cakes made of lightly fermented rice-flour. *Apem* are to be eaten with *kincah* (a dark brown liquid made of palm sugar and coconut milk). According to Man Syapi'i (62 years), an ex-farmer and trader, *ngapem*, a special feature for *slametan* on Sapar, is just like any other *slametan*. Along with its social function of maintaining brotherhood and community bonds, it has at least two other functions. The offering itself is religiously meritorious because it is one form of *sedekah*. The type of food, as in other *slametan*, contains a symbolic message. In this case, a pair of *apem* and *kincah* remind recipients, neighbours and close kin, to be cautious because it is *Sapar*, the month with many misfortunes. *Apem* symbolises the flesh or the

[27] For the scriptural bases (the hadith) and their explanations for the merits of doing these things, see: *Nazhat al Majalis*, vol. 1, pp. 173–175.
[28] Ad-Dairaby, S.A. (n.d.), p. 74.

body. When it is eaten it must be put into the *kincah* symbolising blood and thus reminds recipients of the possibility of the body falling into some misfortune.

Another informant said that *ngapem* is a relatively recent tradition initiated and spread from the court (*kraton*). Its root go back to the early decades of the 18th and 19th century Java when the Dutch attempted to suppress Islam and to spread Christianity. Muslims mostly failed in their resistance against the Dutch, the *kafir* (infidel). The failure of the Cirebonese revolt led by Bagus Serit and Bagus Rangin in 1818 is said to occur on Sapar. Because of military inferiority, the *kraton*, to keep functioning, had no choice but to use a double standard. While accepting negotiation and cooperation with the Dutch, it simultaneously spread enmity among the people to encourage them to oppose the Dutch. One means of doing this was to commemorate *Sapar*, the month of misery, by symbolising the Dutch as *apem* which must be crushed to bloodshed, *kincah*.

Because Sapar is a precarious month, a sudden death through accident or whatever is considered quite probable, especially on *Rebo Wekasan*. This is extremely unfortunate if it happens to someone who is in a sinful state. To anticipate this possibility and the coming of *Rebo Wekasan*, Sunan Kalijaga, who was believed to have stayed in Cirebon to learn Islam from Sunan Gunung Jati, carried out an extra bathing for purification with his disciples at the Drajat river in preparation for their religious devotion and repentance including *ratib* or *tahlil*.[29] This act was followed by others in subsequent years until finally it became *adat*. Until now, around *Rebo Wekasan* people go to Kalijaga to perform *ziarah* at the *petilasan* (a remnant of dwelling) of Sunan Kalijaga. After *ziarah*, those who wish can go up the river in decorated boats, which is a recent development, and bathe at the site where Sunan Kalijaga and his disciples were believed to have bathed. This *adat* is called *ngirab* meaning originally, 'shake something to remove the dirt on it.' In this case it probably means removal of one's sins, a symbolic act of repentance. Currently, there are some people who take this *adat* as having serious spiritual meaning, but for the majority it is just a cheerful picnic or a form of annual recreation to forget about the miserable month of *Sapar*.

The story of *Sapar* would be incomplete without touching upon the *Rebo Wekasan* which is its most crucial day. There is nothing special with the day except that, from the break up of night prayer (*Isya*) until dawn (*subuh*), youngsters, especially those who usually sleep in the *tajug* where they study the Qur'an (*ngaji*), split into groups of four to ten, and march from house to house chanting repeatedly in front of each door in chorus. Whenever they reach a house they chant: "*wur tawur nyi tawur, selamat dawa umur*", meaning "sow

[29] There is a *Desa* in Southern Cirebon called Kalijaga, where Sunan Kalijaga is believed to have stayed. The Drajat river passes this *desa*. Local people, until recently, relied heavily on this river for their water supply, especially for bathing and washing.

up Madam, may you be safe and have long life."[30] The host then opens the door and, before giving them some money, asks: "Whose *santri* are you?" The group members answer by mentioning their Qur'anic teacher from whom they learn the Qur'an or, when they do not belong to any *tajug*, they answer: "Blok-an," meaning "on a Block-basis," and then mention the name of their hamlet. This means that the group is formed on a local basis, the hamlet where they live, rather than on a *tajug*. They do this mostly for fun taking advantage of the prevailing *adat*. The money they get is distributed among themselves and used for their own purposes, most of them say for "*jajan*" (buying snacks).

The story of the origin of this practice is probably more interesting than the *adat* itself. The practice is generally attributed to the legendary figure of Syeikh Siti Jenar also known as Syeikh Lemah Abang alias Syeikh Datuk Abdul Djalil alias Syeikh Jabaranta. Once, according to legend, he was a member of the council of *Wali Sanga* (Nine *Wali* or Saints). But later he was sentenced to death by the wali tribunal for being accused of teaching Sufi doctrine publicly, including to laymen who were really unprepared to receive it. This resulted in the laymen misunderstanding the real Sufi doctrine. They by-passed the *syare'at* (*syari'ah*), the prerequisite for taking a mystical path. His teaching therefore was thought by the wali council to be dangerous for the establishment of *syare'at* and the development of Islam as a whole. At a trial held at the Agung Mosque, it was said, Syeikh Lemah Abang could not deny this allegation, thence the death penalty was decreed and Sunan Kudus carried out the execution using Sunan Gunung Jati's *keris* (dagger), *Kentanaga*. Syeikh was buried at Pemlaten, a grave complex in the southern city of Cirebon. After his death many of his followers, the *abangan* (followers of the teaching of Lemah Abang) felt a deep loss and emptiness.[31] Sunan Kalijaga suggested and it was agreed by Sunan Gunung Jati that under the guise of miserable *Rebo Wekasan*, the *abangan* group were advised to wander from house to house praying for the safety and long life of the villagers; in return the villagers were also advised to provide them with alms. Year after year such a practice was performed not only by the followers of Lemah

[30] In Sundanese villages the word *nyi* (madam) is replaced by *ji*, which stands for *Haji*, a reference or title for those who have been to Mecca; it is used here as an honorary reference to the host(ess), irrespective of whether or not the host(ess) is *haji*.

[31] One informant, who claimed that the term *abangan* refers to the followers of Syeikh Lemah Abang, explained that they (the *abangan*) do believe in one God and Muhammad as the apostle of God but are still reluctant to do religious duties for various reasons, mostly due to their ignorance about Islamic doctrine. They only do *slametan* because this is the easiest way to express their belief and sense of piety. Man Akmal (57 years) a trading commissioner (*palen*), a supposed *abangan*, did not deny such characterisation while advocating the principle of *padu bener bae* (just doing right). He said: "*Wong iku padu bener bae, rukun karo tangga, guru ratu wong tuwa karo kudu diormati; kanga apa sembayang jungkal-jungkel ari tindak lakune bli bener?*" ("The most important thing for an individual is committing good conduct, living in harmony with neighbours, respecting teachers, king (ruler) and one's parents; what is daily prayer for, if the daily conduct is improper?"). In daily life, at least during my field-work, the term *abangan*, if known, was hardly heard. Man Akmal, identifies himself as a *wong bener* (rightful people), not as *abangan*.

Abang but also by the students at many *tajug* and other youngsters as well and, at last, became an *adat*.

The story of Syeikh Siti Jenar or Lemah Abang seems to be the most obscure of the many legends of Javanese *wali*. He is very popular but nothing is known about him except his heretical mysticism and his open spreading of it. An example of the mystical flavour of Lemah Abang's heresy is indicated in the episode of how the *wali* council called Lemah Abang to come to the *wali* court. This episode is fairly well known in Cirebon, and dominates the whole story. The following is a concise summary of the episode given by Siddique:

> He was accused of publicly teaching a doctrine which could be summarised thusly: All that exists is a reflection of God, and because man exists, he is also a reflection of God. He was accused of heresy, and was invited to the *wali* council to explain his actions. He replied: "Syeikh Lemah Abang is not here, only God is here." The council sent another messenger to address himself to God, whereupon Syeikh Lemah Abang answered: "God is not here only Syeikh Lemah Abang is here." They then sent a messenger to ask for both God and Lemah Abang, and he had no choice but to follow them. At the meeting he failed to prove that his teachings had not led his pupils to false practices, like ignoring the five prayers, he was condemned to death and executed by Sunan Kudus ...[32]

Beside these stories, it is interesting that along with the probable connection between his name (Lemah Abang) and the well known term *abangan*,[33] some other intriguing questions remain unresolved.

Based on *Pustaka Negara Kretabhumi*, one of the many Cirebonese Chronicles, T.D. Sudjana wrote an historical novelette about the political turmoil in Cirebon which happened preceding the execution of Lemah Abang. In his account, among other things, the army commander of the Kingdom of Cirebon, Adipati Carbon, son of Pangeran Cakrabuana (the founder of Cirebon), son of Prabu Siliwangi of Pajajaran, faced a serious dilemma having to choose between loyalty to his king and to his mystical teacher (*guru* or *Syeikh*) to whom he had performed *bai'at* (religious vow). While the king, his own cousin, Syarif Hidayatullah, had earnestly entrusted him with the security and welfare of the whole kingdom, the *Syeikh* (Lemah Abang), on the other hand, urged him to take power by overthrowing the ruler. To show that it was serious, Lemah Abang, on this

[32] Siddique (1978), Relics of the Past? p.143. According to de Graaf and Pigeaud (1989), Sheik Lemah Abang was executed in the Demak Mosque. See their *Kerajaan-Kerajaan Islam di Jawa: Peralihan Dari Majapahit ke Mataram*, Jakarta: Grafiti Press, especially p. 262.

[33] The term *abangan* is established in literature by Clifford Geertz and became popular under his tri-cothomy thesis, "santri-priyayi-abangan". For detail, see: Geertz, C. (1976), *The Religion of Java*, Phoenix Edition: University of Chicago Press.

occasion, came to Cirebon Girang, where Adipati Carbon resided, with Kebo Kenanga, Lord of Pengging (Central Java), and his army. The reason advocated by Lemah Abang for overthrowing the ruler was appealing. Adipati Carbon's father, Pangeran Cakrabuana, who had established the Cirebon kingdom, had been at fault in giving the throne to Syarif, his nephew, rather than to his son, Adipati Carbon himself while, in fact, it was he who was the right heir of Cirebon and the great Pajajaran kingdom. In his puzzle, the Adipati performed a prayer and then **tawajuh** (meditation to recall his *Syeikh*). He saw, in his contemplation, the figure of his *Syeikh* smiling at him cynically, but then the figure grew smaller and smaller and finally, turned into a jasmine (*melati*) before the figure disappeared, leaving only the jasmine fragrance, which he could still smell even when he was completely awake. After meditation, he felt, his inclination to follow his *Syeikh's* instruction to rebel weaken. No sooner, had he decided what to do than his deputy, Ki Gedeng Cirebon Girang, brought him a message calling him to come immediately to the Agung Mosque where the *wali* council held an assembly. He went there immediately and found his *Syeikh* had already died. After burial he proposed a name for the site where his *Syeikh* was buried, "Pemlaten" or "Kemlaten", meaning the place of *melati* (jasmine), in commemoration of his sight of the *Syeikh* during his contemplation.[34]

The reliability of this story as an historical fact, whose main source is *babad*, is open to question, but the story illustrates the possibilities of new interpretations of Syeikh Lemah Abang. It is widely believed that all *wali*, including Syeikh Lemah Abang, were Sufi but, unlike other *wali* who were Sunni, Lemah Abang was said to belong to the *Syi'ah Muntadzar* sect who hold 12 Imam as their legitimate leaders. He came to Java from Baghdad and held a doctrine that claims that the *Imam* should be the supreme political figure in the state. Beside, Lemah Abang is considered to have held the *wujudiyah* Sufi doctrine, the same doctrine held by Al-Hallaj.[35] In the Babad Tanah Jawi he is said to have won converts of a number of rulers and their subjects in Pengging, Tingkir, Ngerang and Butuh.[36]

Muludan and Rajaban

M(a)uludan means celebrating *m(a)ulud* (from Arabic, **mawlid**, meaning birthday), the birth of the Prophet Muhammad on 12 **Rabi'al-Awwal** (*Mulud*), the third month of Javanese Islamic calendar. Although the Prophet is also

[34] See: Sudjana, T.D. (n.d.), *Kemelut di Bumi Pakungwati: Sebuah Novelette Sejarah Bersumber dari Naskah Negara Kretabhumi*, unpublished mimeograph, Cirebon: Seksi Kebudayaan, Kantor Departemen Pendidikan dan Kebudayaan, Kotamadya Cirebon.

[35] Al-Husayn b. Mansur Al-Hallaj (244/857-8-309/922) is a famous, indeed notorious, mystic whose utterances, actual or alleged, provoked much controversy both in his lifetime and later. He was cruelly executed in Baghdad for saying "I am the (Divine) Truth," although there must have been both religious and political motivations behind this execution (Netton, 1992, *A Popular Dictionary of Islam*, London: Curzon Press).

[36] See: *Babad Tanah Jawi*, Gravenhage: M. Nijhoff (1941), p.33.

believed to have died on the same date of his birth date, his death is not significant in this celebration. *Rajaban*, on the other hand, means celebrating the event which happened on *Rajab*, the *isra'-mi'raj* or the Ascension of the Prophet Muhammad from the mosque of Al-Haram in Mecca to the mosque of Al-Aqsa in Jerusalem, and then to seven heavens, which occurred when the Prophet was 51 years and 9 months old, on the night of 27 **Rajab** (*Rejep*), in the seventh month of Javanese Islamic calendar. Both months (*Mulud* and *Rejep*) are probably, the two most significant months in Cirebon after the Fasting month.

Like *Grebeg Mulud* or *Sekaten* at the courts of Yogyakarta and Surakarta in Central Java, Cirebon has its own *Grebeg*, called the *Panjang-Jimat* festival, held simultaneously at the three *kraton*, Kesepuhan, Kanoman and Keceribonan on the 12th of *Mulud* each year.[37] The festival, which attracts many people, from almost every stratum of Cirebonese society, has been described by Siddique who interprets it as a part of the machinery for the maintenance of the symbolic universe of Sunan Gunung Jati.[38]

The festival consists of highly ritualised procedures pregnant with symbolic expressions. In the first place, it represents an expression of both solemnity and gaiety at the same time, due to the birth of the Apostle of God in this world. The focal point of the festival is a ceremony in the *Kraton*, followed by a carnival carrying the *panjang jimat* (long amulets), and other *pusaka* (heirlooms) from the Bangsal Agung Panembahan to the Langgar Agung at 9.00 p.m, and back to the Bangsal Agung Panembahan at 11.00 p.m. At the Langgar Agung, before returning to the Bangsal Agung, *aysraqalan* is held led by the *kraton* religious officials (*Penghulu Kraton*).[39] *Sega rasul* (literally means 'apostle rice,' a special rice cooked with turmeric and spices), is then served to those present. The crowd struggles eagerly to get a portion, even a small one, of this rice for its *barakah* (divine blessing).[40] The preparation for the whole procession begins on the 15th of Sura with the cleansing and painting of the *kraton* and the heirlooms (*pusaka*), done mainly by voluntary workers.[41]

The main item exposed at the carnival is the *panjang-jimat*, the main *pusaka*, large oval Chinese porcelain plates, with symmetrical decoration of *kalimat syahadat* (**Kalimah Syahadah**), written in ornate Arabic scripts, which are believed to have been brought by Sunan Gunung Jati himself. Concerning the festival, Pakuningrat S.H, the Sultan of Kesepuhan, in his speech on the ceremony

[37] The word *grebeg* is probably derived from Javanese *anggrubyug*, meaning to escort.

[38] See: Siddique (1978), especially pp. 108–148.

[39] *Asyraqalan* refers to the chanting of *asyraqal badr 'alaina*, the Arabic hymn exalting and praising the Prophet, written by Ahmad al-Barzanji, concluded by a *du'a*)

[40] Some informants explained that the rice resembles *rahmat* (divine mercy). Islam was sent to mankind via Muhammad as divine mercy for the whole universe. Eagerness to get a portion of the rice thus resembles an eagerness on the part of the people to obtain divine mercy.

[41] This cleansing itself, according to some informants, involves not only physical purification but also spiritual of the hearts of the *kraton* officials.

at the *kraton* main hall, Bangsal Prabayaksa, on September 10, 1992, explained among other things that the festival is nothing but a reminder to all. He said *panjang* means long or unceasing, *jimat* stands for *si* ***(ji)*** *kang diru* ***(mat)*** , the one that is solemnly preserved that is, the *Kalimat Syahadat* as it is written on the plates. The *Panjang-jimat* festival, thus, symbolises our concern for life-long and unceasing preservation of the *Kalimat Syahadat*, or the religion of Islam.

The carnival is basically an allegoric dramatisation of the momentous event when the Prophet was born. There are at least 19 important items at the carnival; one item follows the other and each is preceded by someone carrying lighted candles. The first is a man with a lit candle stick in his hand, who acts as a servant (*khadam*) walking to give light to the second item, two men who walk after him. One man carrying a spear, represents Abu Thalib, the Prophet's uncle, and the other, an older man, represents Abd al-Muthalib, the Prophet's grandfather. They are walking at night time to send for a midwife. Next comes a group of men bringing ornamental decorations called *manggaran, nagan*, and *jantungan* symbolising the honour of Abd al-Muthalib's personage. A woman with a brass bowl (*bokor*) containing coins comes next, symbolising the dignity of the midwife; after her is a woman, bringing a tray with a bottle of distilled rose fluid (*lenga mawar*) to symbolise amniotic fluid (*ketuban*). This fluid is placed preceding the dignified newly born baby who is represented by the Sultan himself.[42] A tray containing *goyah* flower, paste and the powder of traditional herRebo Wekasan medicine held by a woman follows to symbolise the placenta. The *penghulu kraton* is seen acting as the one who cuts the umbilical cord. The core of the carnival is the exposition of *panjang jimat*, which comes to be the 12th item in the procession, like the 12 **Rabi'al-Awwal** or *Mulud*, the birth-day of the Prophet, whose mission is to propagate the *syahadah*. Each plate is cared for by two men with two escorts signifying a great concern with the *syahadah*; all of the carriers are *kaum* (care takers) of the Great Mosque, whose special duty is to be the guardians of the enactment of *syahadah*. The *panjang jimat* are seven in number signifying the *kalimah syahadah* is everyone's safe guide to pass the seven stages of the eschatological ladder (*martabat pitu*), one of the main doctrines of the Syattariyah order, the order traditionally maintained by the *kraton*.

After the *panjang jimat* come a succession of other items; two men carrying jars containing beer to resemble the after-birth blood, followed by another two, each carrying a tray with a bottle on it, containing another type of beer which symbolises phlegm. A *pendil* (rice-cooking pot) containing *sega-wuduk* (spiced rice cooked with coconut milk), is carried by a man to symbolise the suffering of the mother at giving birth. Next to the *pendil* comes a *tumpeng* (rice-mount) with roasted chicken, called *sega jeneng* (the rice of naming) symbolising thanksgiving (*syukuran* or *slametan*) for the birth of the baby. This *slametan*, at

[42] When unable, he authorises some one to take this position for him.

which the baby's name is given, is usually offered when the umbilical cord dries and is pulled off (*puput*).

The last three items at the carnival are first, eight *cepon* (huge bamboo baskets) signifying the eight attributes of the Prophet. Four of these attributes are *sidiq* (truthful), *amanah* (trustworthy), *tabligh* (conveying), *fathanah* (intelligent). All are the 'must attributes' (*sifat wajib*) attached to the Prophet. The other four are the negation of these attributes, the 'must not attributes' (*sifat mustahil*). They are *kidzib* (false hearted), *khianat* (betraying), *kitman* (corrupt), *baladah* (stupid). Each *cepon* is full of rice indicating prosperity and God's Grace for the whole world (*rahmatan lil-'alamin*). Next, come four *meron* or *tenong* (large round containers), representing mankind as created from the four elements, soil, water, air and fire. Another informant said they represent the four closest companions of the Prophets, the four Caliph, Abu Bakr, Omar, 'Utsman and 'Ali. Finally, there are four *dongdang*, also a type of large container, symbolising the spiritual elements of mankind consisting of Spirit (*ruh*), Words (*Kalam*), light (*Nur*) and witnesses (*Syuhud*) for the existence of God the greatest. Another informant said, they symbolise the four schools of Islam (*madzhab*): Maliki, Syafi'i, Hanafi and Hanbali.

Similar festive processions of smaller size and different style, mainly centred on the cleansing and exposition of *pusaka* to the public also occur at some *kramat* (shrines), such as Astana Gunung Jati on the 11th, at Panguragan on the 12th, at Tuk on the 17th and at Trusmi on the 25th of Mulud each year.

People in the villages also celebrate *mulud* in their own ways. The most common features are *marhabanan* (the ricital of **marhaba** or 'welcome'), which is similar to *asyraqalan*, and *pengajian* (public speech). *Pengajian* range in intensity from the simplest and informal, involving only a small group and a local *kyai* sitting together at a *tajug* or a mosque, to a glaring festive and formal assembly, attracting thousands of spectators with a famous speaker.

Rajaban

Another important month after Mulud is Rajab, which is commemorated by means of *Rajaban*. In Cirebon, *Rajaban* mostly involves *pengajian* but unlike *muludan* whose main theme is the birth of the Prophet, the main theme of *rajaban* centres around the Ascension of the Prophet from Mecca to Jerusalem on which the Qur'an (S 17:1) says:

> Glory to (Allah) who did take His servant for a journey by night from the Sacred Mosque (Masjid al-Haram, in Mecca) to the Farthest Mosque (the mosque of al-Aqsa), whose precincts We did Bless, in order that We might show him some of Our signs: for He is the One Who hearth and seeth (all things).

Concerning the Ascension of Muhammad to heaven, Adnan mentions among other things a tradition transmitted by Al-Ghaiti as a scriptural basis, saying:

> "And then he (the Prophet) was given (by God) means of Ascension to where the spirits of Adam's descendants go."[43]

While there is a disagreement among intellectuals on the nature of the Ascension, whether it involved physical or spiritual Ascension, the local belief definitely follows the traditionalist contention advocated in many *pengajian*, claiming that the Ascension involved the whole entity of Muhammad's human nature as a "servant" which therefore comprised both his spiritual and physical elements. They consider the phenomenon of Muhammad's Ascension as a catalytic test-case to determine whether or not a believer is sincere. An example of a sincere believer is Abu Bakr as-Shidq (the first Caliph) who accepted the story without reserve merely because the story came from the Prophet. Many others did not believe because it was technically impossible. What had happened during the prophesy, it is said, can also happen now. The phenomenon is, according to Pak Sa'id (53 years), an office clerk at Kecamatan Weru, unthinkable and thus, beyond human rationality. Sincere believers will accept it, whereas non-sincere may reject it. For those who believe in it regard the Ascension as the work of God, rather than the work of Muhammad. Nothing is impossible when God wishes it. Many proponents use the achievement of advanced space technology, which was unthinkable a few decades or centuries ago, yet has now become reality, as support for the acceptability of the Ascension. Traditional *pengajian*, on the other hand, taking the event for granted as a part of Islamic belief, recount a detailed story of the Ascension, including how the Prophet underwent a heart operation from Jibril prior to his Ascension, met with the previous prophets in the heavens during the journey and then went back to Mecca with a prescription from God for the Muslims to observe the five daily prayers. The name of the month *Rajab* (**Ra-Ja-B**) itself, which they claim as consisting of three Arabic letters *ra* [**R**], *jim* [**J**] and *ba* [**B**], substantiates the event. Each letter stands respectively for **R**-*asulullah* (the Messenger of Allah), **J**-*ibril* (Gabriel) and **B**-*uraq* (the vehicle for Ascension).

With respect to *asyraqalan* (the *recital of asyraqal badru 'alayna*) or *marhabanan* conducted mainly during the month of *Mulud* and *Rajab*, it may be requested by an individual who invites his neighbours to come to his house or *tajug* for that purpose, or by common agreement, it may be held at the *desa* mosque. In either case, the participants sit together on mats in rectangular formation. In their midst there is a jar containing pure water and a tray containing flowers and perfume. Some Arabic books, *Al-Barzanji* are placed on benches or pillows in neat cases. When they think that most expected participants are present, the

[43] Adnan, K.H.M. (1969), p. 27.

performance starts. There is a lack of formality in it although the solemnity is significant. Sometimes, men and women are simultaneously involved, but they are separated by a curtain. In most cases women have their own group and do it at different occasions. When it is about to start, incense is sometimes burned and the fragrance helps intensify the spiritual atmosphere.

A set of *Al-Fatiha* is recited whose merit is directed to the Prophet, his wives, his descendants, his companions, and his followers dead or alive. Then the leader, one who is well acquainted with *Al-Barzanji* and having a good chanting voice, takes the first recital of Arabic lyrics of twelve verses taken from *Al-Barzanji* or *Mawlid al-Diba 'i*. Each contains appeals to God to give the highest dignity to the Prophet, his ancestors and his descendants, and merit to his companions, his followers, participants in the gathering and all Muslims. The first verse reads as follows:

> *Oh God [please] exalt Muhammad - oh God [please] exalt him and give him peace.*[44]

This verse is repeated by others in chorus; the same verse is also chanted in response to the leader each time he finishes reciting each of the twelve verses. When this is over, they move to reciting the poetic narrative of the family background of the Prophet before he was born: of his parents, his ancestors, his clan and the situation of Mecca at that time. The recital is done by several people one after another in turn and when the recital comes to a verse which speaks of the eventual birth of the Prophet, all participants rise up, standing to show spontaneous respect, honour and joy, while chanting another verse in chorus:

> *Allah exalts Muhammad, Allah exalts him and endowed him with peace.*[45]

While standing solemnly, the leader chants the following verse and the others repeat:

> *Welcome the light of the eyes, welcome grandfather of Husein,*
> *Welcome and best regard, welcome the best propagator.*[46]

This verse is repeated again and again by all participants in response to the leader each time he chants a verse. Sometimes a participant takes the initiative to change the melody, after shouting in Arabic: "O God, (please) exalt Muhammad," the other reply: "(Certainly) God exalts him and endows him with

[44] The text reads: '*Ya rabb salli 'ala Muhammad - Ya rabb salli 'alaih wa sallim.*'
[45] The verse reads: *Salla-'llah 'ala Muhammad, salla'llah 'alaih wa sallam* (2x).
[46] It reads:

> *Marhaba ya nur al-'ain, marhaba jadd Al-Husein,*
> *Marhaba ahla wa sahla, marhaba ya khair al-da'i.*

peace." Then he starts with further chants in a new melody. The first four verses of the lyrics translate as follow:

> *O, Prophet peace be upon you, O, Apostle peace be upon you,*
> *O, Beloved peace be upon you, Allah's exaltation be upon you.*
>
> *Already arises the full moon upon us, thence [all other] lights are dimmed, the most beautiful thing we have seen, is the sight of you oh the most cheerful face*[47]

No less than 22 verses are chanted in various melodies before they sit again to conclude the performance with a *du'a*. When the *du'a* is finished, some participants take some flowers and/or drink the water; foods are also served by the host. After eating and chatting they stand up asking permission to leave the house, and the host answers them with thanks. Some hosts provide *brekat* some others do not.[48]

Ruwahan

Ruwahan commemorates *Ruwah*, the eighth month of Javanese calendar which coincides with Sya'ban, the eight month of the Islamic calendar. The Javanese *ruwah*, may be derived from Arabic **ruh** (pl. **arwah**), meaning spirit. According to popular belief, on the night of 15th, the mid of the *Ruwah* (**Nisfu Sya'ban**) the tree of life on whose leaves the names of the living are written is shaken. The names written on leaves that fall indicate the mortals who will die in the coming year.[49] Not surprisingly, a number of people use the day to commemorate the dead or to visit the graves.[50]

Conforming to this tradition, a hadith transmitted by Tirmidzi states that on the night of *Nisfu* (mid of) *Sya'ban* God descends to the lowest heaven and calls the mortals in order to grant them forgiveness. An informant in Cirebon called this month *panen pangapura* (the harvest time of forgiveness) and thus, it is a good time for those who wish forgiveness. After sunset prayer of the 15th day of the month (*limalase ruwah*) or *Nisfu Sya'ban*, the devout will read the *Surat Yasin*

[47] The verses read:

> *Ya Nabi salam 'alaik, ya Rasul salam 'alaik,*
> *Ya Habib salam 'alaik, salawat Allah 'alaik.*
> *Ashraq al-badr 'alaina, fakhtafat min-hu 'l budur, Mitsla husnik ma raayna, qatt ya wajh al-surur.*

[48] The word *brekat* is derived from Arabic: *baraka* (pl. *barakat*); it refers to food given to the guests to be brought home),

[49] Cf: "Sya'ban", in *Shorter Encyclopedia of Islam*, and Ahmad Qodhi, A. (1992), *Nur Muhammad, Menyingkap Asal Usul Kejadian Makhluk (Tarjamah Daqooiqul Akhbar)*, Bandung: Al-Husaini, p. 33.

[50] Traditions to visit a grave is embedded in a *hadith* transmitted by Muslim, Abu Dawud and Tirmidzi from Abi Huraira, stating that the Prophet recommended visiting graves (not only on Sya'ban) as it may remind the visitor about life after death. See for example: Rasyid, S. (1988), *Fiqh Islam*, Bandung: Masa Baru, pp. 182–183.

(Sura 36 of the Holy Qur'an) three times and fast on the day. For most village people, *Ruwah* is known as the month for *dedonga* (to utter *du'a*) and *ngunjung* (literally meaning 'to visit'). Led by the *Kuwu* (Desa Chief) and elders, they visit the graves of their ancestors, especially the founder of the *desa* called the *Ki Gede* or *Ki Buyut* if the founder was a man or *Nyi Gede* or *Nyi Buyut* if the founder was a woman. Sometimes this procession turns into a carnival.

In Kalitengah, the villagers held *ngunjung* by making a marching visit. They took a six kilometre route from the *desa* to the Astana Gunung Jati grave complex, where the founder of the *desa*, Nyi Gede Kalitengah, is buried, just outside the east wall of Sunan Gunung Jati's shrine. The one-hour march was attended by approximately 300 people, men and women of various ages, led by the *kuwu* and local elders. The focal point is not the march itself but the *dedonga*. Some people carried foods partly to be offered to the key bearer (*juru kunci*) of the Astana grave complex, partly for their own consumption after the break up of *dedonga*. At Astana they first visited Sunan Gunung Jati's grave, sat on the floor in front of the third door of the nine-door shrine and prayed there by reciting *tahlil*. The door is normally closed but on this occasion, as a service to Kalitengah people, it is opened. No one is allowed to step beyond this limit, they only look at the ascending pathway to Sunan Gunung Jati's tomb.

After this, they went to Nyi Gede Kalitengah also to perform, *tahlil*, the same thing as they did in front of Sunan Gunung Jati's tomb. One of the elders, Pak Suganda (57 years), an army veteran, explained that the purpose of the *ngunjung* is to express thankfulness to Nyi Gede, who first came to Kalitengah and settled there. At this *ngunjung* ceremony they ask God to pardon all her sins and give her a good life in the hereafter. Beside this, they also believe that by carrying out this action, if God so wishes, it is not only Nyi Gede who will obtain merit but also those who pray for her and inhabit the *desa* because what they do is a good thing.

The reason for choosing *Ruwah* for carrying out this ritual, according Pak Suganda, is unclear except that it has become their *adat*, and they feel there is no reason to change or abolish it, as "there is nothing wrong with such an *adat*." I saw there were also groups from other *desa* who did the same thing and explained its purpose in about the same way. As an expression of their respect some groups even choose this event as a good moment to renovate their Ki/Nyi Gede's shrine. Another informant said that taking the middle of Ruwah to visit the graves has its root in various traditions of the Prophet. One of these traditions is based on a story telling that once, on *Nisfu Sya'ban*, the Prophet secretly went to Baqi' (a grave complex in Medina) and prayed there so intensely with his tears flowing. Ali, his companion and son-in-law, followed him secretly and watched from a distance what the Prophet did. Seeing that the Prophet cried, Ali came and asked why. The Prophet explained that it was the night of forgiveness of sin (**lailat al-bara'ah**) and he (the Prophet) was praying for forgiveness from God for his ancestors and believers who might have sins. This indicates also that Islam, in its own way, has a form of ancestor cult.

Syawalan

Along with the traditions surrounding the fasting month (*Ramadhan*) and *riaya*, there is *Syawalan* or *Raya Syawal* for celebrating *Syawal* (**Syawwal**), the tenth month of Javanese Islamic calendar. For the pious, beginning on the day after the end of Ramadan, they fast for six more days. *Raya Syawal*, the 8th day of *Syawal* marks the end of the fast. The celebration is made by going to the Astana Grave complex for a *ziarah* (visit). On this occasion all the nine doors along the ascending pathway to Sunan Gunung Jati's tomb are opened to give way for the three Sultans of Kesepuhan, Kanoman and Kecirebonan and their families, who make a visit to Sunan Gunung Jati's tomb. The visit is made after attending a ceremony at each of the *kraton*. They come there still in their formal *kraton* clothing. Upon their return from *ziarah* to the *kraton*, a crowd struggle to shake hands with them. Sultan Kanoman and his family, in particular, hold a *slametan* attended by Astana custodians. Siddique (1978:136) claims that through this procession and visitation, the sultans' position at the apex of the religious hierarchy among the *kraton* milieu is reaffirmed.

Among the mass of the populace who come and go there on that occasion, flocking around the burial complexes, at the square, at the mosque, at *Gunung* Jati, on the street, numbering as many as 150,000 people, most people pay no attention to the Sultans and their consorts. Along with *dedonga*, they would rather take the occasion as a recreational opportunity to enjoy the gathering and to see the beautiful panorama toward the sea from the top of Gunung Jati. It is true that the presence of Sultans is a special attraction for many people, but more importantly the two *lawang pungkur* (back doors) at the left and right wings of the grave complex, leading to the graves of Ki or Nyi Gede of various *desa* are also opened and thus they can ascend and descend around the grave complex at the top of Gunung Sembung from one *lawang pungkur* at the east wing to another one at the west. They therefore come to Astana on *Raya Syawal* for *dedonga* at three tombs: at Sunan Gunung Jati's, at the Ki or Nyi Gede's who are buried at Gunung Sembung, and then across the main road up to the hill of Gunung Jati, at Syeikh Datuk Kahfi's. Syeikh Datuk Kahfi is known as the first Islamic teacher who came from Arabia to Cirebon in the early 15th century and resided at Gunung Jati where Rarasantang, Sunan Gunung Jati's mother, and her elder brother Walangsungsang, learned Islam. Upon his death the *Syeikh* was also buried there. Another occasion like *Syawalan* also occurs on the 11th of *Mulud* and the 10th of *Raya Agung*.

CELEBRATION AND COMMEMORATION OF THE LIFE CYCLE: SLAMETAN

Another type of *adat* that prevails in Cirebon is the celebration or commemoration of the stages of the life cycle. Like other forms of celebration, most life-cycle celebrations transform their main feature into a *slametan*. As a part of *adat* among Muslims, *slametan* is a wide spread practice among both devout and non-devout, high ranked and common people, rich and poor. Its essence involves performing *sedekah* (**sadaqa**) and *Donga* or *do'a* (**du'a**) on certain important occasions. Thus it is essentially Islamic; its roots can be found directly or indirectly in the formal Scriptures, the Qur'an and the Hadith.[51] In fact, Islam recommends continuous **sadaqa** and **du'a** to its followers even while facing or doing something of minor importance or even a technical activity. Removing an obstacle in, or while using, a path-way is a form of *sadaqa*. Doing anything, including going to the toilet, has its own *du'a*.

The nature and pattern of Slametan

It seems clear that the Cirebonese share with other societies in the belief that life evolves through stages: before birth, birth and after birth, death and after death; each stage also has sub-stages. Turner (1964), who worked on van Gennep's "The Rites of Passage", describes the importance of the liminal period because at that period the neophytes, in terms of social structure, are either removed or invisible.[52] In Cirebon, the movement between stages is also considered important because it is either critical or precarious. People hope that moving from one stage to another goes safely and smoothly without trouble. Unfortunately, they can do very little, because in most parts, it is beyond the control of human endeavour. To hope something will go safely or to celebrate something that has already gone safely and peacefully, people perform *slametan*. The word *slamet* is borrowed from Arabic **salamah** (pl. **salamat**) meaning peace or safety. Other words akin to *slametan* and in many cases used interchangeably are *kajatan, syukuran* or *tasyakuran*, and *sedekahan*, each of which is also borrowed from Arabic, respectively, from the word **hajah** (pl. **hajat**) meaning a need, **syukr** meaning thanking, **tasyakur** meaning to thank, and **sadaqah** meaning to give alms or something to others.

In Cirebon, the term *kajatan*, originally meaning to have *kajat* (a need, or an expectation) is used to refer to a performance similar to *slametan*, but it also has an important or cheerful connotation; more specifically it refers to the

[51] An anthropologist who brought the *slametan* issue to the literature is Clifford Geertz (1960) in *The Religion of Java*. His strong preoccupation with Hindu-Buddhist-Animistic-syncretic thinking about Javanese Islam, however, together with his lack of essential knowledge of Islam, distorts the issue considerably. Along with claiming that *slametan* are the main business of *abangan*, he implies *slametan* are the reflection of a Hindu-Buddhist-Animistic syncretism of Javanese Islam.

[52] Turner, V.W. (1964), "Betwixt and Between: The Liminal Period in Rites De Passage", in Lessa, W.A. and Vogt, E.Z. (1979), pp. 234–243.

expectation of well being after a ceremonial occasion such as a boy's circumcision or a marriage.[53] *Syukuran* or *tasyakuran*, on the other hand, means a celebration, large or small, for expressing thankfulness (to God) or gratitude because something (not limited to stages of the life cycle) has gone through safely and peacefully, such as a release from a difficulty including recovery from a serious sickness, success in doing something important, having something beneficial happened, or obtaining good luck. Whereas *sedekahan* means to perform *sedekah*, it has about the same meaning and connotation as *slametan*. In many context the words *slametan, kajatan, syukuran* and *sedekahan* are interchangeable. Their focal point is expecting other people to pray (to God) for the well being of the individual concerned; in return the individual provides foods either to be eaten where the *slametan* is held, to be taken home by the people who prayed, or both. Thus, following Marcel Mauss, there is a sense of reciprocity in this performance.[54] That is, the gift (prayer or *du'a*) and the return gift, the food; or, it may also go in the opposite direction with the foods being the gift and the prayer being the return gift. The first occurs when a host, referred to as the lord (*majikan*), who expects safety (*sokibul kajat*) invites people of other households, mostly neighbours and kin, to come and sit together at his house to pray or to participate in invocations led by a leader, after which food is served, either with or without *brekat*. For those who can not attend the gathering for some acceptable reason, their food or *brekat* is sent to their homes.

The second occurs when a *sokibul kajat* makes no invitation; rather, he sends an assistant to bring the food (*sedekah* or alms) directly to the recipients (neighbours and kin), at their homes. The structure and arrangement of the food bears a symbolic message of the purpose implied and the type of *slametan* being requested and implicitly say what the sender means. If he is ignorant, the recipient will ask the carrier: "*Seng sapa*?" (Who sends this?) and/or "*Apa-apa-an kiyenkih*?" (What is he/she doing by this?), to which the carrier will give the necessary answer on the sender's behalf. To this, the recipient may or may not utter a prayer, but this is of less importance because the nature of sending the food is *sedekah*. The religious function of *sedekah*, for those who believe in it, is either to repel, drive away or prevent disaster and difficulty, or to express thankfulness to God. The scriptural basis for the first function is found in a hadith that states: "Giving alms repels disaster" (**as-shadaqah tadfa' al-bala'**).[55] Whereas the latter is implied in the Qur'an saying: "If you thank (for what I giveth), I (shall) give you more" (**la in syakartum la azidannakum**). Either

[53] The Cirebonese, as do other Javanese, pronounce k for h, such as kaji for haji, Imam Kambali for Imam Hambali.

[54] Mauss, M. (1980), *The Gift*, London: Routledge & Kegan Paul. In this work the importance of gift exchange and the structures of reciprocity in social organisation are stressed.

[55] My informant said that he certainly found the hadith in *Khazinat al-Asrar*, once when he was in pesantren, but he could not give further details of the book because he did not have it.

type of *slametan* therefore is essentially Islamic and has a significant scriptural basis.

The Occasions for Slametan

In reference to the stages of the life cycle people usually perform *slametan* (or *syukuran, kajatan, sedekahan*) on the following occasions:

Pregnancy

In Cirebon there are normally three occasions on which *slametan* in relation to pregnancy (*wetengan*) occurs: the fourth, the seventh and the ninth month. In Cirebon to be pregnant is called *meteng* or *ngandeg*. The *hadith* transmitted by Bukhari and Muslim from Abi 'Abd al-Rahman ibn Mas'ud states that the early process of pregnancy (*nyidam*) turns the ovum into a thick liquid, then into a clot of blood, then into a clot of flesh. Each stage, according to the *hadith*, takes 40 days for maturation. The time after the third of the 40 day periods, that is, after 120 days or four months is considered critical because at this stage, a very important event occurs. It is the time when God breaths a soul into the flesh and animates it, and designates its fate and death. The Cirebonese call this event, "entering the *alam arwah*, the fourth stage."[56] During these early stages of pregnancy the mother is often characterised as having a strong desire to eat sour things, especially young fruits; as showing strange behaviour, and having strange feelings, anxieties or wishes.[57] To commemorate this event, and at the same time for hoping the well being of both the pregnant mother and the potential child, a *slametan* called *ngupati* is performed. The *slametan* is usually signified by the presence of *kupat* at the *brekat*.[58] The *ku-**pat*** is said to resemble *papat* meaning four, signifying that the *slametan* is either because the fourth month of pregnancy has arrived or because the flesh in the womb has reached the fourth stage of creation.

The next *slametan* held during pregnancy is performed at the seventh month; it is called *ngrujaki, mitui* or *pepitu*, from the word *pitu* meaning seven (in Central Java: *tingkeban*). The number '7' is held to be very important so it is highly recommended that the start of a *mitui* ceremony be at 7.00 a.m. on the 7th or 17th or 27th day of the month. It is believed that at this stage the foetus in the

[56] The preceding three stages of the total seven stages conception of creation are called *alam ahadiyat, alam wahdat* and *alam wahidiyat*. The other three stages are *alam mitsal, alam ajsam* and *alam insan kamil*. See: Chapter Three.

[57] One informant told me that when his wife was about three months pregnant, one night she told him that she wanted to eat/drink young coconut (*dugan*). She refused either to have it from a shop or delaying her desire for the next day and urged instead her husband to climb and pick one by himself from his neighbour's tree that very night. A quarrel occurred between him and his wife until finally, after being mediated by his neighbour, he climbs the coconut tree and picked one for his wife, a task which he had never done before.

[58] *Kupat* (Ind: *ketupat*) is boiled rice wrapped in a woven container of young coconut leaves in a square shape.

womb has already grown into a full human being, a young baby. The traditionalists describe it as entering the seventh stage, the world of the perfect human being (*alam insan kamil*), the world wherein the baby, as a human, as well as having a complete bodily structure, is also completely pure and, free from sin of any sort. This state of purity and sinlessness becomes an exemplary condition to which the pious direct their spiritual endeavours.

The *mitui* ceremony involves a more elaborate procedure than that of *ngupati*. Its central point, however, centres on bathing the pregnant mother to symbolise the intention of a complete purification. The water to bath with, which is taken from seven different wells, is put in a big jar or a large tank with seven species of flowers and other herbal substances in it. The mother sits on a chair, dressed only in a new batik garment (*tapi* or *kain panjang*) of the nicest kind which covers her from above her breasts down to her legs. During the bathing this garment is replaced seven times with other new ones. A young yellow hybrid coconut, carved with Qur'anic verses and sometimes also with favourite *wayang* figures along with some coins inserted here and there, is put on her lap just below her pregnant abdomen. The young coconut resembles the child who is hopefully to be either handsome or attractive, whose personage is idealised by the *wayang* figure, living happily with abundance signified by the inserted coins, and with certainty of being safe in the hereafter as the carved Qur'anic verses would imply. Placed on the ground beside her, is a special ceramic clay jar called *buyung* containing water and flower, including *manggar* (coconut flowers), and valuables, especially gold and jewellery, symbols of dignity and prosperity that await the birth of the child.

The bathing is initiated by an old woman known to be wise and pious who, by using a water dipper, pours the water from the tank onto the mother's head. Preferably the old woman should also have been successful in raising children who have become well to do. After this old woman, follows the husband of the pregnant woman, and then the others, mostly older men and women who pour the water for bath. This bathing ceremony ceases when all the elders have had their turn and the garment has been changed seven times. After the bathing, the gold and jewellery in the clay jar beside her are taken out; her husband takes the jar to a strategic place where many people usually pass and he smashes the jar on the ground. Seeing the jar broken to smithereens children and youngsters applause with a yell: "hooray!" My informant explained that the breaking of the jar in such a place represents a wish for an easy delivery for the mother and wide social recognition for the child.

When her husband returns home, her mother or an appointed woman performs *curakan*, throwing coins mixed with rice and flowers towards a crowd of boys and girls each of whom eagerly struggles to get the sown money more than his/her fellows. The *curakan* expresses an expectation that the child should not be stingy and should care for others, especially the needy. After *curakan* an ordinary *slametan* is held in the house, either by reciting *tahlil* or *marhabanan*. The *brekat* served in the *slametan* is signified mainly by the presence of *rujak* (fruits salad) among the dishes, from which *ngrujaki*, meaning to treat with *rujak*, the name of the ceremony, is derived. *Rujak*, my informant said, serves as a reminder to both the expectant parents and society. *Rujak* is composed of various fruits and spices, with a great variety of flavours: sour, sweet, hot, salty, bitter and many other tastes. If it is properly mixed, it becomes delicious. People who eat *rujak* will taste all these things. In its allegorical meaning, as soon as a women bears a child and becomes a mother, and as soon as a man becomes a father, they are considered to be fully functional as social beings. They have various tasks and responsibilities to carry out for their own household and for the society; they are at the same time parents, guardians, teachers, feeders, protectors and members of the society. They will eventually experience a great variety of emotions and feelings as indicated by the *rujak*; sadness, gladness, happiness, grief, dissent, annoyance, cheerfulness, pleasure, displeasure. All have potential for causing problems; yet, if handled wisely and generously, they can entail real happiness. It is the hope for wisdom and generosity, delicacy and happiness which is implied in the *ngrujaki* ceremony.

Although a baby at the age of seven months in the womb has become a complete human being, it still needs a process of maturation which normally takes about two months and then, at nine months, it is born. Giving birth, especially for the first time, is a precarious event for a woman. Both her own and her child's safety are at stake. To expect an easy, smooth, less painful and safe birthing process, in the ninth month of pregnancy people pray to God by means of a *slametan* called *nglolosi*. *Ngolosi* involves offering *bubur lolos*, to be distributed among neighbours and kin.[59] *Nglolosi* belongs to the second type of *slametan* already described. There is no invitation, no gathering and no formal *du'a* in the house, only hope and desire in the heart accompanying the offering or *sedekah* in the form of *bubur lolos*.

Birth and after birth

Although more and more people prefer to give birth in hospital, or in a special clinic (*Klinik Bersalin*), or send for a trained nurse (*bidan*) for help, there are many others who do not do so for a certain reason or because they are unable to afford the cost. When pregnancy is around seven months, a midwife (*dukun bayi*) is contacted. After that she makes periodic visits to the pregnant woman, her new client, and makes the necessary diagnosis and treatment (mostly by

[59] *Bubur lolos* is sweetened rice-flour porridge, heavily oiled with boiled coconut milk, wrapped cylindrically in banana leaves with both ends are left open. When it is put vertically in standing position, the porridge is instantly loosened and fall down. This clearly symbolises an expectation of an easy and instant child bearing. The word *nglolosi* itself is derived from *lolos*, meaning to slip off easily.

massage) to set the baby into the proper position. Her crucial role comes when the birth takes place.[60] After this eventful occasion a small *slametan*, or more properly a thanksgiving called *bancakan* is offered.[61] Rice and other foods are put together in flat containers (*cekedong*) made of banana leaves, to be distributed to young boys and girls from neighbouring households as if announcing that there is a new junior child among them. This is the first *slametan* offered on the occasion of a new born child. The second *slametan* is *puputan*, performed when the navel cord falls off (*puput*). This *slametan* involves offering *sega bugana* (tasty rice cooked together with coconut and chicken), to be distributed among the neighbours. The word *bugana*, derived from corrupted Arabic *bi-ghina* meaning with abundance, is said to represent the hope that God will nourish the child with abundance. For some, *puputan* is also used as an occasion for naming the child.

The next *slametan* is in relation to the "hair-shaving." The first "hair-shaving" is when the child is 40 days old; on this occasion, red and white rice porridge (*bubur abang-putih*) is offered in the morning (around 10.00 a.m) as *bancakan*. In the evening, especially for well to do parents, a formal *slametan* called *kekah* (from Arabic *'aqiqah*), a purely Islamic offering explicitly established by the Prophet for naming and shaving, is performed. On this occasion one goat or sheep for a female and two for a male baby are slaughtered. The ceremony takes the form of *marhabanan*, with precisely the same things as performed in *muludan*, as are used to commemorate the birth of the Prophet. When the participants chant *marhaba* (while standing), the father takes the baby amidst the participants, followed by an assistant who brings a tray with flowers, perfume and a pair of scissors. First, the most distinguished participant performs a symbolic shaving by cutting some of the baby's hair, then the father moves with the baby slowly to the other participants one by one, each of whom takes a turn in the symbolic shaving. In the meantime his assistant gives a flower and sprays the perfume over the one who has just taken his/her turn to cut the hair. When everyone has taken his turn the baby is carried back to the bedroom. In practice the real "hair-shaving" is done the next morning. The hair is weighed, then its weight is equated with the weight of gold whose current price becomes an amount of money that the parents, on behalf of the baby, should offer to the needy.

Further "hair-shaving" occurs at intervals when needed. When the time comes, *bubur lemu, bubur kule* and *sega aking* is respectively offered as *bancakan* at the second, the third and the fourth of hair-shaving.[62] Finally, a *slametan* called

[60] This is an event which goes nearly the same thing as Wessing describes in reference to the Sundanese. See: Wessing, R. (1978), *Cosmology and Social Behaviour in West Javanese Settlements*, Ohio University: Centre for International Studies, South East Asian Series No.47.

[61] *Ibid*, pp. 127–130.

[62] *Bubur lemu* is rice porridge mixed with palm sugar liquid (*kincah*) and coconut milk, *bubur kule* is sweetened rice porridge, and *sega aking* is second cooked rice. It comes from uneaten cooked rice. When

ngundun lemah is held to celebrate the child touching the ground for the first time. This is a fairly large *slametan*, carried out only by the well to do, usually in the morning. Its special features appears at the *brekat* where a ladder shaped stick with an artificial flower on the top is planted on piled rice. In addition, in the midst of the dishes there are a number of toys representing either womanly or manly work tools, such as an artificial bolo knife (*golok-golokan*), scissors, needle, comb, and mirror, depending on whether the child is female or male. These toy tools signify the hope that the child will grow into a diligent and handy worker and the mirror signifies the hope that the child will be an independent and introspective individual.

Circumcision

Although Shrieke, B. (1921, 1922), as quoted by Wessing (1978:132), speculate that circumcision in Java already existed before Islam came, on Java the practice of male circumcision, or the removal of the foreskin, is an indication of the triumph of Islam over the long established earlier religious traditions. Its current prevalence and the idea that circumcision is a sign of being a Muslim is clear evidence of this triumph. It is true that circumcision is not mentioned in the Qur'an and is observed not only by Muslims but also by other communities as well, especially Jewish and non-Muslim communities in eastern Indonesia, but the fact is that on Java and other Muslim worlds, circumcision has become a sign or hall-mark of Islamic practice. In Islam, its roots are embedded in the hadith that states that Abraham, the great prophet, was circumcised when he was 80 years old.[63] The Cirebonese literary traditions even say that circumcision was initially practiced by Adam as a sacrifice, to express gratitude as soon as God accepted his repentance. In addition, as the traditions imply, Adam did this as an outward expression that he would always keep his bodily organs clean. This outward expression is to show that his inward repentance was sincere and everlasting.

Almost everyone in Cirebon, as is the case in Java, considers circumcision (*sunat*) as a requirement since in this way a Javanese becomes a Muslim, regardless of whether or not he will later fulfil the standards of piety. Another refined Javanese word (*krama*) for circumcision is *nyelamaken* meaning to Islamise. Thus, for a Javanese, one could stay single or always be poor throughout life, but to stay uncircumcised is unthinkable.[64] A boy of circumcision age will be deeply embarrassed when his playmates tease him for being a Chinese because he has not been circumcised. It is a common expression in Cirebon that a boy who has

it is roasted or fried it is called *cengkaruk*, when it is recooked or steamed it becomes *sega aking* to be eaten with dishes, like ordinary rice. I was unable to discover the symbolic meaning of these *bancakan*, except that *bubur lemu*, meaning *ambir lemu*, expresses the hope that the child will grow healthily, whereas sega aking resembles the hope that the child will be nourished with abundance surplus.

[63] See: "Circumcision" in *Shorter Encyclopedia of Islam*.

[64] Wessing, R. (1978), p. 132.

no courage or is reluctant to be circumcised will later become a Chinese (*dadi Cina*). The notion of being a Chinese does not refer to being ethnically, racially or socially Chinese; rather, it is a form of mockery in that, to be a Chinese is to be a non-Muslim and this, in their religious terms, is quite an embarrassment despite the fact that materially most Chinese are rich.[65] As a result of this peer group pressure it is often the boy himself rather than the parents who proposes his circumcision. Parents may propose a circumcision but in most cases the decision is made when the boy himself shows willingness or even asks his parents. Usually, it comes when he is between seven and ten years old. The ceremony may range from a simple or just safe one (*padu slamet bae*), to a large and elaborate celebration, depending on the parents' material well being and social standing.

Once a decision is taken the necessary preparation is made. The first thing is to set the date, which is usually decided by discussion between the boy's parents, grandparents, or other elderly close kin. Consideration may be based on *pitungan*, common sense or convenience. Next, talks will be held concerning how elaborate the ceremony should be, the approximate costs, the number of people to be invited or involved, and other technical details. When everything is decided the house is cleaned, a practitioner either a physician, a paramedic, or a specialist (*dukun sunat*) is contacted. A few days before the due date, close kin and relatives come with contributions of raw materials such as rice, sugar, beans, coconuts and chickens. A festive atmosphere around the house begins to develop two days before the celebration while overall preparations continue.

One day before the circumcision, early in the afternoon, the child is bathed and dressed in either fancy aristocratic or *santri* clothes. If both are to be worn, one set is worn in the afternoon and the other in the evening. The boy is treated like a king or a groom called the *penganten sunat* (circumcision groom). Led by an elder, he is put on an ornamented horseback or a *becak* to visit and put flowers (*ngembang*) on the graves of his parents' closest deceased kin. On this occasion, on the way to and from the grave complex, he is publicly paraded with a festival manner, usually accompanied by drums (*genjring*) or other musical performance, *barong sae* dance or the like, to attract more on-lookers along the way. Participants are mostly boys and girls especially his playmates, peers, and kin.

Most circumcisions are held either in the evening after *ngembang* or in the morning around 7.00 a.m of the next day. At either time the boy is first bathed, ceremonially dressed and taken to the site for circumcision. Some people prefer going to a physician or a paramedic to circumcise their children, either for reliability or for prestige; others prefer a *dukun* for both reliability and cost. In

[65] Certainly there are many Chinese, now and in the past, who are Muslims. On Java however, most Chinese are non-Muslims. In Cirebon there are also a few of Chinese Muslims, including Yoe Keng, a conglomerate who has a large *Majelis Ta'lim* (Center for public learning). The Chinese Muslims are called *Cina selam* and considered as exceptions.

Kalitengah, Pak Surur's son was circumcised by a *dukun* who was paid Rp. 15,000.00 (approximately A$. 12.00) for the operation. The process took just a few minutes, and within four days the wound healed and the boy was able to wear pants. Pak Jaelani's two sons were circumcised in hospital for Rp.25,000.00 each (about A$ 20.00) plus the additional cost for a car rented to go to the hospital; the wound took two weeks to heal.

Traditionally, if the circumciser is a *dukun*, the operation is done in the yard of the house. The boy is put on his father's or an authorised individual's lap. The *dukun* squats down facing them, teaches the boy the proclamation of faith, utters a prayer and circumcises the boy. If the circumciser is a medical doctor or a paramedic, the boy is taken by car to the operation room, lies down on a mattress, is circumcised and taken back to the house. After being circumcised, the boy is laid down on a mattress in the front room. His friends and peers come to congratulate him with presents, so do the adults who come and give him some money while saying: "Congratulations, you are called a real male" (*Slamet ya, sira wis lanang bener*).

The evening after *ngembang* is the real celebration, the peak of the circumcision feast at which, for those who can afford it, there is some sort of entertainment such as an orchestra or *wayang* performance. Special guests, mostly men, come along that evening. They are welcomed and led to sit on chairs to enjoy the entertainment, if any, and are served with foods. When a guest asks permission to leave for home, while shaking hands for fare-well, he passes a named envelope containing some money as his contribution to the host who is holding the *kajatan*. Women guests, on the other hand, mostly come for *bebuwuh* or *kondangan* in the afternoon, pass their contributions to the hostess; in return, unlike their male counterparts, they are provided with a small *brekat*. An ordinary *brekat* is served at the *slametan* held the next morning to conclude the celebration. All guests at the *slametan* are men and are specially invited to recite prayers led by an *imam* who is usually the most prominent local *kyai*. After finishing reciting prayers, either *marhaba* or *tahlil*, they are served with food along with the *brekat* which is specially provided to be taken home. After the *slametan* the celebration of the circumcision is completed.

Marriage

Although a girl is also circumcised, usually as an infant, her circumcision does not have ceremonial significance, probably because it is largely symbolic. It is her marriage which is of important ceremonial significance. The intensity of the ceremony is at least comparable with a boy's circumcision.

There is no clear limitation on the age at which one is allowed to marry but there are certain restrictions concerning whom one can marry. Older people say that the minimum age of *akil-balig*, legal responsibility, is after a girl's first menstruation (around twelve) and after a boy's first ejaculation during dreaming (around fifteen years old). Currently, a girl rarely marries before seventeen, whereas a boy will marry after being able to produce enough cash (*wis bisa menggawe*) and be potentially independent. A sign of this potency is when he stops bothering his parents for money for his own basic expenses, although he still lives and has meals with his parents. A clearer sign is when he occasionally gives his parents, especially his mother, a present of money.

As in other parts of Java, the first marriage in Cirebon is basically arranged by parents, although today, unless the parents have a very strong argument, the boy's voice is mostly heard. Parents usually, directly or indirectly, keep a close watch on whom their children fancy and they will show their agreement or disagreement. In accord with Islamic marriage law marriage among siblings, including half siblings and one's breast siblings (*sedulur sesusu*), and relatives across the generational lines, are prohibited.

The first step in a marriage arrangement is *nakokaken* or an inquiry about the current status of the girl. The boy's parents or their authorised agents come to the girl's parents asking formally whether the girl is available and whether there would be any objection if they take the girl to be their in-law. The degree of formality in the procedure depends on how acquainted the parties are; the more acquainted the less formal is the procedure. However, compared with other Javanese (Geertz, 1976:53–54) or Sundanese (Wessing, 1978:141–142) the Cirebonese seem to be more direct and to have less metaphorical expressions in dealing with this matter. In most cases a set of preliminary and informal talks is carried out by a mediator, usually a middle aged man or woman, called *jomblang* who goes to and fro on behalf of both sides.[66]

When an agreement is reached the *nakokaken* process becomes more straightforward and it is only a sort of formality as the real decision is already known. This leads to the next step called *nglamar* (formal asking) which is taken a few days later. Although basically *nglamar* means to ask for, in practice, in Cirebon, its meaning has turned into a declaration that the boy and the girl are formally engaged (*bakalan*). *Lamaran* and engagement may be very simple involving only two or three people coming to the girl's parents, or it may be elaborate involving a large number of people, depending on the social standing of both sides. Its focal point is the presentation of a gift from the prospective groom to the prospective bride which ties them to a commitment to marry. The tying-gift (*penetep*) can either be jewellery, usually a ring, money, or both put in decorated boxes, accompanied by other things especially food; all are presented

[66] Rejection from the girl's parent is expressed rather directly but subtly; the words may be: "We are very glad to hear that proposal, but the girl is still too young" or "still wants to stay untied" or "refused to think about marriage." Whatever the answer the boy's parent will fully understand what it does really mean.

on trays. Except among some urban dwellers, in Cirebon, a ring is only provided for and worn by the girl and thus, the so called *tukar cincin* (exchange of rings) ceremony to signify the engagement rarely occurs because their *syari'ah* discourages men from wearing gold.[67]

After the engagement, both sides must still meet to discuss the marriage date and other related matters, especially when these things have not been decided at the *nglamar*. When everything is agreed upon, the next step is the marriage contract (*kawinan*). To celebrate the completion of this contract, a wedding party or ceremony is held, first in the bride's family's house called *munggah* (in Central Java, *kepanggihan* or *temon*) and, a few days later, in the groom's family's house called *ngundu mantu*. It is this celebration, whose intensity ranges from very simple (*padu slamet bae*) to the most elaborate (*gedean*, meaning a big feast). The simplest form involves inviting neighbours, close relatives and selected friends, to come and be served with food. The most elaborate procession is an enactment of court marriage traditions.

The current Indonesian Marriage Law (No. 1/1974 Part-I, article 2) states that a marriage contract is valid only when the couple has passed through the religious ceremony which, in fact, is a long established practice. The government records the occurrence and gives the necessary advice and service to ease the procedure. For Muslims, especially in Cirebon, the marriage contract is usually concluded at the girl's house; it can take a day or more before the wedding or be on the same day just a few hours before the wedding ceremony. From his household, the groom and his group leave for the bride's family house. They are welcomed and led to sit on carpets or mats on the floor at the front room of the bride's house or in a nearby *tajug* where the contract will be concluded and where elders and distinguished persons of the bride's family, usually local *kyai*, who will witness the contract or *'akad nikah*, are present.

Along with the marrying couple the Islamic law necessitates the presence of a *wali* (legally responsible guardian according to Islamic law) and two witnesses. At the due time, an official of the Ministry of Religion at the Kecamatan level (*naib*, literally meaning substitute) assisted by a Desa official called *PPN (Pegawai Pencatat Nikah*, the desa official who is in charge of recording marriages) comes and inspects the required documents for the marriage registry. When everything is correct he calls the groom to sit closely facing him. He also calls the bride and asks her whether the marriage accords with her own will; if so, she is required to say verbally that she will marry the groom, and pronounces the declaration of faith (*syahadat*). Then the *naib* asks the *wali* whether he (the *wali*) himself

[67] If, for one and other reasons, the engagement is ruined and the marriage is cancelled, especially when the cancellation comes from the bride's side, the gift (the jewellery or/and money, but not the food) are returned to the groom. Often to show or ensure her family's respectable standing the gift is also returned even though the cancellation comes from the groom.

would like to administer the procedures of the contract (*akad nikah*) or trust it to him (the *naib*). A distinguished *kyai* usually prefers to perform the ceremony by himself whereas most ordinary people prefers the *naib* to do it. The *akad nikah* consists of the *ijab* and *kabul*, shortened into *ijab-kabul*. *Ijab* is the utterance of the *wali*, or the *naib* on behalf of the *wali*, stating that he marries the bride to the groom; the words may be like this: "Brother so and so (he mentions the name of the groom), I marry the girl (or the woman) named so and so (he mentions the name of the bride) to you with the marriage gift (*mas kawin*) consisting of such and such (he mentions the amount, volume and value of the gift), paid in cash (or debt). *Kabul*, on the other hand, is the groom's response, either in Arabic or the local language to the *ijab*, saying that he accepts the marriage of the bride to him with the marriage gift as stated by the *wali*. In local Cirebonese language it may be: "*Trima kaula nikahe or kawine si Anu* (the name of the bride) *kalian mas kawin kang kesebat wau*," (I accept marrying so and so with the marriage gift as stated). The witnesses observe the groom's utterance and proclaim it adequate, thus, making the marriage valid. After *ijab kabul*, the *ta'lik talak* (a vow entitling the wife to divorce from the husband in case of his mistreatment), is uttered by the *naib* and the groom repeats word by word. The procedure is concluded with a prayer for the well being of the new couple and their marriage. The prayer is led by someone, usually a *kyai* or the *naib*. Then the groom kisses the *wali's* hands, shakes the hands of those who are present and, finally, food is served. When the wedding party is not held immediately, the groom and his party go back to their home until the time when a group, sent by the bride's family, come to the groom's house to fetch (*mapag*) the groom and bring him and his group to the bride's house where the wedding ceremony is held. After that the groom stays in the bride's family until a group sent by his family come to fetch the new married couple (*penganten*), for another similar celebration (*ngundu mantu*). The couple stay with the groom's family for *ngundu mantu*, then they return to the bride's family and stay there for an undetermined period. It is common to find a new family with two or three children living with the bride's parent's household.

The purpose of the wedding ceremony is to express both joy and thankfulness as well as the expectation of well being. One purpose is the display of the newly married bride and groom to the public proclaiming that their relationship is lawful. After 4.00 p.m, dressed in either traditional court or European style wedding clothes prepared by *dukun paras* (wedding stylist), the couple are seated on a double seated chair in the fully decorated front room of the house. After giving their gifts, guests, mostly the bride's and groom's friends, come to offer congratulations. With a short break around sunset this exposition continues until late. On the evening of the wedding day, well to do parents sponsor an entertainment group such as an orchestra, *wayang, tarling* opera *or sandiwara* (theatric play). In this case, the guests, mostly the parent's guests, are seated on chairs set under a decorated tent built in the front yard. While enjoying the performance they are served with food. Upon leaving, the guests pass an envelope containing money to the host while they are shaking hands (*salam tempel*), as occurs at a boy's circumcision. The money is their contribution to the host who is holding the ceremony. Each contribution is carefully recorded and will be repaid (as a returned gift) at least at the same value sometime later when the contributor holds a similar occasion.

A *slametan*, is held the next morning around 8.00 a.m., The invited guests consist of neighbouring household heads, relatives, elders and distinguished *kyai*. Wearing *sarung*, shirt and *topong* (cap), they sit on mats on the floor in a rectangular formation facing foods and dishes in the front room of the house where the bride and the groom were displayed the afternoon and evening before. Other guests sit on chairs, with one line facing the other, separated by tables, on which *brekat*, food and dishes are also laid. On several occasions I saw no less than 60 or 80 people at the gathering. When the time comes and there are no more guests to arrive, without any formal speech, the host or the authorised person requests the appointed *kyai* to begin the proceedings with either *tahlil* or *marhaba* concluding with a *du'a*. On one occasion, only the *du'a* was recited, after which the host requested the guests to eat by saying: "*Mangga dikresakaken mawon sawontene*" ("Please have what is provided"). The guests start eating, while talking together. When they have eaten they then ask permission from the host to leave the gathering. They shake the host's hand while bringing with them the *brekat*, that is the basket(s) containing the food specially provided to be taken home.

Variations occur in procedures before the bride and the groom are seated. There are rituals such as *siraman* (bathing), *kerikan* (shaving eyebrows or other parts of facial hair), *tuggak jati leluhur* (visits to ancestors' graves), *sungkem* (prostration on the parents' lap), *nugel lawe* (cutting threads), *ngidek endog* (breaking an egg with the foot) and *sawer* (chants of advice). These rituals, which are really enactments of royal traditions, may or may not be included in a wedding ceremony, depending on individual preference and social standing. The *akad nikah* or *ijab kabul*, the religious procedure which legitimates the relationship of the couple, the actual act of the marriage contract, is the core of the marriage process among Muslims, whether they are devout or only statistical Muslims. Without it there is no marriage; other sections of ritual, before and after *akad nikah* or *ijab kabul* such as *lamaran, ta'liq thalaq*, prayer, various forms of celebration and wedding party, elaborate or simple, including *slametan*, large or small, are secondary rituals which can be left out without jeopardising the validity of the marriage. All these belong to *adat*.[68] Islam recommends such a

[68] Some anthropologists dealing with Indonesian Muslims, especially on Java, fail to understand fully the function of each element in the marriage procedures. A clear example of this concerns the *ijab-kabul*,

celebration although the way of the celebration is not specified and thus, provides room for local *adat*.[69]

It is interesting however, to ask, why most people, the Javanese Muslims in particular, tend to make the marriage celebration important, elaborate, and in fact, costly. One answer may be drawn from Pak Mardjuki:

> For Muslims, the union of husband and wife is sacred or holy. Unlike eating and drinking which end up in producing dirty residue, the husband-wife relationship is to produce descendants. As a noble undertaking, generating descendants should not be done at any time and anywhere at will. A newly married couple are the ones who will start such a sacred and noble thing, producing descendants and, thus, the parents should make all possible efforts to create an atmosphere where the new couple feels honourable and happy. This is to signify an expectation of good, honourable and happy descendants. As the most honourable and happiest individuals known on earth are a king and queen who are just, wise and thankful to God, the bride and the groom are also supposed to be treated like such a queen and king.[70]

Death Rituals

Eickelmann may be right in stating that deaths and funeral ceremonies in their essence show the most consistent features throughout the Muslim world, more so than the other rites of passage.[71]

the most essential element in Islamic marriage in any Muslim society. Bewildered by elaborate marriage procedures among the Sundanese, Wessing (1978:146), misunderstands and uses the term *ijab-kabul* to refer to a person -without even specifying who and what he/she (*ijab kabul*) really is- rather than to a part of the process. Geertz, on the other hand, does worse. He describes the so called "*idjab*" procedure (p. 56) but nothing in his descriptions belongs to *ijab*. Further, he falls into his own *abangan-santri-priyayi* trichotomy and imposes clear-cut religious differences among them; one of which is his exposition, as if *santri* do not think celebration important or *abangan* think celebration is much more important than *ijab kabul* itself. In other words, for the *abangan*, following Geertz, marriage is valid even without *akad nikah*, provided a party with elaborate ceremony is performed while in fact, be it among *abangan, santri* or *priyayi*, there is no marriage and there will be no wedding party of any kind without *akad nikah* or *ijab kabul*. Neither is there a marriage only by *ijab* (without *kabul*); the latter, *kabul*, is one thing that Geertz missed.

[69] In a *hadith*, narrated by Bukhari and Muslim, the Prophet, addressing Abd al-Rahman, said: "Celebrate your wedding, even by having only a lamb." For those who are invited to a wedding are required, by another hadith narrated by the same persons (Bukhari and Muslim), to come. See for example, Rasyid, S. (1988), *Fiqh Islam*, Bandung: Sinar Baru, pp. 368–369.

[70] Interview (19-5-1992): "Munggu wong Islam, kumpule wong laki-rabi iku mulya lan suci, sabab bli kaya mangan lan nginum kang dadie kotoran, hubungan laki-rabi iku dadine nekakaken turunan. Krana nekakaken turunan iku barang mulya lan suci, dadi ya bli kena sembarangan, kapan bae lan Ningi endi bae nglakonane. Penganten anyar iku wong kang arep ngawiti barang mulya lan suci, yaiku nekakaken turunan; dadi ya kudu dibahagiaaken lan dimuliaaken sebisa-bisane wong tuwa, maksude kanga nglambangaken cita-cita yen turunan kang arep teka iku supaya bagus, mulya lan bahagiya. Krana wong kang dianggep paling mulya lan bahagiya Ningi dunya iku ratu lan raja kang adil wicaksana sarta gelem syukuran Ningi Pyengana, penganten anyar uga baguse kudu digawe cara ratu lan raja kang mengkonon."

[71] See: "Rites of Passage: Muslim Rites," in *Encyclopedia of Religion*.

In Cirebon, as in other parts of Java, when someone is seriously ill, neighbours, friends and relatives feel obliged to see and cheer the ailing person (*tetilik*, meaning to have a visit), usually bringing something (*gegawan*) the ailing person likes to eat, especially fruit. When the illness is thought about to bring a death, the Testimony of Faith is whispered in the ailing person's ear and he is expected to repeat it (*nyebut*). His/her bed and lying position is adjusted so that the head is at the east and the feet at the west enabling the face to turn to Mecca. The Qur'an is also continuously recited especially Surah Yasin (QS. 36), to ensure that the person, if he dies, would die in a fully religious atmosphere. At the point of death the eyes are closed, the jaw is bound with the binding going over the top of the head so that the mouth is also closed. The arms are put over the lower chest, the right palm over the left in a position as in prayer and the whole body is covered with a sheet (*tapi* or *kain panjang*). The *lebe* (desa religious official) is sent for and the relatives and neighbours are informed.

When a Muslim dies the *syari'ah* requires the living to bathe the corpse, wrap it with white clothes in a certain manner, pray for it, bring it to and bury it in a Muslims burial complex. Not surprisingly, when someone hears that a person has died he feels that he should come to the dead person's house; women, in particular, bring a bowl or container covered with handkerchief. It is filled with rice and some money conveyed to the dead person's family as a contribution for the funeral. This visit is called *nglayat*. Along with *nglayat* people work together to care and bury the corpse; this working together is called *rerewang*. The funeral, if possible, is carried out quickly on the same day the death occurs. When the death occurs late in the afternoon the burial is postponed until the next day but the caring of the corpse is done early in the evening keeping the corpse over night ready for burial.

A divan for bathing the corpse is put near the well where a tankful of water containing herbs and flowers is ready. The corpse is laid on the divan, pillowed on three sections of a banana tree trunk at the nape, waist and legs. The bathing, during which the corpse's genitals are never let exposed, is led by a specialist or *lebe*, involving the dead person's close relatives, especially the older children. After the bathing is finished the corpse is taken and put on mats in the front room of the house, the head is at north and the feet south. All bodily orifices are closed with cotton and the whole body is perfumed, embalmed with herbs and wrapped in seamless clothes of white sheets and tied in around its feet, waist and top of the head. A litter is placed along the west-wall of the house onto which the corpse is placed. A long garment is spread to cover the litter; flowers in strings are put across on the litter to honour the dead, with the ends hanging loose on both sides. A funeral prayer (*salat jenazah*) is performed over the corpse together led by either the *lebe* or, most commonly, a local *kyai*, followed by a short speech on behalf of the dead person's family requesting people to forgive the deceased. If the deceased had some debt, the debtor is requested to contact the family for repayment. Then, accompanied by people chanting the confession of faiths, the corpse, shaded with an umbrella, is carried to the grave yard where a grave has been dug and is ready for the burial. Three people jump into the grave, the corpse is lifted from the litter and passed on to the three people standing in the grave who, after the call for prayer (*adzan*) is recited, put the corpse on its right side in the smaller hole in the grave facing the west. The head is on the north and the feet on the south; the tie of the shroud is loosened and the face is exposed so that the cheek touches the ground. Planks are laid to cover and protect the dead body from the dirt that is pushed into the grave raising the grave mound about 30 centimetres above the ground. Two wooden poles as grave markers are erected, one in the north, about the chest, another one in the south about the knees of the buried body. When all is completed, *talkin* and *tahlil* are performed.[72] Concluding with a *du'a* for the well being of the deceased and the survivor family, the burial comes to an end after which all the mourners return to their homes or jobs.

In the evening after burial people gather at the dead person's family's house (*ta'ziyah*) to cheer the surviving family and pray for them and for the deceased's well being. They recite the Qur'an, especially Surah 36 (Yasin), and then *tahlil*. On the third day after the death (*nelung dina*), food is served in a *slametan*. The *ta'ziyah* proceeds for seven nights and on the seventh night (*mitung dina*), food is again served along with *brekat*. This *slametan*, in which *tahlil* is performed, is again held on the 40th day (*matang puluh*), 100th day (*nyatus*), first anniversary (*mendak pisan*), second anniversary (*mendak pindo*) and finally, 1000th day (*nyewu* or *mendak ping telu*) or third anniversary, with the last *slametan*, marked by the erection of a brick tomb with grave stones over the grave.[73] Some informants relate the practice of the commemorative *slametan* to the decaying process of the dead body before it finally dissolves altogether into the soil. In normal conditions, it proceeds through seven stages; the first stage is three days after burial when the corpse is believed to swell. The second stage is at the seventh

[72] *Talkin* is addressed to the deceased to explain what will be going on in the grave soon after the last mourner has left and what the deceased should do or say when the two angels come to examine him/her. *Tahlil* on the other hand, (literally means saying "there is no God but Allah), refers to a complex prayer formula. It starts from a set recital of the opening of the Qur'an (*Fatiha*), merits of which is conveyed to a wide range of deceased persons. The first *Fatiha* is conveyed to the Prophet, his companions, his wives, descendants and ancestors. The second is conveyed to all God's prophets and messengers, the angels, the martyrs, scholars, leaders, teachers and the distinguished figures especially 'Abd al Qadir al Jilani and other saints. The merit of the third *Fatiha* is conveyed to parents and ancestors, all deceased Muslims male and female, all believers, male and female especially the one for whom the present *tahlil* is performed. The *tahlil* itself consists of the recital of some selected surah or verses of the Holy Qur'an, exaltation of God and the Prophet, *dzikr* (recollection that there is no God but Allah), begging forgiveness, well-being and safety, concluding with a *du'a*.

[73] Geertz (1976:72) identifies this last *slametan* as *kekah*, which my numerous informants of Central and East Javanese natives denied. *Kekah* (from Arabic *'aqiqah*), among the Javanese, is similar to *slapanan*, a *slametan* for shaving and naming the newly born baby. At *kekah* a goat or a sheep, rather than a fowl, as Geertz points out, is slaughtered when the baby is female; when it is male two goats or sheeps are slaughtered. (See also: "Birth Ritual", earlier in this Chapter).

day when the swelling reaches its culmination and explodes. After that the flesh dissolves and begins to decay. After forty days (third stage) the decaying process of the flesh is accompanied by a slow but sure movement of the body. The head becomes erect, as do the knees while on the 100th day (fourth stage) the decaying body turns from a lying to sitting position. The process goes on until the feet move backward and the head forward. In one year's time (fifth stage), the head reaches the knees. In two years time (sixth stage), when the flesh has completely disappeared the feet reach under the bottom and the head comes to the knees until finally, in three years time or 1000 days (seventh stage), all the bones are gathered together before finally dissolving gradually into the soil. The gathering together of the bones in the dissolving process, especially the movement of the head, is believed to repeat, in the reverse direction, the growing process of a baby (also in seven stages) when it was in the mother's womb. According to local traditions of eschatology rooted in Sufi doctrine (Syattariyah), this dissolving process has mystical significance. Each stage deserves concern and it is for that reason the *slametan* are performed.[74]

[74] The mystical significance of this process, which is basically of the Sufi tradition, see: Simuh (1988), especially pp 255–269. In fact, "Wirid Hidayat Jati" is akin to "Ngelmu Sejati Cirebon" and "Tharekat Syatariyah" held by Cirebon Kraton circle. For details see: Sulendraningrat (1978, 1980, 1982), Simuh (1988), Kartapraja (1978). However, Kartapraja (himself is a Modernist), wrongly associates this "*ngelmu*" with Sheikh Lemah Abang and accused it as a deviation from Islam.

Plate 10: Pagersari-kraton on "Muludan" ceremony prior to the "Panjang Jimat" procession.

Plate 11: Kraton religious officials on "Muludan" ceremony prior to the "Panjang Jimat" procession.

Plate 12: A group of circumcision grooms.

Plate 13: A circumcision groom on becak returns from "ngembang" at his elders' graves.

Plate 14: A circumcision ceremony.

Plate 15: A circumcision groom on display.

Plate 16: A carnival to fetch the groom for "munggah" ("marriage ceremony").

Plate 17: Seated: The bride, the groom and the Penghulu at a marriage contract.

Plate 18: A seven month pregnant woman is bathed at "Ngrujaki" ceremony.

Plate 19: Water with flowers, and a young yellow hybrid coconut crafted with Qur'anic verses and coin inserted used at the "Ngrujaki" ceremony.

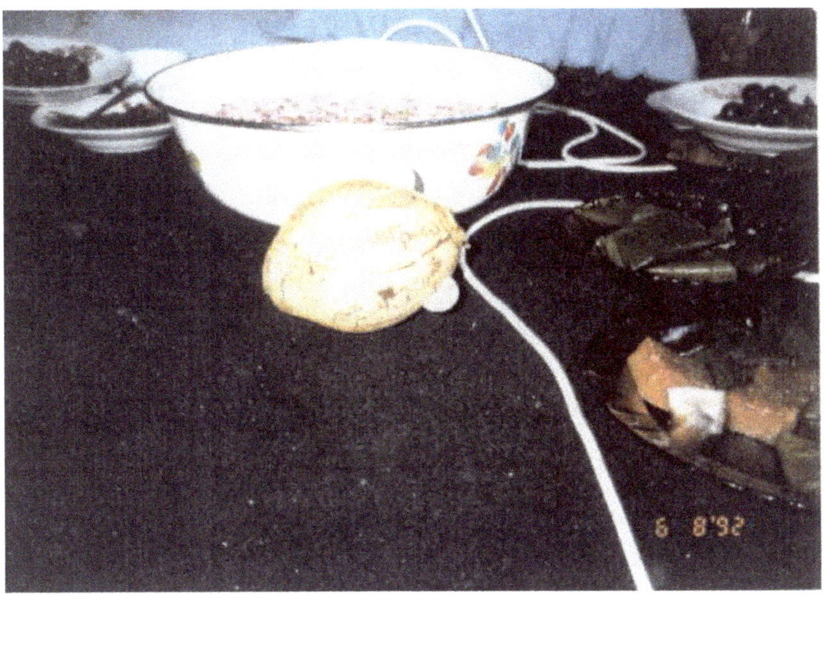

Plate 20: The bathed pregnant woman at "Ngrujaki" ceremony.

Plate 21: Chanting "Marhaba" to honour the pregnant woman.

Chapter 6: The Veneration of Wali and Holy Men: Visits to the Shrines

GENERAL FEATURES OF VENERATION: INTRODUCTION TO ZIARAH

Along with the ritual practices already discussed in the last two chapters, there is another ritual practice belonging to *adat* which is critically important: the veneration of *wali* (saints) and holy men. Part of this *adat* has been touched upon in the preceding chapters but many important aspects of it are still to be considered. Due to its place in the life of the people, and to its complexity, this practice deserves separate treatment.

Wali veneration is a long established practice throughout the Muslim world. Only since the influence of Ibnu Taymiyah and his student, Ibnu Qayyim, has this practice encountered serious challenge.[1] When Saudi Arabia was taken over by Ibnu Sa'ud, a Wahabi ruler in AH 1344, *wali* veneration was strongly condemned and stigmatised as idolatrous. Harsh measures through various means were taken to wipe out this practice throughout the country and the Arabian peninsula.[2] Despite all these attempts, *wali* veneration persists and flourishes in most parts of the Muslim world along with the flourishing Islam itself. Even in Arabia where the attack against this practice has been the most severe and strong, this practice has not been totally wiped out. Moreover, within the Traditionalists' line outside Saudi Arabia, the practice of *wali* veneration is almost unshaken. The world-wide occurrence of the practice of *wali* veneration is discussed for example by Goldziher, Patton, and Arnold.[3] Although South East Asia is not included in their accounts, this region is no exception to the continuation of this practice. In Indonesia, especially on Java, *wali* veneration, and in particular visits to their tombs, is a well established practice. Its wide-spread performance and its relation to the wider context of Javanese tradition (in which *wali*

[1] Ibn Taymiyya (661/1263–723/1328) was a distinguished Hanbalite jurist and theologian. He was born in Harran and later established himself in Damascus where he studied, taught and died. He is known as a literalist in understanding the Qur'an and famous for having said in a Friday sermon that "God comes down from heaven to Earth [to hear prayers] just as I am now coming down [the steps of the pulpit]." He championed the proposal that the gate of **Ijtihad** remained open and he had profound impact on the rise of Wahhabi movement in Saudi Arabia. He attacked many authorities in Islam including al-Ghazali, the Sufis, especially Ibn 'Arabi, stormed against innovation in religious practice and even questioned the competence and authority of the Patriarchal Caliph, Umar and 'Ali. (See: Concise Encyclopedia of Islam).

[2] Subhani, S.J. (1989), *Tawassul, Tabarruk, Ziarah Kubur, Karamah Wali, Termasuk Ajaran Islam: Kritik Atas Faham Wahabi*, Jakarta: Pustaka Al Hidayah, p.7.

[3] Goldziher, I. (1971), *Muslim Studies*, vol.2, ed, by M. Stern, London: George Allen and Unwin, pp. 277-341. Patton, W.M, "Saint and Martyr" in *The Encyclopedia of Religion and Ethics*; also Arnold, T.W, under similar heading in *ibid*.

veneration is an expression of piety among many Javanese) is stated by Fox.[4] Strong condemnation from the Modernists launched since the mid-1920s seems to have had relatively little impact on the persistence of its practice on Java.

In Cirebon, in particular, *wali* veneration takes various forms; the most prominent one of which this chapter will pay a greater attention is *ziarah* (visits) to the sacred places (shrines), of local *wali* or holy men, be they the tombs or the relics of these venerated figures. Other forms of wali veneration worth mentioning are *hadiwan, manaqib* and *hawl*. I shall touch briefly upon these types of veneration.

Hadiwan and Manaqib

Each of these forms of veneration is concerned with addressing the spirits of the *wali* or holy men. The revered figures in *hadiwan* or *manaqib* are the *wali* of foreign renown of whom, Syeikh 'Abd al-Qadir al-Jilani, the founder of the Qadiriyah order is of special prominence. *Hadiwan* is basically an invocation to God by reference to, or by asking the support from, the *wali*. It is conducted by a group of people led by an *imam*. *Manaqib*, on the other hand, is similar to *hadiwan* but its core is the recital of the biography of the *wali*.[5]

With respect to *hadiwan*, its procedure starts with asking forgiveness three times from God, followed by reciting the *Fatihah* (the first Surah of the Holy Qur'an) nine times. The merit of the first recitation of the *Fatihah* is to be conveyed to the spirit of the Prophet Muhammad; the second is to the spirits of the previous Prophets, angels, martyrs (*syuhada*) and good doers (*shalihin*). The third is to the spirits of Adam and Eve and all their descendants who excel themselves in religious work throughout the history of mankind until the Day of Judgement. The fourth is to the companions of the Prophet, their followers, followers of these followers and those who are linked with them throughout the history of mankind until the Day of Judgement. The fifth is to the spirits of the exegetes, jurists, theologians, *Sufis* and those who take their paths. The sixth is to the spirit of the Syeikh 'Abd al Qadir al-Jilani, and the seventh is to the spirits of his teacher and those who are linked with them by the chain of intellectual genealogy to Ali bin Abi Talib and then to the Prophet Muhammad. The eight is to the other *wali* such as As-Syadzili, An-Naqsabandi, Al-Ghazali and the nine *wali* of Java. The last Fatihah is to be conveyed to the spirits of the parents, teachers, and all Muslims wherever and whoever they are, dead or alive. A number of prescribed *Surah* of the Holy Qur'an are also recited, followed by a

[4] Fox, J.J. (1991), "Ziarah Visit to the Tombs of Wali, the Founder of Islam on Java" in Ricklefs, M.C, ed, *Islam in Indonesian Social Context*, Melbourne: CSEAS, Monash University. pp. 19-38.

[5] During field work I was not able to find an example of *manaqib* in practice and thus I wish to exclude it from my discussion. The only occasions of *manaqib* I could find were those among the Tijani followers at Buntet with reference to the founder of the order, Sheikh Ahmad Tijani, which was performed as an additional item to their routine gathering (*pengajian*). The biography of Ahmad Tijani which is composed in poetical form is read verse by verse by the *imam*, and the audience follows it in chorus.

full concentration of the mind to ask the help and support of all the *wali* in an invocation to God. This is done in a meditating manner by murmuring such words as: "Oh our master Al-Syeikh 'Abd al-Qadir al-Jilani, help us, help us, help us in acquiring our needs ... (at this moment each participant mentions his own special individual as well as his group's needs).

Usually, *hadiwan* or *manaqib* is held on Thursday night (*bengi Jum'ah*) at the request of a certain household and thus, it is performed in the house or *tajug*, attended by neighbouring households or members of the congregation of that prayer house (*jama'ah tajug*). This ritual is called *hadiwan*, probably due to the fact that although the procedures of the ritual, especially the litany is fairly complex, its core involves addressing God by His names a hundred times or more, "**Ya Hadi, Ya 'Alim, Ya Khabir, Ya Mubin** (Oh the Guiding, oh the Knowing, oh the Omniscient, oh the Clearest)." *Hadiwan* is concluded with a *du'a* recited by the *imam*, while the others support him by saying "Amen" repeatedly until the *du'a* ends. The content of the *du'a* basically involves begging God to fulfil the needs of those who pray by mentioning God's sovereignty and the fact that He has endowed numerous marvels to those who excelled themselves in religious works, especially the *wali*, and asking the *wali* for support so that God would fulfil what they need in this world as well as in the hereafter. After the *du'a*, food is served; while eating the participants chat and talk together in a way that is similar to the practice of other *slametan*.

Hawl and Ngunjung

Still another form of the veneration of holy men is the **hawl** or *haul*. This refers to the commemoration of the anniversary of the death of an important figure, possibly *a wali* but more frequently the founder of a *pesantren* or a renown *kyai* or even a commonly known ancestor of a certain descent group. The intensity of *haul* ranges from a simple gathering for *tahlil* or assembly to a big festival with a set of activities including a bazaar. An example of this is what happens with the *haul* at *Pesantren* Buntet which is held to commemorate its founders and lasts about a week. Finally, there is also *ngunjung* which, while basically the same thing as *ziarah*, has for its revered figure the founder of a village (*desa*) whose title *Ki* or *Nyi Gede* (male or female founder) is placed before the name of the *desa*, as is the case of Kalitengah.[6] The ancestors termed as *Ki* or *Nyi Gede* are included in the list of holy persons because they are now considered as the early propagators of Islam in the village. Any *ziarah, hadiwan, manaqib, haul* or *ngunjung*, is intended as a reminder to the performers who consider the personages they are venerating as exemplary models whose piety and behaviour deserve imitation and appreciation. By becoming involved in these rituals participants express a sense of piety. It is this function that many forms of *wali*

6 See the preceding Chapter.

veneration in Cirebon seem to occupy. Without disregarding other forms of veneration, the discussion that follows concerning *wali* veneration is focused on *ziarah*, mainly due to the fact that *ziarah* is the most prominent form of the practice. It is performed by many people from all strata of society and can be seen everyday in various places, locally called *kramat* (holy place).

BABAD NARRATIVE ACCOUNTS OF SOME CIREBONESE HOLY MEN

Wali veneration exists, in the first place, because there are people who render veneration. People are not satisfied to show respect by mere recollection of these figures at home, or by ritual such as *hadiwan* and *manaqib*. To show profound reverence, people seek, whenever possible, opportunities to visit the tombs and relics of important personages. This is further accentuated by the belief that the 'fragrance' of their honour still remains posthumously and thus such places contain *berkah* (divine blessing).[7] Thus visits to these places may also bring *berkah*. It is therefore critical to identify those personages who have attained local, even supra local reverence, by examining various biographical narrative accounts. As the number of the revered figures is very large, I shall confine my account to looking at those whom, I think, are the most widely known.

Certainly, there is a different degree of esteem among these figures. Each may be considered of higher or lower importance relative to the other but by and large their level of virtue is relative to a single figure, the most venerated *wali*, Syarif Hidayatullah (Sunan Gunung Jati). He is the centre of veneration because he is considered as the key figure responsible for the overall process of Islamisation throughout West Java, the Land of Sunda (*Tanah Sunda*). Other figures are peripheral and have their importance as either the patrons, disciples, descendants or assistants. The difficulty in recounting their biographies is that most of them are known locally through popular accounts either written or oral. Except possibly Sunan Gunung Jati, these other figures are more mythical than historical. Even concerning Sunan Gunung Jati himself, the historians disagree.[8] Because of the lack of historical evidence my account of the venerated figures is, thus, based on local sources especially the *Babad* (Cirebon Chronicles). But even to follow these sources a difficulty still arises because there are so many versions of the *Babad*. These Babad, however, can be broadly divided into those

[7] See further section.

[8] Considering the nature of local sources, which are mostly blended with legendary tales, historians such as Husein Djayadiningrat (1983), are reluctant to take them as sources for their accounts. The foreign (European) sources, such as Pinto (1692), a Portuguese, of questionable accuracy on whom historians prefer to rely on, says little about Cirebon and nothing about the figures under consideration. Beyond the main figure of Sunan Gunung Jati, de Graaf and Pigeaud (1989), for example, mentions only Pangeran Pasarean, Panembahan Ratu and Pangeran Girilaya, the 1st, the 3rd and the 4th descendants of Sunan Gunung Jati. These figures, however, have almost no significance in the *wali* veneration in Cirebon.

which have been collected, and those which are still in the hands of private owners. Among the former are those which are in the collection of either the Manuscripts Division of the National Library, National Archives in Jakarta, or the University of Leiden. There are at least 16 volumes in the National Library in Jakarta alone, one of which is a recent addition donated by Tjokrosubroto, an army Lieutenant from Cirebon. Some versions of the *Babad* are available in the market in Cirebon, some others are not. Examples of these *Babad* are as follows:

1. *Babad Tjerbon,* edited by J.L.A. Brandes and D.A. Rinkes (1911), collection No. 36, Deel LIX, Batavia: Albrecht.
2. A comment from linguistic and historical perspectives of this Brandes' edition is given by Ekajati (1978), *Babad Cirebon Edisi Brandes: Tinjauan Sastra dan Sejarah,* Bandung: Fakultas Sastra, Universitas Pajajaran.
3. *Tjarita Purwaka Tjaruban Nagari* by Pangeran Arya Tjarbon supposedly written in 1720, which has been partly translated by Atja (1972).[9] Atja has also made an overall revised edition with an introductory comment which appeared in 1986 as *Carita Purwaka Caruban Nagari: Karya Sastra Sebagai Sumber Pengetahuan Sejarah,* Bandung: Proyek Pengembangan Permuseuman Jawa Barat.[10]
4. *Perjuangan Wali Sanga, Babad Cirebon (Pasundan),* by H. Mahmud Rais and Sayidil Anam (1957), reprinted more than once and available in the market. My own copy is a 1986 reprint.
5. *Babad Tanah Sunda, Babad Cirebon,* by P.S. Sulendraningrat (not clearly dated), also available in the market, my copy is a 1984 reprint.
6. *Babad Cirebon Asli,* by P.B Ardiningrat, a mimeographed version dated 1913. I suspect my copy is a recent reprint although its reprinting date is not indicated.
7. *Babad Cirebon* (of 'Klayan manuscript,') a newly found version owned by Taryadi Tjokrodipuro from Klayan, Cirebon. This version has been transcribed into Roman script with an introduction and summary by S.Z. Hadisutjipto (1979), entitled *Babad Cirebon,* Jakarta: Proyek Penerbitan Bacaan dan Sastra Indonesia dan Daerah, Departemen Pendidikan dan Kebudayaan.

For convenience, my recount of Cirebonese holy men is mainly based on *Babad Tjerbon* of the Brandes' collection (No.1 above). This is an older edition among

[9] Ricklefs (1993), casts a doubt on the authenticity of this version, especially due to its ostensible solution of the problems of distinguishing Sunan Gunung Jati from Faletehan. See his comments in his *A History of Modern Indonesia Since c. 1300*, 2nd ed, London: MacMillan, p. 38.

[10] Atja takes some other historical sources into account, including Ricklefs' sceptical warning (see the preceding note). Part of his introductory comment is his positive attitude on the value of taking *Babad* narratives in general, and *Carita Purwaka Caruban Nagari* in particular, as a source of an historical account through careful selection.

other *Babad* and already known to Western scholarship. I will refer further to this *Babad* as '*Babad Tjerbon.*' In addition to this I shall also take into account oral explanations from *Juru Kunci* (key bearers or custodians) of the *kramat* site(s) in regard to figures on whom the *Babad* tells only very little.[11] The figures I wish to include in this discussion are: Walangsungsang, Rarasantang, Syarif Hidayatullah (Sunan Gunung Jati), Pangeran Bagus Pasei, Syeikh Kahfi, Pangeran Panjunan, Nyi Mas Gandasari and Syeikh Magelung. These personages are among the most important focus of *wali* veneration in Cirebon. The first four are buried at Gunung Sembung; Syeikh Kahfi is at Gunung Jati, Pangeran Panjunan at Plangon, Nyi Mas Gandasari at Panguragan and Syeikh Magelung at Karang Kendal.

Walangsungsang (Cakrabuana) and Rarasantang

Babad Tjerbon recounts that Walangsungsang (Cakrabuana) and his sister Rarasantang, mother of Sunan Gunung Jati, were the children of the king of Pajajaran from his marriage to a woman from Singapura (4 km north of Cirebon).[12]

Cakrabuana took Rarasantang with him on pilgrimage (to Mecca). When they were in Arabia they made a visit to Baitulmaqdis (*Beta 'lmoeqdas*) at the time when the ruler of Bani Israil in Egypt (*Mesir*), Maulana Mashuda or Huda, was in mourning because his wife had just passed away.[13] Maulana Huda instructed his minister (*qadi* or *penghulu*), Qadi Djamaluddin and his family, to find for him a woman whose appearance was like his former wife. It happened that the *qadi* met with Cakrabuana and Rarasantang who were on their way to Baitulmaqdis. The minister found that Rarasantang and Maulana Huda's former wife were alike and reported the matter to Maulana. Upon learning this Maulana Huda asked the minister to summon Cakrabuana and Rarasantang to his palace and thence, after Rarasantang stated her requirements and the *maulana* granted them, the marriage occurred. Among the requirements was that Rarasantang wished to have a son to become a *wali* who would preach Islam on Java. After his pilgrimage Cakrabuana took a new name, Haji Abdullah Iman (haji Ngabdoellah Dzoe'liman); Rarasantang, upon marriage, took the new name, Syarifah Mudaim (syarifah Moeda'im). After marriage, Maulana Huda and Mudaim went to Mecca on another pilgrimage. They reached Medina in the month of Rabi'ulawwal,

[11] Reliance on this *Babad ('Babad Tjerbon')*, however, posed further difficulty because, as we will see, it tells very little about Cirebon and the Cirebonese holy men. More over, some ambiguities also appear in this *Babad*. This leads to and allow various interpretations both scholarly and popular. Encountered with this shortcomings, some other sources worth considering. For clarity purposes, I shall also consider some other *Babad* known locally.

[12] In *Babad Tjerbon* (p 29), Walangsungsang is identified as 'radja Tjakra boeana,' Rarasantang as 'nji dalem Satang,' and Sunan Gunung Jati as 'Soenan Gunung jati poerba' or 'molana Jati.' Their brother, 'radja Sengara' which this Babad also mentions, has little significance in present day *wali* veneration in Cirebon.

[13] *Beta'lmoeqdas* must be the **Bayt al-Muqaddas** (Dome of the Rock in Palestine), the former direction of Muslims' prayer. The reference of *molana* must be an Arabic *maulana* (our master), a reference to a dignitary (king, ruler, prophet, etc).

visited the Prophet's tomb and stayed in Medina until the month of Shawwal. They continued their journey to Mecca and did an *umrah*.[14] They stayed in Mecca for a period of time where, on the month of Safar, Mudaim bore a child, Syarif Hidayatullah (Hidajat sjarif). When Syarif was 40 days old, they returned to Egypt.[15]

After acting as the *wali* at Rarasantang's marriage to Maulana Huda, Abdullah Iman returned to Java but not to Pajajaran (Pedjadjaran) but instead, to Cirebon. He married Riris, the daughter of a local *Kuwu* and upon the *kuwu's* death he took his father-in-law's office and position as *Kuwu*, with the new name Pangeran Carbon (pangeran Tjerebon). From this marriage Pangeran Carbon had a daughter, Pakungwati, who later stayed at the Great House of Jalagrahan (*dalem agung Padjalagrahan*). Pangeran Carbon himself stayed at Cirebon Girang although his office was at Lemah Wungkuk.[16]

Syarif Hidayatullah (Sunan Gunung Jati) and Fatahillah

Babad Tjerbon goes on to recount that Maulana Huda passed away when his sons Syarif and Nurullah, were still infants, and thus the sultanate was taken care of by Maulana's brother, Raja Ongkah (radja 'Oenqah). When Syarif passed adolescence Ongkah took him to a special room where a box, the heirloom from the *maulana* was stored. Upon opening the box Syarif found a book about the Essence of *Muhammadiyah (haqeqat Muhammadiah)* written in golden ink.[17] This book inspired Syarif to asked his mother's permission to leave the palace to seek the knowledge about the essence of *Muhammadiyah*. He told his mother and Ongkah to give his rights to the sultanate to his brother, Nurullah. He then set off on an adventure.[18]

[14] *Umrah* is the pilgrimage to Mecca outside the Hajj season.

[15] *Babad Tjerbon*, pp 29-36. The *Babad* says that the date of their return to Egypt is '*waktoe tatkalaning babar hedjrah rasoeloe'llah lagi pitoeng atoes sangang poeloeh lilima poenjoeling warsi doerjataning kanabijan kang estoe Moehammadihi*,' suggesting that it was AH 795 (p 36).

[16] *Babad Tjerbon*, pp 37-38.

[17] What seems to be indicated is a *Sufi* book with a message from the *molana* advising his son to study Sufism.

[18] *Ibid*, pp 39-42. The *Babad* recounts at length (pp 43-64) about Syarif's spiritual journey in search of the real truth or *haqeqat Moehammadiah* which involved wandering from place to place. On this journey he found strange things and had strange experiences. For example, after 7 days of his journey, he reached the sea-shore and found a speaking dragon and had a conversation with it. After passing south of Syam (*Esjam* or Syria) and after another 7 days he met a hermit named 'Afani, who approached him from the sea and suggested to him that they go together to visit the tomb of Salomon; hence, he started a spiritual ascendancy (*a kind of mi'raj?*). He met satans, reached the country of jinns, met the Prophets Hidr (*Hidhir*), Ilyas (Elias), Nuh (Noah), and finally the Prophet Muhammad. The latter gave to Syarif a name. 'Sayid Kamil,' and taught him among other things, not to prostrate to anyone other than God ('*adja soedjoed pada anjar*'), told him to find teachers, try to become a just '*chalifah rasoel*' (vicegerent of the Messenger). The story is narrated in mythical flavour. As the mythical story tells about spiritual journey, I think, the *Babad* should be interpreted, as telling about a religio-mystical experience rather than a purely physical one.

After his spiritual adventure, Syarif returned to Egypt for a reunion with his mother, uncle and other family members. He did not stay with the family for long as he soon asked permission from her mother to leave the palace to study religion from distinguished teachers. First he went to Medina to visit the Prophet's tomb, then to Mecca and studied with Syeikh Tadjmu'ddin al-Kubri. After studying with this *Syeikh* he moved to another *Syeikh*, named Ata'ullahi Syadzili, then to another teacher, Maulana Datuk Siddiq at Surandil and took an initiation in the Khalwatiyah order (*'sjoeghoel chalwati wirid'*). From Surandil he continued his journey to Java via Banten where he found a Muslim community there due to the work of Sunan Ampel. From there he went to Kundul to see Syeikh Madzkur and to Kudus to see Datuk Bahrul who taught him the whole corpus of Islamic religion comprising the *syare't, tarekat, haqeqat* and *ma'rifat (ma'rifatoe'llahi Ta 'ala*). Datuk Bahrul authorised and suggested him to start preaching the Islamic faith, but Syarif said that he needed to contemplate first at Banyu Putih, ('banjoe Poetih,' literally meaning white water) where Maulana Dhofi did the same thing.[19]

When Syarif (Sayid Kamil) visited Sunan Ampel, the *sunan* advised him to go to Cirebon and to stay first at 'Gunung Jati Sembung.' Syarif took the advice and went to Cirebon. On his voyage to Cirebon he met Patih Keling and his men who numbered 100. Syarif asked them to embrace Islam saying that he would be responsible if the conversion angered Patih Keling's master. Patih Keling and his men were convinced and embraced Islam, then escorted Syarif to Cirebon and stayed at Gunung Sembung.[20] In Cirebon Syarif met, and was welcomed with warmth and cheer by, his uncle and all of his family, including Nyi Dalem Pakungwati, daughter of Kuwu Carbon, who later became his wife. Pangeran Cirebon Girang and Kuwu Carbon held a meeting and decided to cease paying the tribute of shrimp paste' (*terasi*) to Pajajaran. This angered of the king of Pajajaran who sent a group of inspectors and soldiers to investigate the matter. When the group reached Gunung Kromong by night they saw a light shining at the peak of Gunung Sembung. This light guided them. Before they reached Gunung Sembung however, at the mount Patahunan, they were mysteriously rendered lame, trapped by the marvel of *'kalimah syahadat'* and were finally converted to Islam.[21]

[19] *Ibid*, pp 64-68. Molana Dhofi, probably refers to Sheikh Idhofi or Datuk Kahfi who was traditionally known as an Islamic teacher predating Syarif.

[20] Converting Patih Keling was therefore, Syarif's first work in his career of preaching Islam and Patih Keling and his men were thus his first disciples (*Ibid* pp 79-80). Later, the descendants of Patih Keling and his men become the hereditary custodians of the Astana Gunung Jati grave complex where Syarif and others were buried (see the next section).

[21] Ibid, pp. 80-81. This is the first event for which the *Babad* uses the reference of *Maulana Jati* ('molana Djati') to replace, *Sayid Kamil* which was the previous reference for Syarif Hidayatullah. It seems open to assume the possibility that *Babad* might have combined various stories about different figures and associated them all with Syarif Hidayatullah. The story about the (Chinese) pregnant girl Nio Ong Tin,

Haji Abdullah Iman told Maulana Jati to take power and to claim authority as the heir of Pajajaran, to an area from western end of Java (Ujung Kulon) eastward to Cipamali in Brebes (Central Java). Beyond that border eastward, he said, Maulana Jati was not heir (*'dede waris kita'*), but the land belonged to Majapahit. Maulana Jati, however, did not take power immediately but left it instead to his uncle, Haji Abdullah Iman, because he wanted to go to Egypt first and bring his mother to stay with him in Java. Moreover, he said, he also wished to visit the Prophet's tomb in Medina for his blessing and Baitulmaqdis for other prophets' permission.[22] Before going to Egypt he went with Pangeran Maqdum and met Ki Gede Babadan whose daughter, Nji Mas Babadan, he married.

On his way to Egypt Maulana Jati stopped in Johor where he obtained a disciple, 'Abdulrahim. From Johor he went to China to fulfil an invitation from the Chinese emperor who wished to test Maulana Jati's saintship. The emperor summoned his daughter, Nio Ong Tin, and asked Maulana Jati to say whether or not "the unmarried girl's confession that she was pregnant" was true. Maulana Jati answered that it was true that the girl was pregnant. The emperor laughed and said that Maulana Jati was not a true saint, because he was unable to recognise the truth that the girl was not really pregnant. He even denounced Maulana as a liar and asked him to leave China immediately. The *Babad* recounts that after Maulana Jati had gone the emperor found that his daughter, who had been referred to as "the unmarried girl" was really pregnant. Feeling deeply embarrassed by this affair, he sent a ship with his daughter on board (to Cirebon) at night to avoid detection. He told his daughter to surrender herself to the Maulana.[23]

In Egypt Maulana Jati settled all his family business including the passing on of his rights to the throne to his brother Nurullah, then asked his mother to return with him to Java. Returning from Egypt with his mother, Maulana Jati stopped at Surandil to fetch his friend, raja Lahoet; he landed at Muara Jati. He stayed there to preach Islam and found the Chinese emperor's daughter was already there. He converted her to Islam along with others such as Babu Dempul, Adipati Cangkuang and Patih Gering. Maulana Jati travelled with Adipati Cangkuang through Pajajaran. He reached Banten where Maulana Jati met Putri Kawunganten, married her, and took her to Cirebon to stay at Muara Jati village. From this marriage he had a son Sabakingking, and a daughter Ratu Winaon.

Afterward came hostile white men, who caused serious disturbances. Patih Keling thought that they were from Keling sent to support Pajajaran. Pangeran

associated with Syarif Hidayatullah goes parallel with the story about Ajar Cempaka with a pregnant woman appears in Babad Tanah Jawi, pp 11-12.

22 *Ibid*, p. 83-84. This, probably, marked the foundation of Cirebon ruling house by Cakra Buana predating *kraton*.

23 *Ibid*, pp 88-90. In the Babad it is written *'angaoela ing kakoeng'* which literally means to enslave (herself) to the man (p. 90). See also Chapter Three.

Carbon, Patih Keling and Adipati Cangkuang made up the necessary preparations and went to battle until all enemies were driven away.[24]

Along with the appointment of the other *wali* in other places, Maulana Jati was appointed ruler of Cirebon ('Tjerebon') by the Wali Council. From this time on Maulana Jati became Sunan Gunung Jati. The Wali Council was mainly concerned with theological issues and was attended by Sunan Bonang, Syeikh Majagung, Sunan Gunung Jati, Sunan Kali Jaga, Syeikh Bentong, Maulana Maghribi, Syeikh Lemah Abang, Sunan Giri and Pangeran Kudus.[25] Soon after his appointment, Sunan Gunung Jati erected the great mosque, *(Sang) 'tjipta rasa,'* located at *'tegal pangalang-alang'* (the field of wild grass). At that time, another mosque had been erected in Demak, the region where Raden Fatah was the ruler.[26] *Babad Tjerbon* also says that Sunan Gunung Jati was involved in the defeat of Majapahit by Demak in which he (Sunan Gunung Jati) was responsible for mounting the siege on the west front. The war between Demak and Majapahit is described by the *Babad* as a total war involving not only physical force but also mystical power, where the superiority of *karamat* (honour from God) over *istidraj* (magic) was attested.[27]

Babad Tjerbon recounts Sunan Gunung Jati's marriage to a woman from Tepasan Adi from whom he had a son, Pangeran Pasarean, and a daughter, Ratu Ayu, while from his royal wife (*garwa jati*) he had Pangeran Kelana Adi and Pangeran Gung Anom (Sedang Lautan). Sunan Gunung Jati entrusted his position to his son, Pangeran Pasarean, while Sunan Gunung Jati himself went about to preach Islam. He converted the people of Bandung, Cianjur, Sumedang, Bogor and Jakarta ('Djaketra') but the ruler of Galuh, Kuningan and Ciamis showed animosity toward him. Some of the converts became religious hypocrites (*munafik*) so that he was forced to send representatives. He appointed Raja Lahut

[24] *Ibid*, pp. 90–94. The coming 'white men enemies' might be the Portuguese and thus the battle into which they were involved may be what is traditionally known as the defeat of Sunda Kalapa. Historians note that in 1522 the Portuguese had agreed with Banten to establish a port on its eastern border as a barrier to the Muslim forces from the east. This caused Pajajaran's second port, Sunda Kalapa, to be taken by the Muslims and renamed Jayakarta, meaning 'prosperous victory' (Ricklefs 1993:37).

[25] While other *wali* are well known, Syeikh Majagung and Syeikh Bentong, are not. *Babad Tjerbon* does not specify who they are. The name Majagung is probably identical to Maja Agung, a place in East Java, suggesting that Syeikh Majagung might be an East Javanese *wali*. Syeikh Bentong, on the other hand, is described in some (recent) versions of Cirebon Cronicle as one who first met Syarif Syam alias Syeikh Magelung alias Pangeran Karang Kendal. Syeikh Bentong, according to these *Babad*, advised Syarif Syam to see Sunan Gunung Jati to have his hair cut [See for example, Mahmud Rais and Sayidil Anam, *Perjuangan Wali Sanga Babad Cirebon (Pasundan)*], unknown publisher, pp 144–146.

[26] *Ibid*, pp 101–104. When Maulana Jati became Su(suhu)nan Gunung Jati, he held the position as *'ratoe pandita'* suggesting that besides being a (territorial) ruler he was also a religious leader. This is different from the position of, for example, raden Fatah in which the Babad says: '... *maring Demak para wali arsa ngangkat* raden Fatah *djoemenenga ratoe djawi* (... the *wali* appointed raden Fatah the ruler of Java),' suggesting he was only a territorial ruler, not a spiritual leader (p. 104).

[27] Ibid, 104–110. *'bala boeda mahabara sakti sarta istidradj bala islam sakti poenjoel linuwih sarta karamat'* (the Buddhists army was powerful with its magic, the Muslim army was more powerful with *its karamat'* p. 107).

his representative in 'Djaketra,' Sabakingking (Seba-kingkin) in Banten, Haji Abdullah Iman in Pajajaran and Raja Sengara in Tegal Luar.[28]

Sunan Gunung jati strengthened his relationship with Demak by establishing a marriage alliance.[29] Sunan Gunung Jati's son, Gung Anom, married Raden Fatah's daughter, Ratu Nyawa. Not long after the marriage, Gung Anom died at sea, becoming known as Pangeran Seda(i)ng Lautan: the prince who died at sea; he was buried at Mundu. Pangeran Pasarean, another Sunan Gunung Jati's son, replaced Gung Anom to become Ratu Nyawa's husband and stayed in Demak.[30]

Figure 6.1: Marriage alliance between Sunan Gunung Jati and Raden Fatah

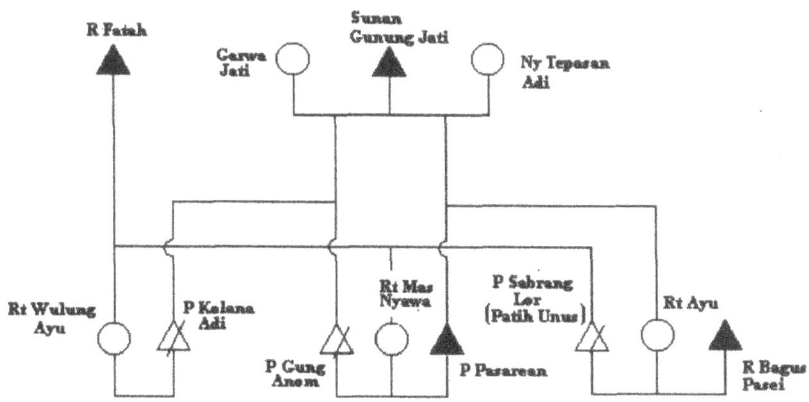

This alliance was still further strengthened when Sunan Gunung Jati's daughter, Ratu Ayu, married Sultan Demak, the successor of Raden Fatah, from whom Ratu Ayu inherited a set of musical instruments ('*gamelan sekati*'). After the Sultan of Demak died, Ratu Ayu remarried a 'noble from overseas' (*wong agoeng sabrang*), named Ratu Bagus Pasei ('ratoe bagoes Faseh'), and had a daughter, Ratu Nawati Rarasa. Nawati Rarasa married son of Pangeran Pasarean, Dipati Pakungja or Dipati Ingkang Seda(i)ng Kemuning. They begot a son, Pangeran

[28] Ibid, pp. 98–100. *Garwa djati* was probably, Nyai Pakoengwati, daughter of Pangeran Cakrabuana (Haji Abdullah Iman), the founder of *kedaton* (Cirebon ruling house). The *Babad* also mentions Sunan Gunung Jati's marriage with *poetri ratoe Tjina* (traditionally known as Putri Cina, Nio Ong Tin or Rara Sumanding, daughter of the Chinese emperor), and that this marriage was short lived because the *poetri* soon passed away. For her honour, a grave complex was established at gunung Sembung employing ki Goesa, an architect from Karawang. After this site became a grave complex, Sunan Gunung Jati moved to Pakungwati palace in the city of Cirebon (p. 114).

[29] One established relation between Sultan Demak and Sunan Gunung Jati was religious. Sultan Demak was Sunan Gunung Jati's disciple having taken an oath (*be'at*). He followed Sunan Gunung Jati's religious (*Sufi*?) way. The *Babad* (p 112) states: "*soeltan Demak ... mlebet be'at ... maring kandjeng sinoehoen Djati*' (soeltan Demak ... took an oath ... to the master *sinoehoen Djati*). The Javanese word *be'at* must be from Arabic **bay'ah** which, according to Danner (1988:233) refers to "the initiatic pact between the Sheikh and his disciple that implies rebirth and entry into the Path. In return Sultan Demak assisted Sunan Gunung Jati in the construction of the city and palace in Cirebon by sending Raden Sepat, an architect from Majapahit (*Babad Tjerbon*, p. 112).

[30] *Ibid*, p 113.

Agung Pakung Radja who, upon Sunan Gunung Jati's death, succeeded to rule Cirebon.[31] The noble man from overseas, named as Ratu Bagus Pasei, is identified by some writers, especially Babad commentators, as Fatahillah, Faletehan or Fadhilah Khan.[32] There is disagreement among some writers, especially historians, on whether or not Syarif Hidayatullah (Sunan Gunung Jati) and Fatahillah alias Faletehan alias Tubagus Pasei alias Tagaril alias Fadhilah Khan are the same person.[33]

Syeikh Datu Kahfi and Pangeran Panjunan

According to local commentators, Syeikh Datu Kahfi is locally equated with Syeikh Idhofi, whose tomb is at Gunung Jati (the former Amparan Jati hill). He is believed to have been a religious teacher predating Sunan Gunung Jati. *Babad Tjerbon*, however, says very little about him. He is referred to firstly as 'Molana Dhofi,' the one who had a place of spiritual seclusion (*petapan*) at 'banjoe poetih' (?) Sayid Kamil (Maulana and later Sunan Jati) used this site for meditation before he started preaching Islam.[34] Secondly, the *Babad* mentions Syeikh Datu Kahfi ('shekh datoe Kahfi') in relation to Pangeran Panjunan. Pangeran Panjunan followed Syeikh Datu Kahfi from Baghdad to Java.[35] *Babad Tjerbon* does not clearly state who Molana Dhofi and Syeikh Kahfi were, nor whether both names refer to the same or to different persons.

According to the *Babad Tjerbon* the original name of Pangeran Panjunan was Maulana Abdul Rahman. He led a group of Arab immigrants from Baghdad including his own sister, Siti Baghdad, and brother, Syeikh Abdul Rahim.[36] They came to Java in three ships and settled separately in Sembung, Muara Jati, Junti (17 km north of Cirebon) and Japura (13 km east of Cirebon). They followed Datu Kahfi who came to Java much earlier and who settled at Muara Jati. Ratu Hud, Pangeran Panjunan and Sunan Gunung Jati were said to have a kinship relation where Sunan Gunung Jati was Panjunan's cousin ('*sederek misanan*'). Pangeran Panjunan initially adopted the Jabariyah school of theology but after

[31] Ibid, 124–125. The 'soeltan Demak' (p. 124), husband of ratoe Ayoe, probably refers to the traditionally known as Pangeran Sabrang Lor son and successor of Raden Fatah. He is identified by historians such as Kartodirdjo (1987:38), as Pate (Patih) Unus, the ruler of Jepara. He died in an expedition to Malacca against Portuguese in the new year of 1512/3.

[32] See for example, Hadisutjipto S.Z. (1979), *Babad Cirebon*, Departemen Pendidikan dan Kebudayaan, especially pp viii–ix; Atja (1986), *Carita Purwaka Caruban Nagari: Karya Sastra Sebagai Sumber Pengetahuan Sejarah*, Bandung: Proyek Pengembangan Permuseuman Jawa Barat. Sulendraningrat, S. (1985) *Sejarah Cirebon*, Jakarta: P.N. Balai Pustaka. Abdurrahman, P.R. (1982) *Cerbon*, Jakarta: Sinar Harapan).

[33] Husein Djajadiningrat (1913), for example, who based his argument on *Babad Banten* (Brandes' collection No. 269), concluded they were the same person, whereas *Babad Tjerbon* (and some other versions of Cirebon Chronicles) distinguishes between these personages. (Consider note 11).

[34] *Ibid*, p 68.

[35] Ibid, p 94.

[36] The story of pangeran Panjoenan appears in *Babad Tjerbon* (pp. 94–98). Siti Baghdad is locally known as Syarifah Baghdad, she became Sunan Gunung Jati's wife and took a new name, Nyai Mas (Syarifah) Panata Pasambangan.

having been involved in a theological debate with Sunan Gunung Jati, he took an oath (*be'at*) to follow Sunan Gunung Jati's way.[37] He and his families, who were engaged in making pottery (*awangoen gegetak*), were given homage at Panjunan, a site in the city of Cirebon. The Panjunan mosque, one of the antiquities in Cirebon, is attributed to him. Until now, his descendants (local Arabs) who live around this mosque still retain their pottery making traditions. It is said that they do this to preserve their hereditary occupation which lays stress on spiritual rather than economic values. Upon his death Pangeran Panjunan was buried at Plangon (12 km south-west of Cirebon) and thus came to bear the name of Pangeran Plangon ('pangeran ing Pelalangoen'). His tomb attracts visitors, especially on 27 of Rajab (*Rejep*) when a festival is held annually.[38]

Nyi Mas Panguragan and Pangeran Karang Kendal

The locally well-known Nyi Mas Panguragan or Nyi Mas Gandasari and Pangeran Karang Kendal or Syeikh Magelung are important because their tombs have become popular foci of *wali* veneration in Cirebon outside the Astana grave complex where Sunan Gunung Jati and others are buried. *Babad Tjerbon*, however, tells very little about these figures. It only recounts that not long after Maulana Jati married Nyi Mas Babadan, he met a young saint (*pandita*), whose name was Pangeran (ing) Karang Kendal. This *pangeran* willingly became Maulana Jati's disciple and agreed to travel together to preach Islam.[39] Later, they met a woman, an Egyptian princess (*'poetri Mesir'*), younger sister of Tubagus Pasei. The princess requested Sunan Gunung Jati to help her make a decision.[40] Sunan Gunung Jati agreed to help her by saying that if she would rather wait (to marry?)

[37] In the *Babad* Pangeran Panjunan is described as *'angangken kadjabariah'* (p. 96), suggesting that he adopted Jabariyah, an Islamic school of theology which held that God compels man to act as he does and thus, man's actions are completely predetermined. Jabariyah emerged as a response to and thus the firm opponent of Qadariyah, which held the doctrine of absolute human free will. Pangeran Panjunan finally learned and followed Sunan Gunung Jati who was supposedly an Ash'arite Sunni. (*'molana Djati woewoesane ahli soeni kang woeroek ming pangeran Pandjoenan.'* p. 97). Al-Ash'ari (d. 324/944) was a religious thinker who adapted certain rational methods to Suni Islam. He was originally a Mu'tazili, the seemingly neo-Qadariyah school of theology. This school sought to apply reason to a broad range of questions by using the methods of argument, reasoning and dialectic. Al-Ash'ari abandoned this school as it did not reflect an adequate understanding of spiritual reality. (See: "Kalam," *The Concise Encyclopaedia of Islam*).

[38] *Ibid*, p. 98. The name 'Plangon' is said to have been constructed from *pe-langu-an*, meaning the place of *lelangu* (seclusion) where pangeran Pandjoenan is said secluded himself when he was alive.

[39] Ibid, p. 85.

[40] *Babad Tjerbon* recounts: *'noeli ... teka ajoeh wong wadon atas poetri Mesir ... rajine toebagoes Paseh' anoehoen toeloeng ing djeng molana panjinge ing sawargane ...'* which means: 'then came a beautiful lady, an Egyptian princess, younger daughter of Tubagus Pasei, begging help to lord Maulana to lead her to heaven.' (*Ibid*, p.86). It is not clear who 'poetri Mesir' (Egyptian princess) really was but local narratives indicate that she was Nyi Mas Panguragan or Nyi Mas Gandasari who was about to make a decision about her marriage (to Pangeran Karang Kendal).

in the hereafter, whereas in this world, she would become Maulana Jati's disciple.[41]

As the *Babad Tjerbon* does not indicate clearly who the Egyptian princess was (except that she was Tubagus Pasei's sister) a rather intricate explanation about these figures was given by *juru kunci* (custodians) at Panguragan where Nyi Mas Gandasari was buried. It was said that Gandasari was an Achenes who had been taken by Cakrabuana upon his return from his pilgrimage to Mecca when she was still a child.[42] At fifteen she learned Islam from Sunan Gunung Jati and began to follow the *Sufi* way under the guidance of Sunan Gunung Jati. Although she was a woman, she was very much interested in and paid special attention to acquiring the art of self defence and had an instrumental role in the defeat of Rajagaluh a vassal-state of Hindu Galuh-Pajajaran. Due to her beauty and with high competence in the art of self defence she could fool Prabu Cakraningrat, the then ruler of Rajagaluh who, in the hope of attracting and then marrying her, took her and showed her everything about the marvels and excellence of Rajagaluh, including the detailed security of the kingdom. This paved the way for Cakrabuana, the army commander of Cirebon, to make the necessary plans to bring about the fall of Rajagaluh. Gandasari was buried at Panguragan and from this the name Nyi Mas Panguragan is derived.[43]

In 1991, her tomb and musoleum were thoroughly renovated with the construction of permanent stone buildings with modern ceramic tiles which cost about Rp 200,000,000.00 (more than A$ 120,000.00). The funds came from a donor named Hellina Ratu Handia, a rich Central Javanese business woman staying in Jakarta who felt obliged to do this for her success in business.[44] According to Pak Yamsir, the key bearer, Ratu Handia was once a visitor at this *kramat*. She is a business woman initially engaged in jewellery making, who

[41] Maulana Jati said: '... *tatapi deng ridha besoek ing achirat bae doepi ing doenja soenakoe baboenira*' which means: '... but you have to be generous that you wait (to marry) in the hereafter, while in this world I take you as my disciple.' (*Ibid*, p. 86).

[42] In more recent *Babad*, Nyi Mas Panguragan was said as foster daughter of Pendeta Selapandan. This *pendeta* (hermit) obsessed to have a pious child. Due to this obsession he performed a meditation under a '*pudak*' tree (a tree which is grown for its scenty flower). He gave up his meditation when a (*pudak*) flower fell onto his lap. Upon his return home he was entrusted to take care Nyi Mas Panguragan under his guardianship. See for example: *Babad Tanah Sunda/Babad Cirebon*, p.60; *Perjuangan Wali Sanga Babad Cirebon (Pasundan)*, p.134. For a fairly long story about her and her relation with 'Pangeran Magelung,' see also: *Babad Cirebon* (Taryadi's manuscript), pp.77-82. These *Babad* do not tell who Nyi Mas Panguragan really was nor where she came from. It is her relation Syeikh Magelung (Pangeran Karang Kendal) which indicates that poetri Mesir was Nyi Mas Gandasari.

[43] The story of Nyi Mas Gandasari may remind us to the 'Feminine Element in Sufism' described by Schimmel, A. (1975), especially pp. 426-435. Schimmel states among other things that Sufism was more favourable to the development of feminine activities than were other branches in Islam. Beside the fact that the first true Muslim saint was a woman, the well known Rabi'ah 'Adawiyah (713-801), there were many others whose sainthood position was comparable to men. Maryam of Basra, Rihana, Sayyida Nafisa and Fatima of Nishapur were few examples. Further account on women saints in Islam, see: Smith, M. (1928), *Rabi 'a the Mystic and Her Fellow in Islam*, Cambridge.

[44] According to the *juru kunci*, this name may not be her original name.

opened a construction firm and won a tender valued at a billion rupiah. Feeling that her success had some relationship with *barakah* from her visit to this *kramat*, she offered to fund the renovation.[45]

The legend of Gandasari would be incomplete without incorporating Syarif Syam alias Pangeran Soka alias Syeikh Magelung alias Pangeran Karangkendal. Pak Chaeruman, the *juru kunci* at Karang Kendal, did not reveal who Syeikh Magelung really was, only that he came from Syam (Syria), hence his name Syarif Syam. He had already adopted the *Sufi* way when he was young and his presence in Cirebon was as a *Sufi* wanderer. He is said as to have had very long hair which, when it was loosened, would reach the ground and so he always knotted (*gelung*) his hair. As a result he was called Syeikh Magelung (the Syeikh with knotted hair). The reason for having the long hair was because no one could cut it. The hair was invulnerable to all cutting devices. He wandered from place to place in search of someone who would be able to cut his hair. Should he find someone, he would be willing to surrender to him and become his disciple. He finally arrived in Java (Cirebon) where, at a site in the city of Cirebon, he found an old man who was able to cut his hair quite easily. The old man was Sunan Gunung Jati; thence Syarif Syam happily became Sunan Gunung Jati's disciple and his name was changed to Pangeran Soka (from *suka*, meaning 'like' or 'happy'). The place in the city of Cirebon where his hair was cut is called Karang-getas ('the land easily cut').[46] He lived in Karangkendal, 19 km North of Cirebon, and after he died he was buried there and from then on, he was known as Pangeran Karangkendal.

His relation with Nyi Mas Gandasari started when he wandered westward from Cirebon and he found a crowd for whom Nyi Mas Gandasari was the centre of attention. Upon completing her learning of *tasawuf* from Sunan Gunung Jati, Nyi Mas Gandasari was advised to think about taking a husband. There were many offers of marriage, making it hard for her to make a choice. To make the decision easier she announced a competition by which she declared that any man who could beat her in a fight, would be the one she would take as her husband. The watching crowd was made up of both spectators and competitors

[45] Unfortunately, according to the Cultural Section Officer at the Regional Office of the Department of Education and Culture, the renovation was made merely by pulling down and rebuilding everything without taking note of the historical value of the previous buildings. Now, he claims, there are no more important artefacts, as almost everything with any historical value has already disappeared. What now exists is a set of new buildings with new structures. The case would probably be different if his office have been consulted prior to renovation. In that way both renovation and the preservation of historical relics could have somehow been combined. From the kramat side, Pak Yamsir said that what he had in mind was how to do the best for the *kramat*. He did not really understand nor feel it necessary to have such a consultation. Moreover, he said, much involvement of government officials might even make things complicated and difficult.

[46] Some informants told me that a river in the city of Cirebon which passes Karanggetas, the 'Sukalila' river, as bearing its name in remembrance to Magelung's surrender. The name "Sukalila' is said to have been derived from '*sukarela*' meaning 'willingly' or 'suka lillah' meaning 'willing for the sake of God.'

attempting to win her. There were many princes and knights who attempted but no one succeeded. Pangeran Soka introduced himself and challenged Gandasari to a fight. Although their powers were really equal and balanced, Gandasari, who was exhausted, jumped behind Sunan Gunung Jati to hide from Magelung's attack. Disregarding the fact that there was someone sitting between them, Magelung tried to grab Gandasari and almost hit Sunan Gunung Jati's head; but before his hand reached the head he fell down powerless. Sunan Gunung Jati helped him and mediated by declaring that neither one was winner or loser.

Plate 22: A gate at Kramat Nyi Mas Gandasari.

Plate 23: The tomb of Nyi Mas Gandasari.

Nevertheless, since the contest was intended to find a partner, while in fact both contestants were *Sufi* and were not really willing to marry, it was agreed that they would marry not in this world but in the hereafter.[47]

As the association of these figures with Sunan Gunung Jati is limited, it is difficult to judge how important these personages were to him. What these legends reveal is that both Gandasari and Magelung represent Sunan Gunung Jati's sincere disciples. Both are considered as *wali* but are peripheral figures. They somehow had kinship relations with Sunan Gunung Jati and their share in the process of Islamisation was considered instrumental, especially in the defeat of Rajagaluh and Talaga, vassal states of Hindu Galuh-Pajajaran.[48]

THE OBJECT OF ZIARAH: TWO EXAMPLES OF KRAMAT

A visit to a sacred place using a particular procedure is called *ziarah*. The word is borrowed from Arabic **ziyara** meaning visit. Its original use basically applied to almost any visit to any object, be it a place or a person. Used as a local term *ziarah* refers to formal visits to a revered person (such as a distinguished *kyai*) or a sacred place (tomb or relics of *wali* or holy men) implying a hope for *barakah* (*ngalap berkah*). Although visits to living individuals such as distinguished *kyai* also take place, this does not constitute a significant practice but rather ordinary reverence. To this extent I shall confine my discussion to visits to sacred places.

In Cirebon sacred places where visits are made are called *kramat* (shrine). A shrine's physical form is usually a building that houses a sacred object which may either be a tomb or relics (*petilasan*) such as the remnants of a dwelling, like the *Umo Gede* (the Great House) of Mbah Buyut Trusmi at Trusmi, springs like *Kramat Cimandung* at Cimandung (11 km South West of Cirebon), a collection of sacred *objects such as Kramat Tuk* at Tuk (4 km West of Cirebon). In most cases a *kramat* contains a combination of these features. The simplest *kramat* is a building where a revered object is kept or situated, with a hall for visitors to stay at least for a moment. A large *kramat*, on the other hand, may incorporate a number of buildings with different functions, including a prayer house (mosque

[47] The story of fighting competition appears in many locally known *Babad* suggesting another feminist tone of Gandasari legend (see note 43).

[48] Talaga is located about 40 km south-west of Cirebon, in the regency of Majalengka. A kinship relation between the princess (Nyi Mas Gandasari/Panguragan), Tubagus Pasei/Fadhilah Khan/ Faletehan, Pangeran Karang kendal/Syarif Syam/Syeikh Magelung, and Syarif Hidayatullah appears in Sulendraningrat, P.S. (1985), *Sejarah Cirebon*, Jakarta: Balai Pustaka, pp. 27-28. It states that Syarif Syam was son of Abdurrahman Rumi, son of Ali Zainal Alim, son of Barkah Zainal Alim. Nyi Mas Gandasari was sister of Fadhilah Khan, both were children of Mahdar Ibrahim, son of Abdul Ghafur, son of Barkah Zainal Alim. The latter was younger brother of Ali Nurul Alim, grandfather of Syarif Hidayatullah. This may be a recent construct. Habib Lutfi of Pekalongan (Central Java) however, acknowledged (in personal talk) this kinship relation although he revealed a different version from that of Sulendraningrat. (Habib Lutfi is known by many people as pious, genius and knows a lot about *wali* on Java. He is associated with four *tarekat*: Syattariyah, Tijaniyah, Qadiriyah wan-Naqsabandiyah and Syadziliyah. He has many guests for his blessing. Kyai Fu'ad Hasyim of Pesantren Buntet, who took and introduced me to him, was among those who were close to the *habib*).

or *tajug*). Other parts of the building may also be divided into sections and each section may have different sub-sections.

Originally, in Cirebon, the word *kramat* refers to anything 'holy' which may either be a word, an object, a person or a place. Etymologically, its special reference to a 'holy place' may be traced through the Arabic word **haramat** (plural form of **haram**), meaning 'sacred' or 'forbidden,' or **karamat** (plural form of **karamah**) meaning honour or regard (from God). Referring to the first word, **haramat**, the replacement of **h** with **k** is common among Javanese. **Haji** becomes *kaji*, **hajat** becomes *kajat*, **halal** becomes *kalal* and **haram** becomes *karam*, **haramat** becomes *karamat* and then *kramat*. In Islam there are three places formally acknowledged as sacred, the two in Arabia called **haramain**, meaning the two sacred (places), and another one in Palestine. The first two are the Sacred Mosque (**Masjid al-Haram**) in Mecca which contains the most revered object, the **Ka'ba**, sometimes called The House of God (**Bayt Allah**); another one is The Mosque of the Prophet (**Masjid al- Nabawy**) in Medina where, after his death, the Prophet was buried. The other which is in Palestine, is the mosque of **Al-Aqsa** (Dome of the Rock), the former direction for Muslims in prayer and a place where the Prophet stopped on his night journey (*Isra' mi'raj*). The official acceptance of the existence of these holy places may have given rise to the belief that some local sanctuary places, especially the tombs and relics of local *wali*, should have some degree of sanctity, although their sacredness is far less than the three officially accepted holy places.

The sanctity of such places is further accentuated by the notion of *karamah*, the marvels wrought by the *wali* which God brings about in the corporeal world. This Arabic word **karamah** (pl.. **karamat**), meaning honour or regard (from God) is sometimes also corrupted by Javanese into *kramat*. Thus, both words **haramat** and **karamat** combine to form a single term *kramat*, implying that the place itself is *holy* (*haram*) and divine marvels (*karamat*) brought about by the *wali* can be expected there.

To illustrate what a *kramat* looks like, I shall present examples from two sites, Astana and Trusmi. Astana, which contains the tomb of Sunan Gunung Jati is the most prominent object of visitation in Cirebon. Sunan Gunung Jati is regarded as one of the nine saints who initiated the preaching of Islam on Java. Sunan Gunung Jati had a number of local associates with whom he worked. These associates, due to their links with Sunan Gunung Jati are considered to have been invested with the honour and fragrance of his saintship. Although they are considered to be saints, they rank lower than Sunan Gunung Jati himself. As many of his associates were buried in different places, this gives rise to the emergence of sacred places outside the Astana grave complex. Currently the number of such places in Cirebon is said to number over 300.

Map of Desa Astana

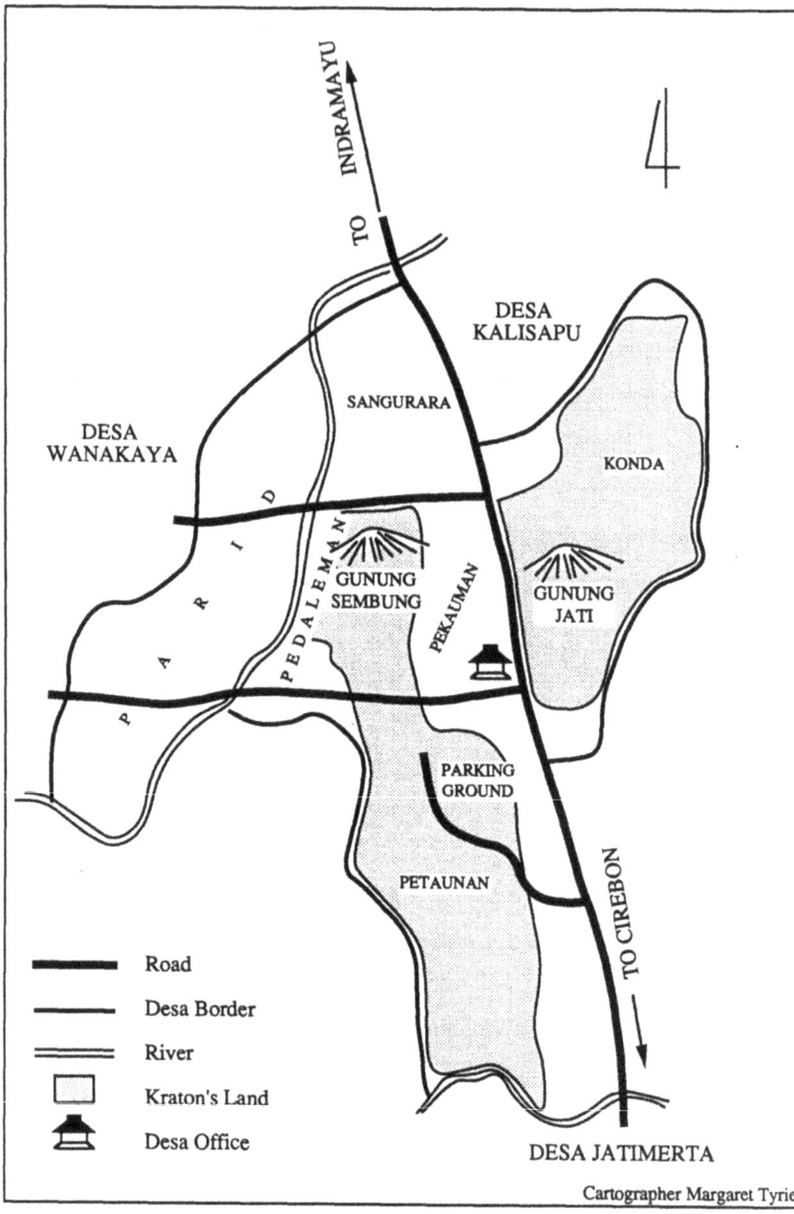

Astana Gunung Jati

The Astana Gunung Jati grave complex, the biggest and the most revered place of visitation in Cirebon, is located at the village of Astana, in the sub-district (*kecamatan*) of North Cirebon, 5 km northward along the main Cirebon-Indramayu road. The complex is made up of two compounds, separated by the main road. Driving from Cirebon, Gunung Jati is on the right of the road whereas Gunung Sembung is on its left. From the foot of Gunung Jati hill we can walk through an ascending pathway where graves of various associates are found, but these have no familial link with the *kraton* family. Up on a hilly plot near the summit covered by high trees lies the tomb of Syeikh Datu Kahfi. He is known as the religious teacher of Sunan Gunung Jati's predecessor. Following another path to the top of the hill is *puser bumi* (centre of the earth), a plateau which was once the crater of a formerly active volcano, from which there is a clear view of the sea. Close to the peak there is a cave (Arabic **kahfi**) which, it is said, Syeikh Kahfi used for contemplation. As a result the Sheikh's name, Master of the Cave (Datu Kahfi) has become associated with it.

Despite the fact that his tomb is an important object of visitation, little is known of Syeikh Kahfi. According to legend, on the North-Coast of West Java there were two Qur'anic schools run by teachers of Arab stock. One was in Karawang led by Syeikh Quro and the other was in Gunung Jati led by Syeikh Nurjati. One of Syeikh Quro's student was Nyai Subanglarang, daughter of Ki Jumajan Jati, the ruler of Singapura (now Mertasinga). She married Prabu Siliwangi, King of Pajajaran and their descendants are significant in later traditional accounts of the history of Cirebon.

Syeikh Nurjati, on the other hand, due to his age and physical condition passed on his work to his student, also of Arab origin, named Syeikh Datu Kahfi or Datuk Khafidh who came to Pasambangan with a contingent of 22 people, two of whom were women. He and his companions were accepted with honour by Ki Jumajan Jati, the then Harbour Master of Amparan Jati who allowed them to settle there. They became the students of Syeikh Nurjati. Later Syeikh Datuk Kahfi was appointed by Syeikh Nurjati, to take his place to teach Islam.[49] When Syeikh Kahfi was leading the school, some new students commenced their study, among whom were Prabu Siliwangi's children from Nyai Subanglarang. They were Walangsungsang, his wife Indang Geulis, and Rarasantang, younger sister of Walangsungsang. It was these students who increased the importance of Syeikh Kahfi's role. These students, Walangsungsang and Rarasantang were

[49] Some other traditions equates Sheikh Nurul Jati with Datuk Kafi; both names, according to these traditions belong to the same person. Some informants speculated that the name Kafi is probably from Arabic **kahf**, meaning cave and associated him with the cave adjacent to the supposed site of his school, now his tomb. He is then thought of as the master of the cave because he is said to have used it as a place of seclusion. The name Khafid, on the other hand is associated with his function as a Qur'anic teacher who himself was a *khafid* (one who memorises the whole Qur'an).

instrumental in the further development of Cirebon and Islam in West Java. It was Walangsungsang who, after studying with Syeikh Kahfi, became the forebear of Cirebon and its kingdom.

Across the main road from Gunung Jati hill is the precinct of the former Pasambangan village where the Gunung Sembung grave complex lies.[50] Some custodians said that formerly Gunung Sembung was a guest house but after Nio Ong Tin (Nyai Rara Sumanding), Sunan Gunung Jati's Chinese wife, died and was buried there, it grew into a grave complex. The name Sembung is said to have been derived from *sambung*, meaning 'added' because to build it up a large amount of soil from various places was added to the existing hill.

Across the Cirebon-Indramayu main road in front of the *Desa* office there is a paved road about 500 metres long leading to the Astana square with the grave complex of Gunung Sembung lying on its North. The date of construction of this complex is indicated by a *Candra Sangkala* (memorial statement) written in Javanese letters, saying "*Sirna Tanana Warna Tunggal,*" implying the Saka Era (SE) 1400.[51] At the square there are two buildings, one is *Pendopo Ringgit*, a hall where puppet plays (*wayang*) or other performances are held; at its western side is the wooden house called *Mande Mangu* or *Mande Tepasan*, with *the Candra Sangkala "Singa Kari Gawe Anake,"* indicating that the *Mande* was constructed in SE 1402(?) as a present, it is said, from Ratu Nyawa, the daughter of Raden Fatah from Demak, who married Gung Anom (Pangeran Bratakelana), son of Sunan Gunung Jati who passed away at sea on his way to Cirebon. The first entrance to the *kramat* is through either one of the two unroofed gates (*candi bentar*), named respectively *Gapura Wetan* (Eastern gate) and Gapura Kulon (Western gate). The word *gapura* meaning entrance or gate is symbolically associated with the Arabic ***ghafura***, meaning forgiveness suggesting that by passing through the gate, one obtains forgiveness. A few steps through the East gate, inside a half metre high wall that separates the grave complex from the square at the right of the gate, there is a well called *Sumur Jati*. At the left side of the gate, three buildings stand parallel. The first of these is *Mande Cungkup Danalaya*, a wooden hall belonging to the villagers of Danalaya (8 km west of Cirebon) who use it to make preparation for their *ngunjung* ceremonies. The next is a museum where the collection of presents from foreign rulers for Sunan Gunung Jati given over centuries are kept. It includes tens of Chinese jars from the Ming dynasty as well as other valuables. The third building is *Mande Cungkup Trusmi*, a wooden hall which belongs to the people of Trusmi which is used for a similar purpose as that of Danalaya.

[50] Now the name Pasambangan refers only to the *Pekemitan*, a watch hall for the caretakers of the grave complex.

[51] The *Candra Sangkala* (memorial statement) of *Sirna* (disappear) *Tanana* (nothing) *Warna* (four) *Tunggal* (one), according to *Juru Kunci*, refers to the number of 0041 which is to be read from right to left. It indicates the Saka Era (SE) which starts at AD 78.

Entering the second entrance, a gate near a water jar from which ablution is taken prior to *ziarah,* there is the *Pendopo Soka* which was used as an assembly hall but has now become a resting room for pilgrims. Next to it is Siti Hinggil, an elevated floor where the Sultan used to keep a watch across the square. A wooden building called *Mande Budi Jajar* or *Mande Pajajaran* with the *Candra Sangkala "Tunggal Boya Hawarna Tunggal,"* indicating that it was constructed in SE 1401(?) stands next to Siti Hinggil. The *Mande* is said as to have been brought by Dipati Jagabaya from Pajajaran and to be used by the Dipati on behalf of Prabu Siliwangi to install Pangeran Cakrabuana (Walangsungsang) as regent of Cirebon under the suzerainty of Pajajaran.

The main gate leading to the pilgrims' destination is *Gerbang Weregu* through which the visitors pass by way of a corridor to *Pekemitan,* a pillared hall used as the quarter for the care-takers called Pasambangan.[52] Pasambangan is divided into two sections the *Paseban Bekel* (place for *bekel*) at the West and *Paseban Kraman* (place for *wong kraman*) at the East. Here the caretakers stand on duty; they are dressed in the Cirebonese traditional way with *iket* (batik headcloth) on the head, white *kampret* shirt at the top for the *Bekel* or *kutung* (chest wrap) for the *Kraman,* and *tapi* (batik garment) as their lower garment. Turning left along the corridor is a hall called *Gedongan Raja Sulaeman,* which was erected by Sultan Sepuh IX and later became his graveyard. The wall throughout these sections is decorated with Dutch and Chinese porcelain plates. The platform to which the pilgrims are led to sit for *ziarah* is next to this *gedongan.* This *is the ziarah* platform which lies between *Gedongan Raja* Sulaeman on the East and *Pelayonan* on the West, and with *Lawang Krapyak* on the South and *Lawang Pesujudan* or *Siblangbong* on the North. The two *lawang* (gates) are part of the nine gates standing one after another in a straight line from south to north, along the ascending pathway from the square to the tomb of Sunan Gunung Jati at the top of the hill. In order, they are: 1) *Gapura Kulon,* 2) *Krapyak,* 3) *Pesujudan* or *Siblangbong,* 4) *Ratnakomala,* 5) *Jinem,* 6) *Ráraroga,* 7) *Kaca,* 8) *Bacem* and 9) *Teratai.* Except for *Gapura Kulon,* all the gates are kept closed; they are opened only on the eve of *Syawalan* to make way for the Sultans and their consorts. *Krapyak* is opened on Thursday night *Kliwon* (*Jum'at Kliwon*) after the *tahlil* ceremony, the main item of *ziarah,* to allow the flocking pilgrims to pass through leaving the *ziarah* platform, whereas *Pesujudan* is also open on Thursday night *Kliwon* during the *tahlil* ritual, not to allow the pilgrims to pass through it but only to allow visibility towards the ascending pathway leading to the hill top. To the West, next to the *ziarah* platform is the *Pelayon* or *Mande Layon,* a wooden hall where corpses are put for a rest prior to burial. After this, there is a section where many Chinese pilgrims burn incense sticks in reverence to Nio Ong Tin

52 This main gate however, does not constitute one of the nine gates leading to Sunan Gunung Jati's tomb. (See the sketch of the grave complex).

(Nyai Rara Sumanding), and finally, at the West end of the complex, stands *Gedong Kaprabon*, a hall used only by the Sultans and their families when a visit to Astana is made (see diagram).

Gedong Raja Sulaeman is the only block of the kraton family grave site to which access is allowed for ordinary visitors. The other blocks behind *Lawang Pesujudan* along the East and West sides of the elevated path-way to the top of the mount are beyond normal reach. Only the three Sultans and their families, or individuals who get special written permission from the Sultans are allowed to enter. The main block called *Gedong Jinem Gusti Syarif* is located at the top of the hill where lies Sunan Gunung Jati's tomb, along with 17 other important figures including Walangsungsang (Pangeran Cakrabuana), Fadhilah Khan (Faletehan), Rarasantang (Syarifah Mudaim), and Nyai Ratu Tepasari (Tepasan). Over the roof of this *gedong jinem*, there is a *memolo* (the top) called *kendi petula* ('emerald pitcher') coated with pure gold. Behind the wall outside the 29 blocks are buried numerous *Ki* and *Nyi Gede* of various *desa*. This section is open to the public on the eve of *Syawalan* and *Raya Agung*.[53]

Along with the *Sumur Jati (Jati* well), there are two other wells which attract visitors, the *Kesepuhan* and *the Kanoman*, located at the West end of the complex. There are still others, however, one of which is the *Kejayaan* well located at the mosque at the North-Eastern section of the *complex*; many visitors including Chinese, bathe at the seven well (*adus sumur pitu*) by going from one well to another. The purpose of this bathing is to release dirt from the body (*ngirab*), a symbolic intention of washing away all sins and bad luck (*mbuang kekebel*). Two of the preferred wells for this ceremony are *Tegang Pati* and *Jala Tunda* located on Gunung Jati hill.[54]

The care for the whole of compounds, both Gunung Jati and Gunung Sembung, is managed by a group of custodians with a fairly complex organisational structure. The overall operation is under the responsibility of *Ki Jeneng*, the principal, who coordinates 120 staff. He directs 4 senior assistants (*Bekel Sepuh/Tua*), 8 junior assistants (*Bekel Anom/Nom*) and 108 technical assistants (*Wong Kraman*). The *Bekel Sepuh* and *Anom* reflect the two *kraton*, Kesepuhan and Kanoman, while the whole structure of the custodians reflects the continuation of the duty set forth in the traditional organisation of the ship's crew, captained by Patih Keling, before their ship was wrecked. Working in rotation, everyday there are always 14 people on duty consisting of *Ki Jeneng* himself, one *Bekel Sepuh*, one *Bekel Anom* and 12 *Wong Kraman*. Along with other duties, the *Bekel Sepuh* is especially responsible for care around the grave

[53] See Chapter Five. A detailed list of prominent occupants at this complex, see: Atja (1986), Carita Purwaka ..., pp. 105–112.

[54] The names of the seven wells (*sumur*) are thus: 1) Jati, 2) Kesepuhan, 3) Kanoman, 4) Kejayaan, 5) Tegang Pati 6) Jala Tunda, and 7) one whose name I missed. It is located within the mosque precinct, next to the women's resting/bath room.

of Pangeran Raja Sulaeman, *Bekel Anom* for care of *Jinem Gusti Syarif*, and the *Wong Kraman* are responsible for caring for the whole complex. Three of the *Wong Kraman* on duty are separately named. One is *Penanggap*, responsible for care for the block of Pangeran Manis graveyard, the other two are *Jemlodi* for Panembahan Ratu, and *Penjangkar* for Sultan Syamsuddin. They are on duty 24 hours for a period of 15 days at each rotation. Thus, only *Ki Jeneng* works everyday as the coordinator. A *Bekel Sepuh* works only once every 45 days, a *Bekel Anom* works once every 105 days and a *Wong Kraman* works only once every 120 days. *Jeneng* and *Bekel* are recruited from the descendants of Patih Keling (Adipati Suramenggala), formerly the captain of ship-wrecked sailors, who later became Sunan Gunung Jati's faithful servant, his body guard and a triumphant warrior at the same time. *Wong Kraman*, on the other hand, are recruited from the descendants of his men sailors. Each rotation (once every 15 days) is marked by a ceremony called *tampan* (handing down the duty) from the former group to the successor in a semi traditional military procedure. This procedure is preserved including the wording which is kept intact. The following is an example of how a *Bekel Sepuh* reports to *Ki Jeneng* at the initiation:

> "Yes Kyai, I was entrusted by *Kyai* to care for the tomb of Sultan Sepuh Raja Sulaeman; now, I have just handed the duty onto *Bekel Sepuh* named (...he mentions the successor) who has taken my job. I would like to report that there has been nothing wrong in and around the site. I apologise if there is something that does not satisfy you. I hereby ask your permission to do *ziarah* at the tomb of Sunan Gunung Jati".[55]

[55] Its original Javanese reads: "Inggih sampun Kyai sakala wau kula dituwawi dumateng Kyai kangge ngormeni Gusti Sultan Sepuh Pangeran Raja Sulaeman, sapuniki sampun kula tampiaken dumateng Bekel sepuh ingkang nami (...) ngagolong pedamelan dalem. Lan malih ngaturi uninga salebete lan sajawine pangubeng Dalem boten wonten salah sawios. Bilih wonten salah sawios kirang penggarapan nyuwun dituwakup. Sinareng saniki kula permios nyuwun izin bade ziarah."

Figure 6.2: Sketch of Astana Gunung Jati Grave Complex

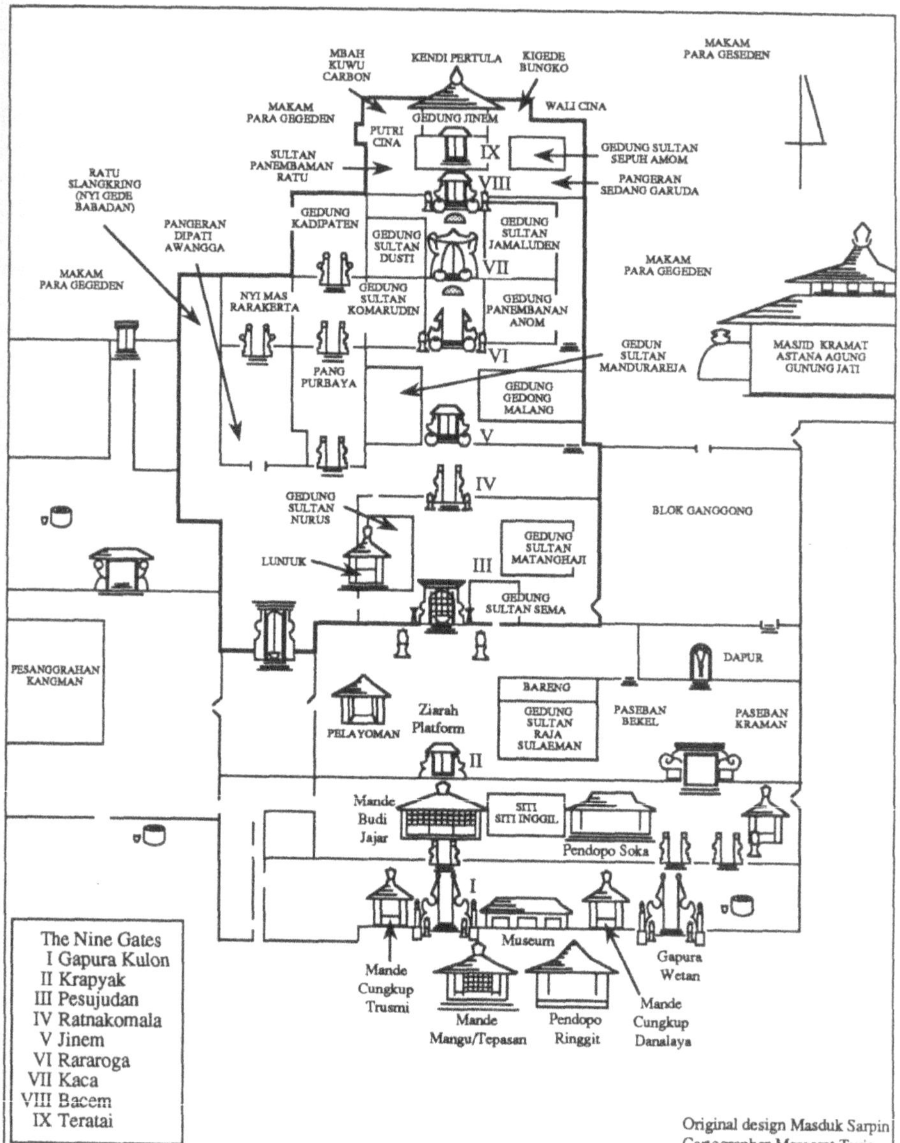

Along with this graveyard custodian there is also a group of mosque caretakers called *kaum*, headed by a *penghulu*.[56] He is assisted by 12 staff consisting of 3 *ketib* (**katib**), 4 *modin* (**muadzin**) and 5 *kemit* (technical assistants). They work in rotation on a weekly basis from Thursday to Wednesday. Everyday the *penghulu* directs 3 staff, a *ketib*, a *modin* and a *kemit*. The Penghulu gives a sermon and leads (*ngimami*) the Friday prayer and the *tahlil* at Pasambangan on Thursday night with Ki *Jeneng*. The *ketib* (secretary) is his direct assistant who represents the *penghulu* in case the latter is unable to do something and to lead daily congregational prayer at the mosque. Outside the mosque he cares for the corpse when a death occurs. The *modin* strikes the *kentong* and *bedug* followed by the call for prayer to signal to the surrounding villagers every time prayer time comes; whereas the *kemit* is in charge of doing technical work in general, including taking care of and cleaning the mosque. All personnel, both for the grave complex and the mosque, are named by the Sultans of Kesepuhan and Kanoman and, thus, they formally work for the sultans. In fact most of the land at Desa Astana is owned by the *kraton*.[57]

Kramat Trusmi

The complete reference for *Kramat Trusmi* is *Kramat Mbah Buyut Trusmi*. It is located in *Desa* Trusmi in Weru Sub-District, about 7 km West of Cirebon and 1.5 km north of the Cirebon-Bandung or Cirebon-Jakarta main road. Public transport to this *kramat* is plentiful and available from Cirebon by taking a small passenger car to Plered, the main town of Weru, then from Plered directly to the *kramat* by *becak*. This *kramat* is the second most important site after Astana in terms of visitors and traditional festivals, although in size it is smaller than Astana. Unlike Astana, which is under the direct control of the *kraton*, Trusmi is now independent, although formerly it also belonged to the *kraton*. Recruitment of the custodians, requires that each candidate should be the descendant of a past custodian, but in many cases, the final decision on who is appointed, involves the *desa* officials, especially the chief (*kuwu* now *kades*), rather than the *sultan*. When this sort of independence commenced is unclear.

The revered figure of this *kramat* is known as *Ki Buyut* Trusmi from which the *kramat's* name is derived. *Buyut* means great grand-father, but the term *Ki Buyut* refers to the ancestor, the founder of the *desa* where the *kramat* is located. Who is really meant by *Ki Buyut* Trusmi is still unclear. Whether it is Walangsungsang, the owner and the founder of the *kramat*, Ki Gede Trusmi, the ancestor or the first settler at Trusmi, or Pangeran Trusmi, grandson of Ki Gede Trusmi and Walangsungsang does not appear to be known. According to the legend the

[56] The present *penghulu* is Kyai Qasim, descendant of Sunan Gunung Jati. He is also local *mursyid* of Qadiriyah wan-Naqsabandiyah order. Most of his followers come from Bekasi, Subang, Karawang and Indramayu regencies.
[57] See map of Astana.

name Trusmi is derived from *terus* (instantly) *semi* (spring up). Thus *terus semi* means 'to spring up instantly.' It is said that once Ki Gede Bangbangan, the first settler in the area, was sitting in front of his cottage enjoying with pride a site around the cottage he had just cleared. Suddenly he heard a mysterious voice saying: "*Assalamu'alaikum* (peace be upon you)." Immediately all the weeds and trees he had just cleared sprang up again and returned to their former condition thus spoiling all his hard work. While he was looking around with a mixture of sadness and astonishment two men walked toward him with a greeting saying: "*Assalamu'alaikum.*" The voice and tone of the two men saying the words was precisely similar to what he had mysteriously heard. A dialogue occurred between Ki Gede Bangbangan and the two men and it turned out that the men were Pangeran Cakrabuana and Sunan Gunung Jati. As a result of this unexplainable event Ki Gede Bangbangan finally embraced Islam and the area became known as Trusmi; Ki Gede Bangbangan became Ki Gede Trusmi.

Sketch of the site of Kramat Mbah Buyut Trusmi (1926).

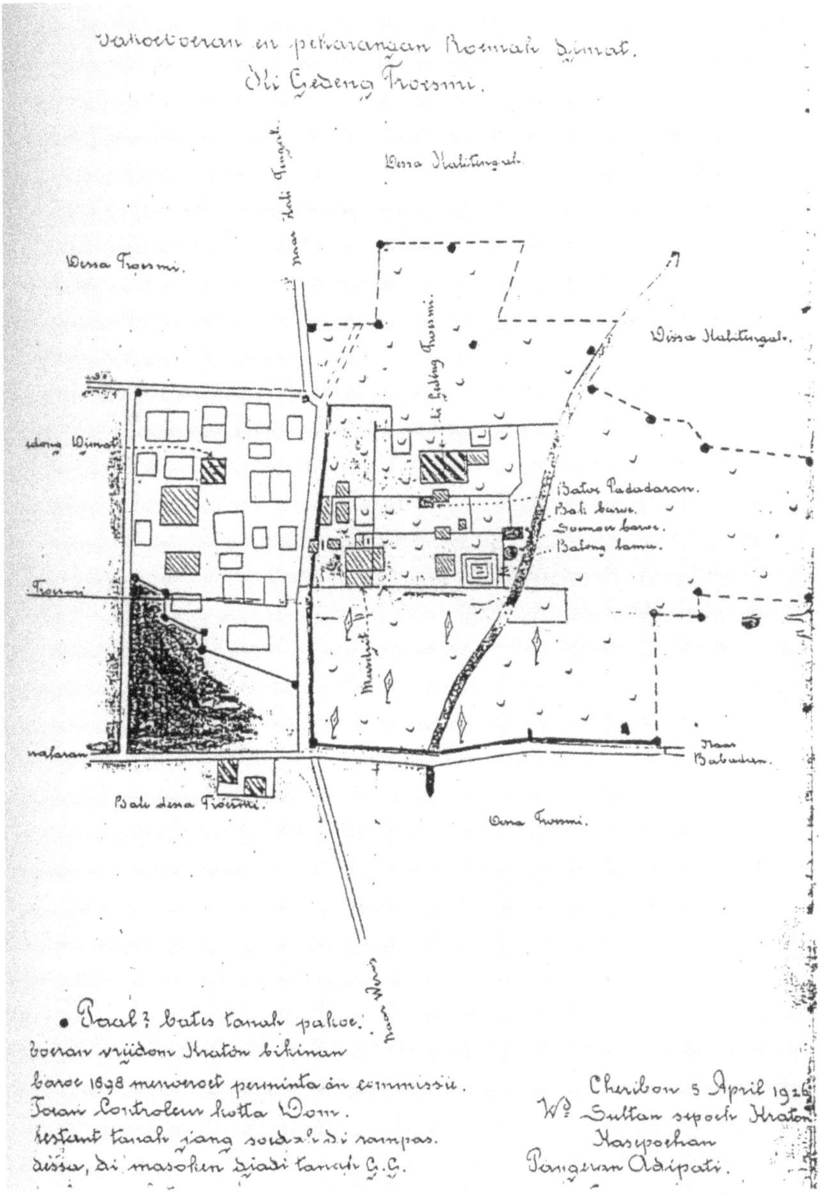

Figure 6.5: Sketch of Kramat Mbah Buyut Trusmi (1995).

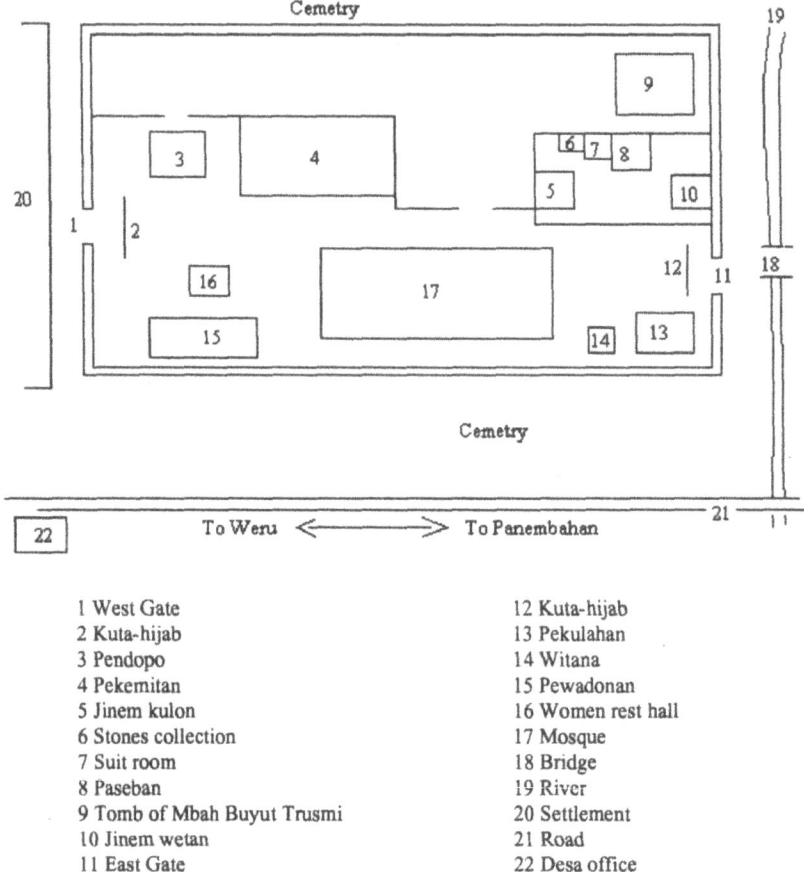

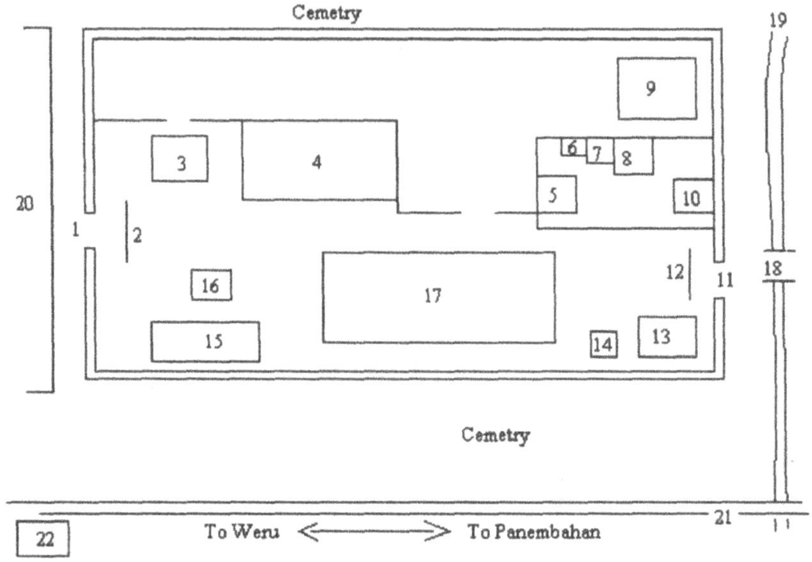

1 West Gate
2 Kuta-hijab
3 Pendopo
4 Pekemitan
5 Jinem kulon
6 Stones collection
7 Suit room
8 Paseban
9 Tomb of Mbah Buyut Trusmi
10 Jinem wetan
11 East Gate
12 Kuta-hijab
13 Pekulahan
14 Witana
15 Pewadonan
16 Women rest hall
17 Mosque
18 Bridge
19 River
20 Settlement
21 Road
22 Desa office

Like many other sites, *Kramat* Trusmi consists of two sections, one section is separated from the other by a space which functions as a pathway from the West entrance of the *kramat* to the East entrance. The first section is in the south, comprising the mosque and its annex, whereas the other section is to the north being the tombs section where the revered figures, Ki Gede Trusmi and Pangeran Trusmi, are buried. Both sections are surrounded by a wall two metres high made up of an uncemented stack of ancient bricks. The sacredness of the complex, although unclear, is attributed more to Walangsungsang (Pangeran Cakrabuana), the founder of Cirebon, who is said to have built the complex. Walangsungsang, the founder of Cirebon, stayed at Cirebon Girang but his son, Pangeran Carbon, married Nyai Cupluk, daughter of Ki Gede Trusmi and had a son named Pangeran Trusmi or Mangana Jati who stayed at Trusmi. The oldest building Walangsungsang erected is called *witana*. This stands for *wiwit ana* meaning the first that existed (was built). Witana was used by Walangsungsang to rest in and to teach Islam. It lies next to *pekulahan*, a pond for bathing and ablution which is watered from the adjacent river. Next to *witana* lies the mosque, one main part of the *kramat* which, although it has undergone extensive renovation, still maintains its antiquity by the preserved structure of the building, the style of its wooden roof (*sirap*), *pillars, and memolo* (peak), its pulpit and the water jars (*padasan*) for ablution.

The tomb section consists of a *pendopo* (a hall to receive guests), *pekuncen* (quarters for key bearers on duty), two *jinem* (stands for *si-**ji** kang ne-**nem***, one consisting of six) on the West and East, each of which accommodates pilgrims who stay overnight, a stone room where a collection of 17 stones are kept, a room where key bearers change their clothes, *paseban* (the hall where the pilgrims doing *ziarah* go), and the *gedongan* ('brick building') where the tombs of Ki Buyut Trusmi and Pangeran Trusmi lie. All are under the responsibility of a group of 9 caretakers called *kuncen* headed by a *sep* (key bearer in chief) who is recruited by election in the same way as a *desa* chief is elected. The present *sep* is the 15th generation since Walangsungsang (Cakrabuana). The 10th of which was Ki Thalhah, who is a prominent *mursyid* of the Qadiriyah wan Naqsabandiyah order in West Java and student of Syeikh Khatib Sambas, a Jawah who lived in Mecca, and the founder of the order.[58]

The *sep* is assisted by four *(juru) kunci* (key bearers) and four *kyai*, assistants to the *kunci*; each being appointed by the *Sep* from among the descendants of previous *kuncen*.[59] The total number of nine for the custodians (according Ki Turdjani, one of the *kunci* at Trusmi), has a double reference. One reference is to the work of the nine *wali*, the founders of Islam on Java, and the other is to the nine world founders of Islam comprising The Prophet, the four Caliphs who succeeded the Prophet's (Abu Bakr, Umar, Utsman and Ali), and the four Imam, founders of the schools of *syare'at* who followed the Caliph (Hanafi, Maliki, Hanbali and Syafi'i). In this hierarchy, the *kunci* rank higher than the *kyai*. This is analogous to the fact that the *Caliph* rank higher than the *imam* of the four schools. Along with the *kuncen* there are also *kaum* and *kemit*. *Kaum* are the mosque custodians headed by a *lebe* who has a similar function *to* the *penghulu* at Astana. He is assisted by a *ketib* and two *modin*. The *kemit* consists of four people who are engaged in technical work for both the graveyard and the mosque. The total number of custodians is therefore 17, representing the total

[58] *Mursyid* is a leader who has an authority to initiate a new follower of a *tarekat* (Sufi order). Khatib Sambas (d. 1875) was a prominent 19th century Indonesian scholar in Mecca, born in Kalimantan. (For a short description, see: Dhofier, 1985:85–87). He is regarded as the one who combined Qadiriyah and Naqsabandiyah doctrines into a single order, the Qadiriyah wan Naqsabandiyah. This order might have had a stronghold at Trusmi and Astana. The present *penghulu* Astana mosque grave complex is a local *mursyid* who traces his spiritual genealogy through Ki Thalhah. Aba Sepuh, father of Aba Anom of Pesantren Surialaya (Tasikmalaya, southern West Java) was also initiated by Ki Thalhah. See: Nasution, H. (1990), ed, *Thoriqot Qodiriyah Naqsabandiyyah: Sejarah Asal-Usul, dan Perkembangannya*, Tasikmalaya: IAILM.

[59] At Trusmi the way to refer to *juru kunci* (key bearer) is by just using the term *kunci* or *Ki Kunci*, meaning key. The word *juru* (holder or bearer) is omitted. A group of *kunci* is called *kuncen*.

number of units of five prescribed prayers. The *Sep* at Trusmi, like the *Jeneng* at Astana, works everyday; the others work in shifts of a week each from Thursday afternoon each week and thus, everyday there are always 5 persons on duty: a *sep*, a *kunci*, a *kyai*, a *kaum* and a *kemit*.

The physical structure of the *kramat* and the traditions within it, Ki Turjani said, also conveys symbolic messages which lay stress on recounting the meaning of Islam as a religion of peace (*rukun/damai*). The total length of the surrounding wall for example, is 60 *depa*; the number, 60 alludes to the number of the prophets known by most Muslims, 25 of whom are messengers (*rasul*) for whom the Prophet Muhammad serves as the seal (the 25th). The notion of 25 messengers and the seal is signified at the traditional Maulid festival (*muludan*) at Trusmi held on 25th of *Mulud*. The use of *depa* (stretching the two hands apart making a straight line of approximately 1.75 metre long) as a way of measuring a unit of length is to reflect that each prophet led mankind onto the straight path (***sirat al-mustaqim***), the only way man can live safely in this world and the hereafter. On the wall throughout the complex there are also 60 domes of piled brick (*candi laras*) to represent the idea that among the messages brought by each of the 60 prophets is the idea of living in harmony (*selaras*) with each other, and with nature and, above all, with God.

The entrance to the *kramat* is called *gapura* (forgiveness) meaning that the main purpose for everyone visiting the place is to seek forgiveness from God both for himself and for others (the living and the deceased). Passing through the eastern entrance which leads to the mosque, one encounters a 'veil' in the form of a brick wall (*kuta hijab*) which obstructs one's view. This wall which is about 2 metres wide and 2 metres high signifies that if someone has an intention to perform *ibadat* (going to the mosque) that person should have made a firm decision and be generous, only for God's sake, not for any other reasons. The same understanding should be held when passing through the western entrance leading to the *pendopo* to meet people and to the *pekuncen* (place of *kunci*) for *ziarah* (visit) or *sedekah* (offering) or other means of establishing a relationship with people, dead or alive. The notion of generosity is further accentuated when inside the *kramat*, close to the well, one will find *kapianjing* and *blimbing wulu* trees standing side by side. The *kapianjing* tree is to signal that anyone who enters (*manjing*) either the mosque or the grave-site must first be clean hearted and spiritually pure. The outward expression of this is indicated by taking a ritual ablution (*banyu wulu*) represented by the *blimbing wulu* tree. The first section of the *kramat*, the mosque, represents *syare'at*, the worldly life; whereas the second, the grave, resembles *hakekat*, life after death. Life in this world, should be used to prepare for the life after death.

The *jinem* which stands for *(si)***ji** *kang (ne)***nem** (one which contains six) alludes to the Decrees of Faiths which are six in number (Belief in God, the Angels, the

Messengers, the Holy Books, the Day of Judgement and God's Pre-destination). *Jinem* lies at both West and East, meaning that wherever and whenever one goes or stays, eastward or westward, at the place where the sun rises or at place where the sun sets, the faiths must be preserved. The enactment of the faith is the holding of the Five Pillars of Islam, the most important of which is the observance of the five prescribed daily prayers whose total number of units is 17, signified by the 17 persons who are custodians, and the collection of 17 stones put on the ground. The stones are of different size from the smallest of 60 grams to the largest of about 27 kg. The largest one, which alludes to the *tauhid* (the unity of God), the key of Islamic religion, is surrounded by the others.

It would be a long list if everything in this complex were to be enumerated. But the important thing is, according to Ki Turjani, there are sufficient grounds to deduce from these examples that Islam is a religion of peace. Islam has been presented by the *wali* to local people in peaceful and subtle ways, using a gradual approach, indirect persuasion and exemplary models. In this way aspects of Islam as a religion of peace and harmony were strongly emphasised. To this end the use of allegorical expressions, mythical stories, and symbolic representation in conformity with the existing condition, world view and traditions have inevitably become a major feature.

THE PROCEDURE OF ZIARAH

Along with the physical structure and historical aspect of the *kramat*, how *ziarah* proceeds, what happens in the *kramat* and how the caretakers and the visitors interact requires careful examination. From the eyes of the caretakers, visitors to *kramat* are of various kinds: first, there are *pengunjung biasa* (ordinary visitors) who come to *kramat* mainly for profane purposes such as to see its historical relics, the architectural structure and the artistic dimension of the buildings. Tourists, researchers and government inspectors belong to this category. Secondly, there are *wong ziarah* (pilgrims), the visitors who come to *kramat* not only to know its physical dimensions but more importantly with a spiritual purpose in mind in hope of obtaining *barakah*. These are the majority of visitors. They come from various places and various backgrounds, with different occupations, status and education. Their knowledge of Islam also varies from very knowledgeable to very rudimentary.

They are broadly of two categories, the *wong ziarah* proper and the *wong nyepi*. The former are those who come for a short visit, pray, look around and go home. The latter are visitors who stay overnight or for some days or even weeks. Some are newcomers, some others are well accustomed to visit the place. The reasons for their coming also vary; some stay only for *dedonga* (praying), to seek or maintain well being in general, some others have some specific purpose and make the visit as an *ikhtiar* (effort) to find divine guidance (*'alamat*) for the solution to a particular problem. An example of this type of visitor is Rohiman

(38 years), a farmer from Gegesik (40 km north west of Cirebon), who had stayed for four days (when I spoke to him) and would stay for at least seven days at Trusmi. He wanted to change his life by applying for a job to work in Saudi Arabia via an agent in Jakarta. Substantial cash was needed for the arrangement along with the administration cost paid to the agent. He covered the total amount by selling part of his *sawah* (paddy field). When the date to finalise his passport and visa came he had to return to Cirebon for some reason and came back to the agent two days later. Unfortunately when he visited the agent, his place had been allocated to someone else who paid more than he did. Instead of refunding his money the agent promised him another arrangement. He visited the agent several times but all the promises were nothing but empty words. He was fooled by the agent, had lost his *sawah*, money and hope. He had no money to pay a lawyer, and had no one to help him. What remained, he said, was faith and belief that God at last would repay his patience with His grace. So he came to the *kramat* for recompense. This was his third visit.

Some other visitors told of different problems but with similar flavour; attempting a restoration from mental breakdown, economic difficulties, family problems, marriage failures, and many others including anxiety to have a child after a long marriage, after consulting many doctors, or being unable to afford such a consultation. For them the *kramat* becomes a mental hospital (*rumah sakit mental*) where self-treatment within a spiritual atmosphere is made. Not all visitors however, come to the *kramat* with such hardships. For example, Pak Sanusi (36 years) and his wife from Semarang (Central Java), came to Astana and stayed there for 40 days not for a redemption. Pak Sanusi slept at the mosque, his wife at Pasambangan. Unlike Rohiman, they were staying there to express thankfulness (*syukuran*) after gaining certain worldly merits. Pak Sanusi had just returned from working in Saudi Arabia as a driver for three years. He had managed to make substantial savings and decided to buy a piece of land, renovate his house and start a new life by opening a shop with the hope that what he had received and what he would be doing would be endowed with *berkah*. He was also praying for his daughter who was staying at *Pesantren* at Mangkang (Central Java). He wanted his daughter to become a person (*dadi wong*), meaning he wanted her to be a proper adult, to be well off and to find a good husband.

For Kartiman (21 years) a young man from Losari (Central Java), a *kramat* is like a *pesantren*. It is a place where a free hostel is available. After graduating from Religious High School (*Madrasah 'Aliyah*), he had the pleasure of wandering from place to place from Banten in West Java to Banyuwangi in East Java. He had visited various *pesantren* and *Kyai* too. He used the mosques in *pesantren* or *kramat* to stay as long as he wanted. When I met him at Astana, he said that he was lucky enough, he got some money (*sangu*) from his parents six months ago and he still had it. Sometimes a *Kyai* who was very kind would give him some money, another time someone else would.

Beside *wong ziarah* and *wong nyepi*, there are also visitors, difficult to name, who come to the *kramat* and stay over-night for mere seclusion without having spiritual purposes. These are the most unexpected visitors and virtually now their number is quite small. Among these types of visitors are criminals who find a *kramat* to be a safe hiding place to escape from arrest. To avoid the presence of such unexpected visitors security measures have been made through co-operation with the local administration (*Desa* officials). Currently in most *kramat*, visitors who stay overnight are required to give their identity card to the security section and their identity is recorded. If a person fails to produce an identity card he will not be allowed to stay overnight. Given the variety of visitors I wish to confine my discussion to the pilgrims belonging to both *wong ziarah* and *wong nyepi* categories.

Wong Ziarah and Wong Nyepi

A *kramat* caretaker considers all visitors in the first place as guests (*tamu*) who must be treated with honour. Many reasons are given for this. A visitor is a guest not only of his own but primarily of the revered person who sanctifies the place for whom the caretaker works. Here he assumes himself to be the servant (*bujang* or *pelayan*) for his master. In this capacity he feels obliged on behalf of his master to receive, mediate and show respect and courtesy to all guests. From a religious and ethical viewpoint, according to a *juru kunci*, any guest deserves honourable treatment since the Prophet said that whoever believes in God, His messenger and the Day of Judgement, should honour his guest. Considered from the mystical dimension, although a guest is a *barakah* seeker, at the same time he is also a *barakah* bearer who brings *barakah* to the host. Thus, from this viewpoint, there is a sense of exchange and reciprocity of *barakah* between the host and the visitors in the *ziarah* process. Finally, from an economic point of view, a guest, although not always, but more often than not, means a donation for the maintenance of the *kramat*. At least partly, this is a source of income for the *juru kunci* and his associates. In some *kramat* the donations they collect from visitors spill over outside the *kramat* milieu. A medium size *kramat* such as *Kramat Syeikh Magelung* at Karangkendal (35 km North of Cirebon) for example, where Syeikh Magelung is buried, provides a grant of a Rp 1,000,000.00 per annum (1992) to support the *desa* administration. It is not surprising then that visits to most *kramat* are always welcome and thus can be made every day at any time. When the *juru kunci* is not there contact with him can be made at his house and most *juru kunci* will not refuse to serve visitors.

The relation between visitor and *juru kunci* normally starts when a visitor or a group of visitors come(s) to the *juru kunci* explaining whether they have come for *ziarah* or for *nyepi*. For formality sake, some *juru kunci* recommend that a visitor, should come with a parcel of flowers and incense (both, which are not compulsory, usually can be bought from peddlers nearby or around the kramat), take an ablution and go together with the *juru kunci* and enter the *ziarah* platform with standard greetings addressed to the dead in a similar way to the ordinary Islamic procedures for visiting graves.[60] The greeting (in Arabic) reads: "*Assalamu'alaikum ya ahladdiyar minal mu'minin wal-muslimin wa inni insya Allah ma'akum lahiqun nasalullaha lana walakumul 'afiyah*" (Peace be upon you oh, the grave dweller[s] of the believers and surrenderers, verily if God will, we shall be with you soon; we beg God endows us with well being).'[61] Then they sit on mats or on the floor facing the tomb and burn incense. The *juru kunci* then asks if the guest will utter the next prayer by himself or, when it is a group, whether one of the group members would like to lead the prayer or else whether the *juru kunci* himself should lead.

The standard prayer uttered in *ziarah* is the renewal of faith by means of *tahlil*.[62] Prior to the *tahlil* the *fatihah* is recited seven times, the merit of each *fatihah* is addressed to a number of spirits of the deceased.[63] The first is to the Prophet Muhammad and his companions, wives, descendants, dwellers of his house (**ahl al-bayt**); the second is to the four companions (the four Caliphs) and some specified closest friends (Thalhah, Sa'ad, Sa'id, Abd Rahman bin 'Awf, Abi 'Ubaidah, Amir bin Jarrah, Zubair bin 'Awwam); the third is to the founders of the four schools of **shari'a**, their followers, the scholars, jurists, *hadithists*, readers of the Qur'an, exegetes of the Qur'an, the true *Sufi* and those who follow them good heartedly *(ihsan)* until the Day of Judgement. The fourth is to the martyrs (*syuhada*) buried at al-Ma'la, al-Shubaikah, al-Baqi', and the believers in general who already passed away in the East and in the West, on land and at sea. The fifth is to all *wali* in the East and in the West, on the ground and in the sea, especially Abd al-Qadir al-Jilani, Junaid al-Baghdadi, Ahmad al-Badawi,

[60] Some informants said that in one sense flowers are used as a symbolic expression of love, affection and sincerity. In another sense, putting flowers on graves is deduced from the example given by the Prophet who once put palm date leaves on the grave he visited. With regard to incense, there are many things enumerated about it, one of which is that it is a symbol of "ngarwah" to address to the spirits. Smoke is a subtle thing which contrary to water, always goes up. The ethereal world where the spirit is supposed to reside is up there and the smoke with incense is the symbolic vehicle which would bring the message. There are also many practical reasons for the use of incense, such as to create spiritual atmosphere, to drive away mosquitoes and other insects, to unite the fragrance brought by various people of various conditions. But those practical reasons, I think, have come mainly as apologies against stigmatisation of its use. According to Kyai Nasir of Pesantren Tarbiyatul Banin at Kaliwadas, burning incense is one of the Prophet's customs, depicted in the *hadith* narrated by al-Nasai and Muslim (i.e.: *Sunan Nasai*, vol 7–8 p.106 and Sahih Muslim, vol 2, p.302).

[61] This procedure is directly derived from a hadith transmitted by Muslim and Ahmad. See for example: Sulaiman Rasyid (1988), *Fiqh Islam*, p.183.

[62] The claim that *tahlil* is a renewal of faith came from a *Juru Kunci*. When I asked about it to Ki Dulah of Buntet, he confirmed that the claim is true. According to Ki Dulah, there is a *hadith* in which the Prophet told his companion: "Renew your faith (continuously)!" His companions asked: "How do we renew our faith?" The Prophet said: "Keep saying as many as you can the words "there is no God but Allah."

[63] This is done in the same manner with *hadiwan* mentioned earlier but the stress to be put is different. In *hadiwan*, the stress is put on addressing the spirit of Syeikh 'Abdul Qadir Al -Jilani whereas in *ziarah* the stress is on the *wali* or holy men being visited.

Ahmad al-Rifa'i, Ja'far al-Sadiq, Abu Yazid al-Busthami, Yusuf al-Hamdani, Hasan al-Harqani, Ma'ruf al-Kurkhy, Sirr al-Saqty, Habib al-'Ajamy and other *Sufi*. The sixth is to a number of prominent figures buried at Gunung Sembung and Gunung Jati, especially Syarif Hidayatullah, Syarifah Mudaim (Rarasantang), Nyai Mas Panatagama Pasambangan (Syarifah Baghdad), Pangeran Cakrabuana (Walangsungsang), Syeikh Datu Kahfi, and Syeikh Bayanillah. This is the case of Astana; in the case of other *kramat*, besides these figures, the figure buried at that *kramat* is added. At Panguragan, for example, an addition is made by mentioning Nyi Mas Gandasari, and at Karangkendal by mentioning Syeikh Magelung and others related to that place.

Having mentioned these figures a special address like that used in *hadiwan* is uttered: "Help us by God's permission and by reference to the *karamat* God endowed to the already mentioned deceased persons, we ask for intercession, blessing, remuneration and safety." The last *fatihah* is addressed to the spirits of parents, ancestors, Muslims, and all believers dead or alive. Then the *tahlil* (testimony "there is no God but Allah") is uttered 100 times, followed by the recital of a set of selected Qur'anic verses, exaltation of God and exaltation of the Prophet Muhammad. Concluding with a *du'a* the palms of the hands are raised up and other participants respond with "Amen." This is similar to *tahlil* at *slametan* or other occasions. Then the flowers are put on the grave between tombstones or at the appropriate place as directed by *juru kunci*. At the end, each visitor contemplates and prays by heart in his own language for any wishes he/she might have, and the *ziarah* is completed. When the visit is made individually, upon leaving the *ziarah* platform the visitor shakes the *juru kunci's* hands and gives him some cash as a donation or puts it into a box provided for it. At Astana where many visitors come and go one after another and usually in groups, the cash is put in front of the *pesujudan* door. When a crowd of people want to give their donation in coins but cannot approach the door because there are too many people, they throw the coins towards the door which will fall down around it. The coins hitting the door thrown by the crowd produces an orchestrated sound. Usually the throwing marks the end of a *ziarah* session. All money and coins will be collected by *wong kraman*.

Many visitors, especially at Astana, feel unsatisfied by merely attending the *tahlil*. Some struggle amidst the crowd, or those who are patient wait until there is enough space, and come forward to take a chance, leaning their chest against the *pesujudan* wooden door; some others kiss it or rub it with their hands, then rub their hands to their face; some brush the door with handkerchiefs; still others pick up and kiss some flowers they put there before *tahlil*. Outside the *tahlil* session there are visitors sleeping between graves, or sitting while their lips are murmuring something, or reciting the Qur'an facing the graves, some even hold a tombstone while doing these things.

Seeing this type of behaviour, observers may gain different impressions from it, some would get an unfavourable one. Of these, especially those who condemn *wali* veneration, usually take it as authentic evidence for their allegations about the idolatrous nature of *ziarah* practices, saying that not only do the pilgrims worship either *wali*, their tombs or both along with God, but also other objects as well such as the wooden door at Astana or other objects elsewhere.

There are many others who see it differently ranging from recommending, agreeing or just not condemning such practices, while they themselves may not do them. They are mostly of the *pesantren* (traditional religious school) stock and the traditional villagers at large. For them faith is in the heart and thus one's faith cannot be judged from outward behaviour only. Some visitors said that what they do is an expression of their anxiety to show respect to *Kanjeng Sinuhun* (a reference to Sunan Gunung Jati); some others said that it was to satisfy themselves emotionally that they were able to come to the place; still others said that it was to ensure earnest praying and to show an eagerness for *barakah*.[64]

For a *wong nyepi*, after the ordinary *ziarah* procedure is concluded, *juru kunci* may lead him to occupy a space available at the *kramat* to stay with others if he is a newcomer, or the *juru kunci* may let his guest take any space he likes if he is familiar with the place. During their stay at *kramat, wong nyepi* usually engage in either one or a combination of fasting, voluntary night prayer, reciting the Qur'an, *tahlil* individually or in group, and doing mental training (*tirakat*) by means of eating only plain staple foods (*mutih* or *ngasrep*) such as rice, cassava and maize, as well as doing other pious practices. Those who cannot do these things, can ask the *juru kunci* for advice. When an individual visitor is unable to take his advice because of serious ignorance, *juru kunci* usually stress the earnestness of the person's concern to keep praying to God, wishing that by virtue of the *barakah* and *karamah* of the figure at the *kramat*, God would answer his prayer. This earnestness should be expressed outwardly in one form or

[64] The situation did not allow indepth talks with visitors who were coming and going to explore their theological outlook. The evidence I could obtain from those who exhibited such behaviour (leaning their body onto the door, rubbing it with handkerchiefs or bare hands, kissing it, etc) is that they feel their visit to this place as an exciting opportunity and do not think of having chance for another visit. They came from far outside Cirebon region, including Lampung (South Sumatra), Bekasi, Subang, Karawang, Indramayu, Cianjur, Sukabumi or other parts of Java. None were regular visitors from surrounding villages. *Ki Jeneng* at Astana was aware of the idolatrous allegation, but he said, such an allegation is too simplistic. Other informants showed similar opinions. Pak Said at Kalitengah for example, said that anyone anywhere can lean on a door or another object, rubbing it and kissing it, but why when these things done at Astana or other *kramat* are they said to be idolatrous while elsewhere they are not? Ki Dulah (of Pesantren Buntet) said, expressions of love, respect, excitement, happiness and sadness vary from person to person. *Sungkem* (prostration to parents) or kissing hands does not mean equating the object with God, neither does kissing a letter from a fiance, rubbing it, pushing it at one's breast, etc. In fact, both groups (those who condemn and those who perform wali veneration hold the same doctrine, the *tauhid* (unity of God). They are, nevertheless, separated by what Wittgenstein (1987:75) calls "an unbridgeable communication gap." They see similar things but each conceives the things differently and uses the things and the sight for different projections.

another like fasting, uttering *du'a* continuously by heart or by tongue in their own language, reciting repeatedly whatever they can do even only the *Basmalah* (In the name of God) and the *Syahadat* (Testimony of Faith). Concentration of the mind (*mancleng*) on God is, above all, strongly stressed.

Ziarah however, can also be performed without formal contact with a *juru kunci* if it is conducted on regular occasions or on the occasion of festivals. At least once a week, usually Thursday night (*bengi Jum'ah*) after evening prayer (*'Isya*), almost all *kramat* in Cirebon routinely perform *tahlil* in which public participation is welcome or even expected. At Trusmi, for example, *tahlil* is held four times a week, on Sunday and Tuesday nights after evening prayer (around 8.00 pm), and twice on Thursday night. Each is carried out after evening prayer and at midnight (12.00 pm). At Astana, on the other hand, *tahlil* is performed once on Tuesday night (*bengi Rebo*) and twice on Thursday night at 8.00 pm led by *Ki Penghulu*, and at 10.00 p.m., led by *Ki Jeneng*. At Astana, each time it is attended by no less than 5000 participants. This number increases substantially to 30.000 on Thursday night (*bengi Jum'at*) *Kliwon*, and several hundred thousand at festival times. Each festival, either at Trusmi or Astana, lasts about a week.

Kramat Trusmi has three main festivals: *muludan* (commemoration of the birth of the Prophet Muhammad), *memayu* (replacement of *welit* or palm-thatch roofs) used on *pewadonan, pekuncen* and two *jinem*,[65] and *ganti sirap* (replacement of *sirap* or wooden roofs) used on *witana*, the mosque, *penyekaran, pesujudan* and *paseban*. The *muludan* is held each year on a fixed date, the 25th of Mulud. *Memayu* is held once a year and *ganti sirap* once every two years; each is held at the beginning of the rainy season. The exact date is determined by the assembly of *desa* officials and *kramat* custodians specially held for that purpose. All materials and labour needed at both *memayu* and *ganti sirap* are provided entirely by the people. The offer of the materials as well as the application for essential voluntary work such as by carpenters and masons comes eventually after the custodian issues an announcement about the matter.

At Astana, as already mentioned, the festival is held four times annually. These festivals are held on *Syawalan* or *Grebeg Syawal* (on the 8th of Syawal), *Grebeg Raya Agung* on 12th Raya Agung, *Muludan* (on the 11th of Mulud) and *Sedekah Bumi-Nadran*, prior to the beginning of the rainy season.[66] All these festivals attract hundreds of thousands of visitors who come by chartered buses or other means of transportations from many places throughout Java and even Sumatra. Folk arts such as *wayang golek* (puppet plays), *wayang kulit* (shadow puppet plays), *topeng* (mask dances), *tarling* (Cirebonese local music), acrobatics, *sandiwara* (play) and Malay orchestra, are performed at these festivals, along

[65] According to Ki Turjani, the word memayu is derived from the *ayu*, meaning beautiful; thus, *memayu* means to make beautiful.
[66] See Chapter Five.

with great carnivals held on the last festive day. The entertaining groups voluntarily come for promotion to entertain visitors without being paid, but their hope of gaining *berkah* from participation in the festival is implicit.

Plate 24: An entrance to Astana Gunung Jati grave complex.

Plate 25: Astana Gunung Jati custodians at the "Pekemitan" hall.

Plate 26: Pilgrims at Astana Gunung: the "Pesujudan" door is closed.

Plate 27: The "Pesujudan" door is open. (The ascending pathway leads to Sunan Gunung Jati's tomb.)

Plate 28: A "wong kraman" serves pilgrims.

Plate 29: Astana Gunung Jati custodians and Kecamatan Administrative officials pray together on a festival occasion.

Chapter 7: The Transmission of Religious Traditions: The Role of Pesantren

INTRODUCTION

Carilah ilmu walau kemana
Walau adanya dinegeri Cina
Itulah sabda junjungan kita
Harus dikejar dengan segera.

Seek knowledge wherever it is
No matter if it is in China
That is what our master (the Prophet) insisted
It has to be sought immediately.

In the preceding Chapters I have discussed the major religious traditions that currently prevail in Cirebon. Some traditions may be independently transmitted by one individual to make it known or accessible to others. An example of this is the accession of "*ilmu ghaib*" or "*ilmu hikmah*" from an owner (master) to a learner. In this Chapter, however, I would like to focus my discussion on how the main corpus of the traditions is institutionally transmitted from one generation to the next in a more formal and systematic manner. It is not difficult to find out the main institutions responsible for this. They are widely known, being found everywhere within the society itself. They are the household, the *madrasah* (modern religious school) and the *pesantren* (traditional boarding school). With special reference to Buntet, the biggest *pesantren* in Cirebon, I wish to focus my attention in this Chapter on discussing the role of *pesantren*.

The verse at the beginning of this Chapter reflects a *pesantren* tradition. The teacher, Pak Nawawi (47 years), who wrote the verse, is a *pesantren* graduate. He composed the verse as a part of the lyrics to be sung by his students at the private primary religious school (*Madrasah Diniyah)* of "Budi Tresna" in *Desa* Panembahan of *Kecamatan* Weru. The first two lines of the verse contain a message which has been derived directly from a well known *hadith* that says: "Seek knowledge, even as far away as China." The last two lines accentuate the fact that the message is indeed derived from the *hadith* and thus its conclusion is that it is everyone's duty because it is an instruction from the Prophet and thus part of the Islamic doctrine. The verse suggests that among the local people the pursuit of knowledge, especially religious knowledge, and its transmission from one generation to the next lie at the very heart of their inner traditions and become something which is always worthy of encouragement.

Islam, following its Judeo-Christian predecessors, is a religion of Scriptures whereby the activity of teaching and learning is an inseparable part of its doctrine. In a real sense, learning is worship, so the study of God's words, the traditions of the Prophet, and the system of law derived from them are part of everyone's fundamental service demanded by God.[1] For Muslims the first revelation which marks Muhammad's prophecy is God's instruction to mankind (via Muhammad) to read.[2] Many verses revealed subsequently also exhort believers to engage in the pursuit of knowledge. To mention a few, there is God's advice to man to pray: "O, my Lord, advance me in knowledge" (QS 20:114). Further, there are God's assertions that those who have no knowledge are not equal to those who have (QS 39:9); that those who do not observe and try to understand are worse than cattle (QS 7:179); that the meaning of revelation becomes manifest to those 'who have knowledge' (QS 6:97) and those 'who have understanding' (QS 6:98); that whosoever has been given knowledge indeed has been given an abundant good (QS 2:269); that the basic qualifications for leadership are, among other things, knowledge and physical strength (QS 2:47); that by virtue of knowledge man is superior to angels and has been made vicegerent of God on earth (QS 2:30), etc.[3]

The enactment of these verses was also exemplified by Muhammad's apostolic career. After the first victory of 300 Muslims over 1000 Meccan Quraisyi unbelievers at Badr in AH 624, for example, Muhammad set all the prisoners free after requiring them to teach skills to the Muslims, especially reading and writing. He then insisted to his followers that someone who leaves his home in search of knowledge, actually walks in the path of God; that seeking knowledge is an obligation for every Muslim, male and female. Also his instruction: "Acquire knowledge, because he who acquires it in the way of the Lord performs an act of piety; he who disseminates it (the knowledge) bestows alms and he who imparts it to others performs an act of devotion to God."[4] Concerning religious knowledge, for which Muhammad himself held the authority, he always insisted his followers should transmit (to others) everything from him.[5] Under this scriptural scheme the Muslims have a legitimate claim to having Islamic ethics for the spirit of seeking knowledge. The verse cited above, which in fact is derived from a *hadith*, is part of this scriptural ethical package. As we will see this package is clearly manifest is popular traditions.

[1] Berkey, J. (1992), *The Transmission of Knowledge in Medieval Cairo*, New Jersey: Princeton University Press, p. 5.

[2] The first revelation is QS 96: 1–5 which translates: "Read in the name of your Lord who created; created man from clots of blood. Read! Your Lord is the Most Bountiful; who teaches by the pen; teaches man what he did not know.

[3] Ahmad, K. ed. (1988), *Islam, its meaning and message*, London: The Islamic Foundation, p. 34.

[4] Ibid.

[5] This insistence manifests in a well known hadith: "Transmit from me even a verse (*Ballighu 'anny walau ayah*)."

In recent versions albeit more popular *Babad*,[6] Walangsungsang's and Rarasantang's being Muslims and their departure to Mecca for pilgrimage, as cited in the previous chapter, did not occur accidentally without precedence as the *Babad Tjerbon* of Brandes edition recounts. The popular *Babad* explain that Syeikh Qura of Pesantren Karawang paved the way for Islam to penetrate the core Hindu Pajajaran ruling house when he encouraged his student, Nyai Subanglarang, to respond positively to the wish of Prabu Siliwangi, the Hindu Pajajaran king, to marry her. This marriage produced Muslim offspring's, Walangsungsang, Rarasantang and Kian Santang. After a long adventure in seeking wisdom, Walangsungsang and Rarasantang finally became Syeikh Kahfi's students at Amparan Jati. Upon completion of their learning, Syeikh Kahfi advised Walangsungsang to open a settlement at a *Tegal Alang-alang* (Field of wild grass) in cooperation with the local elder, Ki Pangalang-alang. After Tegal Alang-alang grew into a busy village, it became Cirebon and eventually needed a sort of government. Ki Pangalang-alang was appointed the *Kuwu* (chief) and Walangsungsang his assistant. Upon Pangalangalang's death Walangsungsang succeeded him and became Pangeran Cakrabuana. Thus, it was after having settled in Cirebon and becoming the Chief's assistant, according to this Babad that Walangsungsang went to Mecca for pilgrimage. What happened with Walangsungsang and Rarasantang during the pilgrimage and later after his return to Cirebon, by and large accord with the scenario of the *Babad Tjerbon* which tells the story of the emergence of Cirebon *kraton*.

In other words, according to this *Babad* version, the Cirebon region, sprang up and developed from the teaching-learning enterprise of *pesantren*-like institutions.[7] Pesantren Krawang (Syeikh Qura) paved the way for Islam to penetrate the core of the Hindu Pajajaran kingdom, whereas Pesantren Amparan Jati (Syeikh Kahfi) paved the way for the establishment of an Islamic kingdom (*kraton*). In return, *pesantren* gained full recognition, legitimation and political support from the *kraton*.

The *Babad* scenario provides even more information than this, however. It says that both Walangsungsang (Cakrabuana) and Sunan Gunung Jati were themselves priest-king (*raja-pandita*), a kind of pre-Islamic title, the ruler and the priest

[6] See Chapter Six. An example of this version of the *Babad* is *Sejarah Cerbon* by H. Mahmud Rais (n.d.), hand-written mimeograph in *pegon* (Javanese Arabic letters) and in Cirebon-Javanese vernacular (18 volumes). This version is now hardly found in the market but I found many people in Kalitengah and Kaliwadas know it. My copy was provided by Pak Akyas (63 years), a tobacco trader of Kaliwadas. A condensed Indonesian version (in Roman letters) of this is entitled *Perjuangan Wali Sanga, Babad Cirebon (Pasundan)* by Mahmud Rais and Sayidil Anam, already mentioned in Chapter Six. This version is available in the market and many people read it which, I think, influences their views about aspects of Cirebon history.

[7] Van Bruinessen (1992) speculates that the oldest *pesantren* was "Tegalsari" in East-Java, established in 1742. No further explanation is given on how and through what institution Islam was transmitted before that period. See his "Pesantren dan Kitab Kuning : Pemeliharaan dan Kesinambungan Tradisi Pesantren," *Jurnal Ulumul Qur'an*, III/4 pp. 73–85).

(*guru*) at the same time whose performances were much more like missionary workers (*Sufi* wanderers) than rulers.[8] Their stories are more centred around preaching than ruling. They tended to use political power to ensure fruitful missionary efforts rather than the contrary, using religion to gain political benefits.[9] During their reign, as far as the *Babad* narrative is concerned, not only did the transmission of Islam enjoy political support, recognition and legitimation from the *kraton* but the *kraton* itself took over and established the mission of the *pesantren*. Such antiquities as Tajug Jalagrahan, Pengguron Kaprabon, the grand mosque of Kesepuhan, the Panjunan mosque and many sites now known as *kramat* are but a few examples that are taken as evidence to substantiate this suggestion.[10] Consequently, the Cirebon *kraton* at that stage is represented as a missionary rather than a political institution. De Graaf's and Pigeaud's assessment may be right in arguing that Sunan Gunung Jati did not have substantial political power although clearly his spiritual charisma was acknowledged and highly respected by the Demak imperium and other Javanese royal circles.[11] This may indicate that Cirebon was not a political institution although to a certain extent it also exercised a quasi-political power. The extent to which Cirebon was known as a centre of learning and piety is witnessed, among others, by Hoadley (1975:10).[12]

This situation was maintained throughout the period when Cirebon stood as a fully independent state. The situation changed dramatically however, when, under Pangeran Girilaya who succeeded Panembahan Ratu, Cirebon lost its independence, being first, controlled by Mataram and then by the Dutch Company (VOC). Girilaya's lack of status as a religious teacher in comparison to his predecessors removed Amangkurat's hesitation in demoting Cirebon from ally to vassal. Girilaya and his two sons were invited by Amangkurat to visit Mataram where they were then held as hostages. During the 1660's Amangkurat sent his governor to rule Cirebon on his behalf and thus Cirebon became the

[8] This may substantiate John's hypothesis that Sufi wanderers were the main individuals who were responsible for the substantial spread of Islam into the Javanese interiors. See: John, A.H. (1961), "Sufism as a Category in Indonesian Literature and History, *Journal of South East Asian History*, vol. II, pp 10–25.

[9] See Chapter Six on Biographical Account of Cirebonese Holy men. Cf: Suleiman, S., et al. (1982), in Abdurrachman, P.R. ed., *Cerbon*, Jakarta: Sinar Harapan. Referring to Cakrabuana (Walangsungsang), the founder of Cirebon, they note: "...he reportedly left the actual rule to his ministers...then went around the lands of Sunda to propagate Islamic faith." (p.33). Referring to Syarif Hidayatullah, they note: "Syarif Hidayatullah, as a religious man, had contacts with the other leaders of Islam of the period, but was not intent on making Cerbon a political force (pp. 22–67). See also Chapter One.

[10] Tajug Jalagrahan (known as the oldest prayer house in Cirebon) and Pengguron Kaprabon (a place of learning, a *pesantren*-like institution within the precinct of the *kraton* at Lemah Wungkuk), both were allegedly being built by Walangsungsang as soon as he founded the settlement. The grand mosque of Kesepuhan is said to have been built by Syarif Hidayatullah as soon as he took his office as the first ruler of Cirebon; the Panjunan mosque is said to have been built by Pangeran Panjunan as soon as he settled there.

[11] See: de Graaf and Pigeaud (1989), pp 143–144; Hoadley, M.C. (1975), pp 9–11.

[12] See Chapter One.

vassal of Mataram.[13] When Java was in chaos due to the Trunojoyo revolt, on April 30, 1681 Cirebon signed a contract for VOC's protection.[14] The cession of Cirebon to the VOC became official when, at the end of the Trunojoyo revolt, the Mataram-VOC contract was signed on October 5, 1705, by which Mataram transferred its suzerainty over Cirebon and Priangan to the VOC.[15]

There is enough grounds to suppose that at the earlier stage predating the *kraton* era, the transmission of Islam in Cirebon was centred in the village (Syeikh Qura at Krawang and Syeikh Kahfi at Amparan Jati). Since Cirebon had its own ruling house under Cakrabuana and then developed into a *kraton* under Sunan Gunung Jati (circa 1570), and his successor, Panembahan Ratu (circa 1650), the centre of religious transmission moved from the village to the ruling house. In 1702 the VOC removed the main traditional function of the *kraton* by forbidding learning activities within it, leaving the *kraton* as a mere ruling house with lands and other possessions but with neither political nor economic power.[16] Religious transmission moved back to the village one hundred years after the death of Panembahan Ratu when Kyai Muqayim, the Kraton Religious Official (*Penghulu Kraton*), fled from the *kraton* to the village and established Pesantren Buntet. The *kraton* became more and more a colonial subject and finally collapsed while the *pesantren*, despite encountering hardships and suppressions, kept its independence and has continued to function until this day. It is on this *pesantren* that further discussions in this Chapter will be focused.

THE GENERAL FEATURE OF RELIGIOUS TRANSMISSION

Before discussing the main issue, I feel that it is necessary to touch upon the general features of religious transmission in Cirebon. In general terms this transmission follows the same tradition of religious education which occurs among the Javanese at large. As Dhofier (1985:18–24) has sketched, every Javanese is taught and formally utters the confession of faith (*syahadat*) at least once in his life time, that is, at marriage. In most cases however, the confession of faith among the Javanese is conveyed to the child as soon as he is born. In Cirebon, as well as in other parts of Java, when a mother is giving birth the father waits outside the room just in front of the door. Soon after the new baby is born, even before it is cleaned, the midwife (*dukun bayi*) puts the baby on a round bamboo tray called *tampa*, symbolising that its presence amongst the family is *ditampa* (meaning being accepted with warmth and welcome) as his presence really means adding to the number of potential believers. Immediately the midwife calls the father to enter the room to utter the *adzan* and *iqamat* (calls for prayer containing the confession of faith) at the baby's right and left ears

[13] Hoadley, M.C. (1975), p 36.
[14] Ibid, p 48.
[15] Ibid, p 53.
[16] Siddique, S. (1977), p 123.

respectively. When the father is unable to do so someone else, or the midwife herself, will do it, witnessed by both the father and the mother. This means that the first sound the child has ever heard in this world is the confession of the faith.[17]

Although the formal utterance of the confession of faith comes later, that is at circumcision for a boy and at marriage for both boy and girl, the child undergoes both informal and formal religious education during his infancy. The informal education is attained through observation of and participation in the day to day village life of which, religious activities of both *adat* and *ibadat* are essential parts. Meanwhile in Cirebon, there are at least three forms of formal religious instruction known to the villagers: *ngaji, mesantren* and *sekolah madrasah*. The intensity of both informal and formal education of the village children, however, depends very much on the parents' knowledge of and commitment to religious precepts.

[17] The uttering of the *adzan* and *iqamat* at the ears of a newly born baby is rooted in the *hadith* transmitted by Ahmad and Tirmidzi, depicting what the Prophet did it when his grand-child, Husein, was born to Fatimah. To the villagers, like Bu Warni (54 years) however, a midwife in Kalitengah, the uttering of *adzan* and *iqamat* is considered as an *adat* practice that has been done since an unknown time. ("*Wis adate seng bengiyen mula gan ari bocah ndau lair iku, ya kudu diadani karo dikomati,*" meaning "it has been a tradition since the old days to utter upon the newly born baby, the *adzan* and *iqamat*).

Plate 30: Two Qur'anic learners at "khataman" ceremony to mark the completion of the whole Qur'an.

Plate 31: Demonstrating the recital of the Qur'an.

Ngaji

One form of formal instruction almost everyone in Cirebon has experienced is *ngaji* (Qur'anic learning). It is a learning process carried on in the household when a child is around six years old. At this age the parents begin to teach their children to memorise step by step the short *surah* of the Holy Qur'an, and the incantations to be uttered in daily prayers. This is usually carried out in the evening after sunset prayer. When the parents are unable to do the teaching by themselves they send or let the children go to a neighbouring household, a *tajug* (prayer house) or the mosque, where such teaching (*ngaji*) is held.

The instruction is basically on an individual basis in which the teacher first recites the short *surah* verse by verse and the child repeats again and again until he grasps it by memory. The recital is presented in melodious format so that the memorisation is made easier and more convenient. At this stage, neither meaning nor understanding of the material is introduced, probably because it is considered unnecessary as the main objective of this early instruction is to give the child an acquaintance with and a basic ability to conform to the minimum requirements for being a good Muslim, especially to be able to perform daily prayers or at least to follow congregational prayers. As all incantations uttered in prayers must be performed without reading any text, the memorisation is therefore crucial. Sometimes, accompanying this instruction, rules of conduct and other religious or ethical dimensions are also added through chants and story telling (*dongeng*) given by the teacher (*ustadz*). The story may be of a real occurrence or fictitious. In many cases, it is taken from a segment or an episode in the life story of the Messengers, *Sufi*, or other exemplary figures.

At around seven years the child is taught the Arabic alphabet and, also step by step, to read the Holy Qur'an. The reading lesson usually starts from the first *Surah* of the Holy Qur'an (al-Fatihah) of the first *juz* (division), then jumps to the last (30th) *juz*. This procedure is taken partly because this *juz* contains short *Surah* (QS 78–114) and also because most of the *Surah* of this *juz* are frequently recited in the prescribed prayers. Learning this 30th *juz* proceeds in the reverse direction, from the shortest *surah* (QS 114) which consists of only a few short verses to the longer ones (QS 78). This procedure allows the child to gain an easy and gradual mastery. The standard text for this initial learning is called *Turutan* (literally meaning 'something to follow'). This text is available in local book shops, containing elementary materials for learning to read the Arabic letters, al-Fatihah and Surah 114 through Surah 78 of the Holy Qur'an. The completion of this text is marked by a minor *khataman* (completion ceremony) in the form of *syukuran* or *slametan*. A *du'a* is uttered at this occasion and food is served. A bigger *khataman* is held upon the completion of the whole Qur'an. Further learning moves from Qur'an to *Kitab* (religious texts) dealing with jurisprudence (*pekih* or **fiqh**), theology (*tauhid*) and ethics (*akhlaq*, part of *tasawuf*). The *kitab* learned at *ngaji* varies considerably from village to village and from individual to individual, but the most commonly used are *Safinah* and *Sullam at-Taufiq* by Imam Nawawi of Banten, which contains a blend of jurisprudence, theology and ethics.

As there is no binding rule, *ngaji* in the village is not so effective. The proportion of 'drop-outs' is high. Only a few children who follow from the start proceed consistently to the completion of a *certain kitab*; many of them do not even complete the *Turutan*. Some factors which contribute to this are that older children are busy with their school work, some teaching sessions are short-lived as the teachers are volunteers, and in addition, especially since the second half of the 1960s, there has been the intrusion of television into village life. Quite often, children are tempted to watch an entertaining program on the television rather than going to the place where the Qur'anic teaching is held. When a child quits and drops out from *ngaji* however, it does not necessarily mean that his religious education in the village terminates. Religion is still taught in public schools; informal education by observation and participation in the village religious activities is an unavoidable process because it is part of the village life. Parents who can afford to and who are more concerned with bettering their children's religious education prefer to send them to *pesantren*, while some others are satisfied with sending them to the nearby *madrasah*.

Mesantren

The local term *mesantren* is synonymous with *nyantri* meaning 'to go to,' or 'to learn in' *pesantren* whose purpose is to become *santri*.[18] A young girl or boy who goes to a *pesantren* gets special treatment from the parents. For example, I found in Plered, a group of three boys and two girls with their suitcases going by *becak* being escorted by a mass of people walking behind them for a distance of seven kilometres from their village to the railway station. The escorting people were walking not because there was no means of transportation but they intentionally did this to express honour to the children going to *pesantren*.[19] The boys and girls were primary school graduates, who for the first time were leaving their village for Yogyakarta to start learning at Pesantren Krapyak.

Pesantren in Indonesia are officially classified by The Ministry of Religious Affairs, into four types, A, B, C and D. Type-A is that which retains the most traditional characteristics where the students (*santri*) stay in a boarding house (*pondok*) around the *kiyai*'s house; there is no set curriculum and thus the *kyai*

[18] In this case the word *santri* can either mean the student of *pesantren* or implying a hope that the child will develop into becoming wong *santri* (a devout individual). For a further account on the meaning of *santri*, see for example, Fox, J.J. (1989), "The memories of village *santri* from Jombang in East Java" (with Prajarto Dirjosanoto) in R. J. May and W. J. O' Malley (eds.), *Observing Change in Asia*, pp. 94–110. Bathurst: Crawfurd House Press. *Santri* in reference to a socio-religious stratum of the Javanese society, see Geertz, C. (1979), *The Religion of Java*, Phoenix ed., Chicago: University of Chicago Press.

[19] Similar treatment is given to someone who is going to Mecca for pilgrimage.

holds full authority over the teaching-learning process including the type and depth of the offered subject matter. The method of teaching is typically 'traditional,' relying on the *sorogan* (individualised instruction) and the *bandungan* (collective learning) methods. In either one the *santri* sits around the *kyai* who reads, translates and explains his lessons, which are repeated or followed by his students. The lessons consist only of religious subjects and Arabic language, usually taken from or using classical religious texts. Type-B *pesantren* includes those which, besides offering the traditional instructions in classical texts with *sorogan* and *bandungan*, have *madrasah* (modern religious schools) where both religion and secular subjects are taught. The *madrasah* has a curriculum of its own or adopts the curriculum set by the Ministry of Religious Affairs. Type-C is a *pesantren* which, along with providing religious education of a type-B model with both traditional instruction (*sorogan* and *bandungan*) and *madrasah* system, has also an ordinary public school administered by the Ministry of Education and Culture such as a Primary (SD) and Secondary (SMP and SMA). Thus, a type-C pesantren is a type-B plus public school. Finally, a type-D *pesantren* is that which provides only boarding accommodation to students. These students go to either *madrasah* or public schools somewhere outside this boarding complex. No formal instruction is given in this type of *pesantren*. The function of the *kyai* is only as a counsellor and spiritual guide to create a religious atmosphere at the complex.[20]

Currently, according to the statistical records issued by the Regional Office of Religious Affairs, there are 133 *pesantren* in the Regency (*Kabupaten*) and 7 in the city (*Kotamadya*) of Cirebon. Following the above classification there are 54 type-A's, 68 type-B's 16, type-C's and none of type-D. Three of the *pesantren* were established in the 18th century, five in the 19th and the rest are of the 20th century stock. Thus, *pesantren* education in Cirebon has evolved for no less than two centuries.

Sekolah Madrasah

In Cirebonese vernacular, the word *sekolah* (which literally means 'school'), can either be a verb or a noun. Used as a verb it means to go to school; as a noun it means the type of schooling (primary, secondary, general, vocational, state owned, private owned, etc). To refer to a school building, the word is *sekolahan* or *sekolan*. Thus, *sekolah* SD and SMP means respectively going to primary school (*Sekolah Dasar*) and Junior High School (*Sekolah Menengah Pertama*), whereas *sekolahan* or *sekolan* SD means the primary school building. The term *sekolah madrasah* therefore, refers to going to *Madrasah* (modern religious school), which can either be *madrasah diniyah* (which gives religious subjects) or public

[20] Aya Sofia and Marwan Saridjo (1988), "Kebijaksanaan dan Program Pemerintah Dalam Pengembangan Pondok Pesantren, official paper presented in *"Seminar Nasional" Perkembangan Program Pengembangan Masyarakat Melalui Pondok Pesantren,"* Ciawi-Bogor, 11–13 June.

madrasah where both secular and religious subjects are given. Each type of *madrasah* consists of three levels, the primary (six years), junior secondary (three years) and senior secondary (three years). The three levels of *madrasah diniyah* are called *Awaliyah, Wustha* and *'Ulya,* whereas the three levels of public *madrasah* are called *Ibtidaiyah, Tsanawiyah* and *'Aliyah*. The proportion for the secular and religious subjects in public *madrasah* varies from one *madrasah* to another but the Ministry of Religious Affairs sets a standard of 70 per cent secular and 30 per cent religious subjects. Any private *madrasah* wishing to follow the Ministry's accreditation should prove that it has fully adopted this standard. The students of a standard *madrasah* are entitled to sit for the national examination and those who pass this examination receive the state issued certificate. This leads to an easier way to continue their education within the educational system and finally to attend an IAIN (The State Institute of Islamic Studies).[21]

According to the 1990 official record, throughout the *Kabupaten* and *Kotamadya* Cirebon, there are 373 *Madrasah Ibtidaiyah* (MI) accommodating 66,504 students, 51 *Madrasah Tsanawiyah* accommodating 9543 students and 20 *Madrasah 'Aliyah* accommodating 5466 students. Most of them follow the curriculum set by the Ministry of Religious Affairs.[22] Only 21 of the schools are *Madrasah Diniyah,* one of which is Madrasah "Budi Tresna" whose song was cited early in this Chapter.

At present, *madrasah* undeniably play an important role in the transmission of religious knowledge both in the urban and rural areas. Their presence in the Islamic educational arena in Indonesia, especially on Java, has involved a long and complex process, but certainly, the *madrasah* system is quite a recent (20th century) development.[23] *Madrasah,* however, stands as complementary to and not as a substitute for the older form of religious learning institute, the *pesantren.* Along with the development of *madrasah,* some *pesantren* may have disappeared but some others have flourished. Although there has been a changing attitude and more and more people rely on *madrasah,* people do not expect too much from it beyond the acquirement of a basic knowledge of religion.[24] Until now

[21] IAIN stands for *Institut Agama Islam Negeri,* a state owned Higher learning institute firstly established on August 9, 1960 by the Indonesian government when K.H. Wahib Wahab, an alumnus of Pesantren Buntet, was the Minister of Religious Affairs. His father, K.H. Wahab Hasbullah with K.H. Hasyim Asy'ari of Pesantren Tebuireng in Jombang (East Java), founded Nahdlatul Ulama, an Orthodox Traditionalist Muslim organisation in 1926.

[22] *Kabupaten Cirebon Dalam Angka* 1990, Cirebon: Kantor Statistik Kabupaten Cirebon; *Kotamadya Cirebon Dalam Angka 1990/1991,* Cirebon: Kantor Statistik Kotamadya Cirebon.

[23] Mahmud Yunus (1960), notes that the oldest *madrasah* in Indonesia was Sekolah Adabiyah in Padang, established by Syeikh Abdullah Ahmad 1909, whereas in Java, it was Madrasah Aniyatus-Saniyah Mu'awanatul Muslimin in Kudus, founded in 1915 by the local Syarekat Islam. See: *Sejarah Pendidikan Islam di Indonesia,* Jakarta: Pustaka Mahmudiah, especially pp 54 and 220.

[24] Although employing the same name the *madrasah* in Java is different from that in the medieval Middle East. The Javanese *madrasah* is designated to provide basic religious education to beginners of school-age

it is the *pesantren* rather than the *madrasah* that is considered to be the real place for acquiring advanced knowledge of religion especially when the student intends to 'know religious rules' (*kanggo ngerti ning hukum*). The people regard the expected result from going to *madrasah*, without learning at *pesantren*, is only fair (*lumayan*), a little better than not knowing anything at all (*tenimbang bli ngerti babar pisan*).[25] Thus, although *madrasah* is important, its depth and intellectual level are considered inferior to the *pesantren*. Even among the IAIN graduates, those who have prior *pesantren* education have more potential depth in their religious knowledge and understanding compared to those who do not.[26] Institutionally too, *madrasah* are also said to be the offspring of *pesantren*. In the next section I wish to concentrate my discussion on the role of *pesantren* in the transmission of religious traditions.

THE ROLE OF PESANTREN: THE CASE OF BUNTET

To demonstrate how *pesantren* in Cirebon have evolved and functioned in the transmission role, I shall present in the following section, the case of Pesantren Buntet.[27] Scholarly work devoted to study this *pesantren*, historically or otherwise is scanty. Siddique (1977:120–123) touches upon it only briefly when she takes Pesantren Buntet as a ready example to support her argument. Despite the fact that the political significance has disappeared, the symbolic universe of Sunan Gunung Jati is still maintained by his descendant groups through organisational structure especially the *kraton* and a number of *pesantren* and *tarekat* (*Sufi* orders). Siddique suggests that the fact that there are many *pesantren* and *tarekat* (*Sufi* orders), not only in Cirebon but also in West Java, led by the descendants of Sunan Gunung Jati who have prestige as a result of being descendants of Sunan Gunung Jati, clearly substantiates this tradition.[28]

children, whereas in the Middle East the *madrasah* is especially intended to provide higher learning. The latter is a natural development from the *masjid* (mosque) in its role as a college of law, and its nearby *khan* as residence of the law students in attendance (*masjid-khan* complex). For detail see for example: Makdisi, G. (1981), *The Rise of Colleges*, Edinburg: Edinburg University Press.

25 At present most *pesantren* have *madrasah* and even, public schools and thus, there are only a few *pesantren* which retain the form.

26 Most current well known Indonesian Muslim intellectuals, such as Nurcholis Madjid, Abdurrahman Wahid and Zamakhsyari Dhofier, received their basic religious education from *pesantren*.

27 A number of works have been devoted to recount the issue of *pesantren*, the most notable one, I think, is Dhofier, Z. (1980), *The Pesantren Tradition: A Study of the Role of the Kyai in the Maintenance of the Traditional Ideology of Islam in Java*, unpublished Ph D. dissertation, Canberra: The Australian National University. The major portion of this work appears as its Indonesian version, *Tradisi Pesantren: Studi tentang Pandangan Hidup Kyai*, Jakarta: LP3ES, firstly published in 1982. My reference to this work is the 4th edition (1985) and has sold over 40.000 copies.

28 It is true that being a descendant of Sunan Gunung Jati carries spiritual (religious) prestige. Among the descendants; however, there is a different stance with regard to this prestige. The *kraton* oriented descendants, demonstratively show it to the public by putting before their names, a dignitary title (Raden, Pangeran, Elang). This reference, I think, has a heavy legitimating connotation by which the users seek for acceptance from others. Their pride probably refers to Sunan Gunung Jati as a ruler. Among the leaders of *pesantren* and Sufi orders this prestige is not claimed. None of them use such a title. Kyai Abdul Jamil (1879–1919), the leader of Pesantren Buntet, is even said to have strictly forbidden

The work which fully recounts the story of Pesantren Buntet is Zaini Hasan's study (1970), which comes with an historical account giving information about the chronological development of the *pesantren* since it was built until around the end of 1960s.[29] Another study is Amidjaja, R., et al (1985), which is a survey study on the life of the *santri* and which, along with providing the background of *pesantren* in general and Pesantren Buntet in particular, gives special emphasis to presenting quantitative illustrations about *santri* who studied there around 1984, with such details as their home origin, socio-economic and parental background, the *santri's* attitudes in relation to their daily routine of the *pesantren* life.[30] Still another one is that by Hisjam Mansur, a staff member of the *pesantren* from 1958 to 1975. In this work Mansur provides both scriptural and ethical reasons for the *haul* (commemorating the death of the founder of the *pesantren*) annually held at the *pesantren*. Then he proceeds to present biographical accounts of the *kyai* who led the *pesantren* and the institutional development of the *pesantren*. By and large Mansur's historical narration tells about the same thing discussed by Zaini Hasan.[31] My subsequent discussion on this *pesantren* relies on these works, together with my own field notes from a short stay at this *pesantren* between July and September 1992 and various visits before and after the stay.

The location and setting

'Pesantren Buntet' is located at 'Buntet Pesantren' (Blok Manis), the northern part of *Desa* Mertapada Kulon, District of (*Kecamatan*) Astanajapura, about 14 km south-eastern of the city of Cirebon.[32] Access to this 127.43 hectares *desa* is possible by taking a bus or mini bus from Cirebon to Ciledug via Sindanglaut. The *pesantren* complex is only 700 metres from the Cirebon-Ciledug main road where the Desa Office lies. The complex is connected with the main road by a paved road (*jalan desa*). *Becak* and passenger motor-bikes (*ojeg*) are available, ready to transport both visitors and residents going in and out of the *pesantren* complex, day and night. Their terminal lies at the junction where the *desa* and the Cirebon-Ciledug main roads meet. In 1992, nearly one third of the 3890 *desa*

his descendants to use such a title. They may be proud of being the descendant of Sunan Gunung Jati, not as a ruler but as a pious and learned individual. Above all they would be proud of their own piety and learning rather than of their ancestors. Hasanuddin Kriyani, descendants of Ki Kriyan, referred an Arabic proverb which says that it is not a real youth who says "here is my father," the real youth instead is one who says "here I am."

[29] Zaini Hasan (1970), *Sekilas Lintas Sedjarah Pesantren Buntet, Tjirebon*, unpublished mimeograph.

[30] Amijaya, R., et al (1985), *Pola Kehidupan Santri Pesantren Buntet Desa Mertapada Kulon Kecamatan Astanajapura Kabupaten Cirebon*, Yogyakarta: Proyek Penelitian dan Pengkajian Kebudayaan Nusantara (Javanologi) Departemen Pendidikan dan Kebudayaan.

[31] Hisjam Mansur, K.H.M. (1989), *Haul di Pesantren Buntet Pesantren: Kajian Sejarah Ringkas*, unpublished mimeograph.

[32] It might be worthwhile to recall the local reference of "Pesantren Buntet" and "Buntet Pesantren." The former refers to the institute for religious learning, whereas the latter refers to the site where the institute (*pesantren*) lies, to distinguish it from the rest of the Buntet village.

inhabitants (excluding the *santri*) made their living as labourers; the rest were engaged in trades, clerical work, agriculture, and crafts. Within the *pesantren* complex itself, there are both *kyai* and *non-kyai* families. The majority are the *kyai* families who are of either the *sohibul wilayah* (the rightful *pesantren* leadership) or *keluarga biasa* (common family who have no rights to leadership).[33] Some of the minority *non-kyai* families are indigenous people who were already there at the time when the *pesantren* was founded, some others are immigrants. Some *non-kyai* families are *pager sari*, (literally meaning 'fence of the core') who work in the service of a *kyai* or the *pesantren*. Some *pager sari* descendants still retain their patronage from the present *kyai*, some others live independently. As the mobility of the population is high their life style is urbanised. Some private and public telephones are available, possession of motor bike, radio and television sets is quite common, there are some parabolic antennas, including some of the *kyai's* possessions in the *pesantren* complex. Although there is no wall which separates the *pesantren* from the rest of the village, two rivers, Kali Kanci at the north and west, and Kali Ciwado at the east, form buffers against unexpected security disturbances rather than separating the complex from the entire village life. Over Kali Ciwado there is a permanent stone bridge providing a crossing for pedestrians and vehicles going in and out of the *pesantren* complex. For security purposes, heavy trucks and coaches are not allowed to pass over the bridge.

The main buildings within the *pesantren* complex are a two storey main *santri*-dormitory (*pondok*), and an antique public mosque (*masjid jami'*) equipped with a high capacity water pump provided by General Benny Murdani in 1987, upon which the mosque and *pondok* rely for their water supply.[34] This main *pondok* accommodates 150 *santri*, mostly the seniors. The other buildings are five *madrasah* buildings with a book shop and a cooperative, and a two storey building used for the *pesantren* office and the small *pesantren* library. Those buildings are maximally utilised all day long with two shifts of schooling. The first shift is from 7.30 a.m through 12.30 p.m, the other from 1.00 p.m through 6.00 p.m. All these buildings stand around a wide multipurpose square, used as a play ground, as a parking ground, for ceremonial undertakings, and for other activities.

[33] Concerning the concept of '*sohibul wilayah*' see the next section.

[34] General Murdani was Commander in Chief of the Indonesian Armed Forces (*Pangab*) who, according to my informants, visited there as part of his political safari to approach a number of key *pesantren* for political purpose.

Table 7.1: Number of Students/Santri at Buntet (1992)

School/Madrasah	Student
Kindergarten	63
Ibtidaiyah (boys)	127
Ibtidaiyah (girls)	186
Tsanawiyah (Mts: boys)	698
Tsanawiyah (MTS: girls	370
'Aliyah (MA: boys)	314
'Aliyah (MA: girls)	312
State owned *'Aliyah* (MAN)	846
Dirosah Diniyah (boys)	71
Dirosah Diniyah (Girls)	67
Other *santri*	1706*
Total	4197

* Includes those who go to public school, mature *santri* who work while studying, university students and *santri kalong* (bat santri).

Map of Desa Mertapada Kulon Kec. Astanajapura Kab. Cirebon

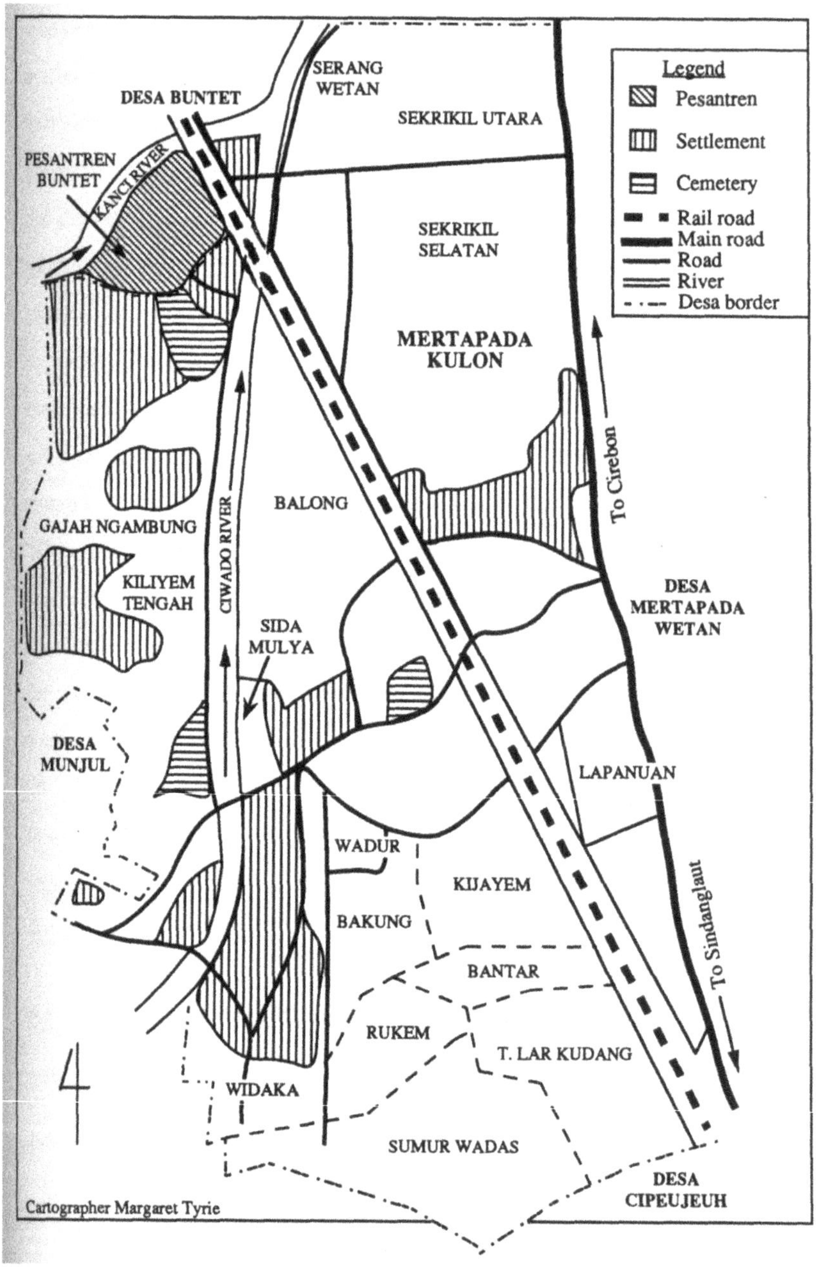

Junior *santri* are required to stay at the many *pondok* scattered throughout the *pesantren* complex owned by the *kyai*. There are currently no less than 40 *kyai* houses with their annexed *pondok* each of which provides accommodation for between 50 to 200 male or female *santri* separately. In 1992 there were 4760 *santri*, about 120 of whom were *santri kalong* (literally meaning 'bat *santri*', who came to the *pesantren* only at night). Most of them are involved in one or a combination of learning activities: *ngaji Qur'an* (Qur'anic learning), *ngaji kitab* (religious texts studies) and *sekolah* (going to public school/*madrasah*). *Ngaji Qur'an* was handled by 64 *kyai* and *nyai* (female *kyai*) whereas *ngaji kitab* was handled by 70 *kyai* and *nyai*. The madrasah school system involved 183 teachers, male and female, about 40 per cent of whom are on government subsidy. Except kindergarten the *madrasah* education in Buntet is non-co-educational where boys and girls study separately. "*Cross-pondok ngaji*" especially *ngaji kitab* is common practice in which a student staying at a *pondok* goes to another *pondok* to study certain *kitab* with another *kyai*.

Because most *santri* are outsiders, the revenue produced by the *pesantren* from the incoming cash, in turn, helps animate the market economy of the district. With few exceptions, in 1992 each *santri* spends at least around Rp.30,000.00 (about A$ 20.00) a month for food and other daily necessities.[35] This means, the *pesantren* injects no less than Rp. 120,000,000.00 (about A$ 80,000.00) cash into the local region each month which, by local standards, is a substantial contribution to the district market economy.

Administration and Leadership

The overall educational activity throughout the *pesantren* is coordinated by the *Lembaga Pendidikan Islam* (LPI) or Islamic Educational Board. The LPI consists of a *Majelis Syuriah* (Steering Assembly) and *Majelis Tanfidziyah* (Executive Assembly). The former is headed by *Sesepuh* (elder), *Pengasuh* (Counsellor) and *Anggota* (Members of Executive Board). The latter is headed by a Chairman, three vice-chairmen, a Secretary General, two other secretaries, a Treasurer and some assistants. Crucial to this organisational structure is the appointment of the *Sesepuh*, the spiritual leader and symbol of the unity for the whole *pesantren*. Acknowledging the *pesantren's* possessions such as lands, buildings and equipments have come from various sources, no one in the *pesantren* is entitled to claim any individual rights of ownership over the *pesantren*. It is envisaged that the *pesantren* will become a public trust (*amanah*) and adopt the principle of so-called "trustee leadership" (*kepemimpinan amanah*). The leader bears a community trust that is to be passed on hereditarily from the *Sesepuh* along the male line to his oldest son. If, under certain circumstances, it cannot be achieved

[35] There are some *santri* who depend for their living on *kyai* or their friends by working or doing something for them.

because the *Sesepuh* has no son, or the son is still an infant, for example, or unable to carry out the function for any other reasons, a *Sesepuh pemangku* (caretaker) is appointed by consensus among the '*sohibul wilayah*' (rightful individuals for the *pesantren* leadership), the male descendants of the founders of the *pesantren* along the male line (see figure 7.1).

Figure 7.1: Genealogy of Sesepuh and Sohibul Wilayah

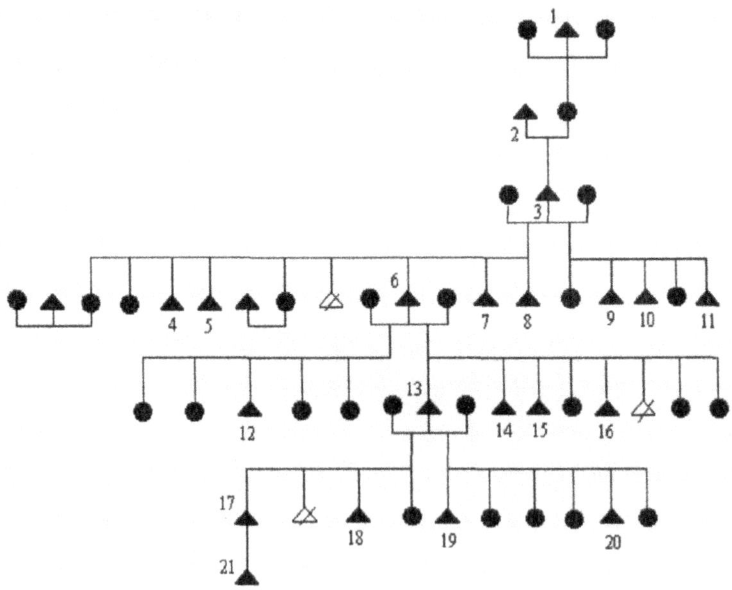

1 Mbah Muqayim
2 R. Muridin
3 Mutta'ad
4 Barwi
5 Soleh Zamzami
6 Abdul Jamil
7 Fachrurrazi
8 Abdul Karim
9 Abdul Mun'im
10 Tirmidzi
11 Abdul Mu'thi
12 Ahmad Zahid
13 Abbas
14 Anas
15 Ilyas
16 Akyas
17 Mustahdi
18 Mustamid
19 Abdullah
20 Nahduddin Rouandi
21 Abbas Sobih

When Kyai Mutta'ad (number 3) led the *pesantren*, all his sons from both wives automatically became the *sohibul wilayah*. His oldest son born by the first wife, Kyai Barwi (number 4) however, married out and stayed in East Java, whereas the second oldest, Kyai Soleh Zamzami (number 5) established a new *pesantren* at Benda Kerep. When Kyai Mutta'ad passed away, Kyai Abdul Jamil (number 6) took the leadership as he was the oldest son staying at Buntet because Abdul Jamil's elder brothers, Kyai Sulaeman (number 7) and another brother, died earlier preceding Kyai Mutta'ad.

In the next generation, upon the death of Kyai Abdul Jamil, the *sohibul wilayah* were his sons from his two wives (numbers 12 through 16), Kyai Abdul Jamil's brothers (numbers 7 through 11) who were still alive and their grown up sons. The *pesantren* leadership in this generation, however, fell onto Kyai Abbas (number 13) because he was Kyai Abdul Jamil's oldest son (born by the second wife). The above principle follows upon Kyai Abbas death whence Kyai Mustahdi (number 17) took the leadership. Upon Kyai Mustahdi's passing away, Kyai Mustamid was appointed *sesepuh pemangku* and then, after Kyai Mustamid passed away, Kyai Abdullah Abbas (Ki Dulah) became the *sesepuh pemangku*.[36] Abbas Sobih (number 21), son of Kyai Mustahdi, shall retake the position of *sesepuh* after Ki Dulah.

The trustee leadership principle adopted in Buntet, according to Kyai Fu'ad Hasyim, finds its root in the Prophetic era, which is especially exemplified by the tradition of key bearer of the *Ka'bah* in Mecca.[37] When the Prophet defeated Mecca and wished to enter the *Ka'bah*, the key was held by 'Utsman bin Thalhah, a Meccan unbeliever. The Prophet asked Ali to take over the key from 'Utsman but the latter refused to pass it on to Ali. 'Utsman argued that by any means he was obliged to keep his traditional right as the key bearer which, since Abraham, was supposed to be passed on hereditarily from one generation to the next. A quarrel between 'Utsman and Ali was unavoidable. When the argumentation was going on, a verse of the Qur'an was revealed to the Prophet saying: "God commands you to hand back your trust to their rightful owners and, when you pass judgement among men, you are to judge with fairness" (QS 4:58). After having this revelation the Prophet approached the quarrelling parties to stop the argument and the Prophet said: "'Utsman, keep the key with you for an undecided duration." On hearing the Prophet's words, which to him were unthinkable, 'Utsman's heart was so touched by surprise and astonishment, that as his tears fell 'Utsman embraced Islam.[38]

[36] See: the next section.
[37] Kyai Fu'ad Hasyim is Kyai Mustahdi's son-in-law from another *pesantren* and thus himself is not a *sohibul wilayah*.
[38] Interview with Kyai Fu'ad Hasyim on August 26, 1992. Kyai Fu'ad Hasyim (53 years) is a prominent supra local public speaker of this *pesantren*. In his pondok stay about 120 *santri*.

The principle of *sohibul wilayah* as practiced in Buntet therefore, does not include female descendants and their heirs into leadership account. This, according to my informants in Buntet, is because in theory, upon marriage, women are taken by and under the auspice and responsibility of their husbands, whereas their descendants inherit their father's heirs.

THE RISE AND DEVELOPMENT OF PESANTREN BUNTET

According to the available sources Pesantren Buntet was first established in 1750 by Kyai Muqayim bin Abdul Hadi, known as Mbah Muqayim, *Penghulu Kraton* or *Mufti* (Court Religious Official) of the Kanoman royal house.[39] Opposing the Dutch intrusion into the internal affairs of the *kraton*, and seeing some *kraton* dignitaries subserviently fall into the embrace of the Dutch rule, some of them even exhibited behaviour which was against the *syari'ah*, such as dancing and drinking alcohol,[40] Mbah Muqayim left his position in the *kraton* in favour of living outside the *kraton* wall. He built a mosque and a hut in the village where he and his followers dwelt and began to teach religion. Bearing his former honourable position as *Penghulu Kraton*, along with his profound knowledge of religion and exemplary behaviour, he attracted many students and soon his hut was full of learners and they had to erect more huts. Finally, it became a learning centre and developed into a *pesantren* complex which evolves until this day.

The early period: Mbah Muqayim

The site where Mbah Muqayim started teaching for the first time was located at Blok Kedungmalang, a hamlet in Buntet. After a few years of operation however, the Dutch came and burned down all his *pesantren* complex. Ki Ardisela, a village headman of Dawuan who knew about the Dutch manoeuvre immediately told Mbah Muqayim so that his family and his *santir* were able to flee to Pesawahan just before the Dutch reached and besieged the *pesantren*. The *pesantren* activities ceased and Mbah Muqayim wandered from one place to another to escape from being arrested. Some of the places where he took temporary refuge were Pesawahan hamlet in Lemahabang village, Tuk in Karangsuwung and Beji in Pemalang (Central Java). After a long adventure he came back to Buntet in 1758 and established a new *pesantren* at a site called Blok Gajah Ngambung, which has now become the *santri* cemetery (*makam santri*).[41] Before deciding on this new site to establish his *pesantren*, it is said that Mbah Muqayim fasted for a twelve months period, doing this in four stages. The merit

[39] This section relies heavily on Zaini Hasan (1970) and Hisyam Mansur (1989). I could not find authoritative historical sources which confirm or reject the claim that this *pesantren* was established in 1750.

[40] The hedonistic tendency evidence among some *kraton* dignitaries probably refers to such persons as Pangeran Arya Carbon, the allegedly writer of *Carita Purwaka Caruban Nagari* (1720). For a short account of him, see for example, Siddique (1977), pp 51–53.

[41] See: Map of Pesantren Buntet Complex, p 315.

of the first three months of the fasting was intended for the pesantren's welfare, safety and continuance; the second three months was for his descendant's well-being; the third was for his *santri* and faithful followers and the fourth, as he was old enough, was for his own personal merit in this world and the hereafter.

One of his *santri* at his newly built *pesantren* was Prince Khaeruddin, son of Sultan Kanoman (Khaeruddin I). When the Sultan passed away in 1798 the Dutch installed Tumenggung Surantaka and sent the actual heir, Prince Khaeruddin, Mbah Muqayim's student, into exile in Ambon. Mbah Muqayim opposed this instalment and was involved in civil unrest to force the Dutch to return Prince Khaeruddin to Cirebon. Partly due to the change within the Dutch administration and policy, Prince Khaeruddin was finally restored to his throne and became Sultan Khaeruddin II.

Mbah Muqayim is said to have married twice. One marriage was to Nyai Randulawang (Nyi Randu), daughter of Ki Enthol Rujitnala a village headman of Situpatok, whom Kyai Muqayim assisted in the construction of an irrigation dam (*situ*). Ki Enthol was a local noble, descendant of Pangeran Luwung. The second marriage was to the daughter of Kyai Salamuddin of Pemalang. From the first marriage he obtained a daughter who married his brightest student, Raden Muhammad.[42] Upon his death he was buried at Tuk, side by side with Ki Ardisela. The date of his death is not told but his tomb at Tuk (30 km south-east of Cirebon) has become an object of visitation. Mbah Muqayim had no son, and after his death the *pesantren* again ceased its operation for some time until Kyai Mutta'ad came.

Kyai Mutta'ad (1785–1852)

Kyai Mutta'ad, son of Raden Muriddin, married Nyai Ratu 'Aisyah, daughter of Raden Muhammad, the brightest student and son in law of Mbah Muqayim.[43] Thus, Kyai Mutta'ad is grandson-in-law of Mbah Muqayim, the founder of the *pesantren*. From this marriage Kyai Mutta'ad had nine descendants, the oldest one was a daughter, Nyai Ruhillah, who married a *Sufi-ulama*, Kyai Anwaruddin Kriyani al-Malebari, known as Ki Buyut Kriyan, whose contribution for

[42] How did his *pesantren* and educational activities look like and for how long the *pesantren* was in operation are not told but Ki Dulah and Kyai Fu'ad Hasyim, in separate interviews said that formerly Mbah Muqayim led a '*pengajian tarekat*' (Sufi learning) of Syattariyah order. This order is locally known as *Tarekat Kraton* (Sufism adopted by the court). Thus, it was said, Mbah Muqayim basically taught Tarekat Syattariyah but because *tarekat* required *syai'ah* and many people had not enough knowledge of this prerequisite, he also taught *syai'ah* and basic knowledge of religion.

[43] Kyai Mutta'ad was son of Raden Muriddin, son of Raden Muhammad Nuruddin, son of Raden Ali, son of Raden Punjul, son of Raden Bagus, son of Pangeran Sutajaya ing Gebang (Sultan Matangaji), son of Dalem Anom (Sultan Senapati), son of Dalem Kebon ing Gebang, son of Pangeran Sutajaya kang seda ing Grogol, son of Pangeran Sutajaya kang seda ing Tambak, son of Panembahan Ratu (Pangeran Girilaya), son of Pangeran Dipati, son of Pangeran Pasarean, son of Syarif Hidayatullah (Sunan Gunung Jati).

development of Pesantren Buntet was considered instrumental.[44] Upon his death, Ki (Buyut) Kriyan as a revered figure was buried at 'Jabang Bayi' grave complex in the city of Cirebon.[45] His tomb attracts visitors, some of whom, according to the *Juru Kunci*, come from Malaysia and Singapore.[46]

Kyai Mutta'ad also married another woman, Nyai Kidul from whom he had five descendants, the oldest one and the fourth were daughters, Nyai Saudah and Nyai Hamidah; the others were sons, namely Kyai Abdul Mun'im, Kyai Tarmidzi and Kyai Abdul Mu'thi. All the descendants from the two wives were *kyai* or married *kyai*. One of his students and also son in law was Kyai Sa'id, the founder of Pesantren Gedongan, another big *pesantren* adjacent to Buntet.[47]

Kyai Mutta'ad is said to have studied with Kyai Musta'in (Jepara, Central Java) and then to have gone to Pesantren Siwalan (Surabaya) for further learning. Soon after taking leadership of Buntet he applied much effort to renew the *pesantren*. With the help of his sons, especially his son-in-law, Ki (Buyut) Kriyan, he left the old *pesantren* at Gajah Ngambung built by Mbah Muqayim to build a new one at Blok Manis in the same village (Buntet) where it remains until now. He translated a number of books into Javanese and rewrote some others including the Holy Qur'an.[48] Meanwhile Ki Kriyan taught *Tarekat Syattariyah* at the *pesantren* and attracted many followers. The number of *santri* and the *Syattariyah* followers increased considerably from tens to hundreds. Later, Ki Kriyan was appointed a religious official (*penghulu*) at Kraton Kesepuhan. After his wife, Nyai Ruhillah passed away, Ki Kriyan married another woman, Nyai Lontangjaya of Arjawinangun (30 km Western Cirebon) and had a daughter, Nyai Sa'diyah.

[44] The second was also a daughter, Nyai Qaumiyah, then successively Kyai Barwi, Kyai Sholeh Zamzami (the founder of Pesantren Benda Kerep), Nyai Mu'minah (a daughter), Kyai Abdul Jamil, Kyai Fachrurazi and Kyai Abdul Karim.

[45] Sulendraningrat (1985) tells us that the name 'Jabang Bayi' (literally meaning 'premature baby') was taken when a baby was born to Nona Delamor (Miss de l'Amour ?), daughter of a French blood Dutch Resident in Cirebon. She had a secret love affair with Prince Raja Kanoman, son of Sultan kanoman and became pregnant. Delamor tried to keep her pregnancy secret, but she finally bore a baby prematurely. In fear of being acknowledged she put the baby in a box and threw it away into the sea. A harbour worker once found the box with a dead baby in it and finally recognised that the baby was of the throne family and buried it at a grave complex, later known as 'Jabang Bayi'

[46] The origin of Kyai Anwaruddin Kriyani (ki Buyut Kriyan) is not recorded neither is the date of his death. According to a legendary tale, he came from Malabar (India), thence the suffix of al-Malebari may have been derived. He was shipwrecked in the Malacca strait but helped ashore by a dolphin. He reached Johor, stayed there for a period of time and had students, some of whom were local dignitaries. He took a voyage to Java and came first to Surabaya. He wandered westward, spent a long time in Semarang before finally, he reached and stayed in Cirebon for the rest of his life. His tomb, although has visitors, does not exhibit extra appearance. It is only built of ordinary bricks and, just like the tomb of the commoners, it has no precinct.

[47] The present *kyai* in Buntet, therefore, trace their lineage to Sunan Gunung Jati through Kyai Mutta'ad. Nevertheless the *kyai* in Buntet do not seem to take pride from this lineage. None of them use a dignitary title like Raden (male) or Ratu (female). Ki Dulah said that his father, Kyai Abbas, and also Kyai Abdul Jamil, prohibited anyone in Buntet from using such a title. Probably, it is to show indifference toward the *kraton* that cooperated with the Dutch and adopted their life style (See note 29).

[48] Now, it is only the handwritten Qur'an which is still kept at the *pesantren* library.

He then stayed at the Kesepuhan court house and took with him his brother-in-law who was still a young boy, Abdul Jamil who later succeeded Kyai Mutta'ad to lead the *pesantren*. Kyai Mutta'ad died when he was 67 years old and was buried at Tuk adjacent to the graves of Mbah Muqayim and Ki Ardisela.

Kyai Abdul Jamil (1842–1919)

The successor of Kyai Mutta'ad was his fourth oldest son, Kyai Abdul Jamil who replaced his elder brothers who were unable to succeed Kyai Mutta'ad because they married out.[49] During his stay with Ki Kriyan, Kyai Abdul Jamil is said to have completed many books. He also studied at other *pesantren*, one of which was Pondok Mayong (Jepara) with Kyai Murtadlo. He went to Mecca on pilgrimage and stayed there for some years. He learned among other things the Qur'anic science (the arts of reciting the Qur'an). Upon his return from Mecca he married Nyai Sa'diyah, Ki Kriyan's daughter. When Kyai Abdul Jamil succeeded Kyai Mutta'ad, Nyai Sa'diyah, his wife, was still a very young girl and Ki Kriyan gave him another wife, Nyai Qari'ah, daughter of Kyai Syathori, religious official of the Dutch administration (*Penghulu Landraad*). From this marriage he had eight children: Kyai Abbas, Kyai Anas, Kyai Ilyas, Nyai Zamrud (Qisthinthoniyah), Kyai Akyas, Nyai Ya'qut, Nyai Mu'minah and Nyai Nadroh. Later, from Nyai Sa'diyah he had five children, one of whom was a son, Kyai Ahmad Zahid.[50]

Kyai Abdul Jamil made many attempts to develop the *pesantren* both in managerial and academic aspects. For this, he maximised the intellectual potency available at the *pesantren* by recruiting all *kyai*, mostly relatives, who stayed within the *pesantren* complex, and senior students for active participation in various development tasks. To overcome the scarcity of text books, efforts were made to reproduce a number of advanced religious texts by handwriting. Among the reproduced texts were *Fath al-Wahhab, Sahih Bukhari, Sahih Muslim, Suzur al-Zahhab, Alfiyah*, etc.[51] Academic activities were expanded. Along with the traditional *sorogan* and *bandungan* classes, he set up a *halaqah* (seminar) class attended by advanced students. *Ngaji pasaran* (open lecture) was also held at least every fasting month using well known quality references such as *I'anah al-Talibin, Fath al-Wahhab, Ihya 'Ulum al-Din, Tafsir Ibn Katsir*, etc. A *takhassus* (specialisation) on religious subjects to be studied by advanced *santri* was set

[49] His oldest brother, Kyai Barwi, married out to Surabaya, whereas Kyai Soleh Zamzami established Pesantren Benda. See also the preceding section concerning the *pesantren* leadership.

[50] See figure 7.1

[51] These texts are considered authoritative, assigned for advanced learners. Fathul Wahhab, written by Abi Yahya Zakaria al-Ansari, for example, is an advanced analysis on Shafi'ite jurisprudence. *Sahih Bukhari* by al-Bukhari and *Sahih Muslim* by al-Muslim are two most authoritative reference on Hadith. *Alfiyah* by Ibnu Malik contains an advanced analysis of Arabic grammar in the form of 1000 poetic prescriptions of Arabic structure.

out and divided into six branches: *Ilmu Kalam* (theology),[52] *Ilmu Tafsir dan Hadith* (exegeses), *Fiqh* (jurisprudence), *Nahwu-Sharaf* (Arabic grammar and word derivatives), *Tasawuf* (Sufism) and *Ilmu al-Qur'an* (Qur'anic science).

To accommodate the increasing number of *santri*, new buildings were erected including a large mosque (*masjid jami'*) whose cost was paid by donors especially well to do ex-*santri*. As the *pesantren* was surrounded by two rivers, it was felt to be rather isolated from the rest of the village. To remove this isolation a bridge was constructed and more *santri* began coming. Under his leadership, the number of *santri* reached around 700, coming from various parts of Java, Sumatera, Sulawesi and Singapore. At the same time, he was also authorised by his brother, Kyai Soleh Zamzami, to be a *mursyid* (*tarekat* leader) to teach and recruit members of Tarekat Syattariyah.[53] Under his leadership by the end of 19th century, this *tarekat* sprang up tremendously attracting thousands of followers. Along with the *kraton* and Benda Kerep, Buntet became another centre (*zawiyah*) of Syattariyah order. This caused the reputation of Kyai Abdul Jamil and his *pesantren* to transcend the local geographic boundary. In 1900, when he was 58 years old he was invited by Hadratus Syeikh K.H. Hasyim Asy'ari to teach at Pesantren Tebuireng in Jombang. He came there with his brother, Kyai Sholeh Zamzami of Pesantren Benda, Kyai Abdullah of Panguragan and Kyai Syamsuri of Wanantara (8 km south-west of Cirebon). They stayed and taught in Jombang for about 8 months.

Kyai Abdul Jamil was also concerned with both short and long term *pesantren* development. For the short term he himself managed the development efforts. For the long term, upon his return from teaching in Jombang, he sent a number of able students, including his sons, Abbas, Anas and Akyas, to study at various *pesantren* throughout Java. Special attention was made to develop the Qur'anic science by sending a number of able *santri* to Yogyakarta and to Banten. Among those who were sent for this purpose were Zainal Abidin (Kyai Zen), Kyai Yusuf and Kyai Murtadlo to study from Kyai Munawir at Krapyak (Yogyakarta), whereas Kyai Hasyim and Kyai Abdul Rauf studied with Kyai Tb.Mansur Ma'mun in Banten.[54]

In the political sphere he was known as a figure who consistently maintained the non-cooperation principle with the Dutch. He had close contact with his

[52] The term *kalam* basically refers to the dialectical style of discussion by putting forth objections and their response. The Mu'tazilah school of theology is credited to use this style of reasoning in the theological speculation based on the dual principle of justice and unity of God. Based on extensive use of Qur'an and the hadith, Al-Asy'ari also used this *kalam* style of rational arguments to maintain his position favouring predestination principle.

[53] As we shall see, Kyai Soleh Zamzami who led this tarekat at Benda Kerep was authorised by his brother-in-law, Ki Kriyan who had moved to *kraton* and became *penghulu*.

[54] When the sending really occurred and for how long are not told, but those who were sent turned to be instrumental potency after Kyai Abdul Jamil passed away. The trio Abbas, Anas, Akyas, brought Pesantren Buntet into its zenith (see next pages).

ex-student, H. Samanhudi, a successful *batik* trader of Surakarta, who in 1911 founded the "Syarekat Dagang Islam" (literally meaning Union of Islamic Trade), a Javanese *batik* traders's cooperative.[55] In this organisation Kyai Abdul Jamil was active on the religious advisory board (*Syuriah*) until he died in 1919. According to Kyai Hisyam, Kyai Abdul Jamil passed away when the *pesantren* was embarking on its remarkable institutional development. His success, to a large extent, was due to both his intellectual and managerial skills and the full support from his assistants such as Kyai Abdul Mun'im, Kyai Abdul Mu'thi, Kyai Tarmidzi, Kyai Muktamil and Kyai Abdullah.[56] Whilst his cousins, Kyai Sa'id and his brother Kyai Sholeh Zamzami, respectively established Pesantren Gedongan at Desa Ender, Astanajapura, and Pesantren Benda at Benda Kerep in the municipality of Cirebon. Upon his death, Kyai Abdul Jamil was buried at the *pesantren* cemetery (*Makam Santri*).

Kyai Abbas (1879–1946)

When Kyai Abdul Jamil passed away, his oldest son from Nyai Qari'ah, Kyai Abbas, seemed to have been quite prepared to take over the *pesantren* leadership. Along with his broad and high intellectual quality, he is described as inheriting his father's leadership competence. He succeeded in marshalling the intellectual potential of other *kyai* who had been sent by his father to study at various *pesantren* and then returned with high intellectual achievement. It is under Kyai Abbas' leadership that Pesantren Buntet is said to have reached its golden age despite the fact that during this period the *pesantren* education encountered nation-wide instability due to the break out of the World War II and its aftermath. Kyai Abbas experienced different phases of political turmoil, pre-war Dutch colonialism, Japanese Fascism, postwar Dutch aggression, and the Indonesian revolutionary struggle for independence. During this course of history both the Dutch and the Japanese military threats and aggression are said as the major sources of unbearable hindrance for the development of the *pesantren*. Several times Buntet became the target of Dutch military raids, which caused damage and unbearable suffering among the people. Many of them fled to the *pesantren* for safety.[57] As a result, Kyai Abbas needed to open up a free public catering (*dapur umum*) to feed the starving people for some period of time. This even established the *kyai's* charisma among the local people. This

[55] For H. Samanhudi and his role in the *Syarekat Dagang Islam* see for example, Vlekke, B.H.M. (1965), *Nusantara : A History of Indonesia*, The Hague: W. van Hoeve, p. 350; Ricklefs, M.C. (1993), A History of Modern Indonesia Since c.1300, Hong Kong: MacMillan, p.166.
[56] See figure 7.1 (genealogy of the *sesepuh*)
[57] Pak Maskira (67 years), a villager at Buntet told: "While the planes were roaring just over the top of the coconut trees, some bombs targeted to the *pesantren* missed and blasted in the paddy field, just around 150 metres outside the *pesantren* complex; some other bombs did not explode, but other villages, including Pesantren Sidamulya, established by his brother, Kyai Anas in 1936, was burnt down."

period was deeply imprinted in the people's memory. For them Kyai Abbas seemed to have been a legendary saviour and unforgettable figure.[58]

Kyai Abbas learned religion firstly with his father Kyai Abdul Jamil, and Kyai Kriyan. Then he went *mesantren* to learn with Kyai Nasuha at Pesantren Sukunsari in Plered, Kyai Hasan at Jatisari in Weru, Kyai Ubaidah in Tegal (Central Java). He was summoned for marriage and after that he went to Mecca on pilgrimage and stayed there for some years for further study. Staying at Syeikh Zabidi's in Mecca, he studied with a number of teachers, one of whom was Kyai Mahfudz of Termas (East Java).[59] Among his Javanese fellow students in Mecca were Kyai Bakir of Yogyakarta, Kyai Abdillah of Surabaya and Kyai Wahab Hasbullah. In Mecca Kyai Abbas also taught and had students, among whom were some from Cirebon such as Kyai Kholil of Pesantren Balerante and Kyai Sulaeman from Babakan Ciwaringin. From Mecca he then went to Jombang (East Java) to learn with Kyai Hasyim Asy'ari at Pesantren Tebuireng.[60] When he was at Tebuireng he worked with Kyai Wahab Hasbullah and with Kyai Manaf and was involved in the establishment of Pesantren Lirboyo in Kediri (East Java).

Under Kyai Abbas' leadership, the *pesantren* management was further improved, academic activities were intensified and facilities were extended. Old buildings were renovated and new ones were erected.[61] But the most notable step Kyai Abbas took was the introduction and inclusion of the *madrasah* system into the *pesantren*. While *sorogan, bandungan* and *ngaji pasaran* were retained, in 1928 he founded Madrasah Abnaul Wathan Ibtidaiyah where secular subjects were taught.[62] Kyai Abbas' revolutionary steps are said to have been inspired by Imam Syafi'i who says:

[58] Such events were always told by older people in Buntet (who are now in their late 50s or over) whom I talked with about Pesantren Buntet.

[59] His other teachers in Mecca were not told.

[60] According to my informants in Buntet, the relation between Kyai Abbas and Kyai Hasyim Asy'ari during the former's stay in Tebuireng was much more colleaguial of about similar standing, involved mostly on discussions, rather than student-teacher (*santri-kyai*) relationship in an ordinary sense. In fact, both *kyai* were about the same age. Kyai Hasyim was only eight years older and lived a little longer (1871–1947) than Kyai Abbas did (1879–1946).

[61] The costs were met mostly by donors, one of whom was H. Kafrawi, a businessman from Brebes (Central Java) who provided a multi purpose building. Another one was a Chief (*kuwu*) of Gegesik (40 km West of Cirebon) who offered the renovation and enlargement cost of the *pesantren* mosque.

[62] The name 'Madrasah Abnaul Wathan,' which literally means School for the Country's Children, is obviously of patriotic flavour used to fit the nationalist spirit of Kyai Abbas' time and his involvement in the nationalist movements. This development might be a result of close contact with Tebuireng. In Tebuireng *madrasah* system was introduced in 1919 but reached its maturity in 1928 when Kyai Hasyim's cousin, Kyai Ilyas, upon finishing a Dutch Primary School (HIS), led the *madrasah*. The pesantren's nationalist spirit was further intensified when in 1929, when Kyai Wahid Hasyim returned to Tebuireng from various learning. The development of Madrasah in Buntet is therefore, parallel with what occurred in Tebuireng. Cf: Dhofier (1985), especially pp. 103–106.

> *"Keep the old values which are good and, take (only) the new ones which are better."*[63]

The curriculum offered by the *madrasah* contained eighty-five per cent religious and fifteen per cent secular subjects. Among the latter were *'ilmu'l-hisab* (arithmetic), *al-Jughrofiyah* (geography), *allughatul wathaniyah* (national language or Indonesian), *'ilmutthabi'iyah* (natural science) and *tarihul wathaniyah* (national history). Later he changed the *madrasah's* name from a patriotic flavour to a more academic one to become Madrasah Salafiyah Syafi'iyah (School of the early Syafi'ite studies) consisting of two levels, the preparatory and the Ibtidaiyah proper, each of which took 3 years to complete. The three years at the preparatory level were called *Tahdhiri, Sifir Awal* and *Sifir Tsani*, whereas the years in Ibtidaiyah were called grades one, two and three.[64] Thus, since Kyai Abbas took the leadership, there have been five different types of educational system applied simultaneously at the *pesantren: sorogan, bandungan, halaqah* (seminar), *madrasi* (madrasah system) and *ngaji pasaran*. The *sorogan* method was open to beginners, whereas the *bandungan* was given to those who passed the *sorogan* and was divided into *Awaliyah* (elementary), *Wustha* (intermediate) and *'Ulya* (advanced). Each level had to complete a certain set of standard texts used in *madrasah*. The first year of elementary *bandungan*, for example, which was equal to grade-IV of *madrasah* had to complete *Safinah al-Najah* (*fiqh* or Islamic jurisprudence), *Qatr-al Ghaits* (theology), *Nasa'ih al-'Ibad* (ethics/*tasawuf*), *al-Ajrumiyah* and *al-Kailani* (Arabic); the second year which was equal to grade-V had to complete *Minhaj al-Qawim* (*fiqh*), *al-Bajuri* (theology), *Bidayah al-Hidayah* (ethics/*tasawuf*), *Syarh Amriti* and *Lamiyah al-A'fal* (Arabic). The third year which was equal to grade-VI had to complete *Tawshih* (*fiqh*), *Syu'ab al-Iman* (theology), *Sullam at-Taufiq* (ethics/*tasawuf*), *Millah al-I'rab* and *Syarh Nazhom* (Arabic), and *Tafsir Yasin* (exegeses). The intermediate and the advanced levels also had a number of texts to master. Al-Ghazali's *Ihya*, for example, was given at the second year of the *'ulya* level.

[63] This phrase is taken until now as the *pesantren's* motto and recounted in the *haul* ceremony held annually. This motto, which in fact embodies the NU's operational principle, according to Ki Dulah, implies that development should grow from the inner traditions. This means, Ki Dulah said, Pesantren Buntet will never adopt a principle of development which is based on condemnation, cutting off and throwing away the good traditions then picking up indiscriminately some new things of worse or unknown quality and totally foreign.

[64] Cf: Dhofier (1985), p. 104.

Figure 7.2: Intellectual Network of Kyai Abbas

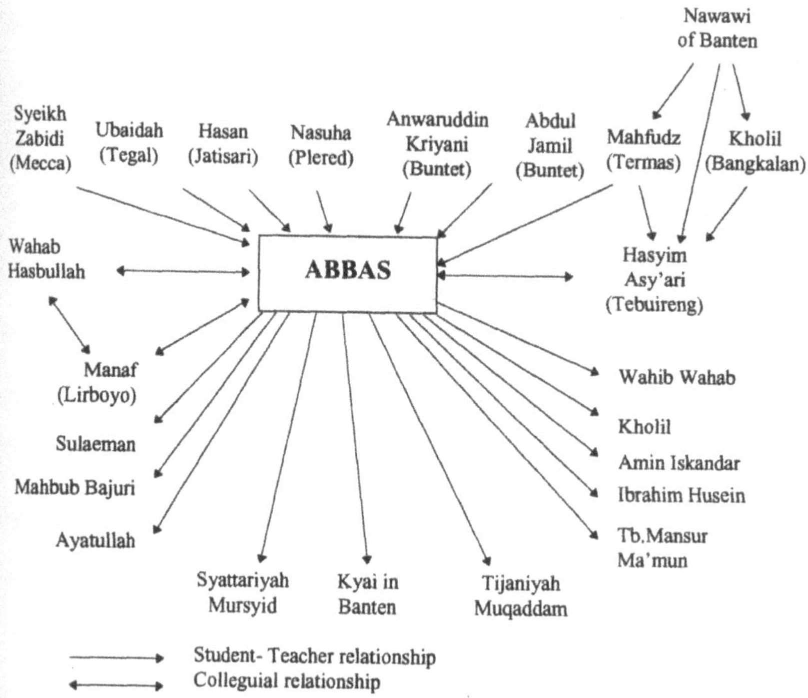

Some advanced students of both *bandungan* and *madrasah*, who were bright enough according to the individual assessment made by the *kyai*, were allowed to attend the seminar class. It is understandable that among about 3000 *santri* coming from various places only a few were fortunate enough to gain admission to this distinguished group. Among those who showed high achievement was Kyai Wahib Wahab (son of Kyai Wahab Hasbullah), former Minister of Religious Affairs who founded IAIN.[65]

The next was Tb. Mansur Ma'mun, a distinguished Qur'an reciter of national calibre of his time. He was then appointed to a high official position at the Jakarta Regional Administration. Another one was H. Amin Iskandar, the former Indonesian Ambassador to Iraq. Still another one was Professor K.H. Ibrahim Husein, the former Rector of IAIN Raden Fatah in Palembang (South Sumatera), the former Rector of Higher Learning Institute of Qur'anic Science (PTIQ), the Rector of the Institute of Qur'anic Science (IIQ) in Jakarta and currently, a member of Indonesian Council of *Ulama* (*Majelis Ulama*). The others are Kyai Ayatullah (Jakarta), Kyai Zuhri (Banten), Kyai Sholeh (Banten), Kyai Abdul Hamid (Banten) and Mahbub Bajuri, the former Regent (*Bupati*) of Cirebon.

[65] Kyai Wahib Wahab was son of Kyai Wahab Hasbullah who in 1926 became the co-founder of Nahdlatul Ulama with Kyai Hasyim Asy'ari of Pesantren Tebuireng, Jombang (East Java).

Figure 7.2 depicts Kyai Abbas' involvement in an extensive intellectual network. First, he, personally, exhibited himself as a true wanderer of knowledge seeker who had learned from many teachers including the distinguished Kyai Mahfudz of Termas.[66] Then he had students consisting of a wide range of individual; some of whom became *ulama*, leaders of *pesantren* and/or *Sufi* orders; some others became politicians and administrators. His close contact with various *pesantren*, and colleguial relationship with other *kyai* (Hasyim Asy'ari, Wahab Hasbullah, Manaf and others), helped the foundation of new *pesantren* (such as Lirboyo) and strengthened the sense of inter-*pesantren* brotherhood. The latter was something which was instrumental for the success of his involvement in the struggle against colonialism, wherein he proved himself to be a figure not only concerned with educational affairs satisfied by his achievement in *pesantren*. Due partly to the political condition of his time, Kyai Abbas was also concerned with national movements.

Figure 7.3: Military Network of Pesantren Buntet under Kyai Abbas.

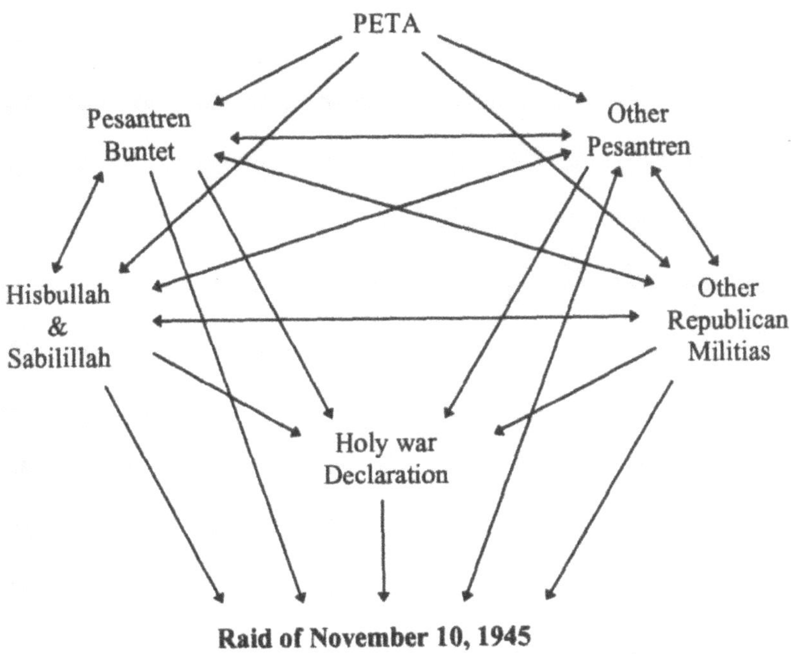

During the Japanese occupation he was a member of the People's Congress (*Sangikai*). Benefiting from the military training provided by the Japanese under the *Pembela Tanah Air* (PETA) or The Country's Defence Corps scheme, he was directly involved in the fight against the Dutch who, after the World War II,

[66] Kyai Mahfudz was student of Kyai Nawawi Banten, both were teachers of Kyai Hasyim Asy'ari of Tebuireng. See: Dhofier (1985), especially pp 86–91.

returned to Indonesia under the Allied Forces umbrella, undermining the Indonesian independence proclaimed by Soekarno-Hatta on August 17, 1945. Kyai Abbas was himself a commander of *Sabilillah* (Fighter in God's path) and then *Hisbullah* (Forces of God), both of which were Islamic wings of the Indonesian revolutionary Defence Corps.[67] He led a contingent consisting of a number of *kyai* and trained *santri* at Surabaya for involvement in the patriotic war against the Allied Forces on November 10, 1945. His contingent came to Jombang early in the morning on November 9, 1945.

Earlier, he had been involved in the assembly responsible for the issuance of the Holy War Declaration (*Deklarasi Jihad*) made by the Indonesian *ulama*. This declaration necessitated every Muslim to fight against the infidel (Dutch) and that the war in defence of fatherland was a Holy War (*jihad*). Kyai Abbas was also involved in the *ulama* assembly deciding the D-date (10 November 1945) to launch the raid against the allied forces head quarters in Surabaya. The raid is always commemorated as the Heroes's Day (*Hari Pahlawan*).[68] The relative standing of Kyai Abbas in the eyes of Kyai Hasyim Asy'ari at that moment is recounted in the following episode:

> When Bung Tomo, the then Commander of the Republican (Indonesian) army, impatiently urged Kyai Hasyim Asy'ari to decide a D-date to launch a raid against the allied forces Head Quarters in Surabaya the *kyai* answered: "...please be patient, we are still waiting for the arrival of a group of *kyai* from Cirebon..."[69]

[67] Under his command were a number of *kyai*, including Kyai Anas, Kyai Murtadlo, Kyai Sholeh, Kyai Mujahid, Kyai Ahmad Zahid, Kyai Imam, Kyai Zen, Kyai Mustahdi Abbas, Kyai Mustamid Abbas, Kyai Hawi and Kyai Busyral Karim.

[68] No matter of the so many lives and material lost, the battle of Surabaya is considered as a successful cry for international recognition that the national state of Indonesia proclaimed in 17 August 1945 was a reality and gained popular support. (See: Ricklefs, 1993:217).

[69] This quotation comes from a personal interview with Kyai Abdullah Abbas (Ki Dulah) of Pesantren Buntet, on August 14, 1992. The "*kyai* from Cirebon" meant by Hadratus Syeikh, according to Ki Dulah, were undeniably Kyai Abbas and his contingent.

Pesantren Bunten Complex

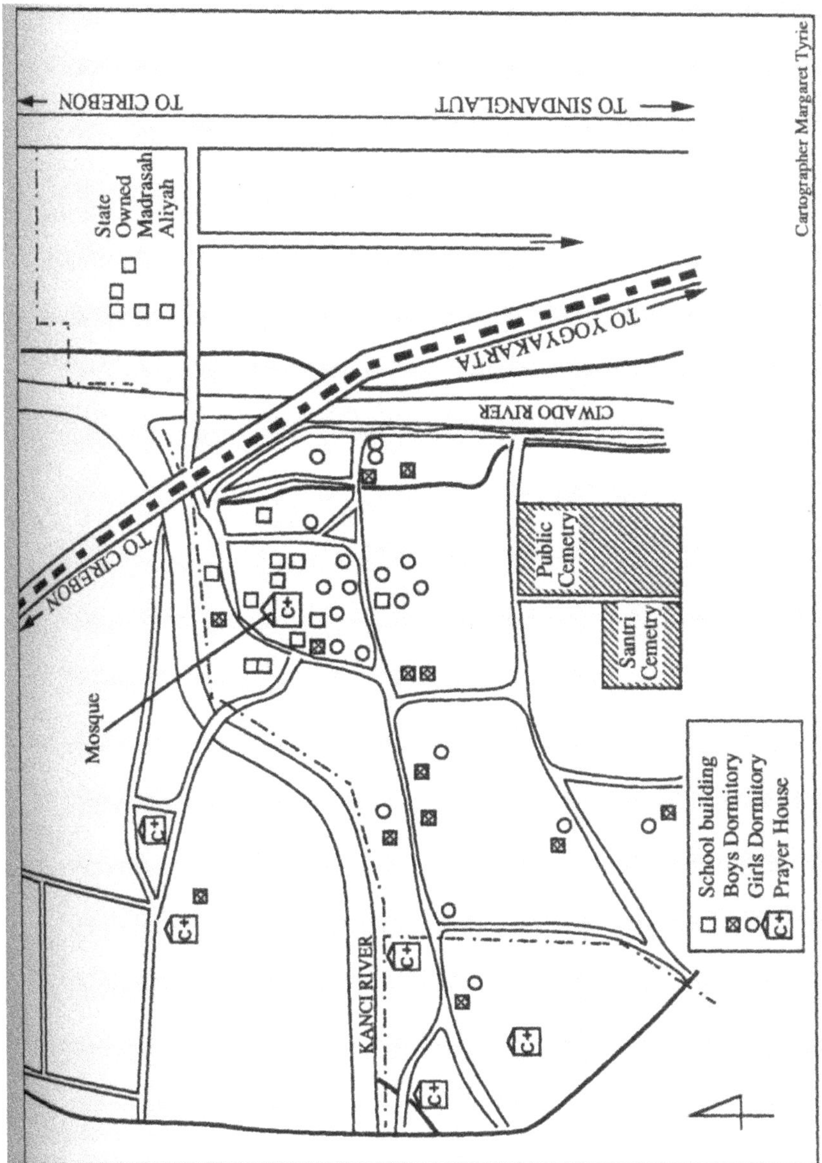

To the end of his life Kyai Abbas was active in both socio-religious and political movements. His involvement in various activities and networks can partly be enumerated as follows: 1) Leader of *pesantren*, 2) Syattariyah *mursyid*, 3) Tijaniyah *muqaddam* 4) Religious adviser of the "Syarekat Dagang Islam" (SDI), 5) Member of the Central Board of *Muhtasyar* (Religious Assembly) of the NU, 6) *Rais 'Am* (Head) of the West Java Provincial Religious Board (*Syuriah*) of the NU, 7) Member of *Sangikai* (Regional People's Congress) and *Sangi-in* (National People's Congress) during the Japanese occupation, 8) Commander of *Sabilillah* and *Hizbullah*, 9) Representative of the West Javanese *ulama* at the Central Indonesian National Committee or the *Komite Nasional Indonesia Pusat* (KNIP).

Figure 7.4: Political Network of Pesantren Buntet under Kyai Abbas.

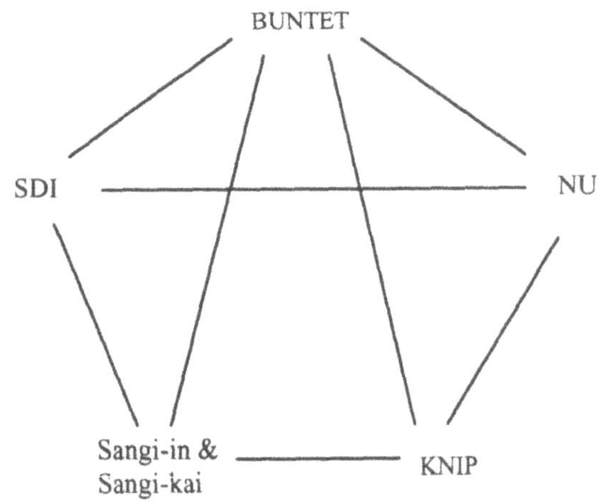

Like his father, Kyai Abbas also married twice. His first wife was Nyai Hafidzoh, with whom he had three sons and one daughter. They were Kyai Mustahdi Abbas, Kyai Abdul Rozak, Kyai Mustamid Abbas and Nyai Sumaryam. With his second wife, Nyai 'Inayah, he had six children, the first and the fifth were sons, namely Kyai Abdullah Abbas (Ki Dulah), who now leads the *pesantren* as *Sesepuh pemangku* and Nahduddin Royandi Abbas who lives in London. The other are daughters (Nyai Hismatul Maula, Nyai Sukainah, Nyai Maimunah and Nyai Munawarah).

With very few exceptions like Nahduddin Royandi Abbas, who first married a French woman then divorced and married a Javanese from Solo, the *pesantren* family practices endogamous marriage. The present generations of *kyai* families at Buntet mostly have multiple familial ties due to both lineality and affinity. Figure 7.5 depicts a set of examples for the occurrences of endogamous marriage where descendants of Kyai Mutta'ad from the first and the second wives intermarried.

Figure 7.5: Sample of endogamous Marriage in Pesantren Buntet.

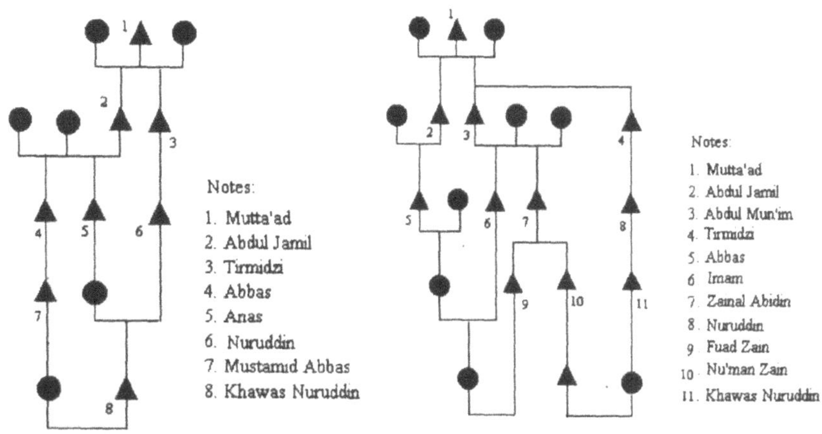

The endogamous marriage, according to informants of *pesantren* circle in Buntet, is advantageous in enabling the *pesantren* to preserve continuous supply of *kyai*. It is said that the offspring resulting from this type of marriage, more often than not, will be raised and educated, at least at their childhood, within the *pesantren* atmosphere. It is hoped, therefore, that even when the child's further education is a secular one, and involves in an occupation which has little relation with *pesantren* life, he or she will be motivated, sooner or later, to participate directly or indirectly in the preservation of *pesantren* tradition.

Kyai Mustahdi Abbas (1913–1975)

Kyai Abbas died in 1946 and was buried at the Buntet Pesantren grave complex (*Makam Santri*). His oldest son, Kyai Mustahdi Abbas was appointed his successor. Kyai Mustahdi learned religion with his father Kyai Abbas and his uncles, Kyai Anas, Kyai Ilyas and Kyai Akyas. He then went to Pesantren Babakan Ciwaringin to study with Kyai Amin, to Termas (East Java) with Kyai Dimyati, to Tebuireng in Jombang with Kyai Hasyim Asy'ari, to Lirboyo in Kediri with Kyai Abdul Manaf and to Lasem to study with Kyai Ma'mun and Kyai Baidlowi. He is said to have been such a genius that once when he was 15 years old, his father, Kyai Abbas, tested him with an assignment to put *syakl* (vowel signs) on the reproduced volumes of al-Ghazali's *Ihya* so that it would become readable to the beginners. The result was amazingly very neat and without a mistake. As a reward Kyai Abbas gave him a wrist watch which, at that time, was a very precious gift.

Kyai Mustahdi married Nyai Asiah, daughter of Kyai Anas, his uncle, and had three daughters and a son. He went to Mecca on pilgrimage and stayed there for some time with (Professor Dr) Kyai Anwar Musyaddad, former Rector of

IAIN in Bandung. He worked with Sayid 'Alawy to complete a number of books, one of which was a book on *tasawuf, Riyadh as-Salihin.*

In leading the *pesantren,* Kyai Mustahdi paid special attention to developing the *madrasah* system. One part of his ambitious activity was to make Pesantren Buntet an integral part of national education. In 1950 he changed the 3 year *madrasah* established by his father into a 6 year *Madrasah Ibtidaiyah* (MI). Influenced by his strong NU mindedness, in 1958 he added to the *pesantren* junior secondary education by establishing a 4 year NU Teacher Training (PGA 4 Tahun NU). In 1960 it became two separate Institutes, each a 6 year Religious Teacher Training Centre, one for boys and one for girls (PGA 6 Tahun NU Putra and the PGA 6 Tahun NU Putri). In 1965 he also established Madrasah Tsanawiyah NU, and in 1968 Madrasah Aliyah NU. Finally in 1970 he established The Islamic University of Cakrabuana with two Faculties, *Tarbiyah* (Education) and *Ushuluddin* (Theology). Later, these faculties became affiliated with the State Institute of Islamic Studies (IAIN) "Sunan Gunung Jati" of Bandung (West Java). Inspired by the success of his *santri,* Fu'ad Zen, who won the National prize in the competition for the Recital of the Qur'an held on the occasion of the 1965 Afro-Asian Islamic Conference in Jakarta, Kyai Mustahdi established a Qur'anic Science Academy (Akademi Al-Qur'an). This academy involved 3 years of tertiary education specialising in Qur'anic Studies.[70]

Kyai Mustahdi also paid attention to developing the *pesantren* management and laid down an organisational structure under which all *madrasah* within the *pesantren* were integrated. The present LPI (*Lembaga Pendidikan Islam* or Islamic Educational Body) is attributed to him. It was firstly established in August 17, 1958. In 1967 he called for all Pesantren Buntet alumni to hold a congress to discuss contemporary issues, especially those which were related to Islamic education. Various issues were raised and an alumni organisation, the *Ikatan Keluarga Buntet Pesantren* (IKBP) or Buntet Pesantren Alumni Union, was set up.

The development of the *madrasah,* although in itself quite an achievement, was not the only thing Kyai Mustahdi was concerned with. As a *pesantren* leader and member of the *Syuriah* of the West Java regional NU, he was a *Mursyid* of the Syattariyah order who frequently travelled throughout Java, especially to Central and East Java, visiting the *zawiyah,* and this, also added to the reputation of his *pesantren.* He worked hard for his *pesantren* until he died in 1975.

[70] Fu'ad Zein from Pesantren Buntet won the first prize and toured some Afro-Asian Islamic countries to demonstrate his ability.

Figure 7.6: Genealogy of Some Kyai in Buntet.

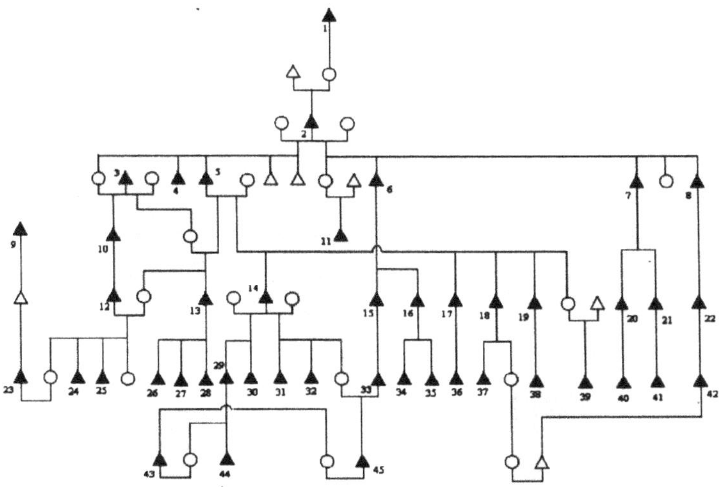

1 Mbah Muqayim
2 Mbah Mutta'ad
3 Ki Kriyan
4 Saleh Zamzami
5 Abd Jamil
6 Abd Mun'im
7 Tirmidzi
8 Abd Mu'thi
9 Amin (Pesantren Ciwarigin)
10 Abdullah
11 Sa'id (Pesantren Gedongan)
12 Abd Rahman
13 Ahmad Zahid
14 ABBAS
15 Anwar
16 Zainal Abidin
17 Anas (Pesantren Sidomulyo)
18 Ilyas
19 Akyas
20 Nuruddin
21 Ahyad
22 Yusuf
23 Amin Sirazi
24 Hasanuddin Kriyani
25 Faqih
26 Izzuddin
27 Nasiruddin
28 Anwaruddin
29 Mustahdi Abbas
30 Mustamid Abbas
31 Abdullah Abbas
32 Royandi Abbas
33 Hawi
34 Fu'ad Zein
35 Nu'man Zein
36 Junaidi
37 Mutta'ad
38 Abdullah Syifa
39 Hisyam Mansur
40 Khawas Nuruddin
41 Abd Aziz (Colonel)
42 Badlowi
43 Fu'ad Hasyim
44 Abbas Sobih
45 Fahim Hawi

Plate 32: Kyai Abbas.

Plate 33: Kyai Abdullah Abbas (in sarong and white cap) before "Haul" ceremony.

Kyai Mustamid Abbas (1975–1988) and Kyai Abdullah Abbas (1988–...)

When Kyai Mustahdi passed away, his son, Abbas Shobih, was still a young child, and thus his brother, Kyai Mustamid Abbas, was appointed his successor. Kyai Mustamid was already 60 years old when he took over the *pesantren* leadership and was already busy enough. He was the *Rais Syuriah* of the West Java Provincial Board of the NU, member of the National People's Congress (MPR), President of Cirebon Branch of the 'Indonesian Pondok Pesantren Union.' His educational experience began at the Madrasah Wathoniyah Buntet Pesantren. He then went to Termas, Lasem, Lirboyo (Madrasah Muballighin) and Kulliyatul Muballighin at Tebuireng, Jombang. Rather than setting up a new policy, he chose to continue his brother's policies. In the meantime the Ministry of Religious Affairs reorganised its religious educational system. This policy had a considerable impact on the overall number and organisational structure of religious education in Indonesia, especially in regard to the PGA (Religious Teacher Training) and tertiary religious education (IAIN). Under the new scheme PGA was transformed into an ordinary public *madrasah*, thence the *madrasah* education operating in Buntet became: (1) Madrasah Wathoniyah Ibtidaiyah Puteri (2) Madrasah Ibtidaiyah Wathoniyah Putera (3) Madrasah Tsanawiyah NU Putera-I (4) Madrasah Tsanawiyah NU Putra-II (5) Madrasah Tsanawiyah NU Puteri (6) Madrasah 'Aliyah NU Putera (7) Madrasah Aliyah NU Puteri and (8) Madrasah Aliyah Negeri (state owned Madrasah Aliyah). The Islamic University of Cakrabuana, including the Qur'anic Science Academy, ceased its operation.

When Kyai Mustamid died in 1988, Abbas Shobih, son of Kyai Mustahdi to whom the leadership should have returned, was still very young and announced his unpreparedness to take over the leadership as *Sesepuh* (*pesantren* elder). A consensus among the *sohibul wilayah* was reached on the 7th day ceremony of Kyai Mustamid passing away and appointed Kyai Abdullah Abbas, son of Kyai Abbas, who is referred to as Ki Dulah, to take over H. Abbas Shobih's position as *sesepuh pemangku* (acting elder). This position is still retained until now (1995).

In his sixties Ki Dulah has not made significant change to the *pesantren* educational structure, but a draft of a ten year (1990–2000) *pesantren* development plan has been produced to build a new complex on a two hectare piece of land alongside the connecting road between the present *pesantren* complex and the Cirebon-Sindanglaut main road.[71]

So far, the relationship between Ki Dulah, Abas Shobih (Kang Obih) and other *kyai* has been good. Recently however, especially facing the 1992 general

[71] A News Bulletin, *Fajar* (literally meaning dawn light), also appeared in 1988 but disappeared by the following year.

elections, an internal friction between the *kyai* arose. Following the nation-wide friction, there arose a division within the NU circle concerning the political support of the NU for the competing parties. Some of the *kyai* favoured GOLKAR, the government party, while the others preferred to keep their traditional support for the former Islamic party, the PPP.[72] In Indonesia, as seen in Buntet and elsewhere, support for political parties is not considered merely as a practical undertaking. It transcends the pragmatic level into the ideological one. Some *kyai* in Buntet, like Ki Dulah, Ki Fu'ad, Kang Obih, Ki Hisyam and others supported GOLKAR in the 1992 elections, whereas Ki Nu'man, Ki Syifa, Ki Izzuddin and others supported PPP despite the fact that this party no longer claimed Islam as its ideological basis. With few exceptions, it happened GOLKAR supporters resided mainly in the east wing of the *pesantren* complex, that is, from the *pesantren* mosque eastward and thus they were referred to as *golongan wetan* (the eastern group). On the other hand, PPP supporters resided in the west and thus they were called *golongan kulon* (the western group).[73] The *golongan kulon* argued that although currently the PPP no longer declared Islam as an ideological basis, this party was still uncontaminated by non-Islamic elements. All its leaders were Muslims and still struggling for Islamic ideals, at least outwardly. It was, they said, therefore a moral obligation for the Muslims to support this party. This group, or at least some of them, became extreme and vocal in accusing the *golongan wetan* of betraying the Islamic ideals and therefore easily forgetting the sufferings and trauma caused by 1971 and the subsequent general elections.[74] The western group claimed that the eastern group needed to renew their testimony (*kudu syahadat maning*). Probably, due in part in the security of standing for the government, the eastern group exhibited a calm and more mature attitude. They argued that they did suffer the 1971 trauma and that the government and GOLKAR's hard measures against Islam especially in 1971 were, to a large extent, due to the key figures of the military personnel who led GOLKAR and the government at that time. Now, they argued, the situation had changed; there were no more such persons as Sukawati, Ali Murtopo and Amir Mahmud.[75] To be fair, they said, the present (GOLKAR)

[72] Currently, Indonesia has three political parties. One is PPP, which stands for "Partai Persatuan Pembangunan" (Development Union Party), is a fusion of former Islamic parties but in the 1992 election it discarded Islam as its operational basis. The next is PDI which stands for Partai Demokrasi Indonesia (Indonesian Democratic Party), a fusion of Nationalists and Christian parties. The third party is GOLKAR which stands for Golongan Karya (Functional Group), is the ruling (the present government) party.

[73] See the sketch of Buntet Pesantren in the previous section.

[74] The 1971 general election was the first one held by the New Order government since it took power in 1966. To keep itself in power the government installed the former non-political organisation, the GOLKAR, to become a political party and compete with other political parties in the election. By various means, including the allegedly hard measures, violence and unfair practices the government forced GOLKAR, the government's party, to win.

[75] During the New Order government, Indonesia has a general election every five years. But each time the election was held, the 1971, 1977, 1982, 1987, unfair practices, including intimidation and violence have been allegedly made to force the government's party to keep winning. The '1971 trauma' therefore,

government had been relatively good to the Muslims and Islam, and they could expect even better in the future. Thus, there was room for the Muslims to respond positively to the changed situation and abandon their irrational oppositional stance. In addition, experience had shown that supporting the PPP had brought nothing except trauma and disappointment to many people. PPP could do nothing for its supporters who sacrificed themselves, being in custody and becoming the victims of election abuse.[76]

Despite this internal friction, the NU was still functioning as a binding force, at least on the surface. This appeared for example, at the occasion when the Cirebon regional branch of NU held an annual congress on November 1992. On this occasion, the *kyai* of Buntet from both sides, the *golongan wetan* and *golongan kulon*, were present, sitting together side by side amidst other *kyai* from other *pesantren* to take part in the proceedings.

THE PESANTREN IN OPERATION: AN EXAMPLE OF DAILY ACTIVITIES

The daily activities which occur in the *pondok* throughout the *pesantren* complex are not homogeneous. They vary from *pondok* to *pondok* but in general the activities are governed by a common central theme which, according to Kyai Hisyam Mansur, is "to guide the *santri* to become knowledgeable and pious individuals, meritorious to themselves, their parents, the nation and religion."[77] To this end the learning activity is geared toward acquiring intellectual and practical acquaintance with religious precepts. To achieve this broad objective most *santri* are to engage in two types of learning activities, *ngaji* in the evening and schooling in the day time. An example of its enactment in a daily practice, can be seen from what occurs in the *pondok* owned by Kyai Hisyam Mansur himself.

Kyai Hisyam Mansur, the writer of *Haul in Pesantren Buntet*, who currently limits himself to having only between 50 to 60 mature *santri* (high school students or older), concentrates on teaching two *kitab* (religious texts). For this, he first requires his *santri* to get up on before dawn (around 4.00 a.m) for the call for

refers to what usually occurred since the 1971 and subsequent general elections. The role of these persons (Sukawati, Ali Murtopo and Amir Mahmud), who were army generals and held key positions, is considered crucial in the allegedly election abuse.

[76] Such a division, which still appeared towards the end of 1992, the last time I visited the *pesantren*, seemed to hamper the realisation of the ambitious ten year (1990–2000) *pesantren* development plan under Ki Dulah's leadership.

[77] Kyai Hisyam Mansur is the writer of *Haul in Pesantren Buntet*, referred to earlier in this section. He, like Kyai Fu'ad Hasyim, belongs to an ordinary *kyai* family (*non-sohibul wilayah*) but he was active in the *pesantren's* Executive Board until 1975. From 1977 to 1982 he was a member of Regional Parliament (DPRD) of Kabupaten Cirebon representing the Islamic Party (PPP). In the 1982 election he was a candidate for the Provincial Parliament but was not appointed and returned to his administrative position as Religious Education Superintendent at the Local Office of the Ministry of Religious Affairs in Kabupaten Cirebon. In 1992 he became a member of the Regional Parliament (DPRD) Kabupaten Cirebon from GOLKAR.

prayer (*adzan*), *puji-pujian*, to perform morning congregation prayer and *ngaji kitab*. The standard (compulsory) texts he sets for his *santri* are *Safinah* (major) and *Taqrib* (minor). Both *kitab* are basically equal texts but they differ in the ordering of the topics into chapters. The students are to split themselves into two groups and each group is further divided into two sub-groups so that there are four sub-groups. Once a week each individual *santri* has to rotate his/her membership from one group/sub-group to another and thus from week to week each *santri* will belong to a different group/sub-group. By applying the *bandungan* method in two shifts Kyai Hisyam teaches one group after another the *Safinah* in an orderly manner from one chapter to the next. Outside the *bandungan* class he requires the *santri* to read the related chapter(s) from *Taqrib* and to consult him or whoever when it is needed. Thus unlike what they do with the *Safinah*, they read the *Taqrib* on a topic rather than on a chapter basis. Once a week two shifts of discussions are held. One sub-group discusses *Safinah*, the other sub-group argues or raises some comments based on *Taqrib*. To support their arguments Kyai Hisyam encourages the *students* to consult the references he provides, consisting of *Hadits*: *Arba'in al-Nawawiyah, Riyadh ash-Shalihin*; *Tafsir* (Exegeses): *Jalalain, Ash Shawi, Ibn Katsir, Qurtubi, Muraghi*); Theology (*Nazham Nur al-Iman*; *Tajwid* (Arabic or Qur'anic reading rules): *Bidayah ash-Sibyan, Tanfir al-Atfal, Jazwiyah*. For *Nahu/Sharaf* (Arabic grammar and word derivatives) Kyai Hisyam urges his *santri* to go to another *pondok* to learn from another *kyai*. By applying this procedure Kyai Hisyam hopes the students will have basic mastery of certain *kitab* with some acquaintance and broadened perspectives.

In his *pondok, Ngaji kitab* is held from 8.00 p.m to 10.00 p.m and from 5.00 a.m to 6.30 a.m daily, except on Friday which is free. Every Thursday evening after sunset prayer, however, Kyai Hisyam still requires his *santri* to perform *tahlil*, and after evening prayer to perform *marhaba* and public speech training. For all these, the *santri* have to organise these rituals by themselves. Through this procedure he hopes that in the future or when they have completed their learning, *santri* will have the necessary training to engage actively in their societal roles.

Plate 34: The main "pondok" of Pesantren Buntet.

Plate 35: Commemorating the Independence Day at Pesantren Buntet.

Plate 36: The Pesantren Mosque in Buntet.

Plate 37: Girlscouts of Pesantren Buntet on exercise.

بسم الله الرحمن الرحيم

سلسلة الطريقة الشطارية

أقول: اخذت الطريقة الشطارية من والدي ومربي الشيخ العارف كياهي مستهدي
عباس وهو من والده الشيخ العارف كياهي عباس بونتت فسنترين جربون وهو من والده
كياهي الحاج عبد الجميل وهو اخذ من اخيه الشيخ كياهي الحاج محمد صالح وهو من
كياهي محمد انوار وهو اخذ من كياهي اشعري كالي ووغو كندال وهو اخذ من الشيخ
محمد سيد مدني وهو اخذ من ابيه الشيخ طاهر مدني وهو اخذ من ابيه الشيخ ابراهيم
وهو من ابيه الشيخ طاهر وهو اخذ من ابيه الشيخ ملا ابراهيم المعلى وهو اخذ
من الشيخ احمد قشاشي وهو اخذ من الشيخ احمد شناني وهو من السيد صبغة الله
وهو اخذ من السيد غوث وهو اخذ من الشيخ حضري وهو اخذ من الشيخ هداية الله سرمت
وهو اخذ من الشيخ قاضي الشطاري وهو اخذ من الشيخ عبد الله الشطاري وهو اخذ من الشيخ عارف
وهو اخذ من الشيخ محمد عاشق وهو اخذ من الشيخ حدا قلي ما وراء النهار في الشام وهو اخذ من الشيخ ابي
حسن خرقاني وهو اخذ من الشيخ ابي المظفر ترك الطوسي وهو اخذ من الشيخ ابي يزيد العشق وهو
اخذ من الشيخ محمد مغربي وهو اخذ من الشيخ ابي يزيد البسطامي وهو اخذ من امام جعفر الصادق
وهو اخذ من امام باقر وهو اخذ من امام زين العابدين وهو اخذ من امام حسين شهيد وهو
اخذ من سيدنا علي ابن ابي طالب وهو اخذ من سيد الوجود سيدنا محمد صلى الله عليه وسلم
وهو اخذ من الله بواسطة الروح الامين .

A sample of "Ijazah" of
Tarekat Syattariyah in
Buntet

Chapter 8: Pesantren and Tarekat: The role of Buntet

INTRODUCTION

On Java, the *pesantren* and the *tarekat*, meaning (mystical) path, is the hall-mark of traditional Islam. The former is a place where *syare'at* (the exoteric dimension of Islam) is transmitted to the next generation; the second, in the strictest sense, is an organisation by which the esoteric dimension of Islam is established, especially among the aged.[1] The *pesantren* mainly prepares the young to cope with their immediate future in social life. It enables them to undertake active and acceptable participation in various societal roles without neglecting the more distant future, the hereafter. The *tarekat*, on the other hand, prepares the aged to cope with their immediate future. It attempts to secure for followers' safety and well being in the hereafter, after they feel that their worldly life is close to its end. In addition, the *tarekat* attempts to open the heavens to the public. It is a way to ensure equity of opportunity for entry to paradise between the religiously knowledgeable individuals and the laymen, and between the rich and the poor.[2]

The *tarekat* is usually associated with *tasawuf*. The objective of joining a *tarekat* comes after a commitment to the *Sufi* way (*tasawuf*) is taken by means of cleansing the heart (*tasfiyatul qalb*).[3] In practice, *tasawuf* is a strict adoption of the Islamic precepts through observance of both obligatory and recommended religious work for attaining God's favour. Although not always, the by-product of doing *tasawuf*, if God's favour is obtained, is the ability of the individual to attain the knowledge of Divine Truths, the Essence (*hakekat*). The attainment of the Truth is *ma'rifat*, literally meaning knowing the Reality (gnosis). *Ma'rifat* (gnosis) is knowing the *hakekat*, the Essence or Divine Truth. This *hakekat* can be attained

[1] *Tarekat* (***thariqah***) can be defined as the contemplative Path of Islam, in contrast with *syare'at* (***syari'ah***), which is concerned with the life of action. *Tarekat* is associated with or even considered synonymous with Sufism and its cognates. In its more restrictive meaning and specialised sense it refers to Sufi orders (Danner, 1988:242). Some informants explained that our life is a journey to common destination, the afterlife world. Everyone who travels must take a certain way. The word *tarekat* bears this notion. The word is derived from Arabic **thariq** and **thariqah**, meaning path or road. It is usually contrasted with *syare'at*, also derived from Arabic **syar'** and **syari'ah**, meaning street or highway. This contrast implies that the former (*tarekat*) is smaller and the latter (*syare'at*) is larger. *Syare'at* is the way that every Muslim should take to reach the general or common destination. As broad or common destination is reached everyone needs a certain path that leads to a specific place to which he wishes to dwell comfortably.

[2] By definition, according to Kyai Fahim Hawi (50 years) a Tijaniyah *muqaddam*, the knowledgeable and well-to-do people have a greater chance to enter paradise because they have the means and knowledge of how and what to do. The majority of laymen, on the other hand, have less chance. Due to various reasons they could not attain similar means and knowledge. *Tarekat* would like to guide them. With minimal knowledge and material means, provided they follow the guidance of the *mursyid*, they could have a similar chance to the knowledgeable and the well to do few.

[3] See Chapter Four.

by following *tasawuf*, cleansing the heart. It is said that to many people, doing *tasawuf*, although not essential, is much easier and more convenient if it is carried out by following a certain *tarekat* (path). Whichever one would choose, the pre-requisite for following *tarekat* is the observance of *syare'at*. As not every Muslim observes the *syare'at*, not every Muslim who observes the *syare'at* wishes to follow a *tarekat*. In turn, not all the Muslims who follow a certain *tarekat* could attain the *hakekat* and thus experience *ma'rifat*. In local popular uses *syare'at, tarekat, hakekat* and *ma'rifat* form a sequence to characterise the degree of piety in which the first is the lowest, and the last is the highest. Because of either individual or societal factors only *wali* are thought to be likely to reach *ma'rifat*.

EARLY TAREKAT IN BUNTET: SYATTARIYAH

Pesantren Buntet gives homage to two *tarekat*, the Syattariyah, which came earlier and the Tijaniyah which came later. Both belong to the *tarekat mu'tabarah* (accepted *tarekat*).[4]

Although since its first stage Pesantren Buntet has been associated with *Tarekat Syattariyah* (the Syattariyah Order),[5] the formal introduction of this *tarekat* within the *pesantren* circle is said to have been announced publicly only after Kyai Anwaruddin Kriyani al-Malebari (Ki Buyut Kriyan) arrived. When Kyai Mutta'ad led the *pesantren*, Kyai Anwaruddin, married Nyai Ruhillah, daughter of Kyai Mutta'ad; after that he publicly set up the *tarekat* in Pesantren Buntet.

Trimingham describes Syattariyah's origin as being obscure. The *tarekat* is claimed to be in Taifuri traditions but its foundation is attributed to 'Abdallah al-Syattar, a descendant of Syihab ad-Din as-Suhrawardi. According to Trimingham 'Abdallah was sent by his *pir* (a leader of the order), Muhammad 'Arif, to India; first to Jawnpur, then to Mandu where he died in 1428/9. His Path was spread by his pupils, especially Muhammad 'Ala', known as Qazan Syattari of Bengal. Its full development as a distinctive order is attributed to Shah Muhammad Ghawth of Gwalior (circa. 1517) who was succeeded by Syah Wajih ad-Din (circa. 1018/1609) who, in Gujerat, was known as a great saint.

[4] According to Ki Dulah, at least two requirements should be met for a *tarekat* to be considered as *mu'tabarah*. One is that its litanies and teachings do not oppose the *syari'ah*, and that it had an unbroken spiritual chain (*silsilah*) to the Prophet. This would ensure that the teaching really comes from the Prophet.

[5] See note 29.

Table 8.1: The Spiritual Genealogy *(Silsilah)* of Tarekat Syattariyah at Buntet

1. *The Prophet Muhammad*
2. *Ali bin Abi Thalib*
3. *Husein*
4. *Zain al-'Abidin*
5. *Al-Baqir*
6. *Ja'far Shadiq*
7. *Abi Yazid al-Busthami*
8. *Muhammad Maghribi*
9. *Abi Yazid al-'Ashaq*
10. *Abi Mudhaffar Turki at-Tusi*
11. *Hasan Khirqani*
12. *Hadaqly*
13. *Muhammad 'Asyiq*
14. *'Arif*
15. *Abdillah Syattari*
16. *Qadhi Syattari*
17. *Hidayatillah Sarmat*
18. *Hudhari*
19. *Al-Ghawth*
20. *Sibghatillah*
21. *Ahmad Syanani*
22. *Ahmad Qasyasyi*
23. *Malla Ibrahim al-Mu'alla*
24. *Thahir*
25. *Ibrahim*
26. *Thahir Madani*
27. *Muhammad Sayid Madani*
28. *Kyai Asy'ari*
29. *Muhammad Anwaruddin Kriyani (Ki Buyut Kriyan).*

Although its chain clearly links with Suhrawardiyah, this *tarekat* does not regard itself as an offshoot of any order. In Iran and Turan Syattariyah was known as 'Isyqiyah, and in Ottoman Turkey as Bisthamiyah.[6] It was brought to Indonesia (Aceh) by Abdul Rauf Singkel, who brought with him the theosophical doctrines of the seven stages of creation (*Martabat Tujuh*). Among his students was Syeikh Abdul Muhyi who brought the *tarekat* to south Priangan (West Java) via Cirebon.[7] Although it is said that before going to south Priangan Syeikh Muhyi married and lived in Cirebon for some period of time, Tarekat Syattariyah in

[6] Trimingham, J.S. (1971), *Sufi Orders in Islam*, Oxford: The Clarendon Press, p. 97–98. The Taifuri tradition refers to Abu Yazid al Bustami (d. 261/872 or 264/877–8), a famous medieval Sufi. He spent most of his life in Bustham and died there. Trimingham's characterisation of Shattariyah's obscurity seems to stem from his inability to discover the identity of Muhammad 'Arif who sent 'Abdallah to India.

[7] Santrie, A.M. (1987), "Martabat Alam Tujuh" in Hasan, A.R. (ed.), *Warisan Intelektual Islam Indonesia*, Bandung: Mizan, pp 105–129. Syeikh Muhyi was buried at Pamijahan (Tasikmalaya, West Java). His tomb attract many visitors from various places.

Buntet has no link with him nor with Abdul Rauf Singkel because the Syattariyah came to Buntet from a different source.

Figure 8.1: Recruitment of Syattariyah Mursyid in Buntet

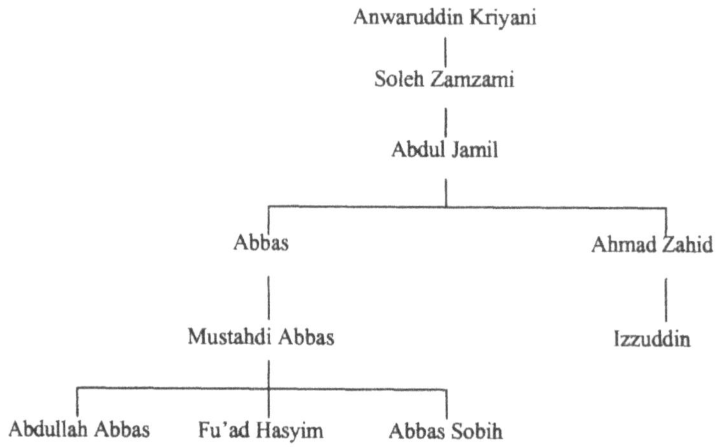

In Buntet, Kyai Anwaruddin Kriyani al-Malebari (Ki Buyut Kriyan), the founder of the Syattariyah order in Buntet received his authority as a *mursyid* (leader) from Kyai Asy'ary of Kaliwungu (Central Java). Table 8.1. shows the spiritual genealogy (*silsilah*) of Kyai Asy'ari to whom Kyai Anwaruddin in turn traced his authority. The latter therefore, is the 29th in the genealogical chain that relates him spiritually to the Prophet. As a Syattariyah *mursyid*, Kyai Anwaruddin in turn authorised Kyai Muhammad Saleh Zamzami, the founder of Pesantren Benda at Benda Kerep, to become a new *mursyid* when Kyai Zamzami was 57 years old (1317/1898). Kyai Saleh Zamzami authorised his brother at Buntet, Kyai Abdul Jamil, who authorised first Kyai Abbas and then Kyai Ahmad Zahid. Kyai Abbas authorised Kyai Mustahdi, who authorised Kyai Abdullah Abbas, Kyai Fu'ad Hasyim and Abbas Shobih (Kang Obih). Kyai Ahmad Zahid, on the other hand, authorised Kyai Izzuddin (Figure 8.1).

In addition to this, Tarekat Syattariyah is said to have been part of *kraton* traditions but it seems to have a different genealogy. The present Syattariyah *mursyid* within the *kraton* circle is P.S. Sulendraningrat of Kaprabonan at Lemah Wungkuk. He is a 15th descendant of Sunan Gunung Jati and the writer of *Sejarah Cirebon* and *Babad Tanah Sunda, Babad Cerbon*.[8] Mbah Muqayim who was *Penghulu Kraton*, the founder of Pesantren Buntet, is said to have been a *mursyid* of Syattariyah *kraton* although in Buntet he did not recruit members or, if he did, it was not publicly. In Buntet Tarekat Syattariyah had won thousands of followers but after the death of Kyai Mustahdi its organisational

[8] For a brief account on Syattariyah at *kraton* see: Siddique (1978), especially pp. 122–124.

significance has diminished considerably.[9] Now, this *tarekat* still persists and is still strong in Benda Kerep, but in Buntet it seems to be left as a mere individual observance rather than an organised group.[10]

TAREKAT TIJANIYAH

Currently in Buntet, another *tarekat*, the Tijaniyah, is much more dominant than Syattariyah. Tijaniyah seems to gain more and more attraction among the Javanese and thus, with special reference to Buntet, it deserves a special attention. In addition to this, as we shall see, Buntet has been one of the important door-ways for the further spread of this *tarekat* to other parts of Java, especially West Java. It is this special role that in the subsequent discussion I wish to stress.[11]

The Origin of Tijaniyah

Tarekat Tijaniyah was founded by Abu-'Abbas Ahmad who claimed to be the 21st descendant of the Prophet Muhammad. He was born in 1150/1737 at 'Ain Madi in south Algeria. His father, Muhammad bin Mukhtar, is said to have been a pious man of learning who lived and taught at 'Ain Madi, whereas his mother, "Sayidah 'Aisyah binti Abdullah bin Al-Sanusy-Attijany" was of the original Tijani tribe of 'Ain Madi and thus the name At-Tijani for Abu-'Abbas Ahmad is derived from his mother.[12]

At seven years of age, Ahmad at-Tijani is said to have read the whole Qur'an well, especially in Nafi' style (*qiraat Nafi'*). He then studied various religious subjects. He learnt *Mukhtashar al-Syeikh Khalil*, a summary of Malikite jurisprudence, read *Risalah Jama'ah as-Shufiyah bi bilad al-Islam* by Abu'l Qasim al-Qusayri, studied *Muqaddimas* of Ibn Rusyd and al-Akhdari and became a learned figure. He taught a number of students and gave *fatwa* (legal judgement) when he was 20. At 21 years of age he felt a call to the *Sufi* life and started travelling. He came to Fez in 1171/1757–8 in search of *Sufi syeikh*, studied the

[9] H. Abbas Shobih of Buntet speculates, probably it is because upon his father's (Kyai Mustahdi's) death, Kyai Mustamid who succeeded Kyai Mustahdi was already old and unable to make extensive travel visiting the *zawiyah* (branches).

[10] According to Kyai Fu'ad Hasyim, Tarekat Syattariyah in Cirebon and elsewhere came into two formats. One was in fully Arabic the other was explained in Javanese. Syattariyah in Buntet and Benda Kerep (and *pesantren* other as well) represent the first, while Syattariyah *kraton* represents the second. Both are equally *Mu'tabarah*.

[11] For the early stage of the rise of Tijaniyah in Java, see: Pijper, G.F. (1987), "Timbulnya Tarekat Tijaniyah di Pulau Jawa" in G.F. Pijper, *Fragmenta Islamica: Beberapa Studi Mengenai Sejarah Islam di Indonesia Awal Abad XX*, Jakarta: UI Press, pp 79–101, translated from *Fragmenta Islamica, Studien over het Islamisme in Nederlanndsch-Indie*, Leiden: E.J. Brill, 1934 by Tujimah. For a general account on Tijaniyah, see: Abun-Nasr (1965), *The Tijaniyya: A Sufi Order in the Modern World*, London: OUP. My own local Tijani sources are Fathullah, K.H.F. (1985), *Biografi Alquthbul Maktuum Saiyidul Awliyaa: Syeikh Ahmad Attijaniy dan Thariqatnya Attijaniyah*, Pasuruan: (anonymous publisher); *Al Masyrabul Kitmani Lil Khotmil Muhammadiy Syekh Ahmad bin Muhammad Attijani*, a pamphlet from Panitia Idul Khotmi Attijani Ke: 199, 9/10 Shafar 1413 H = 8/9 Agustus 1992 M, Leces-Probolinggo (East Java).

[12] Fathullah, K.H.F. (1985), p. 52.

Prophetic traditions and joined three *Sufi* brotherhoods, the Qadiriyah, the Nashiriyah and the *thariqah* of Ahmad al-Habib bin Muhammad.[13] Among the *Sufi syeikh* whom Ahmad at-Tijani met was Muhammad bin Hasan Al-Wanajaly a great *wali* of his time who, at mount Zabib, said that At-Tijani would have a position (*maqam*) equal to Asy-Syadzily. Ahmad at-Tijani became a real *Sufi* at 31 after contemplation (*riyadhah*) for a period of time.[14]

Table 8.2: Ancestral Genealogy of Abu Abbas Ahmad at-Tijani The founder of Tijaniyah order

1. *The Prophet Muhammad*
2. *Ali bin Abi Thalib*
3. *Hasan al-Sibthi*
4. *Hasan al-Mutsanna*
5. *Abdullah*
6. *Muhammad an-Nafs az-Zakiyah*
7. *Ahmad*
8. *Ali Zain al-Abidin*
9. *Ishaq*
10. *Idris*
11. *Abdul Jabbar*
12. *Abbas*
13. *Abdillah*
14. *Ali*
15. *Ahmad*
16. *Ahmad al-'Alwani*
17. *Salim*
18. *Muhammad*
19. *Mukhtar*
20. *Muhammad*
21. *Abu 'Abbas Ahmad at-Tijani*

Ahmad at-Tijani went to Tunis, then to Mecca on pilgrimage in 1186/1772–3. On his way to Mecca he stopped at Azwawi, a town near Algiers and took an initiation into the Khalwatiyah order with Mahmad b 'Abdul Rahman. He spent a year in Tunis, teaching the *Kitab al-hikam* of Ibn Ata' Allah, then went to Egypt to meet Syeikh Mahmud al-Kurdi, the Khalwatiyah chief in Cairo. He reached Mecca on Syawwal 1187/1773–4, then performed his Hajj. In Mecca he tried to meet a great Indian *Sufi* Ahmad bin Abdullah al-Hindy. Although he failed to meet him in person, via al-Hindy's servant, At-Tijani received a written message from him saying that At-Tijani inherited all al-Hindy's occult mystical learning, and that At-Tijani would reach an equal status with Abu'l Hasan Asy-Syadzily. Two months after that al-Hindy died.[15]

[13] Abun Nasr (1965), pp. 16–17.
[14] Fathullah (1985), p. 55.
[15] Ibid, pp 55–59.

After finishing his pilgrimage At-Tijani went to Medina to visit the Prophet's tomb and met Syeikh Abdul Karim as-Samman, the Sammaniyah chief (a branch of Khalwatiyah), who foretold his potential for becoming the dominant *qutb* (pole). At-Tijani left Arabia in 1191/1777–8 for Africa via Egypt where Mahmud al-Kurdi authorised him to preach the Khalwatiyah order in North Africa. He did not return to 'Ain Madi however, but went to Fez then settled in Tlemsen (Algeria) until 1196/1781–2. From Tlemsen he went to Syallala and settled in Sidi Abi Samghun, an oasis 75 miles south of Geryville. There, in that year (1196/1781–2), he marked the foundation of the Tijaniyah order when he announced to his followers that the Prophet appeared to him in daylight while he was fully conscious and in active mind (*yaqdhah*), not dreaming. The Prophet, he said, authorised him to start a new work of *at-tarbiyah* (spiritual guidance) and assigned him his order's *wird* (litanies), consisting of *istighfar* (asking God's pardon) 100 times and *shalawat* (exaltation of the Prophet Muhammad) 100 times.[16]

In AH 1200, At-Tijani claimed, the Prophet reappeared and completed the litanies with *hailalah* (uttering there is no God but Allah). Fourteen months later, on Muharram AH 1214 At-Tijani claimed to have reached a position of 'the pole of (*wali*) poles' (*al-qutbaniyatul-'udhma*) which means that he obtained the 'highest rank of the highest' within the current *wali* hierarchy. On 18th Shafar of the same year he attained another position, 'the hidden seal of all poles' (*al-khatm wa'l-katm*) or 'the hidden end of the highest pole.' This implied that there would be no more *wali* pole whose position is higher than himself.[17] Bearing simultaneously two positions, At-Tijani relinquished his former affiliation with the four orders with the assertion that along with teaching him the litanies for his order in person, the Prophet himself also ordered At-Tijani to give up all his former affiliations with the other orders. This was an official proclamation that At-Tijani only recognised the Prophet as his master and hence the Tijaniyah adherents claimed their order as *at-Thariqah al-Muhammadiyah*, a name similar to that claimed by the followers of Sanusiyah and Kittaniyah for their own *tarekat*.[18] At-Tijani died on 12 Syawwal 1230/22 September 1815 when he was 80 years old. He was buried in Fez.

Some Tijaniyah's Essential Doctrines

There are some essential doctrines which mark Tijaniyah as being distinct from other *tarekat*. I wish to mention briefly some of them before discussing the specific role of Pesantren Buntet with regard to this *tarekat*. Trimingham characterised Tijaniyah as belonging to the 19th century revival movement mainly because:

[16] Ibid, 55–63; Abun Nasr, pp 18–19.
[17] Ibid, 63–64.
[18] Abun Nasr, p 37.

> He (Ahmad At-Tijani, the founder of the tarekat) imposed no penances or retreats and the ritual was not complicated. He emphasised above all the need for intercessor between God and man, the intercessor of the age being himself and his successors. His followers were strictly forbidden, not merely to pay the *'ahd* of allegiance to any other shaikh, but to make invocations to any *wali* other than himself ...[19]

It is common belief among the *Sufis* that their *syeikh* are organised in a spiritual hierarchy, hence a *Sufi* of high reputation of sanctity and learning, could claim to have attained a certain rank in the hierarchy. His followers had only to accept on trust what their Syeikh's claimed.[20] In this context, At-Tijani took the liberty of claiming to occupy two of the highest positions simultaneously, one being *Qutb al-Aqtab* (the Pole of the Poles) the other being *Khatm al-Wilayah al-Muhammadiyah* (the Seal of Muhammadan Sainthood). This twofold position in relation to other *wali* is drawn parallel to the position of the Prophet Muhammad vis-a-vis other prophets. The Prophet Muhammad was the *Khatm* (seal) of the prophets in the sense that he was to complete all marvels of the other prophets, and that there would be no prophet sent to earth after him. At-Tijani on the other hand, was the *Khatm* of the *wali* in the sense that he bears a complete and perfect embodiment of *wilayah* before and after him, and that if ever there may be other *wali* after him, none would surpass or supersede at-Tijani in rank.[21]

At-Tijani is not a unique claimant of the *Qutb al-Aqtab* and the *Khatm al-Wilayah*. This position had been claimed by Muhyi ad-Din ibn al-'Arabi for himself. He was the famous Andalusian *Sufi* in the 13th century whose theosophical concepts influenced much of At-Tijani especially regarding the concept of *al-khatm*.[22] The position was also claimed in the 14th century by an Egyptian 'Ali bin Wafa for his father, Muhammad bin Wafa, and by the founder of Kittaniyah order, Muhammad bin al-Kabir al-Kittani of Morocco in the 19th century.[23] The Tijanis however, assert that later on, Ibn al-'Arabi found that he himself had been mistaken and thus he wrote in his *Futuhat al-Makkiyah* that the *Khatm al-Wilayah al-Muhammadiyah* would be a man of noble Arab origin, living in his (Ibn 'Arabi's) own time, in Fez, and when God would try to locate this man among people, they would not believe him. Beside the fact that no one else in Fez had

[19] Trimingham, J.S (1971), p 108. (Words between brackets are my own).

[20] Ibid, pp 27–28; The existence of spiritual hierarchies among *wali* was first set forth by Abu 'Abdillah al-Tirmidzi during the 11th century. It became an established belief due to the work of Ibn al-Araby (1164–1240) and gained wide spread acceptance after 'Abdul Rahman al-Suyuti (1445–1505), a Hadithist, gave Prophetic traditions for this belief.

[21] Abun Nasr, p 32.

[22] Ibid, p. 32. It says: "The *Khatm*, who will be the standard of *wilaya*, will be the end of the line and its completion. He has been a *Khatm* without being known, and has the command which cannot be repeated or dispensed with ... Should a *wali* appear after him, he will be one of the followers, companions, or attendants (of the *khatm*) ..."

[23] Ibid, p 28.

announced such a claim, except that "the *Khatm al-Wilayah* would be living in his (Ibn al-'Arabi's) time," all points to Ibn al-'Arabi's formal disavowal for his own status to be taken over by the Tijani to confirm At-Tijani's position.[24]

Claiming this superior position above other *wali*, along with giving up his affiliation with other orders At-Tijani posited his own order to excel the others. This claim, in turn, was formed into a doctrine which requires that all Tijani followers should neither join any other orders nor seek for *barakah* from other *wali* by visiting them, dead or alive. Further, as every Tijani is required to bind his heart completely to his own Tijani *Syeikh*, no Tijani follower is allowed to associate membership with any other order at the same time. Thus, anyone who would like to become a Tijani should be spiritually free. If he is a member of a certain order he has to give up his membership in his former order. The prohibition for a Tijani to join another *tarekat* is however accompanied by the Tijaniyah rejoicing doctrines. *Kitab Ar-Rimah* affirms At-Tijani's assertion that (by the will of God) his faithful companions shall not enter the *mahsyar* with other laymen.[25] While being at the *Mahsyar*, Tijaniyah followers will not encounter suffering even for a second until they are settled in the highest heavens. On the Day of Judgement faithful Tijani companions will not stay at the stations amidst the mass of laymen; instead they will rest under the shadow of God's Throne. In addition, the Prophet himself had taught At-Tijani in words, the *shalawat* **Jawharat al-Kamal**, and affirmed that whoever recites this *shalawat*, the Prophet and the Four Companions will be present with him during the recital.[26] All the rejoicing and other doctrines tend to impress exclusiveness, as if the Tijani followers were above the other Muslims and this, certainly, provokes disagreement, even refutations.

Another feature worth mentioning, which distinguishes Tijaniyah from other *tarekat*, is concerned with the notion of a spiritual genealogy chain (*silsilah*). In ordinary Sufi traditions, a *tarekat*, including the already mentioned Syattariyah, will produce a long list of names by which the present *Syeikh* and the founder of the *tarekat* are linked together spiritually in terms of master-to-master lineage, back to Al-Junaid or al-Busthami and via 'Ali or Abu Bakr, to the Prophet Muhammad. It is this *silsilah* that validates that its rituals come from the Prophet and that ensures the flow of *barakah*. Contrary to this, At-Tijani produced no *silsilah* because, as At-Tijani himself claimed, and as 'Ali al-Harazim puts it in his *Jawahir al-Ma'ani* (an official Tijani reference), the Prophet appeared to him when he was awake (*yaqdhah*) and instructed him in all the litanies and the

[24] Ibid, p 30.
[25] *Mahsyar* is a plain where all the dead, after resurrection, get together to receive a fair judgement.
[26] Fathullah (1985), pp 110–111.

number of times they were to be repeated.[27] Thus, if present *muqaddam* (Tijaniyah *syeikh*), have a *silsilah*, it will be much shorter than what is ordinarily known for a *Sufi silsilah*.[28]

Currently Tijaniyah has become an established order throughout the Muslim world including Indonesia, especially Java. With all its peculiarities and crucial points it has encountered opposition and rejection over time. An early serious rejection came from Muhammad al-Khidr bin Ma Ya'ba (1927). In his *Musytaha al-kharif al-jani*, al-Khidr devoted a full chapter to recount the absurdity of At-Tijani's claim. He also attempted to prove that At-Tijani's claim has no grounds in the Prophetic traditions. The Tijanis, on the other hand, consider that what had happened with their master and the presumed direct communication with the Prophet while he was awake was a sign of the Prophet's favour and thus ensured the status of the *tarekat* as being above others.[29] In addition, Al-Khidr's attitude towards the Tijaniyah seems to have been motivated, at least partly, by a political outlook rather than purely on theological grounds. This is due to the fact that upon the death of At-Tijani and the collapse of the Turkish rule, At-Tijani's successors, for their own reasons (probably due to the opposition from other *tarekat*), brought Tijaniyah into subservient co-operation with French colonialism in Algeria at that time.[30]

When Tijaniyah was brought to Java at the end of 1920s and in the early 1930s, similar refutations also came from some already established orders such as Naqsabandiyah, Qadiriyah, Syattariyah, Syadziliyah and Khalwatiyah.[31] The most notable one came from Sayid Abdullah bin Shadaqah Dahlan, an Arab who settled in Java, the nephew of Sayid Ahmad bin Zayni Dahlan, a distinguished Syafi'ite Mufti in Medina. In the same way as Muhammad al-Khidr bin Ma Ya'ba did, Sayid Abdullah referred to the crucial points contained in the Tijaniyah doctrines. He recounted the fallacies of the doctrines and denounced them by saying that some *ulama* in Morocco, Egypt and Hejaz had accepted Tijaniyah as untrue.[32] The crisscrossing argumentations for and against Tijaniyah that prevailed at that time called for intervention from the NU, the traditionalist Muslim organisation that takes a number of *tarekat* under its umbrella. In its 6th Congress on August 1931 held in Cirebon, in which Kyai Adlan Ali, a prominent figure of Pesantren Cukir, Jombang (East Java) was appointed

[27] Abun Nasr (1985), p. 38. The rites consists of both the compulsory (*lazim*) and recommended (*ikhtiari*). The compulsory consists of *wird lazimah* (litanies), *wadzifah* (office) and *hailalah* (participation in Friday afternoon *hadra* or seance). See Abun Nasr, pp 50–57; Fathullah, pp 129–139.

[28] See: the subsequent section.

[29] Detailed early refutations and counter refutations see Abun Nasr 1965, especially pp. 38–41.

[30] Ibid, pp 72–75.

[31] Strong reaction against Tijaniyah in Buntet came from Benda, the *pesantren* established by Kyai Soleh Zamzami of Buntet, the elder brother of Kyai Abdul Jamil. Since Kyai Abbas era, until now, Benda-Buntet opposition is unreconciliable.

[32] Pijper (1985), *Fragmenta Islamica*, pp 89–96.

Chairman, the Tijaniyah issue was included in the agenda. After a long and exhausting debate chaired by Kyai Hasyim Asy'ari, the Congress finally agreed that Tijaniyah is *mu'tabarah*. This, nevertheless, did not end the anti-Tijaniyah campaign especially outside the NU circle. Further refutation, for example, came from Kyai Muhammad Ismail of Cracak (Cirebon), a distinguished *Syeikh* of the Qadiriyah wan-Naqsabandiyah order who personally was not affiliated to the NU Through his pamphlets, he raised renewed and sophisticated arguments similar to those expounded by earlier anti-Tijaniyah proponents.[33]

Quite recently, another refutation even came from within the NU circle when Kyai As'ad of Pondok Kramat in Pasuruan (East Java) issued a 94 page manuscript.[34] The manuscript was a translation in Madurese vernacular of the *Wudhuh ad-Dalail*, originally written on 26 Rabi' ats-Tsani 1930/19–20 (September 1930). Through this translation he turned the Tijaniyah issue from being a scholarly concern into a public concern. The polemic became complicated, albeit degraded, because some *non-ulama* became involved in the affair.[35] In a session held on December 1984 at Pesantren Nurul Qadim, Probolinggo (East Java), Kyai As'ad demanded that the NU review the Cirebon decision regarding the legitimacy of the Tijaniyah. In the session which was part of the 27th NU Congress centred at Pesantren Asem Bagus, Situbondo (East Java), Kyai As'ad encountered strong opposition from other *kyai* and failed to have his demand put into effect.[36] The result was that the status of Tijaniyah as being *mu'tabarah* remained unshaken.

Under seemingly continuous opposition, Tarekat Tijaniyah keeps growing. It relies on simple rites relative to other *tarekat*, yet promises its adherents high spiritual efficacy and merit. Together with its friendly attitude towards worldly life rather than the ascetic tendency usually exhibited by other Sufi orders, "Tijaniyah is suitable for every one, even the busy people of modern times; it is even suitable for civil servants," said Kyai Abdullah Syifa, a Tijaniyah *muqaddam* at Buntet. Currently, Tijaniyah enjoys wide acceptance from many people ranging from *ulama*, state dignitaries, and intellectuals to ordinary laymen.[37]

[33] Ibid, pp 98–100

[34] This Kyai As'ad is to be distinguished from Kyai As'ad Syamsul Arifin of Pesantren Asem Bagus, Situbondo (East Java), former Chairman of *Syuriyah* NU.

[35] Fathullah (1985), pp 140–141. In this work (*Biografi Alquthbul Maktuum*) Without mentioning its writer, Fathullah devoted a full chapter entitled "Fasal Tambahan" (Additional Chapter) to counter the *Wudluh ad-Dalail*.

[36] The 1984 Situbondo Congress is well known for producing *Khittah 1926*, by which NU returned to the principle initially adopted when NU was established in 1926. This means that officially NU abstains from direct involvement in politics and is solely concerned with social and religious affairs.

[37] This was claimed by Kyai Fahim Hawi and Kyai Abdullah Syifa, two Tijani *muqaddam* in Buntet. An example of Tijaniyah's wide acceptance was given by Kyai Fahim Hawi in recounting a number of figures in Tijaniyah. Some of them are Sayid Alfa Hasyim, a Hadithist in Medina, Syeikh Hasan Yamani, father of Zaki Yamani, former petroleum Minister of Saudi Arabia, Mr. Muhammad, a Senegalese envoy

The Role of Buntet

In his special account on the rise of Tijaniyah on Java, Pijper states that Tarekat Tijaniyah was not known in Java before 1928. A wandering Arab, born in Medina, Syeikh Ali bin 'Abdullah at-Thayyib al-Azhari, is held responsible for the introduction of this *tarekat* to Java, especially through his work, *Kitab al-Munyah fi 't-thariqat at-Tijaniyah*, Tasikmalaya: 1349/January 1928, a treatise on *Munyat al-Murid*.[38] Pijper points out further that from the age of nine years, Syeikh 'Ali at-Thayyib had studied in Cairo where he remained for 20 years; he then stayed and taught in Mecca for six years. He returned to Medina and worked as a *mufti* for about ten years, then came to Java. First he stayed in Cianjur, then successively in Bogor, Tasikmalaya and back in Cianjur. In Java he lived from teaching and extensive travel from Banten to Surabaya selling religious books, including his own work, *Kitab Misykat al-Anwar fi shirat an-Nabi al-Mukhtar*, Tasikmalaya: (undated). Pijper claimed that he had met Syeikh 'Ali at-Thayyib at his house on the slope of mount Gede in Cianjur.[39]

According to local Tijani sources, the spread of Tijaniyah on Java is mainly attributed to two figures, one was 'Ali at-Thayyib al-Madani, an authoritative scholar in Medina who formed the gate for West Java by recruiting seven West Javanese *muqaddam*, the other was 'Abd al-Hamid al-Futi, also a distinguished scholar in Arabia who formed the gate for East Java by recruiting two East Javanese. Table 8.3 shows that 'Ali at-Thayyib al-Madani, who was held

to Jakarta on February 1985 who met President Suharto on behalf of the Senegalese President. All, he said, are Tijaniyah *Muqaddam*. There are also a number of distinguished figures at Al-Azhar in Cairo. Wide acceptance by many Javanese was shown by the huge number of participants in the festivals held to commemorate At-Tijani's spiritual ascendancy, the *Idul Khotmi At-Tijani*. One of which was performed at Jakarta's main stadium in 1990 had around a 100,000 participants. At a similar festival, the 199th *Idul Khotmi*, held on 8–9 August 1992 in Leces, Probolinggo (East Java), around 60,000 participants were present. I was among the contingent from Cirebon.

[38] Pijper, G.F. (1985), Fragmenta Islamica, Jakarta: U.I. Press, p 82.

[39] Ibid, pp 86–87. Inspite of his claim of having met 'Ali bin 'Abd Allah at-Thayyib in Cianjur in 1929, Pijper seems to give a quite puzzling explanation. It is rather naive to think that a distinguished scholar holding a prestigious position for ten years in Medina, migrated to Java to become a petty trader of religious books. Pijper also says that when he met, 'Ali bin 'Abd Allah at-Thayyib was already old, did not have disciples from the nearby areas, etc. This contradicts his biographical account stated above, whereby 'Ali at-Thayyib should have been 45 when he came to Java (from the age of 9 years old, he stayed in Cairo for 20 years, then in Mecca 6 years, and in Medina 10 years). According to Kyai Fahim, among the key figures for the development of Tijaniyah on Java was Syekh 'Ali bin 'Abdullah at-Thayyib al-Madani (an Al-Azhar graduate from which the addition of al-Azhari may be derived). He was a prominent scholar with high authority in religious affairs, staying in Medina, not in Java. He, however, visited Java several times to see his son, Muhammad bin 'Ali bin 'Abd Allah at-Thayyib, an Arab immigrant who also had studied at Al-Azhar but stayed in Java (Bogor). The latter became a Tijaniyah *Muqaddam* with whom Kyai Fauzan Fathullah, the writer of *Biografi al-Quthbul Maktuum*, one of my references, was initiated. (Syeikh) Muhammad bin 'Ali bin 'Abd Allah at-Thayyib of Bogor lived in the same period with Kyai Abbas, Kyai Anas and Kyai Akyas, three *muqaddam* from Buntet. They were all authorised as *muqaddam* by Syeikh 'Ali at-Thayyib al-Madani, father of (Syeikh) Muhammad bin 'Ali bin 'Abdullah at-Thayyib of Bogor. If Kyai Fahim is right, Pijper might have confused the two names, Syeikh 'Ali bin 'Abdullah at-Thayyib al-Madani (al-Azhari) who stayed in Medina, and his son, Syeikh Muhammad bin 'Ali bin 'Abdullah at-Thayyib (al-Azhari) who stayed in Bogor.

responsible for the spread of Tijaniyah in West Java, traced his spiritual genealogy with Ahmad at-Tijani through two different sources: Syeikh Adam bin Muhammad Shaib al-Barnawi and Syeikh Muhammad Alfa Hasyim.[40] This spiritual link can also be seen from Figure 8.2

Table 8.3: Spiritual genealogy of Syeikh Ali At-Thayyib al-Madani (West Java gate of Tijaniyah)

Chain-1	Chain-2
1 Ahmad at-Tijani	1 Ahmad at-Tijani
2 Muhammad b Qasim al-Bisri	2 Muhammad a-Ghala
Abd Wahab al-Ahmar	
3 Ahmad al-Bani a-Fasi	3 Amr b Sa'id al-Futi
4 Adam b Muhammad Shaib al-Barnawi	4 Al-Haj as-Sa'id
5 Ali at-Thayyib al-Madani	5 Muhammad Alfa Hasyim
	6 Ali at-Thayyib al-Madani

The seven West Javanese *muqaddam* recruited by Syeikh Ali at-Thayyib were his own grandson, Syeikh Muhammad bin 'Ali bin 'Abd Allah at-Thayyib (Bogor), Kyai Asy'ari Bunyamin (Garut), Kyai Badruzzaman (Garut), Kyai 'Utsman Dlamiri (Cimahi, Bandung) and three brothers Kyai Abbas, Kyai Anas and Kyai Akyas (Buntet). It was these West Javanese 'magnificent seven' who were in turn, responsible for the further spread of Tijaniyah, not only in West Java but also in Central and East Java because later, many other Javanese *muqaddam* were initiated by one or more of them. Among the Tijani, this *silsilah* grew into a complex crisscrossing spiritual chain as some *muqaddam* for various reasons, either for seniority or intellectual considerations, took initiation from more than one superior *muqaddam* (*muqaddam min muqaddam*). Kyai Hawi, father of a current *muqaddam* at Buntet, Kyai Fahim, for example, took initiation from Kyai Saleh, Kyai Abbas, Kyai Anas, Kyai Akyas and, when he went to Mecca, from a very senior *muqaddam*, Syeikh Muhammad Hafiz at-Tijani. The latter had only two *Syeikh* that spiritually linked him with Ahmad at-Tijani, the founder of the order.[41]

[40] Cf: Pijper (1985), p 87.
[41] I could not get the two names because despite I made several visits, I failed to meet Pak Gani, a Maderise businessman in Jakarta who, according to Kyai Fahim Hawi, keeps the document.

Figure 8.2: Main Entrance of Tijaniyah to Java.

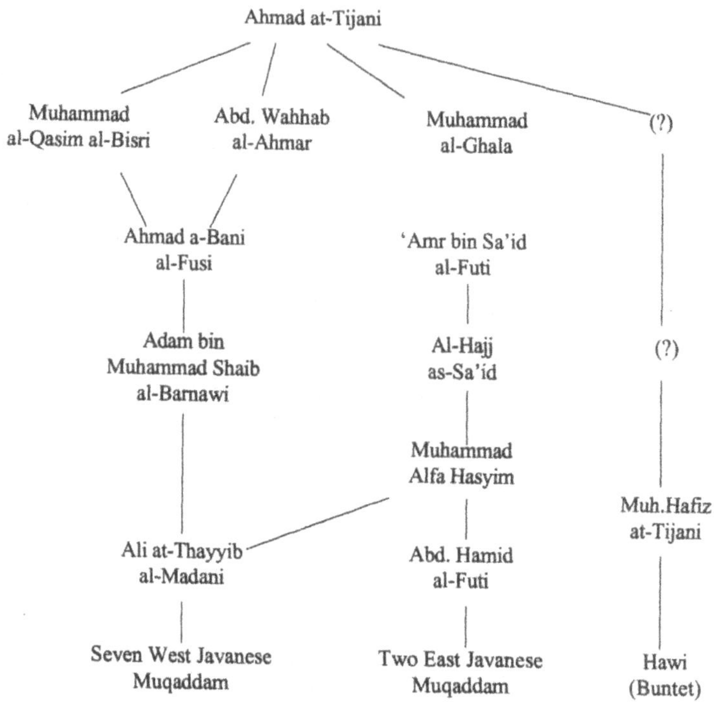

Kyai Abdullah Syifa, another current *muqaddam* at Buntet, took his initiation from Kyai Hawi and Kyai Akyas. Kyai Fauzan Fathullah (Sidagiri, Prussian, East Java), the writer of *Biografi Alquthbul Maktuum*, took initiation from Kyai Khozin Syamsul Mu'in (Probolinggo), Kyai Muhammad bin Yusuf (Surabaya) and Syeikh Muhammad bin 'Ali bin 'Abd Allah at-Thayyib (Bogor).

Syeikh Abd al-Hamid al-Futi, the main gate for East Java, traced his authority from Muhammad Alfa Hasyim (source 2 number 4 of table 8.3). In turn, 'Abd al-Hamid al-Futi, initiated two East Javanese, Kyai Khozin Syamsul Arifin and Kyai Jauhar. Kyai Khozin Syamsul Arifin initiated Kyai Mukhlis (Surabaya), whereas Kyai Jauhar initiated Kyai Muhammad Tijani (Madura). Thus, even a *muqaddam* who took initiation from only one superior *muqaddam* will automatically inherit multiple *silsilah* because through Syeikh 'Ali bin Abd Allah at-Thayyib, he can trace at least two lines, those of Syeikh Adam al-Barnawi and Syeikh Muhammad Alfa Hasyim. How complex the *silsilah* is can be observed from Figure 8.4.

Within the Buntet line, the persons who are considered the most instrumental and are held responsible for the spread of Tijaniyah, are Kyai Anas (1883–1945) and Kyai Abbas and, for the next generation, Kyai Hawi. Kyai Anas was the son of Kyai Abdul Jamil, younger brother of Kyai Abbas. Like Kyai Abbas, Kyai

Anas first studied with Kyai Nasuha at Pesantren Sukunsari (Plered), then with Kyai Agus (Pekalongan), and Kyai Hasyim Asy'ari at Tebuireng (Jombang). Together with Kyai Abbas, he was also involved in the foundation of Pesantren Lirboyo (Kediri) led by Kyai Abdul Manaf. He went to Mecca for both pilgrimage and study while his brother, Kyai Abbas, led Pesantren Buntet. It was due to Kyai Abbas' advice that Kyai Anas took Tarekat Tijaniyah. Kyai Abbas himself met Syeikh 'Ali at-Thayyib in Medina but, despite his interest in Tijaniyah, he did not take an initiation at that time because he bore responsibility as a Syattariyah *mursyid*. Kyai Anas took his brother's advice and upon his return he publicly established tarekat Tijaniyah and thus, there were two *tarekat* in Pesantren Buntet at the same time, the Syattariyah led by Kyai Abbas, and Tijaniyah led by Kyai Anas. Eventually, when both *tarekat* grew larger, Kyai Abbas took Tijaniyah initiation, not from his younger brother, Kyai Anas, but from Syeikh 'Ali bin 'Abd Allah at-Thayyib al-Madani when the latter visited Java (Bogor) in 1937. In 1939 Kyai Anas moved from Buntet and established his own *pesantren* at Kilapat, an adjacent village south-east of Buntet, where adultery and burglary were common. He named his *pesantren* 'Sidamulya,' meaning 'to become lofty.' Later, the name Kilapat for the village, where the new *pesantren* is located, was also renamed Sidamulya, following the *pesantren's* name. The earlier reputation of the village gradually vanished and it gained a reputation as a *santri* village.

Figure 8.3: Recruitment of Tijaniyah Muqaddam from Buntet

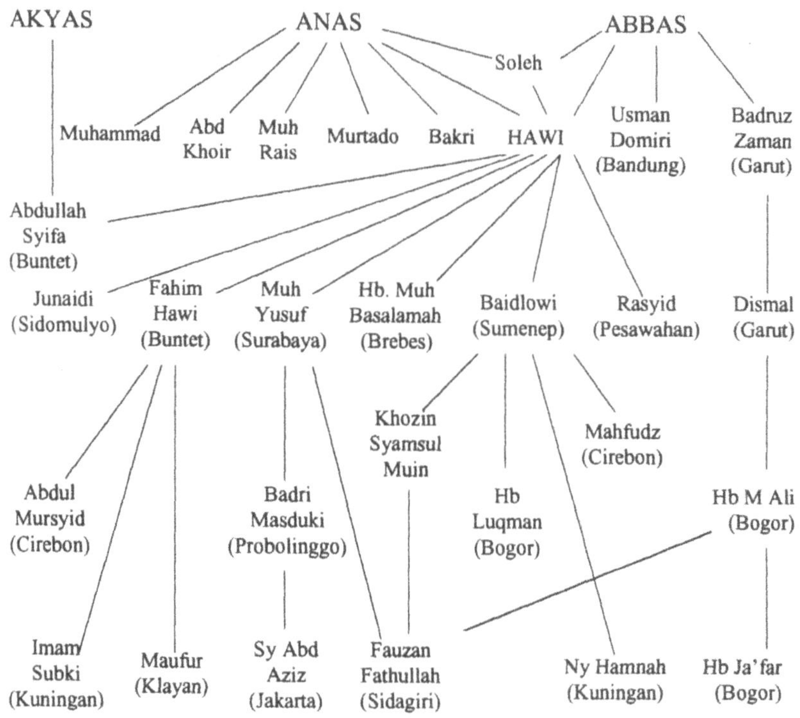

Figure 8.4: Spiritual Genealogy of Some Tijaniyah Muqaddam in Java

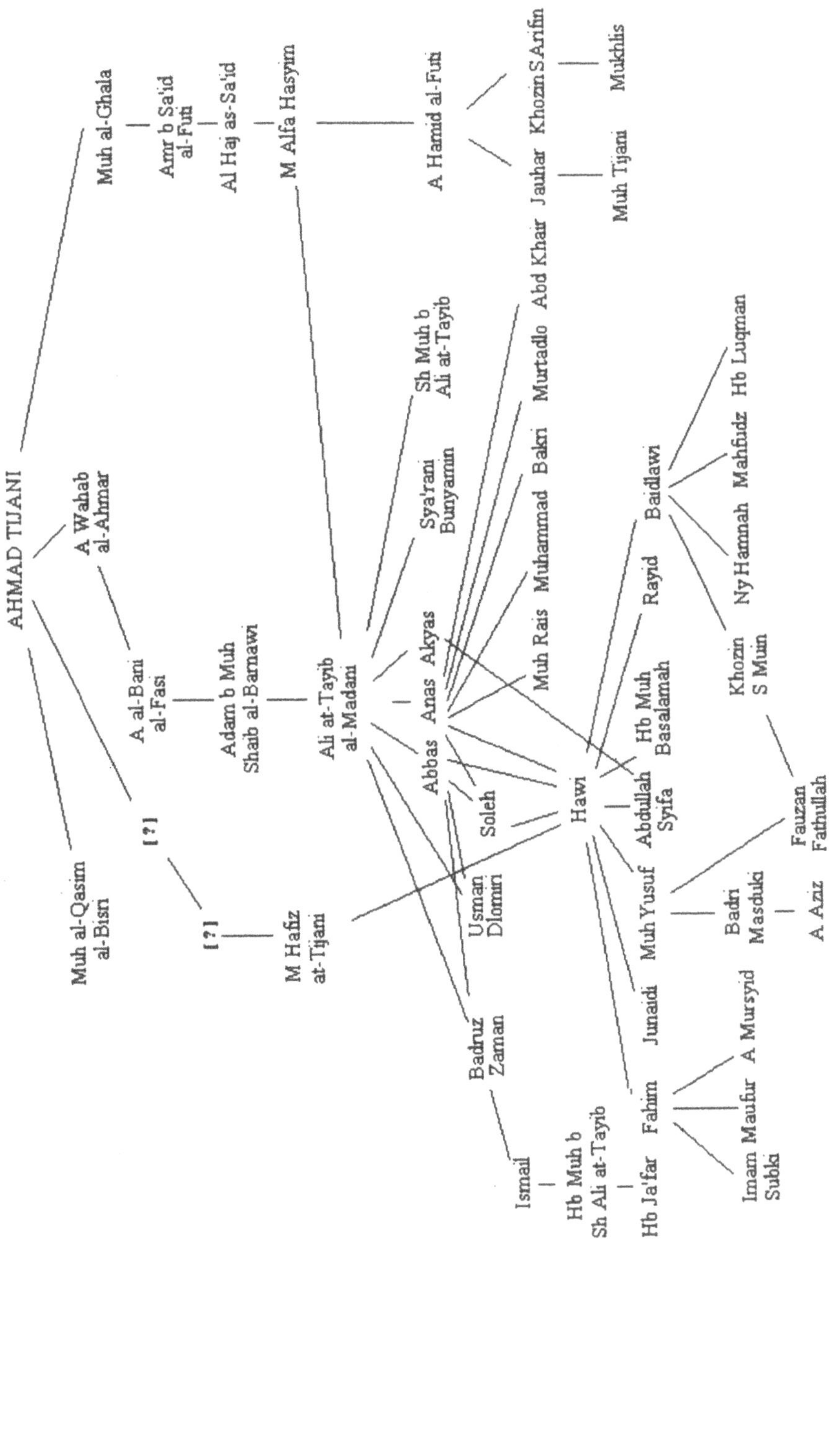

By then, Kyai Abbas was associated with and led the two *tarekat*, becoming *mursyid* of Syattariyah and *muqaddam* of Tijaniyah at the same time. To some people this seemed to show the extent of Kyai Abbas' leadership capacity and open-mindedness. Not only did he successfully lead the *pesantren* but also two *tarekat* centred at his *pesantren*. To others it was puzzling how Kyai Abbas managed his association with the two *tarekat*, considering Tijaniyah necessitates every Tijani to abandon other orders. Kyai Abbas himself as a Tijaniyah *muqaddam* broke the Tijaniyah rule because he did not give up his association with Syattariyah. When I asked about the matter, informants in Buntet of either Syattariyah or Tijaniyah always referred to this as an exception due to both Kyai Abbas' intellectual and spiritual excellence. Moreover, it was said that it was necessary especially after Kyai Anas, the *muqaddam* of Tijaniyah, had established his own *pesantren*, while in Buntet both *tarekat* were growing larger. No one directly raised the issue, especially not even Syeikh Ali at-Thayyib himself, the initiator of Kyai Abbas, suggesting that in certain circumstances, Tijaniyah strict rules could also have exceptions.

In their career as Tijaniyah *muqaddam* Kyai Anas and Kyai Abbas produced a number of new *muqaddam*. Kyai Anas initiated Kyai Muhammad (Brebes), Kyai Bakri (Kesepuhan, Cirebon), Kyai Muhammad Rais (Cirebon),[42] Kyai Murtadlo (Buntet), Kyai Abdul Khair, Kyai Hawi (Buntet) and Kyai Soleh (Pesawahan). Repeating the initiation made by Kyai Anas, Kyai Abbas initiated Kyai Soleh and Kyai Hawi (Buntet). He also initiated Kyai Badruzzaman (Garut) and Kyai Utsman Dlomiri (Cimahi, Bandung) before both *kyai* repeated an initiation from Syeikh 'Ali bin 'Abd Allah at-Thayyib al-Madani when the latter made another visit to Java. Among the *muqaddam* initiated by Kyai Anas and Kyai Abbas, Kyai Hawi excelled himself by producing seven more *muqaddam*. He initiated Kyai Abdullah Syifa (Buntet), Kyai Fahim Hawi, his son (Buntet), Kyai Junaidi, son of Kyai Anas (Sidamulya), Kyai Muhammad Yusuf (Surabaya), Habib Muhammad Basalamah (Brebes, Central Java), Kyai Baidawi (Sumenep, Madura) and Kyai Rasyid (Pesawahan, Cirebon). Currently, Kyai Hawi's son, Kyai Fahim Hawi, has initiated three new *muqaddam*, Ustadz Maufur (Klayan, north of Cirebon), Kyai Abdul Mursyid (Kesepuhan, Cirebon) and Kyai Imam Subky (Kuningan). In East Java, Kyai Muhammad bin Yusuf Surabaya initiated Kyai Badri Masduqi (Probolinggo) and Kyai Fauzan Fathullah. Kyai Baidowi (Sumenep) initiated Habib Luqman (Bogor), Kyai Mahfudz (Kesepuhan, Cirebon) and Nyai Hamnah (Kuningan).[43] In turn the new *muqaddam* have recruited many followers and quite likely further recruitment will continue.

It is clear that Pesantren Buntet has played an important role in the spread of first Syattariyah and then Tijaniyah in Java, especially West Java. Not only has

[42] A short description of Muhammad Rais, see Pijper (1985), pp 85–86.
[43] For further detail, see figure 8.4.

Pesantren Buntet now become the largest *pesantren* in Cirebon but it also represents one of the oldest *pesantren* in the area with its inherent mission for the transmission of religious tradition. The notion of 'the oldest' brings further implications in that, firstly, its dynamics and development reflect the dynamics and development of traditional Islam in this area for a period of more than two and a half centuries. Secondly, if the *Babad* narrative is taken into account, Pesantren Buntet finds its roots in the early stages of the Islamisation of 15th century Java, especially of West Java. Traditionally therefore, Pesantren Buntet stands in an unbroken chain of continuous religious transmission over time from the pre-*kraton*, early *kraton, kraton* and post-*kraton* eras. During the *pre-kraton* era religious transmission centred in the village as a free and independent undertaking. During the period of the early *kraton* religious transmission was fully under the auspices of the *kraton*. Not only did religious transmission enjoy political support and legitimation from the *kraton*, but also had the *kraton* homage. Later on, when the *kraton* came under the subjection of foreign rule, religious transmission was banned from the *kraton*. A hundred years after the death of Panembahan Ratu, religious transmission rediscovered its way back from the *kraton* to the village. This was marked by the establishment of Pesantren Buntet. Under considerable strain the *pesantren* endured and developed into its present form. Its present existence within the community therefore, represents the triumph of its spiritual traditions. Thus, what we can see in Cirebon and probably elsewhere on Java, the maintenance of scriptural and cultural traditions continues within the Javanese Muslim society, most notably, through combination of *pesantren* and *tarekat*. By these institutions, religious transmission has never ceased either with or without the support of the political power structure. This is probably one element that contributes to answering Hodgson's question: "why the triumph of Islam in Java was so complete.'[44]

[44] Hodgson, M (1974), *The Venture of Islam: Conscience and History in a World Civilisation*, Chicago: University of Chicago Press, p. 551.

Plate 39: Kyai Fahim Hawi (left), a Tijaniyah Muqaddam of Buntet.

Plate 40: Kyai Abdullah Syifa and his five year old son.

Plate 41: Kyai Fu'ad Hasyim.

Plate 42: Kyai Fahim Hawi among Tijaniyah followers.

Plate 43: Nyai Hammah, a Tijaniyah Muqaddam of Kuningan.

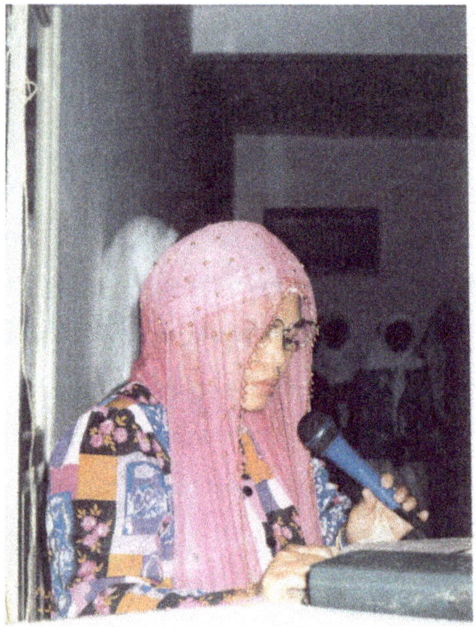

Plate 44: Nyai Hamnah (centre), her followers and Kyai Imam Subki (Nyai Hamnah's husband).

Chapter 9: Concluding Remarks

Throughout this work, I have presented a wide-ranging discussion of Javanese religious traditions as exhibited by people in Cirebon. Major parts of these traditions are readily observable because they are manifest in people's everyday life. The discussion stretches from what the people believe to what they do and how they act. Exceptions might occur but by and large, what the people believe, do and act, are complementary to each other. What they believe motivates what they do and how they act, while what they do and how they act reflects verbal expressions of what they believe. Careful examination of these traditions suggests that almost everything covered in this study can be located in an Islamic tradition, especially traced along the lines of traditional Islamic orthopraxy. As the discussion shows, almost everything has scriptural roots or finds its justification in the basic sources of Islamic doctrine: the Qur'an, the Hadith and the work of the *ulama* where operational meanings of the Qur'an and the Hadith are elaborated. Whether or not this basis and justification is considered applicable and acceptable to other Muslims, it is much more a matter of internal theological debate within the Muslim community than a subject for judgement by observers.

To make it clearer, it is worthwhile to review briefly what the preceding discussions have highlighted. This is useful especially to explore whether some part of the people's core traditions reveal, at any rate, contributions from non-Islamic elements, such as Hindu/Buddhist/Animist elements.

Discussion in Chapter Two, the initial substantive chapter, suggests that central to Cirebon-Javanese ideas is belief in the unity of God and His attributes which explains His self and existence. At the periphery there are other beings, physical and spiritual, malevolent and benevolent to human beings. All these beings are considered as His creation and, without exception, they are fully under His control. This is further substantiated when people refer to their deity. In this reference God is enunciated as the sole Creator, the Sovereign and the Ruler (Governor) of the whole universe and the contents thereof. A striking evidence throughout the discussion is a total absence of core Hindu deities and vocabularies (such as Brahma, Vishnu and Shiva or other names which would share in these crucial deity positions) that might suggest the probable intrusion of Hindu influence.

Another aspect which deserves careful consideration is the question about animism in relation to the belief in the existence of spirits and spiritual beings.[1] Animism, in Tylorian perspective and as Seymour-Smith (1990: 12–13) puts it, presupposes a consideration on the part of the believers that the 'spirit' or 'life' endowed in the natural phenomena should constitute an independent entity or

[1] This is specially crucial in Geertz's delineation of *abangan* spirit belief.

hold an independent power. This is in sharp contrast with the spirits and spiritual beings in which the Javanese hold a belief. To the Javanese, all beings, spiritual or physical, other than God are God's creation and are under His control. Moreover, to the people, the existence of spiritual beings is considered as a necessary consequence of the existence of physical beings. None of the beings are by themselves independent entities nor independent holders of particular powers. Even men, under certain circumstances of God's endowment, can control them or their power. This seems to imply that the people have at least a twofold conviction: one is that the position of these beings relative to the sovereign God is low, the other is the necessary absence of either the character of a deity or any legitimate right on the part of any of the spirits to be treated as a deity. In fact, the belief in the existence of spiritual beings is not the monopoly of a certain tradition such as animism, but it is a common feature of many other traditions, including Islam and Christianity. If reference to Islamic doctrine is required there is a verse in the early chapter of the Holy Qur'an (QS. 2:2– 3), for example, that says that the pious are those who believe, among other things, in unseen things (**ghayb**), which inevitably include spirits and spiritual beings. It is therefore ill founded to consider the Javanese, who believe in the existence of spiritual beings, as necessarily and automatically being specifically animist.

Chapter Three, which deals with mythology and cosmology, reveals quite explicitly the prevailing folk tales about the creation and origin of the universe and the creation and origin of mankind, including the Javanese. Major parts of these myths replicate people's cognitive knowledge and understanding about this matter. Unlike the core of (Islamic) doctrines which are religious constituents, the local people are quite aware of the position of myths which, as tales (*dongeng*), may or may not contain something true. Some parts of these myths, especially those which contain a cosmological outlook, might have been derived from the concept of *Martabat Pitu* (seven stages of creation), part of the theosophical speculation of Tarekat Syattariyah, an orthodox Sufi order, one of whose versions was held by the *kraton* circle. Other parts, especially those which are concerned with the origin of mankind, strongly enunciate the absolute unity and sovereignty of God, and degrading Hindu deities to ordinary non-powerful creatures, the ancestors. If Hindu/Sanskrit names and vocabularies are used in this respect, the tendency is much more for explanatory purposes rather than to teach or enunciate Hindu/Buddhist doctrine. On the part of the *kraton* potentates, parts of these myths, beside their religious purposes, might have been intentionally developed. It may serve as a useful means of educative, legitimating and ruling instruments, especially with regard to the notion of *rukun* (to live in harmony) on the one hand, and the pronouncement of the ancestral standing of the *kraton* potentates on the other.

The assertion of the absolute sovereignty of God again appears in the popular narratives of an eschatological nature. The narratives recount the unescapable mortality of all creatures and the eventual fair judgement revealed to mankind, such as the reward of paradise and punishment of hell throughout eternal life after death. Total mortality, fair universal judgement, reward of paradise and punishment of hell are totally part of Islamic doctrine which stands in sharp contrast with, for example, Hindu/Buddhist's reincarnation, *karma* and *nirvana*, although some sort of ingenious speculative parallelism quite possibly could be drawn. It is similarly difficult to find here anything about the adoption of animistic concepts, considering nothing in animism gives a clear enunciation of a single sovereign deity, life after death, fair universal judgement, or the eventual reward of paradise and punishment of hell.

Turning our attention to the discussion of ritual practices, there is a clear indication that these ritual practices follow the lines of traditional Islamic orthopraxy. There is a set of ideologies on which many of these practices seem to rely. Three of which can be enumerated: (a) the broadly defined concept of "*ibadat*" (b) the crucial position of "*niyat*" and (c) the notion of "*ummat*".

In Cirebon, *ibadat* (devotion to God) is conceived of as having a broad as well as a narrow meaning. While its narrower meaning is clear enough, in that it refers to a set of activities relating to the enactment of the five pillars, the broader meaning of *ibadat* deserves special attention. In this broad sense of the term, *ibadat* is used to embrace a vast variety of activities. It refers to any activity, religious or otherwise, intended as a devotion to God. The traditionalist's understanding of this concept tends not to separate religious and worldly matters. It runs precisely parallel to Nasr's claim that everything is sacred and nothing is profane because everything bears the fragrance of the divine. The only thing which makes an activity religious or non-religious, or in Cirebonese terms "*ibadat*" or "non (*dudu*)-*ibadat*" is the presence or absence of *niyat* (intention). If there is a religious intention attached to an activity (as a form of devotion) this activity automatically becomes *ibadat*. In other words, *niyat* changes the status of an activity from non-*ibadat* into *ibadat*. In Durkheimian terms, a *niyat* brings the "profane" into the "sacred" because *niyat* ensures a flow of the divine fragrance. So important is the position of intention in this ideology that although it is sufficient to utter an intention by heart, a verbal utterance of the intention by tongue, such as by saying the *Bismillah* (in the name of God) or other forms of similar flavour, is credited to contain special merit.

Another point worth mentioning which characterises the traditional nature of Islam in Cirebon is that regarding the *ummat* (community of believers). The main issue concerns "who can be considered as a Muslim." In this context, Abu 'Ubayd, a classic traditionalist proponent, argues that one can be termed a believer on the basis of the statement of faith. Even a Muslim who commits a grave sin is still to be termed a believer and thus belongs to the community of believers.[2] The application of this concept is clearly seen in Cirebon. People in this region and elsewhere consider anyone who uttered the *syahadat* to be automatically a Muslim. The person instantly belongs to the community of believers (*ummat*) and has an equal status as other Muslims do. When that person has trouble or gets sick, other Muslims are obliged to help, and when that person dies it is the duty of other Muslims to care for the corpse, to pray at the burial and to bury the person at a Muslim burial complex.[3] So strong is the sense of brotherhood, at least at the ideological level. The scope of this brotherhood is not confined to relatives or neighbours but extends to any Muslim, living anywhere, in the east and in the west, on earth or at sea. It transcends racial, spatial and temporal boundaries. It even includes those who live at the present time (still alive) and those who lived centuries ago in the past (already died). Special credits and honours are attributed to those who have devoted most parts of their lives solely to the path of God or, exhibited exemplary behaviour in terms of devotion and piety. Various commemorations, celebrations, festivals and feasts encapsulated in the *adat* rituals, including the *wali* and holy men veneration, mostly reflect the sanctification of this *ummat* and the ideas of brotherhood. The presence of people of various strata with various degrees of religiosity in these festivals, through which they express a sense of piety and Muslim identity, can therefore be interpreted as a symbolic representation of such sanctification. On these occasions, uttering prayers for the merits of all members of the *ummat*, whoever and wherever, dead or alive, is institutionalised. In a religious festival therefore, at least three elements intricately mix together: it is an *adat* because it is customarily performed, an *ibadat* because each participant uses it to express a sense of piety and Muslim identity, and a sanctification of notion of *ummat* whereby the internal social bond within the community of believers is strengthened.

It seems clear at this stage that Islam in Java is essentially no different from Islam elsewhere. Its foundation is threefold: *iman* (to have faith), *islam* (submission) and *ihsan* (deference), the same foundation adopted by all Muslims elsewhere.[4] During the Formative Period of Islam (9th–14th century AD) the questions about how *iman, islam* and *ihsan* should be understood and actualised became the subject of a profound and complex body of scholarly expositions. Various schools of thought have emerged in the field of theology with respect to *iman*, jurisprudence with respect to *islam* and theosophy and Sufism with respect to *ihsan*. One school was termed as the "traditionalists" because its followers often

[2] Rippin, A. (1990), *Muslims*, p.63. (The word between brackets is my own).
[3] See Chapter Two.
[4] Hadith transmitted by Muslim (see Chapter Two). Here I need to distinguish between (I)slam, a proper name referring to the religion of the Muslims and (I)slam to mean an act of submission.

called themselves as *"ahl al-sunnah"* meaning "followers of the Prophetic traditions."[5]

Through a complex process of maturation this classical type of Islam, "Traditional Islam," evolved and developed. It spread widely to various corners of the world following the spread of Islam itself. Eventually it reached Java at about the same time when Islam in general reached the archipelago.[6] In Java and elsewhere, this classical type of Islam, the full heritage of Sunni tradition, now better known as the *"Faham Ahlu Sunnah wal Jama'ah,"* contributed to Javanese popular traditions.[7] It presents itself as a religion with a harmonious and peaceful (*rukun-damai*) format. It came as a "grace for the whole universe" (*rahmatan lil-'alamin*) not as a condemnation. Through its genius, any time and anywhere it was ready to accommodate, absorb or be adopted by other traditions. It requires almost nothing but one condition. If there is an element in the absorbed tradition that opposes the principle of *tauhid* (unity of God) and submission to the one God, then such an element must be removed or replaced with an Islamic one. Once this condition is met, everything is acceptable. Coming in this format, "Traditional Islam" influenced the Javanese and shaped their traditions. Also in this format, its triumph in Java has been complete.

[5] In the early Formative Period, this group was generally connected to Ahmad ibn Hanbal (circa AD 855). See: Rippin, A. (1990), p.63.

[6] At this stage I do not think it so important to include an account on when Islam precisely came to Java and the archipelago, who brought it and how. I leave it to the hands of historians.

[7] Dhofier, Z. (1985) rightly states that this type of Islam (*"Faham Ahlu Sunnah wal Jama'ah"* or the "School for the followers of Prophetic traditions and Consensus") is one which holds Asy'arite doctrine of theology, four *madzahib* (schools of thought: Syafi'ite, Malikite, Hanafite and Hanbilite) of jurisprudence, and Ghazalian Sufism. See also: Ali, H.A. (1980), *Ahlusunnah waljama'ah dan Unsur-unsur Pokok Ajarannya*, Semarang: Wicaksana. (H. Amin Ali, the writer of this book, is a Cirebonese Kyai).

Bibliography

Abdalati, H. 1991 *Islam in Focus,* Singapore : The Muslim Converts's Association.

Abduh, S.M. 1966 *Theology of Unity,* translated from Arabic into English by Ishak Musa'ad and K., Cragg, London : George Allen & Unwin.

Abduh, S.M. 1976 *Risalah Ilmu Tauhid,* (Translation from Arabic into Indonesian by H., Firdaus, 6th edition), Jakarta : Bulan Bintang.

Abdurrahman, P.R. 1982 *Cerbon,* Jakarta : Sinar Harapan.

Abu Zayd, A.R. 1974 *Al-Ghazali on Divine Predicates and Their Properties,* Lahore : SH. Muhammad Ashraf.

Abun-Nasr 1965 *The Tijaniyya: A Sufi Order in the Modern World,* London : OUP.

Adnan, K.H.M. 1969 *Peringatan Hari-Hari Besar Islam,* Sala : A.B. Siti Syamsijah.

Ahmad, K. (ed). 1988 *Islam, its meaning and message,* London : The Islamic Foundation

Ahmad Qodhi, A. 1992 *Nur Muhammad, Menyingkap Asal Usul Makhluk (Tarjamah Daqooiqul Akhbar),* Bandung : Al-Husaini.

Ali, H.A. 1980 *Ahlusunnah Waljama'ah dan Unsur-unsur Pokok Ajarannya,* Semarang : Wicaksana.

Amijaya, R.et al. 1985 *Pola Kehidupan Santri Pesantren Buntet Desa Mertapada Kulon Kecamatan Astanajapura Kabupaten Cirebon,* Yogyakarta : Proyek Penelitian dan Pengkajian Kebudayaan Nusantara (Javanologi) Departemen Pendidikan dan Kebudayaan.

(Anonymous author) 1941 *Babad Tanah Jawi,* Gravenhage : Martinus Nijhoff.

Arnold, T.W. 1926 "Saint and Martyr (Muhammadan in India)", *The Encyclopedia of Religion and Ethics,* Edinburg : T. and T. Clark.

Atja 1986 *Carita Purwaka Caruban Nagari: Karya Sastra Sebagai Sumber Pengetahuan Sejarah,* Bandung : Proyek Pengembangan Permuseuman Jawa Barat.

Aya Sofia and Saridjo, M. 1988 "Kebijaksanaan dan Program Pemerintah Dalam Pengembangan Pondok Pesantren" in *Seminar Nasional Perkembangan Program Pengembangan Masyarakat Melalui Pondok Pesantren,* Ciawi-Bogor , 11–13 Juni 1988.

Azra, A. 1992 *The Transmission of Islamic Reformism to Indonesia: Network of Middle Eastern and Malay-Indonesian 'Ulama' in the Seventeenth and Eighteenth Century,* unpublished Ph D dissertation, Columbia: Columbia University.

Bachtiar, H.W. 1973 "The Religion of Java: A Commentary," *Madjalah Ilmu-Ilmu Sastra Indonesia*, Djilid V, No. 1.

Barth, F. 1993 *Balinese Worlds*, The Univ. of Chicago Press: Chicago .

Bekki, A. 1975 "Socio Cultural Changes in a Traditional Javanese Village" in *Life in Indonesian Villages*, Institute of Asian Studies, Tokyo : Rikko (St. Pauls) University.

Bell, C. 1992 *Ritual Theory, Ritual Practice*, New York : Oxford University Press.

Berkey, J. 1992 *The Transmission of Knowledge in Medieval Cairo*, New Jersey : Princeton University Press.

Brown, K. and Palmer, M. 1990 *The Essential Teachings of Islam*, London : Arrow Books.

Buny, al-, S. (n.d) "Riyadlah ayah al-Kursiy wa bayan da'awatiha" in an-Narly, Al-Ustaz as-Sayyid Muhammad, *Khazinat al-Asrar*, Syarikat al-Nur Asia, pp. 150–151.

Dahlan, A. 1988 *Hadits Arba'in Annawawiah*, Bandung : Al-Ma'arif.

Dairabi, ad-, A.A.S. (n.d) *Al-Mujarrabah ad-Dairabi al-Kabir*, Semarang : Al-Munawar.

Danner, V. 1988 *The Islamic Tradition: An Introduction*, New York : Amity House.

De Graaf and Pigeaud 1989 *Kerajaan-Kerajaan Islam di Jawa: Peralihan Dari Majapahit ke Mataram*, Jakarta : Grafiti Press.

Denny, F.M. 1985 "Islamic Ritual: Perspectives and Theories", in Martin, R.C. (ed), *Approaches to Islam in Religious Studies*, Tucson : The University of Arizona Press.

Dirdjosiswojo 1957 *Kawi Djinarja*, Klaten : Pertjetakan Reoublik Indonesia

Dhofier, Z. 1980 *The Pesantren Tradition: A Study of the Role of the Kyai in the Maintenance of the Traditional Ideology of Islam in Java*, unpublished Ph D dissertation, Canberra: The Australian National University.

Dhofier, Z. 1985 *Tradisi Pesantren : Studi tentang Pandangan Hidup Kiyai*, LP3ES: Jakarta .

Djayadiningrat, H. 1983 *Tinjauan Kritis tentnag Sejarah Banten: Sumbangan Bagi Pengenalan Sifat-sifat penulisan sejarah Jawa*, Jakarta : Djamabatan

Ellen, R.F. 1983 "Social Theory, Ethnography and the Understanding of Practical Islam in South-East Asia", in Hooker, M.B. ed., *Islam in South-East Asia*, Leiden : E.J. Brill.

Fathullah, K.H.F. 1985 *Biografi Alquthbul Maktuum Saiyidul Awliyaa: Syeikh Ahmad Attijaniy dan Thariqatnya Attijaniyah,* Pasuruan : (anonymous publisher).

Fox, J.J. and Prajarto, D. 1989 "The memories of village santri from Jombang in East Java," in R. J. May and W. J., O'Malley (eds), *Observing Change in Asia,* Bathurst : Crawfurd House Press, pp. 94–110.

Fox, J.J. 1991 "Ziarah Visits to the Tombs of Wali, the Founder of Islam on Java" in Ricklefs, M.C. (ed), *Islam in Indonesian Social Context,* Melbourne : CSEAS, Monash University. pp. 19–38.

Geertz, C. 1975 *Islam Observed,* Chicago : The University of Chicago Press.

Geertz, C. 1976 *The Religion of Java,* Phoenix Edition, Chicago : University of Chicago Press.

Gluckman, M. 1962 *Essays on the Ritual of Social Relations,* Manchester : Manchester University Press.

Goldziher, I. 1971 "Veneration of Saints in Islam", in Stern, M. (ed), *Muslim Studies,* vol.2, London : George Allen and Unwin, pp. 277–341.

Goldziher, I. 1981 *Introduction to Islamic Theology and Law,* New Jersey : Princeton University Press.

Graham, W.A. 1987 "Scripture", in Eliade, Mircea (ed), *The Encyclopedia of Religion,* New York : MacMillan.

Gunawan, W. 1992 *Industri Gula di Jawa Dalam Perspektif Model "Inti-Satelit," Kasus di Kabupaten Cirebon,* Bogor : Pusat Studi Pembangunan, IPB.

Gunawan, W.et al. 1991 *Pembentukan Modal di Pedesaan, Kasus Kabupaten Cirebon,* Bogor : Pusat Studi Pembangunan, IPB.

Hadisutjipto, S.Z. 1979 *Babad Cirebon,* Jakarta : Departemen Pendidikan dan Kebudayaan.

Hasan, Z. 1970 *Sekilas Lintas Sedjarah Pesantren Buntet, Tjirebon,* unpublished mimeograph.

Hoadley, M.S. 1975 *History of the Cirebon-Priangan "Jaksa College" 0–,* unpublished. Ph D dissertation, Cornell University.

Hodgson, M. 1974 *The Venture of Islam: Conscience and History in a World Civilization,* Chicago : University of Chicago Press.

Hooker, M.B. 1978 *Adat Law in Modern Indonesia,* Kuala Lumpur : Oxford University Press.

Hooker, M.B. 1983 *Islam in South-East Asia,* Leiden : E.J. Brill

Hurgronje, C.S. 1906 *The Achehnese,* two vols, (translated from Dutch into English by A.W.S. O'Sullivan), Leiden : E.J. Brill.

Johns, A.H. 1961 "Sufism as a Category in Indonesian Literature and History", *Journal of South East Asian History*, vol. II, pp. 10–25.

Johns, A.H. 1985 "Islam in Southeast Asia: Problems of Perspective", in Ibrahim, A., Siddique, S., and Husein, Y. (1985) eds, *Readings On Islam in South East Asia*, ISEAS: Singapore .

Kantor Statistik Kabupaten Cirebon 1991 *Kabupaten Cirebon Dalam Angka 1990*, Cirebon : Kantor Statistik Kabupaten Cirebon.

Kantor Statistik Kotamadya Cirebon 1992 *Kotamadya Cirebon Dalam Angka 1990/1991*, Cirebon : Kantor Statistik Kotamadya Cirebon.

Kartapraja, K. 1978 "Ngelmu Sejati Cirebon", *Dialog*, Edisi Khusus, Jakarta : Dep. Agama, March 1973, pp.91–107.

Kartodirjo, S. 1987 *Pengantar Sejarah Indonesia Baru*, Jakarta : Gramedia.

Ki Sura, (ed.) (n.d.) *Buku Primbon Jawa Jangkep*, Solo : U.D. Mayasari.

Koentjaraningrat 1963 "Book Review: Clifford Geertz's The Religion of Java", *Majalah Ilmu-ilmu Sastra Indonesia*, vol. 1, no.2, September, pp.188–191.

Leach, E.R. 1961 "Two Essays Concerning The Symbolic Representation of Time", in Lessa, W.A and Vogt, E.Z. (1979) ed, *Reader in Comparative Religion: An Anthropological Approach*, 4th edition, New York : Harper and Row, pp. 221–229.

Leach, E.R. 1964 *Political Systems of Highland Burma: A Study of Kachin Social Structure*, London : The Athlon.

Lessa, W.A. and Vogt, E.Z. (eds). 1979 *Reader in Comparative Religion: An Anthropological Approach*, 4th eddition, New York : Harper and Row.

Levy, R. 1957 *The Social Structure of Islam*, London : Cambridge University Press.

Mahmud Yunus 1960 *Sejarah Pendidikan Islam di Indonesia*, Jakarta : Pustaka Mahmudiah.

Mahmud, R. and Anam, S. 1986 *Perjuangan Wali Sanga Babad Cirebon (Pasundan)*, unknown publisher.

Mahsun, T. Kh. 1958 *Qisasul Anbiya'*, Surabaya : Makatabah Muhammad bin Ahmad Nabhan wa awladuha.

Makdisi, G. 1981 *The Rise of Colleges*, Edinburg : Edinburg University Press.

Malinowski, B.C. 1935 *Coral Gardens and Their Magic: A Study of the Methods of Tilling the Soil and of Agricultural Rites in the Trobriand Islands*, London : George Allen & Unwin.

Mansur, H. 1989 *Haul di Pesantren Buntet: Kajian Sejarah Ringkas*, unpublished mimeograph.

Mauss, M. 1980 *The Gift: Forms and Functions of Exchange in Archaic Societies,* London : Routledge & Kegan Paul.

Nakamura, M. 1983 *The Crescent Arises Over The Banyan Tree: A Study of the Muhammadiyah Movement in a Central Javanese Town,* Yogyakarta : Gajah Mada University Press.

Nakamura, M. 1984 "The Cultural and Religious Identity of Javanese Muslims: Problems of Conceptualization an Approach," *Prisma,* No. 31, Jakarta : LP3ES.

Nasr, S.H. 1981 *Islamic Life and Thought,* Boston : George Allen & Unwin.

Nasr, S.H. 1987 *Traditional Islam in the Modern World,* London : Kegan Paul

Nasution, H. (ed). 1990 *Thoriqot Qodiriyah Naqsabandiyyah: Sejarah Asal-Usul, dan Perkembangannya,* Tasikmalaya : IAILM.

Ngah, Mohammad Nor Bin 1983 *Kitab Jawi: Islamic Thought of the Malay Muslim Scholars,* Singapore : Institute of Southeast Asian Studies.

Nieli, R. 1987 *Wittgenstein: From Mysticism to Ordinary Language,* New York : State University of New York Press.

Noer, D. 1973 *The Modernists Muslim Movement in Indonesia 1900–1942,* Oxford University Press.

Ormsby, E.L. 1984 *Theodicy in Islamic Thought: The Dispute Over Al-Ghazali's "Best of All Possible Worlds",* New Jersey : Princeton University Press.

Panitia Idul Khotmi Attijani Ke : 199. 1992 *Al Masyrabul Kitmani Lil Khotmil Muhammadiy Syekh Ahmad bin Muhammad Attijani,* pamphlet, Leces-Probolinggo (East Java), 9/10 Safar 1413 H = 8/9 Agustus 1992.

Patton, W.M. 1926 Saints and Martyrs (Muhammadan in India)" in *The Encyclopedia of Religion and Ethics,* Edinburg : T. and T. Clark.

Pijper, G.F. 1934 *Fragmenta Islamica, Studien over het Islamisme in Nederlanndsch-Indie,* Leiden : E.J. Brill.

Pijper, G.F. 1987 Timbulnya Tarekat Tijaniyah di Pulau Jawa" in G.F. Pijper, *Fragmenta Islamica: Beberapa Studi Mengenai Sejarah Islam di Indonesia Awal Abad XX,* (Translation from Dutch into Indonesian by Tujimah), Jakarta : UI Press.

Pinto, F.M. 1692 *The Voyages and Adventures of Ferdinand Mendez Pinto,* (English translation by Henry Cogen), London : J. Macook.

Pranowo, M.B. 1991 *Creating Islamic Tradition in Rural Java,* unpublished Ph D thesis, Clayton: Monash University.

Qodhi, A.A. 1992 *Nur Muhammad, Menyingkap Asal Usul Kejadian Makhluk (Tarjamah Daqooiqul Akhbar),* Bandung : Al-Husaini.

Rais, M.H. (n.d) *Sejarah Cerbon,* (hand-written mimeograph in Cirebon Javanese and in Javanese-Arabic letters), 18 vols, unknown publisher.

Rasyid, S. 1988 *Fiqh Islam,* Bandung : Masa Baru .

Ricklefs, M.C. 1993 *A History of Modern Indonesia Since c.1300,* Hong Kong : MacMillan.

Rippin, A. 1990 *Muslims: Their Religious Beliefs and Practices,* Vol.1, London : Rutledge.

Salam, S. 1960 *Sekitar Wali Sanga,* Kudus : Menara.

Santrie, A.M. 1987 Martabat Alam Tujuh" in Hasan, A.R. (ed), *Warisan Intelektual Islam Indonesia,* Bandung : Mizan.

Schimmel, A. 1975 *Mystical Dimensions of Islam,* Chapel Hill : The University of Carolina Press.

Siddique, S. 1977 *Relics of the Past?,* unpublished PhD dissertation, Bielfeld: Bielfeld Universitat.

Simuh 1988 *Mistik Islam Kejawen Raden Ngabehi Ranggawarsita,* Jakarta : University of Indonesia Press.

Subhani, S.J. 1989 *Tawassul, Tabarruk, Ziarah Kubur, Karamah Wali, Termasuk Ajaran Islam : Kritik Atas Faham Wahabi,* Jakarta : Pustaka Al Hidayah.

Sudjana, T.D. (n.d) *Kemelut di Bumi Pakungwati: Sebuah Novelette Sejarah Bersumber dari Naskah Negara Kretabhumi,* unpublished mimeograph, Cirebon: Seksi Kebudayaan, Kantor Departemen Pendidikan dan Kebudayaan, Kotamadya Cirebon.

Sulendraningrat, P.S. (n.d) *Babarnya Jimat Kalimasada Prabu Yudistira Amartapura,* type written manuscript, Cirebon : Pengguron Caruban Krapyak, Kaprabon.

Sulendraningrat, P.S. 1978 *Beralihnya Pulau Jawa Dari Agama Sanghyang Kepada Agama Islam,* type written manuscript, Cirebon : Pengguron Caruban Krapyak, Kaprabon.

Sulendraningrat, P.S. 1980 *Timbangan,* mimeograph, Cirebon : Pengguron Caruban Krapyak Kaprabonan.

Sulendraningrat, P.S. 1982 *Ghaib,* type written manuscript, Cirebon : Pengguron Caruban Krapyak, Kaprabon.

Sulendraningrat, P.S. 1985 *Sejarah Cirebon,* Jakarta : PN Balai Pustaka.

Suparlan, P. 1976 *The Javanese in Surinam: Ethnicity in an Ethnically Plural Society,* Unpublished Ph D dissertation, Urbana: University of Illinois.

Suparlan, P. 1991 *The Javanese Dukun,* Jakarta : Peka Publication.

Syafi'i, asy-, Abdur-Rahman as-Safuri (n.d) *Nazhat al Majalis*, vol. 1, Beirut : al-Maktaba as-Sa'baniya.

Ter Haar, B. 1948 *Adat Law in Indonesia*, New York : Institute of Pacific Studies.

Tjitrajaya, I. 1989 Contextual explanations: A Methodological Examination," *Berita Antropologi*, Th XIII, No. 45, Januari-Maret, pp. 1–10.

Trimingham, J.S. 1971 *Sufi Orders in Islam*, Oxford : The Clarendon Press.

Turner, V.W. 1964 Betwixt and Between: The Liminal Period in Rites De Passage", in Lessa, W.A and Vogt, E.Z. (1979) ed., *Reader in Comparative Religion*, Fourth Ed., New York : Harper and Row, pp. 234–243.

Van Bruinessen, M. 1992 Pesantren dan Kitab Kuning: Pemeliharaan dan Kesinambungan Tradisi Pesantren", *Jurnal Ulumul Qur'an*, III/4 pp. 73–85).

Vayda, A.P. 1983 Progressive Contextualization: Methods for Research", *Human Ecology*, no.11, pp.265–281.

Vlekke, B.H.M. 1965 *Nusantara: A History of Indonesia*, The Hague : W. van Hoeve.

Watt, W.M. 1979 *What is Islam?*, 2nd ed, London : Longman.

Wessing, R. 1978 *Cosmology and Social Behaviour in West Javanese Settlements*, Ohio University: Centre for International Studies, South East Asian Series No.47.

Woodward, M.R. 1989 *Islam in Java: Normative Piety and Mysticism in the Sultanate of Yogyakarta*, Tucson : The University of Arizona Press.

Encyclopaedias:

Eliade, Mircea, et al (eds). 1987 *The Encyclopedia of Religion*, New York : MacMillan.

Gibb, H.A.R.et al (eds). 1960 *The Encyclopaedia of Islam*, New Edition, Leiden : E.J. Brill.

Gibb, H.A.R. and Kraemers, J.H, (eds). 1961 *Shorter Encyclopaedia of Islam*, Leiden : E.J. Brill.

Glasse, C. (ed). 1989 *The Concise Encyclopaedia of Islam*, London : Atlantic Highlands.

Goetz, P.W.et al (eds). 1986 *The New Encyclopaedia Britannica*, 15th Edition, 32 vols, Chicago : Encyclopaedia Britannica.

Hastings, J. (ed). 1926 *Encyclopaedia of Religion and Ethics*, 13 vols. Edinburg : T. and T. Clark.

Idris Bell, H. (ed). 1989 *The Concise Encyclopedia of Islam,* New York : Harper and Row.

Dictionaries:

Barnhart, C.L. and Barnhart, >R.K, (ed). 1994 *The World Book Dictionary,* 2 vols. Chicago : World Book.

Dirdjosiswojo 1957 *Kawi-Djinarya,* Klaten : Pertjetakan Republik Indonesia.

Echols, J.M. and Hassan Shadily 1982 *Kamus Inggeris Indonesia,* Jakarta : Gramedia.

Echols, J.M. 1982 *An Indonesian English Dictionary,* Jakarta : Gramedia.

Funk and Wagnalls 1984 *Standard Desk Dictionary,* Cambridge : Harper and Row.

Hava, s.j. J.G. 1951 *Al-Fara'id ad-Dariyah fi al-lughah al-'Arabiyah wa'l-Engliziyah, Arabic English Dictionary,* Beirut : Catholic Press.

Netton, I.R. 1992 *A Popular Dictionary of Islam,* London : Curzon Press.

Seymour-Smith, C. 1990 *Macmillan Dictionary of Anthropology,* London : MacMillan.

www.ingramcontent.com/pod-product-compliance
Lightning Source LLC
Chambersburg PA
CBHW060928170426
43192CB00031B/2864
* 9 7 8 1 9 2 0 9 4 2 3 0 4 *